The Politics of Basic Needs

The Politics of Basic Needs

URBAN ASPECTS OF ASSAULTING POVERTY IN AFRICA

RICHARD SANDBROOK

Professor, Department of Political Economy
University of Toronto

HEINEMANN

LONDON   IBADAN   NAIROBI

Heinemann Educational Books Ltd
22 Bedford Square, London WC1B 3HH
PMB 5205, Ibadan · PO Box 45314, Nairobi

EDINBURGH   MELBOURNE   AUCKLAND
HONG KONG   SINGAPORE   KUALA LUMPUR
NEW DELHI   KINGSTON   PORT OF SPAIN

© Richard Sandbrook 1982
First published 1982

British Library Cataloguing in Publication Data

Sandbrook, Richard
  The politics of basic needs.
  1. Poor – Africa
  2. Africa – Cities and towns
  3. Poverty – Political aspects
  I. Title   II. Series
  305.5′6   HC79.P6

ISBN 0-435-96537-9

To my Blythes

Set in 10pt Times by Willmer Brothers Limited,
Birkenhead, Merseyside
Printed in Great Britain by Biddles Ltd., Guildford, Surrey

Contents

Tables

Preface

African poverty persists. Why? Some writers persuasively maintain that this is unnecessary. How might poverty be overcome?

These deceptively simple questions demand that we confront some of the most complex and controversial issues in the political economy of development and underdevelopment. An inquiry into the structural roots of poverty, whether urban or rural, leads to the investigation of the African territories' incorporation into the world economy and, in particular, the imperial priorities that governed this incorporation. It also requires an examination of class formation in the periphery. Pertinent here is the knotty issue of the relationship between this process and the formation of power structures that serve in various ways to perpetuate poverty.

But this is only the beginning; the study of poverty and its eradication demands, as well, an act of imagination. The analysis should not end after an investigation of concrete transnational and national structures and policies. Left at this point, a study risks exacerbating a sense of hopelessness and gloom by portraying material deprivation as a consequence of seemingly overwhelming structural forces. Yet poverty is rarely overdetermined. It is important to understand not only the *status quo*, but also the alternatives that may be immanent in the political consciousness and political struggles of ordinary people. The reader is asked to imagine the feasible shifts in political forces and development strategies that might vanquish the squalor, debilitation and humiliation of poverty. While this quest utilizes various Marxian categories, the conclusions sometimes clash sharply with certain cherished positions of the Left, as well as of the Right.

For reasons that are made clear in chapter 1, the emphasis in the study rests on the urban situation of poverty, economic structure, class formation and power relations. The comparative analysis draws heavily, though not exclusively, upon the experience of the major city or cities in Senegal, the Ivory Coast, Ghana, Nigeria, Zambia, Zaïre, Kenya and Tanzania. I think it is legitimate to compare these cases because they share certain important attributes: a similar colonial heritage, especially with respect to the pattern of urbanization and belated industrialization; similar socio-economic problems and occupational profiles associated in part with a typically high rate of urban growth; and comparable levels of technological and economic development. Not coincidentally, these cases reflect my own field research experience (in Kenya and Ghana) and travel over the past dozen years. They ensure as well a wide geographical representation and an adequate literature for synthesis. Finally (and admittedly largely fortuitously), the countries selected for concentration have also exhibited diverse development strategies and dominant class alliances.

As the notes at the end of each chapter attest, the analysis in this book relies mainly upon the sifting of a mass of widely scattered documentary, historical and social scientific material. The general reader may wish to ignore the voluminous references; they add nothing germane to the arguments in the text. However, any reader interested in gauging the evidential basis for generalizations or constructing a selected bibliography on specific topics (with items as late as mid-1980) should find the notes useful. To enhance readability, I rarely refer the reader to more than one note in a single paragraph.

In accordance with convention, I wish to acknowledge certain debts I incurred in the execution of this study. I could not have written the book without the continuing financial support of the Canada Council, now the Social Sciences and Humanities Research Council. This organization funded research in Africa relevant to this project in 1968–70, 1972, 1975 and 1977. Small grants from the University of Toronto's Research Fund facilitated my work at various stages between 1975 and 1980.

As usual, my Political Economy colleagues at the University of Toronto were a source of ideas and encouragement. Cranford Pratt, Ronald Manzer and Richard Stren read all or most of the manuscript and made valuable comments. Jonathan Barker gave me a critique of chapter 3 based upon his special knowledge of the role of the state in Africa. José Nun contributed insights into the debates on marginality and the 'labour aristocracy' among Latin American scholars. Discussions with Gerald Helleiner helped keep me honest on economic questions and provided me with a wealth of pertinent references. With this sort of assistance, any errors of omission or commission that remain must surely be my responsibility alone.

Finally, I gratefully acknowledge the permission of JAI Press to use in parts of chapters 4 and 6 material that originally appeared in my contribution to volume 1 of *Research in the Sociology of Work* (1981).

Richard Sandbrook
University of Toronto

1   The Poverty Problem

Debates in international forums often suggest that basic-needs
approaches and efforts to achieve a new international economic order
are distinct and even opposed programmes. This is misleading. Any
effective assault on mass poverty will require a restructuring of both the
world economy and domestic development strategies. It would be best if
changes at both levels occurred simultaneously; however, this is
unlikely. But even if poor countries cannot negotiate reformed
international economic arrangements, they have it within their power to
reconstitute their domestic priorities and institutions. The inequities of
the international order surely do not excuse the persistence of social
injustice within the underdeveloped countries. Moreover, I contend,
strategies of basic-needs satisfaction, if widely adopted, would
themselves work many needed changes in the international, as well as
national, orders. It should be clear, therefore, that the focus of this book
on domestic strategies does not imply a disregard for the international
impediments to poverty eradication.

Perhaps the most obvious feature of basic-needs approaches is their
moral appeal. They tend, in the first place, to treat the well-being of the
poor and social equity as the primary goals of development policy, not
just as potential long-term by-products of policies designed to augment
economic growth. In the second place, basic-needs proponents manifest
a laudable concern for the relationship between ends and means in social
change. If the means employed condition the ends, then worthy goals
cannot be sought through unworthy means. For instance, the once-
popular developmentalist view that rapid growth and future welfare
necessitated authoritarian means is now rarely heard. Instead, there are
insistent calls for popular participation in the definition, implementation and benefits of basic-needs strategies. Similarly, national self-
reliance is proposed as both a means and an attractive goal. To break the
North–South linkages that impede an assault on poverty, a society must
rely primarily upon its own resources and co-operation with like-minded
countries. But the enhanced national autonomy and self-confidence that
result are also valuable in themselves.

Practice, however, is rarely congruent with lofty ideals. The ethical
superiority of 'Another Development', as it is sometimes called, will not
by itself dissolve the intractable realities of powerful national and
transnational vested interests. Indeed, the lack of attention paid to the
political conditions for basic-needs approaches has led many to
conclude that these approaches are utopian. Not that the basic-needs
proponents are oblivious to the importance of such political analysis. As
two economists recently declared:

It is quite clear that a major restructuring in political and economic power relationships within a society is a prerequisite for a genuine pursuit of a development strategy aimed at basic needs. Whether this can be managed by most developing countries today, or the extent to which this can be managed in various societies, are some of the most challenging issues we face in this field.[1]

These issues form the subject matter of this book. The geographical focus is tropical Africa: to establish the context I begin by sketching the dimensions of poverty there and the basic-needs approaches advanced to tackle this problem. This provides the basis for a discussion of the precise aims of the study and the rationale for the urban emphasis I adopt.

Growth and poverty

The problem of mass poverty in the Third World is more fundamentally one of the *pattern* of economic growth than the *rate* of growth. This seems to be the conventional wisdom of development economics today. Although per capita income in the Third World rose by more than a third in real terms during the First Development Decade, this expansion provided little or no benefit to perhaps a third of the relevant population. Indeed, the 'very poor' (in the World Bank's terminology) in some countries suffered worsening absolute as well as relative impoverishment during the 1960s. The 'frightening implication' drawn by one study of growth and equity is that

hundreds of millions of desperately poor people throughout the world have been hurt rather than helped by economic development. Unless their destinies become a major and explicit focus of development policy in the 1970s and 1980s, economic development may serve merely to promote social injustice.[2]

The magnitude of the problem facing such development policy has been underlined by the World Employment Programme (WEP) of the International Labour Office (ILO). At least 300 million people are currently unemployed or earning below subsistence incomes; productive employment must be created not only for these, but also for some 700 million persons who will join the labour forces of the underdeveloped world before the year 2000.[3]

The poorest of the poor, tropical African countries have experienced persisting poverty in the context, in most cases, of relatively low and uncertain growth rates (see table 1.1). Several of these countries, however, have attained reasonable economic expansion, as table 1.2 shows. Those with the highest rates – Nigeria, Kenya, the Ivory Coast and Malawi – include both large and small countries, as well as those with a high and low natural resource endowment. Irrespective of some

Table 1.1 *Real GNP per capita growth rates, 1951–75 and projected 1978–85 (% per annum)*

	1961–70	1971–5	1951–75	1978–85
South Asia	1·5	0·5	1·8	1·7
East Asia	4·0	4·8	3·9	4·6
Latin America	2·5	3·7	2·6	3·8
Sub-Saharan Africa	1·6	2·1	2·0	2·4
All developing countries	3·2	3·0	3·1	3·4

Source: Development Policy Staff, World Bank, *Prospects for Developing Countries, 1978–85* (Washington, DC, November 1977), pp. 1, 5

economic success stories, though, tropical Africa contains a disproportionate share of the world's poor, whether these are defined by reference to an absolute or a relative standard.

With respect to an absolute standard, the poor comprise those households whose income falls below a level necessary to satisfy the basic needs of their members in housing, nutrition and clothing. Any stipulation of basic needs will, of course, be arbitrary, but it will at least provide some rough measure of the dimensions of human misery. In the

Table 1.2 *Population, GNP per capita, and average annual real growth rates, tropical Africa*

	Population, 1977 (millions)	GNP per capita 1977 (US$)	Growth rates (%) GNP per capita 1960–77	Growth rates (%) GDP, 1970–7
Nigeria	79·0	420	3·6	6·2
Ethiopia	30·2	110	1·7	2·5
Zaïre	25·7	130	1·1	1·9
Sudan	16·9	290	0·1	5·0
Tanzania	16·4	190	2·6	4·5
Kenya	14·6	270	2·5	6·2
Uganda	12·0	270	0·7	−0·1
Ghana	10·6	380	−0·3	0·4
Cameroun	7·9	340	2·9	3·4
Ivory Coast	7·5	690	3·3	6·5
Upper Volta	5·5	130	0·6	3·3
Malawi	5·5	140	3·0	6·3
Senegal	5·2	430	−0·3	2·8
Zambia	5·1	450	1·5	2·8

Source: World Bank, *World Development Report, 1979* (New York: Oxford University Press, 1979), tables 1 and 2

World Bank's view, for instance, the 'absolute poor' in 1975 included those individuals with an annual 'international purchasing power' of under US $279. While 53 per cent of the world's absolute poor lived in densely populated South Asia, the next highest portion, 20 per cent, resided in sub-Saharan Africa. Approximately half of the latter region's total population was absolutely poor. Probably four-fifths of these people were rural-dwellers.[4]

Palpable relative poverty also characterizes tropical Africa. Needless to say, even if everyone within a country received an income above US $279 (or some other figure) in 1975, it would not necessarily have eliminated poverty. Income cannot validly be divorced from its societal context; people measure their own circumstances in relative terms. It is, moreover, reasonable that they should do so. The meaning of relative poverty – of having much less than others in the way of property and income – is, as so many poverty studies have shown, *humiliation* for the relatively deprived – a sense of powerlessness and lacking dignity. Owing to the positive correlation between economic inequality on the one hand and political inefficacy and social inferiority on the other, relative poverty can be as excruciating for its victims as absolute deprivation. Indeed, the 'culture of poverty' that Oscar Lewis did so much to popularize – the complex of self-destructive attitudes, values, personality structures and family relationships – is in large measure a reflection of, or a way of coping with, the structural constraints on success weighing upon the poor.[5]

It is one thing, however, to perceive relative poverty through living within a society and quite another to prove its existence. There is no universally applicable standard of income distribution that necessarily generates among the poorer a sense of relative deprivation and humiliation. The World Bank proposes that those households with per capita incomes of less than one-third of the average per capita income for a country constitute the 'relatively poor'; but this standard, though useful for illustrative purposes, appears wholly arbitrary. All one can say in general terms is that there is considerable inequality in tropical Africa. What the few cross-sectional studies of income distribution show is that most of the sub-Saharan countries manifest marked inequality in world terms, with the bottom 40 per cent of the population receiving 15 per cent or less of the total income. The least developed countries (for example, Chad, Niger, Uganda) had the least inequality, whereas the more developed ones (such as the Ivory Coast, Senegal, Kenya) evidenced the worst maldistribution. In addition, the few available country case studies arrive at the same sort of conclusions. Studies of income distribution in Kenya, Zambia and Ghana reveal, for instance, that in 1970–2 they ranked among those countries with the most extreme inequality, and that they had all experienced a worsening distribution since independence. In Uganda, living standards for all socio-economic levels rose during the 1960s, but there was no improvement in relative distribution; in both 1961 and 1970 the poorest 40 per cent of the population received only 19 per cent of the country's total income. Doubtless, the lot of the poor deteriorated in 1970–9 under the oppressive rule of Idi Amin.[6]

Tanzania, a case discussed in chapter 3, is one of the few African countries whose government has genuinely sought to reverse the trend toward income inequality. It has achieved some success in this since 1967 by means of selective salary freezes in the public service, tax policies, minimum wage policies, asset redistribution via nationalization and directly productive investment, the expansion of rural infra-structure and the promotion of *ujamaa* (socialist) villages. By 1972, the bottom 40 per cent of the population had increased its share of total income by about 2·5 per cent, the middle 40 per cent by 5·5 per cent, both at the expense of the top 20 per cent households.[7]

But is the trend towards income inequality (and hence, in poor countries, a high incidence of relative and absolute poverty) a cause for alarm? According to the famous Kuznets' hypothesis, economic growth involves – indeed, requires – increasing income inequality. The reasoning behind this is complex, but the essential point is that the wealthier households tend to save, whereas the poorer ones tend to consume. Consequently, any redistribution of income to the poor at low levels of development is likely to reduce savings and investment, and hence the rate of growth. However, at advanced levels, a different economic dynamic obtains, so that the income redistribution then demanded by the increasingly organized and powerful underprivileged classes is congruent with crisis-free economic growth. In short, income distribution tends initially to worsen and later to improve in the course of development.[8]

If such is the natural pattern of all capitalist development, then policy-makers in developing countries could justifiably regard income maldistribution with a degree of equanimity. Inequality and mass poverty now would presumably lay the groundwork for the more equitable distribution of an enlarged economic pie later.

But there are strong grounds for doubting the validity of the Kuznets hypothesis as a guide to policy in underdeveloped countries. In the first place, there is no necessity for income distribution to worsen as development proceeds. Two non-socialist countries, Taiwan and South Korea, have achieved high growth rates at the same time as the poor's share of national income has risen or has at least remained constant. As one recent review of the relevant literature put it,

cross-country data do show less-developed countries have greater inequality than developed countries, but cross-country evidence for a *U* curve [Kuznets' hypothesis] is very weak, and recently available data over time for individual less-developed countries throw even stronger doubt on the inevitability of initially increasing inequality during development.[9]

In the second place, there is no reason to believe that marked inequality and poverty will be temporary phenomena in most underdeveloped countries, as they mainly were in the West. It is noteworthy that the main evidence for the Kuznets' hypothesis is nineteenth- and early twentieth-century data relating to the early industrializers. To contend that development will lead to improving distribution in Third World countries requires one to assume that the conditions in the latter are similar to those in the early developers. But, in fact, the economic and political conditions are quite different. In the trenchant words of Michael Lipton in *Why Poor People Stay Poor*:

> Britain in 1815–1950 is not West Pakistan in 1947–2050. In Britain, inequality threatened stability: political stability as the literate poor organized, economic stability as the unemployed and underpaid proved unable to buy. Hence the dominant capitalist class tolerated a reduction in inequality as the price of stable, crisis-free growth. This involved increasing state responsibility for financing investment, education and other non-consumption expenses, as there were no longer enough very rich people to do so – and as the poor were no longer so weak as to have to accept the priorities of the rich. This process of socialization is still going on.
>
> In today's LDCs [less developed countries], inequality may also be self-destructive in the very long run. It militates against labour-intensive and efficient development paths; and it is at risk from literacy and popular political involvement (though both are generally lower than in the much more urbanized conditions of nineteenth-century North-West Europe). But in the twenty-five-year horizon, inequality assists political stability, because the articulate 'labour aristocracy' of the cities is small enough to be bought off with part of the surplus extracted from the numerous but inarticulate rural poor; and it assists economic stability, because the rest of the surplus can be used to sustain a process of capital-intensive industrialization that, however inefficient and unjust, is thereby enabled to provide growing wages and profits to its few participants.[10]

While I differ with Lipton on certain points, especially his characterization of the labour aristocracy, this statement stands as one of the most concise and cogent explanations of why growth, even if forthcoming, is unlikely in itself to resolve the poverty problem.

In the light of arguments like those just reviewed, conventional knowledge among development economists has shifted. Fewer would now argue that there is a justifiable economic rationale for high and increasing inequality in underdeveloped countries. Instead, there is almost a consensus that some policies designed to enhance social equity will not adversely affect, and under certain conditions will even stimulate, economic growth.[11] The wide acceptance of this view has promoted a deluge of proposals for fostering redistribution, as international agencies, foundations, and individuals have enlisted as shock troops in 'assaults' on mass poverty. But, of course, there are divergent prescriptions as to how this best of all possible worlds is to be won.

Basic-needs approaches

> Increases in national income – essential as they are – will not benefit the poor unless they reach the poor. They have not reached the poor to any significant degree in most developing countries in the past, and this in spite of historically unprecedented average rates of growth throughout the sixties.[12]

With this acknowledgement of the failure of the old development model in 1972, the President of the World Bank, Robert McNamara, inaugurated a new phase in the conventional wisdom of what some call the 'international development community'. New development strategies have since proliferated as each development-oriented international and national agency has sought to differentiate its product from the others. Hence, the World Bank officially shifted from a preoccupation with economic growth to a broader concern to eradicate absolute poverty and to promote 'redistribution with growth'; the United Nations' Environmental Programme moved, in its environmental policy, from a focus upon ecology to a more inclusive approach recognizing an 'inner limit' of minimum human needs as complementary to the ecological 'outer limit'; and the ILO broadened its earlier emphasis upon unemployment to encompass a commitment to the fulfilment of the 'basic needs' of the poor, whether employed or unemployed. Other agencies likewise dedicated themselves to the advancement of 'basic human needs' or 'minimum living standards'.

Should we take these belated professions of concern for the world's poor seriously? It is tempting simply to dismiss them all as slogans whose real function is to legitimize, in changing times, the existence of various international and national agencies. I think such a response is ill advised. Basic-needs approaches are not all the same. Not all the agencies allegedly assaulting poverty are actually so engaged; conversely, not all of them are benighted or devious.

It is important to distinguish between conservative and radical approaches to the poverty problem.[13] This distinction will obviously rest upon the depth of change envisaged: a conservative anti-poverty programme would propose piecemeal reforms within the existing national and international economic orders, whereas a radical one would prescribe a mutually reinforcing set of policies entailing structural change at the national and international levels. Inasmuch as this book adopts an 'underdevelopment' perspective in explaining poverty (see chapters 2 and 3), I take the position that only a radical approach could plausibly eradicate poverty in a non-oil-producing African country within a generation (twenty-five years) or so. Only radical anti-poverty programmes constitute genuine assaults on poverty.

The World Bank is the foremost instance of an international agency wedded to a conservative basic-needs strategy. In making this claim, I do not mean to imply that the World Bank is monolithic: there are obviously competing points of view on development policy within this agency. Nonetheless, the official view of the poverty problem, as reflected principally in McNamara's speeches since 1972, is that it arises largely from factors internal to each developing country, and that its eradication therefore largely depends upon governmental policies and actions directed towards these internal barriers to development. Moreover, the Bank's propensity for developing and prescribing policy on a sectoral basis (rural, urban, education, health and so on) lends itself to a conception of poverty amelioration as isolated, piecemeal reforms. Particular policy reforms and projects are designed to assist 'target groups' among the poor to escape absolute deprivation; but an unreformed modern sector will continue business as usual.* That this agency has adopted a moderate and cautious path is hardly surprising in the light of the institutional constraints under which it must operate. The World Bank must placate not only its major shareholders, the governments of the advanced-capitalist countries, but also its lenders in the international capital markets and its clientele, composed largely of the more conservative governments of the underdeveloped world.[14]

The Bank has been willing to recommend domestic reforms – including such important ones as land reform and the removal of biases in access to some essential public services – though there is no evidence it has pushed these very hard.[15] To motivate conservative governments, McNamara has sought to generate the requisite political will by fostering a fear of the poor. As he stated in his 1972 Address to the Board of Governors, 'policies designed to reduce the deprivation among the poorest 40 per cent in developing countries are prescriptions not only of principle but of prudence' (page 15).

There is no notion in Bank statements that the advanced-capitalist countries bear any responsibility for mass poverty, except insofar as their selfish trade policies restrict the flow of Third World exports. Indeed, the implication is that the rich nations deserve their wealth:

> The industrial base of the wealthy nations is so great, their technological capacity so advanced, and their consequent advantages so immense that it is unrealistic to expect that the gap between the rich and the poor nations will narrow by the end of the century. Every indication is that it will continue to grow. Nothing we can do is likely to prevent this. But what we can do is begin to move now to insure that absolute poverty . . . is ended.[16]

---

*There is a 'progressive' wing of the World Bank that sees the basic-needs approach as an integrated, systemic strategy premised upon structural political change. See Mahbub ul Haq and S. J. Burki, *Meeting Basic Needs: An Overview*, Poverty and Basic Needs Series, World Bank, Washington, DC, September 1980. However, the title page declares: 'the views and interpretations expressed are those of the authors and should not be attributed to the World Bank.'

In this great enterprise the contribution of the industrialized members is to be minor. They are enjoined, on grounds of charity, to increase their Official Development Assistance to 0·7 per cent of their Gross National Products, and to eliminate discriminatory trade barriers to imports from poor countries. The international economic order would remain basically unreformed.

If the ILO has elaborated a more radical (and also a theoretically more adequate) basic-needs approach than the World Bank, how is this to be explained? At first glance, the institutional constraints bearing upon the ILO seem no less onerous than those restricting the Bank. The ILO, after all, emerged in 1919 as a European response to the threat posed internationally by Soviet Bolshevism. In the words of a former ILO official, it 'offered organized labor participation in social and industrial reform within an accepted framework of capitalism'. It has continued to embody a form of tripartism consistent with the corporatist system evolving in industrialized societies. In this system, a doctrine of 'harmony of interest' legitimizes the search for consensus and accommodation among the leaders of big business, big labour and the state, especially with respect to the management of the economy. This is obviously not a propitious environment for the development of a programme dedicated to the eradication of mass poverty.[17]

From its start in 1969, the ILO's World Employment Programme confronted a contradiction in its terms of reference. On the one hand, the emergence of this Programme was to be emblematic of the ILO's readiness to tackle the vital issues of international development. This orientation prompted a creative group of economists to broaden the initial focus upon unemployment to encompass a concern for the creation of more egalitarian societies via the provision of productive employment for all. But the formation of such societies would obviously require structural transformations of national and transnational economic relationships in order to incorporate unorganized and marginal citizens into remunerative activities. On the other hand, the ILO required the WEP to work through the existing structures of the organization; yet these reflected the power of those largely satisfied with the existing pattern of employment and income distribution – the representatives of organized business, organized labour and governments. Precipitated by the American withdrawal from the ILO, the resolution of this contradiction took the form of the emasculation and reorientation of the WEP. This transpired following the World Employment Conference of 1976, when a new management received 'a mandate to reduce the scale of the WEP and to bring it into line with ILO orthodoxy'.[18]

Although the radical impetus of the WEP is now spent, this is no reason to ignore its seminal work associated with the 1976 conference. This constitutes, in my judgement, a plausible model of an alternative pattern of growth or accumulation in underdeveloped countries which is capable of speedily overcoming absolute deprivation and reducing massive inequalities. This model has much in common with other recent visionary approaches, most particularly those produced by the Dag Hammarskjöld Foundation in Uppsala, Sweden, the Fundacion Bariloche in Argentina, and the Foundation Reshaping the International Order (RIO) in the Netherlands.*

The aim of the WEP is to encourage all 'countries' to seek to satisfy the basic needs of their people by the end of the century. While it is part of the ILO's populist rhetoric to contend that the people in each country must themselves determine the scope and priority of basic needs, ILO economists have, in practice, been willing to offer their own definitions. Material basic needs include certain minimum levels of private consumption of food, clothing and shelter, and access to certain essential public services, such as pure water, sanitation, public transport, and health and educational facilities. Technocrats have expended considerable effort in seeking to quantify these needs and to establish national and international targets for each; but these rather arid exercises cannot detain us here. Of more importance is the question of scope. Should an anti-poverty programme concentrate solely upon material needs, or should it include, as well, some basic human rights? The rationale for a preoccupation with the fulfilment of material needs is quite simple: these are the foundation of all other human needs because their satisfaction is essential for survival. Nonetheless, at least one non-material goal – popular participation – is closely connected with any assault on poverty, as an important means as well as an end in itself. As one proponent writes, 'the mass commitment and mobilization that would appear to be essential in most countries to attain basic-needs targets within a reasonable period can only be forthcoming in a system involving mass participation and support'.[19]

What package of mutually reinforcing policies will lead to the eradication of absolute poverty? At the national level, the general approach is to enjoin governments to satisfy material needs not by

---

*The approach of the Dag Hammarskjöld Foundation is presented in two of its publications: *What Now?: Another Development* (1975) and *Another Development: Approaches and Strategies* (1977). The Bariloche working group uses econometric modelling techniques to discern alternative development strategies capable of satisfying the basic needs of populations in various regions of the world. See Amilcar O. Herrera *et al.*, *Catastrophe or New Society* (Ottawa: International Development Research Centre, 1976), and G. Chichilnisky, 'Development Patterns and the International Order', *Journal of International Affairs*, xxi, 2 (1977), pp. 275–304. RIO sketches the main features of a national basic-needs strategy that should accompany movement towards a new international economic order in chapter 5 of Jan Tinbergen *et al.*, *Reshaping the International Order: A Report to the Club of Rome* (New York: E. P. Dutton, 1976).

transfer payments to the poor (which are both intolerably expensive and detrimental to growth prospects), but by the provision of sufficient productive (and presumably remunerative) employment and of essential public services available to all. To achieve these goals, the WEP rightly refuses to furnish a ready-made strategy. The specific set of policies in each country will depend upon such factors as its level of economic development, the pattern of income and wealth distribution, and the local definition of basic needs. Nevertheless, for all underdeveloped countries there are certain principles that must guide economic strategy if this is to achieve the ultimate end. These are essentially three.

In the first place, there must be a redistribution of income in order to create an effective demand for the goods and services that together constitute the fulfilment of basic needs in a particular country. The forms and extent of income redistribution will depend upon the initial pattern of distribution and the rate of growth. But there is little doubt that the satisfaction of basic needs within the short space of twenty-five years will, in most cases, require a redistribution of existing *wealth*, as well as future income. In highly inegalitarian societies it is simply impracticable to redistribute income without redistributing productive resources. This, as Keith Griffin succinctly explains, is

partly because it is difficult to confine the effects of standard price, subsidy, tax and expenditure policies to a particular group and partly because the effects of many standard economic policies ultimately are neutralized by off-setting forces set in motion by the policies themselves. For example, the benefits of a rural road-building programme cannot be limited to small farmers; they inevitably 'spill over' or 'leak' to large farmers as well. Similarly, the imposition of a minimum wage for landless agricultural labourers will have multifarious implications for, say, the costs of agricultural production, the demand for labour, the level of food prices and of prices in general – all of which will tend to counteract the effects of the legislation on the distribution of income. Thus because of leakages and countervailing forces the only way to alter substantially the distribution of income is by altering the distribution of wealth.[20]

For most underdeveloped countries, asset redistribution means, above all, land reform.

In the second place, the state must oversee a reorientation of the system of production to make this accord with the gratification of material needs. The redistribution (or even socialization) of existing productive facilities will not, in itself, facilitate the abolition of mass poverty; there is a need to uproot old economic activities and to create new ones. Essential here is a commitment to innovation in, and diffusion of, 'appropriate technologies'. An appropriate technology is one that is more congruent with a society's needs, resources and physical environment than an alternative. Obviously, basic-needs development requires a shift away from the production of non-essential goods for the relatively well-off and towards the production of basic foodstuffs and simpler consumer and capital goods appropriate to the low incomes of the majority. In addition, if remunerative employment is to be generated for the Third World's 1 billion unemployed and grossly underemployed individuals by the year 2000, many of the technologies employed will need to be capital-saving and labour-intensive. Though highly efficient, modern capital-intensive techniques transferred from industrialized countries cannot supply the needed jobs. This is evident from a calculation of the prohibitive investment involved in absorbing burgeoning labour forces into modern-sector employment by the end of the century. It cost about US $20,000 to create a job in the United States in 1978 and about the same to do so in the modern sector of an underdeveloped country. Investment on the scale required to absorb the poor into high-technology jobs is simply impracticable in the poorer countries. Hence, a necessary condition for an assault on poverty in Africa is the (probably endogenous) development of technologies which 'will raise the productivity of small farmers, create employment for landless labourers, lead to more productive use of labour in public works programmes, and establish labour-intensive industries which rely on local materials and meet local needs'.[21]

All the changes discussed so far will, it is hoped, interrelate and reinforce each other. Production, consumption and resource distribution form a configuration of interdependent elements in which each entails, and is entailed by, the others. A real assault on absolute poverty necessitates the replacement of the existing 'vicious circle' of inappropriate technology, inappropriate products and a highly concentrated income distribution with a 'virtuous circle' of appropriate technology, appropriate products, and a more egalitarian income distribution. The ILO describes this process thus:

High and growing inequality of income generates rapidly increased demand for luxury goods (in particular, expensive consumer durables) but relatively sluggish growth of effective demand for basic foodstuffs and consumer goods. Increased productive employment and higher incomes for the poor will change both the level and rate of growth of demand for basic consumer goods and public services. This shift in the composition of demand should induce a shift in the pattern of production towards goods which in many cases are more suitable for production on a relatively small scale. This may tend in turn to generate higher levels of productive employment, to the extent that the new output mix is characterized by greater labour intensity. Moreover, the new conditions should increase the incentive to search for and use more appropriate technologies.[22]

The most contentious aspect of this economic reasoning concerns expectations about technological change. Is it likely that scientists, engineers and tinkerers can design labour-intensive technologies which are as efficient, or nearly as efficient, as the existing relatively capital-intensive ones? Many economists are sceptical. Some argue that capital-intensive development is more likely to produce sustained growth and eventual productive employment than labour-intensive development. Others contend, more cautiously, that there is no reason to suppose that 'basic' or essential goods (other than foodstuffs) are more susceptible to labour-intensive yet efficient techniques than high-income non-essential or 'luxury' goods. (Poor consumers certainly make good use of *some* capital-intensive products, such as plastic shoes, bicycles, and synthetic fertilizers.) Note, however, that the debate is conducted largely in hypothetical terms. Today the bulk of global research is devoted to the development of increasingly sophisticated technologies. Only the allocation of comparable resources to research in appropriate technology could permit the controversy that surrounds this to be decisively resolved. Yet, ironically, only the incentive provided by a basic-needs commitment in some groups of underdeveloped countries could call forth the indigenous research effort there that is required. Any such effort, it should be emphasized, would *not* require a wholesale rejection of modern technology. Instead, the realistic aim would be to develop a mix of techniques. The probability of designing efficient labour-intensive techniques obviously varies by sector and, within each sector, by process or product. Experience suggests there is a higher likelihood of introducing intermediate technologies into agriculture, the service sector and construction than into manufacturing industries. Within the last sector, products such as petrochemicals, basic chemicals, synthetic fertilizers, steel, heavy machinery and pulp and paper can probably be produced efficiently only using large-scale, capital-intensive technologies. Other products, such as sugar or clothing, provide more scope for the design of labour-intensive techniques. Basic-needs development, therefore, does not imply a harking back to a more primitive technological level; it does involve, as the Chinese say, 'walking on two legs'.[23]

The third and final principle that must underlie a basic-needs approach is the provision of equitable access to expanded and reformed public services. The availability to the poor of appropriate educational and health facilities, clean water, environmental sanitation and adequate public transport is clearly an end in itself; it can also make a substantial contribution to augmenting the productivity of poor people and to promoting their fuller participation in society.[24]

This then, in essence, is the vision of the WEP. The economic logic is plausible, though not beyond debate. What is left unstated are the relations of production and specific development strategies consistent with this anti-poverty programme. While the sorts of structural changes envisaged demand an expanded economic role for the state, the ILO documents coyly steer clear of advocating any capitalist or socialist path. It is at this point that the institutional constraints upon the ILO mentioned above have apparently had their impact.

The radical implication of this approach require little elaboration. The State in underdeveloped countries is called upon to intervene in order to remove class biases in access to public services and redistribute income and probably assets from powerful social classes to those whose economic and political power is currently insubstantial. It goes without saying that in societies with a high concentration of land ownership, a thoroughgoing redistribution of land is a precondition for poverty eradication. But even where no great inequality of landholdings exists a redistribution of wealth is probably necessary. This need is demonstrated in studies designed to assess the efficacy of alternative policies to satisfy the (quantified) basic needs of the bottom 20 per cent of populations by the year 2000. Employing computer models, two such studies conclude that only a development strategy that combines initial *and subsequent* redistribution of income and assets with a growth rate of 6 per cent per annum could eradicate absolute poverty in Africa within the target period. As one set of these authors defensively notes, these findings 'result from a quantitative and regionally disaggregated model, not from any ideological analysis'.[25]

Indeed, the vision has more radical implications than even these projections indicate. Central to basic-needs development is a shift throughout the economy towards more appropriate technologies producing more appropriate goods. But there is reason to believe that this necessary change will not occur smoothly or gradually. Frances Stewart has authoritatively contended that 'the use of advanced-country technology builds up biases in selection mechanisms in favour of its further use; this in turn leads to further decisions in favour of such technology.' Although her argument is complex, the process by which a vicious circle of inappropriate technology perpetuates itself is basically this. Modern capital-intensive technologies are inappropriate to the environment of underdeveloped countries in the ways I adumbrated above and shall discuss further in chapter 2. Despite this, their importation into these countries will continue, in part because their presence moulds the economic infrastructure (for instance, the education and transportation systems) to conform to their requirements, and in part because certain powerful local classes and foreign investors gain a vested interest in their perpetuation. This vested interest arises from the profits made possible by technologies which, by ensuring high labour productivity, permit a concentration of income high enough to create and sustain a demand for the capital-intensive goods produced. (One might add that some people gain a vested interest also in the sort of life style that the prestigious high technologies make possible for a minority.) Moreover, governments, which promote to a greater or less extent the interests of the classes benefiting from the modern sector, support – that is, subsidize and protect – this sector. A consequence is that the local innovation of more appropriate, though still efficient, technologies is discouraged. Underdeveloped countries are therefore likely to remain dependent upon the advanced-capitalist countries, insofar as technical progress ensures the obsolescence of all existing modern technologies.[26]

This is truly a gloomy diagnosis. If one accepts the proposition that the 'inappropriate' technologies now installed in most African countries are in fact appropriate to the economic interests of the ruling groups, then the prospects for significant technological change are bleak. Technology in this perspective is but one element of an interlinked political-economic system Therefore, a precondition for a national commitment to develop an independent technological capability and to foster appropriate technologies is radical structural change. This would need to include a shift both in power towards the poorer classes and in the choice of consumption patterns on the part of the (new?) dominant classes. But what is the likelihood of such profound change in most African countries?

There are also evident radical implications for the international economic order. À propos transnational corporations, a genuine assault on mass poverty would adversely affect their interests in two principal ways. First, this approach would probably end their domination of many manufacturing industries in the Third World. Basic-needs development would nullify, in many product lines, the oligopolistic advantages of manufacturing transnationals, namely, their control over sophisticated technologies and expensive marketing techniques to produce and sell branded, Western-style consumer goods. Transnational corporations in search of profits *could* invent and develop cheap, mass-produced consumer and producer goods to satisfy basic needs. But to the extent that they succeeded in this, they would make themselves dispensable. Local industrialists could easily imitate the transnational corporations' standardized processes and products. Imported technologies would then remain indispensable only with respect to products designed for consumers in affluent countries or to important 'appropriate' products, such as synthetic fertilizers, petrochemicals, basic steel and heavy equipment, whose efficient production probably requires capital-intensive techniques.[27]

Secondly, this basic-needs approach would also threaten the transnational corporations' control over the export trade of the Third World. Since the simpler goods and technologies intrinsic to the strategy would interest mainly the people of underdeveloped countries, there would presumably be an expansion of trade among these and a correspondingly diminished reliance upon less appropriate imports from advanced-capitalist countries. In short, a new international division of labour could emerge, with various Third World countries specializing in particular basic products and capital goods.[28] This would advance the goal of national and collective self-reliance, though probably at the expense of the transnational corporations and the capitalist centres.

These brief comments imply that the challenge to the international economic order transcends the interests of the transnational corporations. Indeed, the 'Declaration of Principles' which emanated (in diluted form) from the ILO's 1976 World Employment Conference makes this explicit. Identifying mass poverty as a 'one-world problem' caused by international as well as national factors, this document cryptically declares that the basic-needs approach is 'only the first phase of the redistributive global growth process'. It is likely that the poorer underdeveloped countries would be unable to provide for mass basic needs within a generation without a substantial, unilateral transfer of resources from the rich countries. In short, basic-needs development, if ever it were widely implemented, would entail a transformation of the international economic order. In the words of one judicious proponent:

> A focus on meeting the basic needs of the people should imply a lessening of the dependence of the Third World on the markets, capital and technologies of the industrialized world; a greater potential for trade expansion among developing countries; an improvement in their terms of trade *vis-à-vis* the industrialized world; a reduced dependence on and role for multinationals and sophisticated technologies; a reorientation of development assistance . . . . [A] basic-needs approach opens up the possibility of autonomous, self-sustained growth for the Third World . . . . [This strategy] would thus appear to be a more potent means of realizing the Third World demands for a restructuring of the world economy . . . than endless, protracted negotiations.[29]

If a concern for one's fellow man ruled the world, radical basic-needs strategies would be in the process of implementation everywhere. Unfortunately, the choice of public policy generally depends upon different considerations.

The politics of basic needs

Utopianism and ideological mystification are related charges which one could lay against the approach just outlined. The first allegation is that exponents adduce no persuasive reasons why dominant classes would agree to open up the polity to mass participation, limit their own privileges, and turn against favoured foreign interests. If the poor represent a threat to their privileges, would not coercion do as well as structural reform in keeping the poor quiescent – and at a lower cost to the rich? The second stricture is that putative 'assaults on poverty' may not only abort but, worse, serve an (unintended) ideological function. There is a tendency for ruling groups to expropriate attractive social doctrines (such as 'democracy', 'socialism'), convert them into slogans, and use these to legitimize inegalitarian and often oppressive social orders. There is no reason to suppose that this fate will not befall basic-needs approaches. Third World regimes may adopt the rhetoric of basic needs, but implement only those marginal reforms (for instance, 'low-cost' housing) required to give credence to the notion of progress and, hence, forestall popular challenges.[30]

The crux of these potential objections is that fighting poverty is as much a *political* as a technical problem. That is, the problem is one of mobilizing the political will to undertake radical change, as well as one of appropriate planning, resource allocation, and so on. Indeed, this is a truth that basic-needs proponents have been willing to accept – in principle. There is no dearth of statements in the relevant ILO documents recognizing the centrality of power structures in the perpetuation of mass poverty. Hence, two political prerequisites for the basic-needs approach are stated as 'an effective, decentralized and democratic administrative structure to translate policies into decisions and action', and 'mass participation in the development process by the poverty groups'.[31] Yet despite these statements, the audience for which the reports seem to be written is made up of planners. There is too much emphasis upon the quantification of basic needs and the elaboration of technically practicable combinations of measures, and too little concern (understandably, given the institutional context) with political strategy and political feasibility.

In consequence, the basic-needs approach does constitute more in the way of a utopia than a strategy. It offers a valuable vision of an alternative society and international order which has abolished poverty through a reorganization of production, distribution, consumption and political institutions. But it does not really connect the 'is' to the 'ought', as any programme must seek to do.

Hence, the contribution of this book. It attempts to provide an analysis not only of what *is*, but also of what *might be*. Without an understanding of the political-economic roots of existing inequality and poverty, there is unlikely to be a successful strategy for transcending these problems. My thesis, implicit in my exposition and critique of the basic-needs approach, is at one level quite simple and even non-controversial. An assault on mass poverty requires a profound restructuring of human relations, especially productive relations. This restructuring would deprive the members of the dominant class or classes and their foreign allies of their privileges. Therefore, they resist the necessary changes, using the repressive power of the state and the persuasive influence of ideology to this end. A political economy of poverty therefore requires an investigation of the class alliances and forms of the state which underpin poverty-generating strategies of capital accumulation. But this alone is insufficient. Left at this point, the analysis might contribute to a sense of powerlessness and hopelessness on the part of those who would strive for a new order. The analyst must also honour, as best he can, an obligation to adopt the optative mood: to suggest what development strategies and associated class alliances may accord with the basic-needs approach, and what the state of struggle towards these strategies now is. In this book the focus is upon tropical Africa, with special reference to the urban areas.

Before proceeding to justify this urban emphasis, I should indicate how the chapters relate to the central themes. Chapter 2 examines the pattern of peripheral capitalist development in urban Africa and, in particular, how this perpetuates marginalization and mass poverty. Chapters 3–6 then explore the politics of basic needs by focusing upon the relationship between the state, class formation, and public policy. The aim, to repeat, is to comprehend the political conditions that retard, or alternatively might foster, a development strategy congruent with the basic-needs vision. The book concludes with a consideration of the feasibility and limitations of particular strategies and political activity to achieve 'Another Development', in light of the analysis of national class formation and transnational influences.

Is an urban emphasis warranted?

'The basic conflict in the Third World', writes Michael Lipton in *Why Poor People Stay Poor*, 'is not between capital and labour, but between capital and countryside, farmer and townsman, villager (including the temporarily urban "fringe villager") and urban industrial employer-cum-proletarian elite. . . .'[32] If this is true, the urban emphasis of this study is a mistake. The towns and cities would constitute part of the *cause* of mass poverty, not part of the solution.

There is no doubt that Lipton provides a useful corrective to the view that equates development with urban-based industrialization and infrastructural modernization. Urban bias on the part of some Third World governments exists; it is typically manifest in controls on food prices, tax policies, subsidies and credit schemes, and public investments and services. The high rates of rural–urban migration are, in large part, a consequence of official neglect of rural economic conditions – despite rhetorical commitments to rural development. An anti-poverty programme must therefore remove this bias by seeking to achieve national self-sufficiency in food, raise agricultural incomes, expand agricultural employment and employment in the smaller towns, and provide basic health, educational and environmental services to rural-dwellers.

It follows that any policies that augment urban bias are likely to compound the poverty problem. Relevant here is the paradox that efforts to expand urban employment in countries with stagnant rural areas will increase urban unemployment and underemployment, a consequence of stimulating greater migration to the relatively prosperous cities.[33] This book therefore does not treat urban poverty as a problem that is soluble in isolation. Instead, it asks: what role do urban elements play in perpetuating mass poverty, and what role might some of these play in its transcendence?

It is unclear whether even this formulation would satisfy Lipton. For him, urban *bias* is the problem, and therefore the primary contradiction lies between privileged urban-dwellers and the impoverished rural masses. Why then would the former play any positive role in alleviating the problems of the latter? But this is a case of an author overstating his case in order to make a point. His political analysis should not stand, for in incorrectly delimiting the range of progressive class alliances, he unintentionally hinders effective political practice designed to eliminate poverty.

In the first place, Lipton's position depends upon two untenable assumptions. These are that the visible urban poor can actually be identified with the rural population, and that the rich landowners generally possess extensive urban connections. This is a convenient view. But it often does not accord with reality. On the one hand, as this book will show, it is just as fallacious for Lipton to identify the urban poor as unemployed or underemployed temporary migrants, as it is for him to label the urban working class a 'labour aristocracy'. The facts are that the so-called 'urban fringe villager' is often a hardworking member of the informal sector, and that he, along with other deprived urban elements (including segments of the working class), is frequently committed to urban living on a long-term basis. For some, there was really no alternative to a fairly permanent cityward migration, owing to population pressure upon land in their rural homes and the rules governing inheritance. For others, the only hope (if slim) for material success lay in the city. On the other hand, Lipton overemphasizes the degree of rural equality. Contradictions exist here too; moreover, they exist not just between the wealthy landowner with urban ties, on the one side, and the rural masses, on the other. The commercialization of agriculture, in Africa as elsewhere, has generated rural differentiation, and hence a minority who would lose, as well as a majority who would gain, from basic-needs development. In short, a simple, dichotomic, rural–urban model of class conflict cannot capture the complexity of actual and potential class alliances (as Lipton recognizes in his less polemical sections).

In the second place, we need to be clear that there *is* a real and growing problem of urban poverty in tropical Africa. If so, stabilized urban classes exist whose *objective* interests would lie in an assault on poverty – even if this necessitated a removal of urban bias in the allocation of resources. Lipton points out that average incomes are higher in urban than rural areas. While this is generally true, one must bear in mind several factors in evaluating the rural–urban incidence of absolute poverty. First, fragmentary evidence suggests that in Africa incomes are more unequally distributed in town than country.[34] Even if average urban incomes are relatively high, therefore, many urban dwellers may still suffer deprivation, absolute as well as relative. Secondly, it is very difficult, as I shall discuss in chapter 4, to compare cash estimates of income in rural and urban areas; not only do prices differ, but urban life also involves extra expenses. Thirdly, though an urban bias in the provision of public services is widely observed, there is no evidence that the poorest third or quarter of urban populations actually have access to them.[35]

Indeed, there is some direct evidence that the basic needs of many African urbanites are not being met. Based on the research carried out by his World Bank staff, Robert McNamara has described the lot of the Third World urban poor as 'unspeakably grim':

> Poverty pervades not only the countryside, but the urban centers of the developing world as well. There, the numbers of the poor are smaller. But the natural increases within the cities, combined with the rapid rate of migration from the rural areas, guarantees that the problem will grow to mammoth proportions in the next two decades, if governments do not begin to take appropriate measures to deal with it.

Although table 1.3 shows that only between 12 and 38 per cent of the populations of the larger African countries is urban (according to national definitions), the rate of urban growth is the world's highest. The United Nations has projected an African urban population by the year 2000 of about 320 million persons, equal to the *total* population of Africa in 1965. The bulk of the rural migrants, according to migration studies, initially settle in the slums and spontaneous settlements in and around the towns and cities.[36]

Table 1.3   *Structure of population, selected African countries*

	% of population urban 1980	Average annual increase		% of labour force in agriculture 1978
		Total population 1970–8	Urban population 1970–80	
Ivory Coast	38	5·6	8·2	81
Zambia	38	3·0	5·4	68
Ghana	36	3·0	5·2	54
Zaïre	34	2·7	7·2	76
Senegal	25	2·6	3·3	77
Nigeria	20	2·5	4·9	56
Kenya	14	3·3	6·8	79
Uganda	12	2·9	7·0	83
Tanzania	12	3·0	8·3	83

Source: World Bank, *World Development Report, 1980* (New York: Oxford University Press, 1980), tables 17, 19 and 20

Consider briefly some facets of the African urban poverty problem. Perhaps the most concrete manifestation of this poverty is the inadequacy of housing and the associated environmental and sanitary services. The squalor of the burgeoning slums and spontaneous settlements, catering for up to half of a city's population, is too well known to require elaboration. Many residential areas contain dilapidated and overcrowded housing whose inhabitants lack access to an adequate supply of clean water and electricity, or to waste and garbage disposal systems, drains and paved roads, and medical facilities.[37] One obvious by-product of these conditions is the prevalence of certain diseases among the residents. While the sparse evidence does not permit one to conclude whether the health of the urban poor is generally better or worse than that of rural people, the former's higher susceptibility to certain maladies is established. In principle, this differential susceptibility should be more than offset by the superior medical facilities available in the towns. In practice, however, these superior facilities are often located far from low-income settlements, and are, in any event, rarely inexpensive to use, even where medical services are nominally free.[38]

Diseases posing special threats to the urban poor are those borne by excreta and passed on through the contamination of water, foodstuffs and soils, and those borne by the air or spread by human contact. Diseases in the former category include gastro-enteric ones, especially diarrhoea (which has the effect of lowering resistance to other diseases), cholera, and parasitic infestations, especially in children. Indeed, intestinal parasites have been found to infest from half to three-quarters of the children examined in low-income housing areas, but a considerably smaller proportion of children from better-quality areas.[39] Tuberculosis is 'primarily an urban slum disease', insofar as its incidence is much higher there than elsewhere in the city or in the countryside. For instance in Kano, northern Nigeria, the infection rate for children in the congested, predominantly poor, central area was almost twice that in the higher-quality housing areas. Tuberculosis is also commonly found in association with other diseases of the poor, such as malnutrition, anaemia and malaria.[40] Pneumonia is another poverty disease. A study in Lagos found that bronchitis and pneumonia were the leading causes of death among children under five years of age (accounting for one-quarter of all deaths!) and adults over seventy-five. Furthermore, the mortality rates from these causes were highest in areas with overcrowded, poor-quality housing, whereas they were negligible in the highest-quality areas – except among servants! Pneumonia was also associated with other diseases of the poor, including kwashiorkor, gastro-enteritis, tetanus, anaemia and amoebiasis.[41]

There is also a possibility that the urban poor are more likely to succumb to psychogenic maladies than others. Their lack of privacy, in conjunction with the stress associated with economic insecurity and self-disparaging comparisons with more successful people, may be conducive to mental illness. Among the Yoruba of Nigeria, for instance, the incidence of mental illness was highest among the long-term urban 'migrant labourers' who were unemployed and lived alone. But the statistical data pertaining to the socio-economic and geographic incidence of mental illness is too sparse to support any hypothesis of differential susceptibility. All one can say with any degree of assurance is that the rapid socio-economic change and the insecurity characteristic of urban life do spawn neuroses that are uncommon in the rural areas.[42]

Good health depends not only upon adequate housing, sanitary services and medical facilities, but also upon access to nutritious food. The available literature allows one to pose two generalizations with respect to African nutritional levels. In the first place, urban-dwellers on the average tend to be as well, or better, fed than the peasant population. In the second place, the nutrition of those living in urban slums and dense, uncontrolled settlements tends to be far inferior to that of people residing in higher-quality neighbourhoods, and worse (or no better) than that of control groups of rural-dwellers. This is so even though the poorest urban households allocate as much as 70 per cent of their total incomes to food purchases. This intra-urban inequality in nutrition is graphically illustrated by a detailed budget survey undertaken recently in Kinshasa. On the basis of a stratified sample drawn from five socio-economic categories, this study found a positive correlation between urban poverty and nutritionally deficient diets. Establishing the food consumption per member in the workers' households as 100, the authors discovered that while the consumption of the unemployed was essentially the same, that of the 'white collar' households was 143, of the 'merchant' households, 175, and of the 'manager' households, 225. The poor also consume many more starchy staples, and many less animal products than the better-off, confirming a trend found elsewhere in the world. There is probably only one rare circumstance where this correlation between low income and malnutrition does not obtain: where the density of a squatter settlement is low enough to permit most households to cultivate their own vegetable gardens.[43]

Children are most adversely affected by malnutrition. Items in the traditional diets of children (such as home-produced goat or cow milk) are often replaced with less nutritious substitutes by poor urban parents – owing to low family incomes and, sometimes, ignorance. Not surprisingly, then, kwashiorkor is more widespread in low-income urban areas than elsewhere in the cities or in most villages. Inasmuch as early malnutrition retards the development of a child's physical and intellectual capacities, this situation leads to an irreversible waste of human resources.[44]

Access to educational facilities is a basic public service at least as crucial for the poor as their access to health facilities. If the children of the poor cannot gain educational credentials, their chances of social mobility are bleak. Yet the unpleasant reality in much of Africa – as in the West – is a marked inequality in access to education on a regional, rural-urban and intra-urban basis. It is generally assumed that urban-dwellers as a whole benefit from the urban bias in the location of schools. Such is often not the case. The World Bank's Urban Poverty Task Force has discovered that, in general, 'while school enrolment ratios in urban areas are typically much higher than those in rural areas, these averages mask marked educational disadvantages for the urban poor, who usually have about the same lack of access to education as their rural counterparts'. The rule is that educational institutions are scarcer and of lower quality in low- than in high-income neighbourhoods. Nairobi epitomizes this trend; here the colonial division of schools on a racial basis has been superseded by a non-racial but elitist three-tier system maintained by differential tuition fees. The three types of primary schools, differentiated in terms of the quality of teachers and resources, reflect in their location the socio-economic spatial structure of the city. In Lusaka, too, according to a World Bank report, the educational systems 'show an elitist bias, favoring upper- and middle-income groups at the expense of the rural and urban poor'. While about half of Lusaka's population lives in squatter areas, all schools (with a single exception) were located elsewhere. It thus comes as no surprise that primary-school enrolment was only 36 per cent of the appropriate age group in the squatter areas, and 90 per cent in the rest of the city, and that drop-out and repetition rates were also highest among the children of squatters. The same differential spatial distribution of schools along socio-economic lines is evident in Abidjan, and doubtless in other cities for which data is lacking.[45] Nonetheless, it must be borne in mind that even the inferior urban schools are superior (and more accessible) than those available in much of the countryside.

In light of these tendencies, one would expect to find a positive correlation between class position and the educational achievement of children. In countries such as the Ivory Coast, Kenya, Nigeria and Ghana, the children of the small, urban, well-educated and mainly administrative/managerial/professional class indeed gain a dispro-portionate access to higher education, and hence to remunerative jobs. In Ghana in 1964, for example, though urban-dwellers (constituting 12 per cent of the total population) obtained nearly half of that country's sixth-form places, some urban classes were even more under-represented at this level than some sections of the peasantry. The managerial bourgeoisie had about fifty times the representation that would have resulted from a random distribution. The unskilled and semi-skilled workers, in contrast, comprised 13 per cent of the country's labour force, yet their children formed only 0·2 per cent of the sixth-form sample and 0·3 per cent of the University of Ghana sample. In the 1960s a rapid expansion of the Ghanaian educational system occurred: enrolment in publicly supported secondary schools grew from 14 000 in

1960 to 56 800 in 1972. Yet this enlargement apparently failed to enhance equality of opportunity. A large-scale sample survey of secondary students in 1974 led to the conclusion that

> recruitment . . . is noticeably less fluid than it was in 1961, despite large-scale expansion that theoretically allows for increased democratization of access. Rather than serving to broaden the base of recruitment, expansion has made it comparatively less likely that children from rural and/or low socio-economic backgrounds would receive places in the nation's secondary schools. This suggests that the secondary level of the educational system is acting increasingly to reproduce social inequality rather than offer opportunities for mobility. . . . It can be argued that [the data] suggest the emergence of a more rigid and closed class structure than existed previously.

It is likely that the children of the rural and urban poor have more equal access to schooling in Tanzania, where public policy genuinely seeks to check class formation. But the data to confirm this proposition are lacking.[46]

To be poor in urban Africa is thus to live in overcrowded and inadequate dwellings and to confront both peculiar health hazards and the possibility of raising malnourished, and therefore mentally and physically stunted, children. Furthermore, the prospects for escaping these conditions are generally not good. The process of class crystallization in much of urban Africa is evident in the manner in which educational institutions, though ostensibly equally open to all, are actually biased against the children of the lower classes.

On this point I have argued, *pace* Lipton, that the notion of the city exploiting the countryside is too gross to guide analysis or political practice. One cannot validly reduce mass poverty to a wholly rural phenomenon. Objectively, many urban-dwellers have much to gain from an anti-poverty programme, whereas some rural classes and strata have something to lose from it. Hence, on these grounds, an urban emphasis in a study of the politics of basic needs is not illegitimate, provided the study recognizes the impossibility of 'solving' urban poverty while rural poverty remains.

But there is also a positive ground for choosing an urban focus. If structural political change is normally a prerequisite for a basic-needs development strategy, then the radical protest that produces this change is likely to emerge first in the expanding cities of Africa. It is here that inequality and exploitation are most visible and oppressive, and oppositional organizational resources most concentrated.

It is a commonplace of sociological studies that alienated urban intellectuals and proletariats frequently lead organized protest or revolutions in largely peasant societies. Peasants, for well-known reasons, normally exhibit very limited class consciousness and solidarity, and rarely engage in sustained, independent class action. The typical peasant protest is the *jacquerie*; this is a spontaneous mass rising animated by either a profound desire to purge corrupt or oppressive elites, or a chiliastic vision. In neither case is peasant rebellion likely to institute a new social order. A basic-needs strategy, requiring a fundamental reorganization of production, distribution, consumption and political institutions, will need anchorage in more conscious and enduring social movements than rural people alone are likely to create. In the specific case of twentieth-century socialist revolutions, urban elements have provided this anchorage:

> the original impetus, organization, leadership and ideology of revolutionary struggle *began* precisely in the more advanced sectors of the peripheral economy: in Russia the Petrograd proletariat led by the Bolshevik Party; in China and in Vietnam in the coastal cities; in Cuba in Havana. In all cases, however, the *success* of the revolution which began in the advanced productive units depended on joining efforts with the bulk of the social forces (peasants) located in the backward areas of the economy.[47]

Even Frantz Fanon, known for his identification of the peasantry as 'the only spontaneously revolutionary force' and his disparaging remarks about urban workers, was, according to one persuasive analysis, 'realistically aware of [peasant] organization and leadership limitations, frankly admitting the revolutionary cadres had to be recruited from urban nationalists and the proletariat'. Indeed, Fanon's alleged 'peasant messianism' aimed more to create a myth, to mobilize revolutionary activists into organizing the peasants, than accurately to portray the real world.[48]

Needless to say, the explanation of the 'joining up' between urban and rural protest is complex. Many studies in the vast literature on the political potential of peasantries stress the importance of rural social differentiation in understanding peasant rebellion. In one popular view, it is the independent 'middle' peasant who – squeezed by the rich farmer or moneylender, and fearing descent into the poor peasantry – is most susceptible to radical appeals. Be that as it may, few would deny the influence of the diffusion of radical notions from the cities in the realization of peasant radicalism. In Africa, the most important animator of peasant wars – in Algeria, Angola, Cameroun, Guinea-Bissau, Kenya, Mozambique, Rwanda, Zanzibar and Zimbabwe – has been nationalism. This has been manifest in wars of liberation against both colonial powers and minority racial or ethnic groups. One mechanism for the diffusion of such political ideas has been circular migration which, in blurring the rural–urban division, has permitted urban-based movements to spread into the countryside.[49]

From this brief survey of the dynamics of radical movements flows a further rationale for an urban emphasis in this book. While the bulk of the poor live in the countryside, movements for the eradication of poverty are likely to emerge in the cities. Yet there are many recent comparative studies of peasant politics, and very few of urban political-economic dynamics. In undertaking this latter task, I seek to move beyond such gross but widely employed categories as 'urban migrants' and 'urban poor' to a more finely honed class analysis.

However, before proceeding to this socio-political analysis, I need first to delineate the pattern of peripheral capitalist development as this relates to urban Africa. Only on this basis will the post-colonial structures and development strategies, and consequently the prospects for basic-needs approaches, be explicable.

Notes

1. P. Streeten and S. J. Burki, 'Basic Needs: Some Issues', *World Development*, VI, 3 (1978), pp. 414–15.
2. Quote from Irma Adelman and C. T. Taft, *Economic Growth and Social Equity in Developing Countries* (Stanford: Stanford University Press, 1973), p. 192. See also pp. 188–9. Information on the First Development Decade: Hollis Chenery *et al.*, *Redistribution with Growth: Policies to Improve Income Distribution in Developing Countries in the Context of Economic Growth* (London: Oxford University Press 1974), p. xiii. See also Michael Lipton, *Why Poor People Stay Poor: Urban Bias in World Development* (Cambridge, Mass: Harvard University Press, 1977), esp. p. 28.
3. ILO *Meeting Basic Needs: Strategies for Eradicating Mass Poverty and Unemployment* (Geneva: ILO, 1977), p. 1.
4. Development Policy Staff, World Bank, *Prospects for Developing Countries, 1978–85* (Washington, DC, November 1977), pp. 5, 7–9.
5. The various meanings of poverty are dealt with well in P. Townsend, 'The Meaning of Poverty', *British Journal of Sociology*, XIII, 1 (1962), pp. 210–17. P. Marris graphically illustrates the meaning of relative poverty in his 'Economics is not Enough', *East Africa Journal*, III (February 1967), pp. 13–18. A good, brief evaluation of Oscar Lewis's views is R. Wade, 'A Culture of Poverty', *Institute of Development Studies (IDS) Bulletin*, V, 2/3 (1973), pp. 4–30.
6. Useful surveys of available sources and knowledge on income distribution in Africa: A. O. Phillips, *Review of Income Distribution Data: Ghana, Kenya, Tanzania and Nigeria*, Discussion Paper No. 58, Woodrow Wilson School, Princeton University Research Program in Economic Development, 1975; and J. P. Powelson, 'Income Distribution within the Developing Countries', *Cultures et développement*, VIII, 1 (1976), pp. 119–36. The cross-sectional worldwide study is that of M. S. Ahluwalia, 'Income Inequality: Some Dimensions of the Problem', in Chenery *et al.*, *Redistribution with Growth* (n. 2 above), esp. table I.1, pp. 8–9. See also, for a comparative perspective, ILO, *Employment, Growth and Basic Needs* (Geneva: ILO, 1976), pp. 20–3. The relevant case studies include: M. Hodd, 'Income Distribution in Kenya (1963–72)', *Journal of Development Studies*, XVII, 3 (1976), pp. 22–8; ILO, *Employment, Incomes and Equality: A Strategy for Increasing Productive Employment in Kenya* (Geneva: ILO, 1972), chap. 5; R. van der Hoeven, *Zambia's Income Distribution During*

THE POVERTY PROBLEM 27

the Early Seventies, ILO Working Paper, WEP 2–23/WP54, March 1977, pp. 30–49; K. Ewusi, 'The Distribution of Monetary Incomes in Ghana', Technical Publication No. 14, ISSER, University of Ghana, 1971, pp. 94, 96; and Charles Elliot, *Employment and Income Distribution in Uganda*, Discussion Paper No. 1, Development Studies, University of East Anglia, 2nd edn., March 1977, esp. pp. 48–9.

7. See Reginald Green, 'Tanzania', in Chenery *et al.*, *Redistribution with Growth* (n. 2 above), pp. 269–70; and Wouter Van Ginnekan, *Rural and Urban Income Inequalities in Indonesia, Mexico, Pakistan, Tanzania and Tunisia* (Geneva: ILO, 1976), pp. 11, 15.

8. S. Kuznets, 'Economic Growth and Income Inequality', *American Economic Review*, XLV, 1 (1955), pp. 1–28. For a review of the evidence relating to Kuznets' hypothesis, see F. Paukert, 'Income Distribution at Different Levels of Development: A Survey of Evidence', *International Labour Review*, CVIII (1973), pp. 97–125.

9. Quote: W. R. Cline, 'Distribution and Development: A Survey of Literature', *Journal of Development Economics*, I, 4 (1975), p. 394. Data on Taiwan and South Korea: G. Ranis, 'Equity with Growth in Taiwan', and D. C. Rao, 'Economic Growth and Equity in The Republic of Korea', both in *World Development*, VI, 3 (1978).

10. M. Lipton *Why Poor People Stay Poor* (n. 2 above), pp. 42–3. For a study that reveals how much poverty still exists in a developed country, see Peter Townsend, *Poverty in the United Kingdom* (Harmondsworth: Penguin, 1979).

11. See, for instance, M. S. Ahluwalia and H. Chenery, 'The Economic Framework', in Chenery *et al.*, *Redistribution with Growth* (n. 2 above), p. 47; chaps. 4–7 of this same book discuss the policy measures likely to promote redistribution with growth. A similar package of policies is discussed at greater length in Charles R. Frank and Richard C. Webb, *Income Distribution and Growth in Less-Developed Countries* (Washington, DC: Brookings Institution, 1977), chaps. 3–11. On the basis of an econometric analysis of seventy-eight non-oil-producing LDCs during the period 1960–73, N. L. Hicks concludes: (1) that 'countries making substantial progress in meeting basic needs do *not* have substantially lower GNP growth rates [than those which are not making progress]'; and (2) that 'the attainment of a higher level of basic-needs satisfaction appears to lead to higher growth rates in the future'. See his 'Growth vs. Basic Needs: Is There a Trade-Off?', *World Development*, VII, 11/12 (1975), pp. 985–94.

12. Robert McNamara, *Address to the Board of Governors* [*of the World Bank*], Washington, DC, 25 September, 1972, p. 8.

13. Compare the 'conservative–radical–revolutionary' typology in R. H. Green, 'Basic Human Needs: Concept or Slogan, Synthesis or Smokescreen?', *IDS Bulletin*, IX, 4 (1978), pp. 10–11; and the 'shallow' vs. 'deep' interpretations of basic-needs approaches in J. Galtung, 'The New International Economic Order and the Basic Needs Approach', in his *The North/South Debate*, WP No. 12, Institute for World Order, New York, 1980.

14. On institutional constraints, see A. van de Laar, 'The World Bank: Which Way', *Development and Change*, VII, 1 (1976), pp. 67–97.

15. For the World Bank's rather limited achievements in reorienting its

lending toward 'low-end poverty' as of 1978, see M. ul Haq, 'Changing Emphasis of the Bank's Lending Policies', *Finance and Development*, xv, 2 (1978), pp. 12–14; E. Jaycox, 'The Bank and Urban Poverty', *Finance and Development*, xv, 3 (1978), pp. 10–13; and L. E. Christoffersen, 'The Bank and Rural Poverty', *Finance and Development*, xv, 4 (1978), pp. 18–22.

16. McNamara, *Address to the Board of Governors* (n. 12 above), p. 26.
17. The quote and the interpretation are from R. W. Cox, 'Labor and Hegemony', *International Organization*, xxi, 3 (1977), pp. 385–424. Quote p. 387.
18. Interpretation from *ibid*. Quote p. 420.
19. Identification of basic needs: ILO, *Employment, Growth and Basic Needs: A One World Problem* (Geneva: ILO, 1976), p. 32. On quantification: D. P. Ghai and T. Alfthan, 'On the Principles of Quantifying and Satisfying Basic Needs', in D. P. Ghai *et al.*, *The Basic Needs Approach to Development* (Geneva: ILO, 1977), pp. 19–59. Quote p. 24. For an excellent discussion of the relationship between 'needs' and 'rights', see P. Streeten, 'Basic Needs and Human Rights', *World Development*, viii, 2 (1980), pp. 107–11.
20. ILO, *Employment* (n. 19 above), p. 49.
21. C. Norman 'Soft Technologies, Hard Choices', *Mazingira: The World Forum of Environment and Development*, 8 (1979), p. 21. On the unlikelihood that measures to reform the system of North–South technology transfers would have much impact upon the employment/poverty problem, see D. Forsythe, N. McBain and R. Solomon, 'Technical Rigidity and Appropriate Technology in LDCs', *World Development*, viii, 5/6 (1980), pp. 371–98.
22. ILO, *Employment* (n. 19 above), pp. 49–50. For an elaboration of this view, see chap. 9 of this report, and Hans Singer, *Technologies for Basic Needs* (Geneva: ILO, 1977), p. 7 and *passim*.
23. Sceptical economists: P. Beckerman, 'Some Arguments for (Moderately) Capital-Intensive Development, Even in Labour-Abundant Nations', *World Development*, vi (1978), pp. 533–43; S. Dell, 'Basic Needs or Comprehensive Development', *World Development*, vii, 3 (1979), esp. p. 300; and Cline, 'Distribution and Development' (n. 9 above), pp. 375, 395. F. Stewart provides a powerful refutation of Beckerman's case in *World Development*, vi (1978), pp. 544–50. Arguments in favour of a 'realistic' mix of technologies in basic-needs development: H. C. Bos, 'The Use of Appropriate Technology: A Survey', in K. Haq (ed.), *Equality of Opportunity within and among Nations* (New York: Praeger, 1978), pp. 104–12; and J. Galtung, *Development, Environment and Technology: Towards a Technology for Self-Reliance* (New York: UNCTAD, 1979), chap. 4.
24. ILO, *Employment* (n. 19 above), pp. 56–61.
25. See M. Hopkins and H. Scolnik, 'Basic Needs, Growth and Redistribution: A Quantitative Approach', and J. J. Stern, 'Growth, Redistribution and Resource Use', both in ILO, Tripartite World Conference on Employment, Income Distribution and Social Progress and the International Division of Labour, vol. I: *Basic Needs and National Employment Strategies* (Geneva: ILO 1976). Quote by Hopkins and Scolnik, p. 37.

26. Frances Stewart, *Technology and Underdevelopment*, (London: Macmillan, 1977). Quote p. 87. See also, L. de Sebastian, 'Appropriate Technology in Developing Countries: Some Political and Economic Considerations', in Jairam Ramesh and Charles Weiss (eds.), *Mobilizing Technology for World Development* (New York: Praeger, 1979), pp. 66–73.

27. This is an extension of the argument found in ILO, *Employment* (n. 19 above), chap. 10, esp. pp. 162–3. See also, P. Streeten, 'Transnational Corporations and Basic Needs', in Mary Evelyn Jegen and Charles Wilbur (eds.), *Growth with Equity* (New York: Paulist Press, 1979), pp. 163–74.

28. *Ibid.*, p. 103. See also, A. R. Khan, 'Production Planning for Basic Needs', in Ghai, *Basic Needs Approach* (n. 19 above), esp. pp. 112–13. For evidence that direct foreign investment by LDCs in other LDCs transfers more appropriate products and technologies, see L. T. Wells, 'The Internationalization of Firms from Developing Countries', in Tamir Agmon & Charles Kindleberger (eds.), *Multinationals from Small Countries* (Cambridge, Mass.: MIT Press, 1977), pp. 133–56.

29. 'Declaration of Principles': ILO, *Meeting Basic Needs: Strategies for Eradicating Mass Poverty and Unemployment* (Geneva: ILO, 1977), pp. 20, 29. Quote: D. P. Ghai, 'What is a Basic Needs Approach to Development All About?, in Ghai, *Basic Needs Approach* (n. 19 above), p. 45.

30. Instance of a charge of utopianism: C. Leys, 'Interpreting African Underdevelopment: Reflections on the ILO Report on Employment, Incomes and Equality in Kenya', *African Affairs*, LXXII (1973), pp. 419–29; instance of a charge of ideological mystification: C. Leys, 'The Politics of Redistribution with Growth', *IDS Bulletin*, VII, 2 (1975), p. 8.

31 ILO, *Employment* (n. 19 above), p. 66. On political analysis more generally, see pp. 64–6.

32. Lipton, *Why Poor People Stay Poor* (n. 2 above), p. 67.

33. This is sometimes referred to as the 'Todaro paradox'. See M. P. Todaro, *Internal Migration in Developing Countries* (Geneva: ILO, 1976), pp. 28–39.

34. For the wide income differentials, see van der Hoeven, *Zambia's Income Distribution* (n. 6 above), p. 30; ILO, *Employment, Incomes and Equality* (n. 6 above), pp. 75–6; and C. J. Fapohunda, J. Reijmerink and M. P. van Dijk, *Urban Development, Income Distribution and Employment in Lagos*, ILO Working Paper, WEP 2–19/WP 13, September 1975, table 3.7.

35. On these three points, see B. van Arkadie, 'Town vs. Country?', *Development and Change*, VIII, 3 (1977), pp. 411–12.

36. Robert McNamara, *Address to the Board of Governors*, Washington, DC, 1 September 1975, p. 37. Chenery *et al.*, *Redistribution with Growth* (n. 2 above) cite a survey of major cities in forty poor countries that found that, in seventeen of these cities, more than half the population were living in 'slums and uncontrolled settlements', while in only twelve were less than one-third of the people living in such areas (p. 151n). The UN statistics come from Economic Commission for Africa, *Urbanization in Africa: Levels, Trends, and Prospects*, 21 July 1972 (E/CN. 14/POP/67), p. 1.

37. For a general discussion, see Charles Abrams, *Man's Struggle for Shelter in an Urbanizing World* (Cambridge, Mass: MIT Press, 1964), pp. 6–8. For African case studies, see Economic Commission for Africa, *Sanitation and Environmental Services in Selected African Cities*, 25 April 1975 (E/CN.

14/HUS/7); F. O. Okediji, 'Socio-Economic Status and Attitudes toward Public Health Problems: A Survey in the City of Lagos', *International Journal of Health Education*, XIII, 2 (1970), pp. 72–82, I. M. Dieng, 'The "Redevelopment" of Nimzatt-Anglemouss (Dakar) and Its Consequences', *Manpower and Unemployment Research*, IX, 2 (1976), pp. 3–16; Michael A. Cohen, *Urban Policy and Political Conflict in Africa: A Study of the Ivory Coast* (Chicago: University of Chicago Press, 1974), p. 57; P. Andrew et al., 'Squatter Manifesto (Lusaka)', *Ekistics*, XXXIV, no. 201 (1972), pp. 108–13; and Andrew Hake, *African Metropolis: Nairobi's Self-Help City* (New York: St Martin's Press, 1977), part II.

38. For the urban health situation in general, see D. M. Wilner and R. P. Walkley, 'Effects of Housing on Health and Performance', in Leonard J. Duhl (ed.), *The Urban Condition* (New York: Basic Books, 1963), pp. 215–28; F. Golladay and C. Koch-Weser, *Health and the Urban Poor*, Urban Poverty Task Force, World Bank, December 1974; and C. C. Hughes and J. M. Hunter, 'Urbanization and Disease in Africa', *African Urban Notes*, IV, 2 (1969), pp. 20–36. For the health situation in Abidjan and Dakar, see Cohen, *Urban Policy* (n. 37 above), p. 57; R. Baylet et al., 'Recherches sur la morbidité et mortalité différentielles urbaines–rurales au Sénégal', in Centre National de la Recherche Scientifique, *La croissance urbaine en Afrique noire* (Paris, 1972), vol. I, pp. 317–37; and M. Sankalé et al., 'Urbanisation et santé', in Groupes d'études dakaroises, *Dakar en devenir* (Paris: Présence Africaine, 1968), pp. 265–98.

39. See Sankalé, 'Urbanisation et Santé' (n. 38 above), p. 228, and S. N. Edimo, 'A Shantytown Area and the Health of the Children: Douala', *Environment in Africa*, I, 1 (1974), pp. 81–90.

40. The quote and much of the information on TB is from Hughes and Hunter, 'Urbanization and Disease' (n. 38 above), pp. 23–4. On Dakar and Abidjan, see Sankalé, 'Urbanisation' (n. 38 above), p. 286; and Heather Joshi et al., *Abidjan: Urban Development and Employment in the Ivory Coast* (Geneva: ILO, 1976), p. 76.

41. G. O. Sofuluwe, 'The Effect of Housing Conditions on the Prevalance of Bronchitis and Bronchial Pneumonia in Lagos', *West African Medical Journal*, XVIII, 2 (1969), pp. 35–40. See also, Sankalé, 'Urbanisation' (n. 38 above), p. 287.

42. General surveys of the relevant literature include Hughes and Hunter, 'Urbanization' (n. 38 above), esp. p. 29; and T. A. Lamb, 'Socio-Economic Changes in Africa and their Implications for Mental Health', in Gordon Wolstenhome and M. O'Connor (eds.), *Man in Africa* (Boston: Little, Brown, 1965), pp. 124–9. The reference to the Yoruba case is in this source. An inconclusive Sierra Leonean case study is that of J. Dawson, 'Urbanization and Mental Health in a West African Community', in Ari Kiev (ed.), *Magic, Faith and Healing* (New York: Free Press, 1964), pp. 305–42.

43. The two generalizations derive from I. S. Dema and A. P. den Hartog, 'Urbanization and Dietary Change in Tropical Africa', *Food and Nutrition in Africa*, no. 7 (July 1969), pp. 31–63. This study is based upon the authors' extensive nutritional research in Ghana and Nigeria, in addition to a synthesis of the relevant comparative research reports on Africa. The incidence of urban malnutrition is also treated in R. G. Henrickse, 'Some

Observations on the Social Background to Malnutrition in Tropical Africa', *African Affairs*, LXV, 261 (1966), pp. 341–9. For case studies, see C. Houyoux and J. Houyoux, 'Les conditions de vie dans soixante familles à Kinshasa', *Cahiers économiques et sociaux*, VIII, 1 (1970), pp. 124–5; C. Mandeville, 'Poverty, Work and the Financing of Single Women in Kampala', *Africa*, XLIX, 1 (1979), pp. 43–7; and G. J. Ebrahim and D. R. W. Haddock, 'Polyneuropathy of Probable Nutritional Origin in Dar es Salaam', Royal Society of Tropical Medicine and Hygiene, *Transactions*, LVIII (1964), pp. 246–54. On nutrition in a low-density squatter settlement, see *Pilot Nutrition Project: Report to the Regional Development Director, Dar es Salaam*, by a Working Team, Dar es Salaam, 13 May 1975.

44. The relative incidence of kwashiorkor is discussed in Dema and Hartog, 'Urbanization' (n. 43 above) and reported in Sankalé, 'Urbanisation' (n. 38 above), p. 288; and Joshi *et al.*, *Abidjan* (n. 40 above), p. 76. A careful study of 200 children suffering from kwashiorkor in Lagos found that the low incomes of parents and mothers' ignorance about nutrition were the most important causes. See O. Ransome-Kuti, W. O. Gbajumo and M. O. Olaniyan, 'Some Socio-Economic Conditions Predisposing to Malnutrition in Lagos', *Nigerian Medical Journal*, II (July 1972), pp. 111–18. The relationship between infant malnutrition and intelligence loss is treated in M. Selowsky and L. Taylor, 'The Economics of Malnourished Children: An Example of Disinvestment in Human Capital', *Economic Development and Cultural Change*, XXII, 1 (1973), pp. 17–30.

45. Report on Urban Poverty Task Force: E. Jaycox, 'The Bank and Urban Poverty', *Finance and Development*, XV, 3 (1978), p. 13. For case studies, see Z. Ergas and F. Chege, 'Primary School Education in Kenya: An Attempt at Evaluation', *Journal of Eastern African Research and Development*, III, 2 (1976); World Bank, *Education: Sector Working Paper* (December 1974), p. 33 (on Lusaka); and Cohen, *Urban Policy* (n. 37 above), p. 57 (on Abidjan).

46. Evidence relating to the Ghanaian case comes from G. E. Hurd and J. J. Johnson, 'Education and Social Mobility in Ghana', *Sociology of Education*, XL, 1 (1967), pp. 55–79; and L. Weis, 'Education and the Reproduction of Inequality: The Case of Ghana', *Comparative Education Review*, XXIII, 1 (1979), pp. 41–51, quote pp. 50–1. See also, P. J. Foster, 'Secondary Schooling and Social Mobility in a West African Nation', *Sociology of Education*, XXXVII, 2 (1963), table 1. For similar findings in other cases: see also, S. Adesina, 'The Development of Western Education', in A. B. Aderibigbe (ed.), *Lagos: The Development of an African City* (Lagos: Longman, 1975), p. 135; J. B. Olson, 'Secondary Schools and Élites in Kenya: A Comparative Study in 1961 and 1968', *Comparative Education Review*, XVI, 1 (1972), pp. 10–23; and Remi Clignet and Philip Foster, *The Fortunate Few: A Study of Secondary Schools and Students in the Ivory Coast* (Evanston, Ill: Northwestern University Press, 1966), p. 158.

47. On the question of the political role of the peasantry and, in particular, its 'low classness', see especially T. Shanin, 'The Peasantry as a Political Factor', *Sociological Review*, XIV (1966), pp. 5–27. Quote from J. F. Petras, 'Toward a Theory of Twentieth Century Socialist Revolutions', *Journal of Contemporary Asia*, VIII, 2 (1978), p. 170. For a wideranging literature

survey supportive of Petras's position, see R. Aya, 'Theories of Revolution Reconsidered', *Theory and Society*, 8 (1979), pp. 39–100, esp. p. 74.

48. Views of Fanon in his *The Wretched of the Earth* (Harmondsworth: Penguin, 1967), esp. pp. 98, 101. Study on Fanon: B. M. Perinbam, 'Fanon and the Revolutionary Peasantry: The Algerian Case', *Journal of Modern African Studies*, xi, 3 (1973), quote p. 437.

49. Theory of the 'middle peasant' has been developed by H. Alavi, 'Peasants and Revolution', *The Socialist Register, 1965* (London: Merlin Press, 1965) pp. 241–77; and Eric Wolf, *Peasant Wars of the Twentieth Century* (New York: Harper & Row, 1970). On the diffusion of radical notions from the cities, see the synthesis of studies of modern revolution by D. F. Ferguson, 'Rural–Urban Relations and Peasant Radicalism', *Comparative Studies in Society and History*, xviii, 1 (1976), pp. 106–18; and I. Wallerstein, 'Migration in West Africa: The Political Perspective', in Hilda Kuper (ed.), *Urbanization and Migration in West Africa* (Berkeley: University of California Press, 1965), pp. 148–59. On nationalism as an animator of African peasant wars: C. F. Welch, 'Obstacles to "Peasant War" in Africa', *African Studies Review*, xx, 3 (1977), p. 125; and R. Jeffries, 'Political Radicalism in Africa', *African Affairs*, lxxvii, 308 (1978), pp. 345–6.

2   Underdevelopment and Urban Poverty

The message is loud and clear. Developing countries, particularly the least-developed, are caught in a poverty trap.

Amir Jamal, Minister of Communications and Transport, Tanzania, 1979

The crux of the employment problem in the developing world [asserts the ILO's Director-General in his report to the 1976 World Employment Conference] lies in the high proportion of the labour force earning inadequate incomes. These persons are classified as underemployed. . . . The proportion of the labour force classified as underemployed is approximately the same as the proportion of the population classified as destitute [using ILO and World Bank statistics]. . . . Thus, problems of employment and poverty are inseparable.[1]

From this viewpoint, the fight against mass poverty translates chiefly into a strategy to expand markedly the utilization and productivity of labour. It is assumed that the spread of productive employment will raise the incomes of not only the unemployed but also the wage-earners, family workers and self-employed whose hard labour currently yields incomes insufficient to satisfy their households' basic needs. Furthermore, the socio-economic changes needed to homogenize productivity levels throughout the economy should, if the basic-needs accumulation model previously discussed is valid, reduce income inequality as well.

This chapter explores the structural roots of the poverty/employment problem in urban Africa. It argues that the imbalance between productive employment and the burgeoning labour force is a facet of the process of underdevelopment.

There are two interpretations of how underdevelopment might relate to this imbalance. According to an early view, underdevelopment constitutes a process of blocked or aborted capitalist development in the periphery. The historical incorporation of dependent territories into a global division of labour entailed a tendency toward economic development in the centres of the world capitalist system, and economic stagnation in the colonies and neo-colonies. This 'stagnation thesis' appears in much of the early writing on underdevelopment and dependency: Paul Baran's seminal work in the field was, after all, entitled 'The Political Economy of *Growth*'. He and many of his followers, most prominently André Gunder Frank, devoted themselves largely to a concern with the disposition of a dependent country's economic surplus. As long as much of this was patriated by foreign capitalists, appropriated by *comprador* classes, and used unproductively, the prospect for sustained economic growth was held to be negligible. Stunted capitalist development at the periphery could therefore not produce the jobs or goods necessary to satisfy the needs of the indigenous populations. Only socialism could.[2]

But, as we now know, peripheral capitalism *can* succeed, and indeed in some cases has succeeded – *on its own terms*. Among Marxist writers, Bill Warren has pressed this point the farthest, arguing, on the basis of evidence that twenty-two Third World countries had achieved high rates of industrial growth, that 'dependency is a myth'. While few would go this far, the new conventional wisdom of underdevelopment theorists is that dependency and industrialization are not antithetical notions. Hence, Fernando Henrique Cardoso speaks of 'associated-dependent development' in Brazil. Others have reclassified the more economically dynamic and developed Third World countries as 'semi-peripheries', lying between the underdeveloped 'peripheries' and the advanced 'core' countries. Why some dependent countries manage to achieve rapid economic and industrial growth whereas others do not is a question of considerable current debate.[3]

Another interpretation of underdevelopment conceives of it as a peculiar pattern of capitalist growth. Peripheral capitalism can expand – but normally at a high and continuing cost for a substantial part (25–50 per cent) of the populations. Disturbing studies have recently emerged which demostrate that even in countries attaining high growth rates, *absolute* as well as relative poverty sometimes worsens. Of course, industrialization has always entailed a high price in suffering on the part of peasants and workers. Yet, in the early industrializing countries, the bulk of the labour force eventually escaped from absolute deprivation as a result of their own organized protests and the rising productivity generated by the revolutionizing of productive forces. This history is unlikely to repeat itself in tropical Africa, unless drastic changes in the pattern of growth occur.[4]

A major divergence in the development paths of early and late capitalism relates to the fate of the non-capitalist modes of production. Robert Brenner has persuasively contended that

> capitalist economic development [is] a function of the tendency toward capital accumulation via innovation, built into a historically developed structure of class relations of free wage labour. From this vantage point, neither economic development nor underdevelopment are *directly* dependent upon, caused by, one another. Each is a product of a specific evolution of class relations, in part determined historically 'outside' capitalism, in relationship with non-capitalist modes.

One must take care not to oversimplify Brenner's intricate argument. However, his essential point is that capitalist development in Western Europe originated, not primarily in primitive accumulation via unequal trade relations with its periphery, but rather in political struggles within each of the major countries. From these emerged a dominant class whose own interests lay in revolutionizing the productive forces in a direction which eventually absorbed much of the labour force into productive employment. This transformation required the conversion of both labour power and the means of production into commodities:

> Only under conditions of free wage labour will the individual producing units (combining labour power and the means of production) be forced to sell in order to buy, to buy in order to survive and reproduce, and ultimately to expand and innovate in order to maintain this position in relationship to other competing productive units. Only under such a system, where both capital and labour power are thus commodities . . . is there the necessity of producing at the 'socially necessary' labour time in order to survive, and to surpass this level of productivity to ensure continued survival. Under the impetus of intense competition in societies where considerable labour had been 'freed' from the land, capitalists perforce had to innovate in order to survive and expand. This dynamic process undermined and destroyed the less productive pre-capitalist modes of production.

It is noteworthy that Brenner's thesis is not inconsistent with some major non-Marxist analyses of the roots of European industrialization, in particular that offered by David S. Landes in his magisterial *The Unbound Prometheus: Technological Change and Industrial Development in Western Europe*.*[5]

In contrast, the principal characteristic of peripheral capitalism is the coexistence and articulation of modes of production on a continuing basis. The introduction of oligopoly capitalism from the outside creates, as Aidan Foster-Carter remarks, a situation where 'capitalism neither evolves mechanically from what precedes it, nor does it necessarily dissolve it. Indeed, so far from banishing pre-capitalist forms, it not only coexists with them but buttresses them, and even on occasions devilishly conjures them up *ex nihilo*.' It is evident that capitalism in the contemporary developing countries tends to be less dynamic than its

---

*Landes, in seeking to explain why industrialization occurred first in Western Europe, cites a variety of conditions that set European development apart from that of the rest of the world: relatively high per capita incomes; the emergence of propitious values; freedom from conquest and war; the structure of trade with dependent colonies an semi-colonies; and the development of a strong bourgeoisie. Landes stresses this last factor: 'The role of private economic enterprise in the West is perhaps unique: more than any other factor, it made the modern world' (p. 15). He contends, furthermore, that imperialism was neither a necessary nor a sufficient condition for industrialization. There had been empires and systematic looting before, but none of these episodes had produced technological improvement and industrial growth. Without a vital bourgeoisie at the centre, empire would not have assisted innovation and growth in the core (pp. 38–9).

earlier variant. Consequently, the fate of a large part of the labour force is exclusion from employment in the highly productive capitalist mode of production or public agencies and relegation on a long-term basis to occupations of a 'marginal' type. These include both employment and self-employment in economic activities characterized by instability of employment, insecurity of income, and very low incomes or profits.[6]

This is not meant to imply that an 'iron law of marginalization' operates at the periphery. Peripheral capitalism is not necessarily a status assigned once-and-for-all. In a few Third World countries – for example, Hong Kong, Singapore, Taiwan and South Korea – the capitalist mode of production *is* decomposing the non-capitalist forms. There are special reasons for their success in this. Hong Kong and Singapore, as city-states, did not confront the problem of a large agricultural sector of low productivity, while Taiwan and South Korea, prodded in each case by a clear external threat and a relatively uninfluential landed class, developed the political will to undertake a radical programme of land redistribution and rural development. In addition, the governments of these countries made shrewd policy choices in the 1950s or 1960s. They sought to transcend the inequality-generating pattern of import-substitution industrialization by means of fiscal and trade incentives to promote labour-intensive and export-oriented manufacturing of consumer non-durables, and later, durables. The experience of these countries is not easily imitated, however. Not only have these 'early' exporters pre-empted many of the existing opportunities in labour-intensive manufactures, but also it is only the small economies that can hope to absorb much of their under-used labour by means of export-oriented industrialization.[7]

But the preponderant tendency is for capitalist development at the periphery not to revolutionize the productive forces throughout the economy. One therefore needs to explain why most of the currently developing countries are unlikely to repeat the pattern of early capitalist development. This is obviously an exceedingly complex task: vague references to 'the development of underdevelopment' will not suffice. Part of the explanation relates to the largely unintended consequences of imperial priorities determining the structure of colonial and semi-colonial economies. A capitalism introduced from outside and governed by external needs is unlikely to generate capitalists who, in Brenner's terms, 'perforce had to innovate in order to survive and expand', thereby undermining the less productive pre-capitalist modes. After political independence, the opportunity theoretically exists to reorient national economies and carry through a bourgeois revolution. But this prospect is rarely realized. Of course, the task is immense: there is a wide range of factors, some specific to the demographic features, location, resource endowment and culture of each Third World country, some generic in the special disabilities facing late developers in the international economic order, that constrain developmental prospects. In addition, in some countries, a compromised *comprador* bourgeoisie is unwilling to undertake a vigorous espousal of national development if this adversely affects the interests of foreign capital. But elsewhere (as I shall argue in chapter 3) class relations and political power are not unconducive to vigorous national capitalist development. The political problem here is that the interests of the dominant classes are identified with an imitative model of development – capital-intensive industrialization at the expense of agriculture – that produces capital accumulation for some and marginalization for many. Yet marginalization is a price that the ruling groups are willing for the poor to pay.

How do class relations tend to underpin this marginalizing model of capitalist development at the periphery? Some marginality theorists, writing on Latin America, seem to believe that the 'marginal pole' of the economy is so crucial to accumulation in the capitalist sector that the ruling classes contrive to perpetuate it.[8] This does not appear to be so in Africa. Rather, marginalization here is a by-product of the limited dynamism of the ruling model of development. Marginalization is however acceptable to the dominant classes and the state because it is not dysfunctional to accumulation in the capitalist mode of production and, indeed, is modestly functional to such accumulation. In the first place, the non-capitalist forms bear the cost of supporting those whose labour is surplus to the requirements of the modern sector. With limited public investment in social services, the bulk of the capital can thus be reserved for productive investment. In the second place, the intensive and cheap use of labour in petty commodity production, petty commerce and personal services allows some capitalist firms to reduce their labour costs, and hence increase profits. In sum, as Bryan Roberts argues in the Latin American context:

> This form of capitalist development is convenient to the dominant classes since it permits economic growth while maintaining high standards of consumption among the wealthy. Such a pattern of growth depends, however, on a political context in which the mass of the population has no effective means of influencing the allocation of resources and thus securing improvements in living standards. The political context is partly produced by authoritarian government and partly by the weak development of political and labour organization among the urban working class, under social and economic conditions that tend to divide and isolate members of this class from each other.[9]

The implications of this analysis are clear. If few peripheral capitalist countries will succeed in generating sufficiently dynamic development to decompose the non-capitalist forms of production, then the eradication of poverty will require an entirely new approach. This is the rationale for a basic-needs approach. However, insofar as this is inimical to the interests of the currently dominant classes, it will only be pursued in the event of a major shift in the class alliances within societies.

The rest of this book seeks to substantiate this general perspective. In this chapter, I trace the development of peripheral capitalism in Africa, with particular reference to the urban areas. I begin with a discussion of how the ·incorporation of dependent territories into an imperial division of labour manifested itself in a pattern of 'dependent urbanization'. Imperial priorities determined the economic functions and even the locations of most of the larger towns and cities. Yet the limited commercial and administrative tasks assigned to these did not prevent the emergence of an urban overpopulation (relative to the productive employment) by the Second World War; I argue that the high rates of rural–urban migration are a reflection of uneven development associated with the restricted penetration of capitalism. This provides the background to an examination of the evolution of the capitalist mode in the expanding cities. 'Dependent industrialization' in post-war Africa did not, I contend, represent a break with the original pattern of dependent urbanization. A consequence of this is the marginalizing tendency inherent in a more-or-less stable articulation of modes and forms of production. The next stage in the argument – that the state represents the interests of certain dominant classes in supporting this pattern of accumulation – receives attention in the following chapter.

Dependent urbanization[10]

Although most of the towns and cities of middle Africa originated or expanded in response to imperial imperatives, some, especially in West Africa, predated European contact. Along the East African coast there are several old trading centres established by Arabs to organize trade across the Indian Ocean – most notably Mombasa and Zanzibar. There are also several ancient and more recent Ethiopian towns, like Aksum and Addis Ababa. In central Africa, few large settlements existed before the colonial period, though the ruins of the vanished city of Zimbabwe attest to the presence of some urban civilization.

The situation is different in West Africa where many traditional urban centres thrived. For instance, Benin City, on the Guinea coast, was first visited by Portuguese explorers in 1486; later visitors reported that it contained streets several times as broad as those of European cities. Now capital of the Benin Republic, Abomey had an estimated population of 24000 in 1772. Kumasi, the capital of the Ashanti Confederacy in what is now Ghana, is another long-established adminstrative/commercial centre. In 1838 a European visitor estimated its population as 25000 people, and commented as well on the opulence of the royal court. There were also perhaps twenty-five Hausa towns containing at least 20000 inhabitants each (at their peak) before the European intrusion. The rulers of these maintained standing armies, collected taxes and tribute, proselytized for Islamic conversions, and organized commerce. Kano is the best known of these towns. Dating from the seventh century AD, it had prospered as the entrepôt for trans-Saharan trade as well as for trade with much of West Africa, and as the centre of thriving handicraft industries and agriculture. There were, of course, other non-Hausa commercial towns along the edge of the Sahara desert, of which Timbuktu is perhaps the most widely known.

But the most traditionally urban of all African peoples were the Yoruba. The largest of the traditional Yoruba towns were Ibadan, Abeokuta, Ife and Oshogbo in western Nigeria; these were described by European expeditions in the early nineteenth century as 'large and extensive', and 'capacious and populous'. Nigeria's last reliable population census, that of 1952, found that fully 47 per cent of the population in the Yoruba region lived in settlements of 5000 or more people. However, it is significant that most of the inhabitants of these towns earned their livelihood on farms to which they commuted for several days at a time. These were clearly pre-industrial as well as pre-colonial towns.[11]

The crux of the urban employment problem lies in the fact that African towns, unlike their European counterparts, did not expand in response to technological changes which supplanted agricultural workers while enlarging an urban manufacturing base. The capitalist impulse was weak in export-oriented, raw-material-producing, colonial economies. Exploitation of mining and agriculture required the construction of ports and the penetration of the hinterland by rail and road. Towns, and later cities, emerged around these ports, at cross-roads along the railways, and at administrative centres established in the interior. Sixteen of the largest fifty-seven African cities in the 1960s were coastal or river ports; almost all the remainder (with the exception of the traditional Yoruba towns) owed their rapid growth to their location on the railway systems. Industrialization played almost no part in the origins of the largest cities.[12]

Dramatic growth of African towns occurred only after the Second World War. In the 1930 there were merely three cities in all of the tropical area with populations over 100 000 – Ibadan, Lagos and Omdurman. Kano and Addis Ababa were next in size, with about 80 000 people each. Dakar, Accra, Luanda and Mombasa registered populations of about 50 000 in 1930, whereas the next largest towns (Nairobi, Salisbury, Douala and Kinshasa) were considerably smaller. The capital cities experienced particularly rapid expansion in the post-war period: Lagos, Kinshasa and Ibadan (a regional capital) each grew to a million people in the 1960s, while many of the rest reached a population of about half a million.[13] The current rate of increase of Africa's primate cities ranges from about 9 to 15 per cent, or between four and eight times the rate of rural increase. Not surprisingly, therefore, the projected growth of some capital cities is little short of

Table 2.1   *Growth of some African cities (000's)*

	1970		1985	
Nairobi	550		1700	
Kinshasa	1100		3300	
Accra	600		1600	
Lagos	3500	(1975)	4500	(1980)

Sources: ECA, *Urbanization in Africa: Levels, Trends and Prospects* (New York, 21 July 1972). For Lagos, see Federal Government of Nigeria, Lagos, Master Plan Unit, Ministry of Works and Planning, *Master Plan for Metropolitan Lagos: Working Assumptions on Population 1952–80* (Lagos, 1976)

extraordinary (refer to table 2.1). Between 1940 and 1960 Africa's overall rate of urban growth – at about 5 per cent per annum – ranked with the world's highest.[14] Urbanization, as table 2.2 shows, has proceeded furthest in North and Southern Africa and least in East Africa. By the year 2000 an estimated 28 per cent of the African population will live in urban areas – not too far below the projected world total of 38 per cent. Africa will be the most rapidly urbanizing region of the world until the end of the century.[15]

This rapid urban expansion owed much to changes in the world economy and in imperial policy. In the immediate post-war period the high world demand for primary products and a sustained imperial effort to promote colonial economic development fuelled an urban employment boom. Incipient industrialization, as we shall see, also played a part in fostering rural–urban migration in the 1950s, notably in the cases of Dakar, Accra, Lagos, Leopoldville (Kinshasa) and Nairobi. Import-substitution industrialization normally received further impetus following political independence, though manufacturing continued to

Table 2.2   *Urban population as percentage of total population, 1970*

	%
North Africa	30
West Africa	14
East Africa	8
Central Africa	12
Southern Africa	25
Africa as a whole	17

Source: ECA, *Demographic Handbook for Africa, 1971*

be dominated by foreign capital and was concentrated in primate cities. To the extent that external impulses still played a major part in determining the expansion and functions of African urban areas, political independence did not obliterate dependent urbanization.[16]

Migration

Urban marginality obviously cannot be understood in isolation from the processes of agricultural change. Not natural urban increase but rural exodus accounts for the accelerated urban expansion in post-war Africa; it is this expansion which, in turn, poses the major problem of urban labour absorption. The historical context of cityward migration is the penetration of capitalism into pre-capitalist agriculture. This penetration has taken one or both of two forms: the establishment of capitalist enclaves in the form of estates, plantations and mixed farms worked by hired labour (as in Rhodesia and Kenya); or the commercialization of household production (as in West Africa), a process that tends to accentuate rural differentiation as some households are in a better position to respond to market opportunities than others. Both forms generate an uneven development that provides the framework within which rural–urban migration takes place.

In the first instance, however, the labour problem in colonial Africa consisted of a labour shortage, not superfluity. What accounts for this original situation, and what determined the transformation of the problem?

COERCION AND THE CREATION OF A LABOUR MARKET

Initially, Africans were reluctant to enter colonial capitalism as sellers of labour. Indeed, such a notion was alien to pre-capitalist African societies. Labour was not a commodity to be sold and bought on the market, but an obligation one owed as a member of a household and kinship unit. Pre-capitalist relations of production involved the allocation of labour to specific tasks on the basis of sex and age. Women undertook certain domestic and farming duties until they became too old to work. Men were assigned tasks not on the basis of capital, skills or strength (as in capitalist society), but on the basis of age. This is clear-cut in the case of societies that operated an age-grade or age-set system. Either mechanism allowed young, single men to be withdrawn from productive activity in order to constitute a fighting force. But in all traditional African societies there was specialization of labour depending upon age. In pastoral societies, for instance, boys at the age of five or so were placed in charge of goats or calves; only the older boys were responsible for large herds of cattle. And the elders would constitute the decision-making unit. Even slaves in African pre-capitalist modes of production were incorporated into the prevailing division of labour. The unit of production was usually the household (especially among agricultural peoples), and particular households and kinship groups simply incorporated slaves into them. There they contributed to production, eventually being absorbed with full rights. Seldom were slaves in Africa permanently denied rights to independence.

The problem confronting newly installed colonial regimes and foreign capitalists was how to pry labour out of these pre-capitalist societies. It was widely held that the lure of high wages would be ineffectual, if not counter-productive. Colonialists tended to ascribe the reluctance of Africans to enter (or stay in) employment to their economic irrationality: inasmuch as Africans worked only to earn a set sum and generally put leisure before work (that is, were indolent), raising wages would merely encourage Africans to leave their jobs sooner. This was the infamous theory of the 'backward-sloping labour supply function'.[17]

In fact there were good reasons why Africans initially resisted incorporation into urban labour forces. The costs of rural–urban migration were generally high before the Second World War. In the first place, the living conditions for Africans in towns were abysmal until water purification and sanitary services were improved in the 1920s and 1930s. The prevalence of disease in the towns made migration a risky venture. For example, the death rate among Africans in Elizabethville (Belgian Congo) in 1911 was an estimated 24 per cent, owing to outbreaks of typhoid fever, influenza, tick fever and pneumonia. It is therefore not surprising that during an outbreak of influenza in Elizabethville in 1913, about half the labourers deserted their jobs. So bad were the conditions for the Mossi migrants of Upper Volta during the early colonial years that they had a saying, 'Nansara toumde di mossé' – 'White man's work eats people.' Mombasa's African population in 1910 had to contend not only with the relatively highest rates (for Kenya) of maleria, tuberculosis and pneumonia, but also with digestive disorders, skin diseases and the threat of typhoid, owing to their consumption of water from polluted wells. While environmental services are still far from good in the low-income areas of African towns, they are generally superior to those provided in the early colonial period.

In the second place, the alienness of town life discouraged labour migrants. Indeed, officials in British central, southern and eastern Africa tended to regard Africans as merely temporary urban residents whose proper place was in the countryside. This was the rationale for paying Africans only the equivalent of a bachelor's wage. In Kenya, for instance, it was not until 1954–5 that the colonial government officially conceded that African workers (of a certain age) should earn enough to support a small family in town. In addition to living alone, African labourers in the early period were subject to the alien laws of the white man (and punishment for infractions could include flogging), and had to pay high prices for staple foods which sometimes were unfamiliar. A third and final cost of rural–urban migration was simply the effort involved in reaching town. In the early period the absence of transport facilities meant Africans had to trek for days or even weeks to find employment.[18]

Unwilling to improve the living conditions and wages of African labourers, colonial regimes turned to coercive measures to secure an adequate labour force. The first of these was compulsory labour, but this, after the first decades, could be used only in extraordinary circumstances because it offended the sensibilities of metropolitan legislators and opinion leaders (except, of course, in Portugal). However, taxation, an indirectly coercive measure, proved equally as effective in levering Africans into the labour market, and less obnoxious to metropolitan governments. As the Governor of Kenya Colony remarked in 1908 (at the time of imposing a poll tax on top of an existing hut tax), 'taxation is the only possible method of compelling the native to leave his reserves for purposes of seeking work'. Of course, many Africans earned their tax money through the sale of cash crops or foodstuffs. But this option was open only to some: those who lived on adequate, fertile land with the appropriate climatic conditions and proximity to transport routes. Even then, in colonies dominated by settlers, the adminstration could further restrict rural opportunities through prohibitions on Africans cultivating designated crops – such as in the case of coffee in Kenya. For the male population unable to grow and market cash crops, the alternatives boiled down to two. They could either evade the payment of taxes (as many doubtless did), or earn money in wage-employment. The amount of work involved in paying taxes was not paltry. In the Belgian Congo in 1911–19, for instance, labourers would have had to work between forty-five and ninety days per year (depending on the tax rate in their home districts) in order to satisfy their tax obligations.[19]

UNEVEN DEVELOPMENT AND RURAL–URBAN MIGRATION

Colonial regimes after the Second World War no longer needed coercive measures to assure adequate labour supplies. Indeed, the labour problem typically became one of controlling the *influx* of Africans into town in search of jobs. One can begin to explain this dramatic change in terms of the lowering of the costs of rural–urban migration which had taken place. Movement to town now became a more casual matter with a decline in the urban mortality rate owing to mass vaccinations and improved public health facilities, with the extension of railway and road transport systems, and with the residence in town of kin or friends who could provide assistance to the newcomer. The improvement of transport and communications facilities, in particular, lessened the

physical and cultural gap between town and country. While a Frafra
migrant (from northern Ghana) had to undergo a two- to three-week
trip on foot to Kumasi in the 1930s, today Accra is only a day's lorry ride
away for him.[20]

But these conditions merely facilitated the move to town; they do not
explain it. One sort of explanation has focused upon the considerations
entering into an individual's decision to migrate. A major problem
with this behavioural approach is that it takes as given the existing
spatial and social distribution of opportunities, and as problematical
only the specification of the factors entering into a person's rational
response to this historical reality. Yet this structure of opportunities –
which largely, though not entirely, determines individual migration
decisions – itself surely requires explanation.

Imperialism introduced widespread socio-economic change into the
African countryside. Perhaps the most important force for change was
the extension of the cash-based market. Only in the areas of European
farming or plantation agriculture (most prominently in parts of the
Rhodesias, Kenya and South Africa) was the capitalist impulse strong
enough to supplant pre-capitalist relations of production. But almost
everywhere the desire to earn cash – initially to pay taxes, later to
purchase new goods and services – led to modification in pre-capitalist
modes of production in the direction of 'peasantization'. Peasants
entered the market economy as sellers of raw materials and sometimes
cheap labour as well. Characteristically, however, capitalism generated
uneven development on both a regional and social-structural basis.
What this essentially meant was that social strata emerged for whom
migration appeared attractive, and other strata for whom it appeared
almost unavoidable.[21]

Consider briefly uneven regional development and the creation of
'labour reserves'. While the existence of high-grade land, appropriate
climate and access to transport facilities fostered a flourishing cash-crop
agriculture in certain regions, the absence of those circumstances
elsewhere obstructed development. For people in the latter regions,
entry into the cash economy generally required migration to more
prosperous areas. This migration is not necessarily to towns; in West
Africa, for example, the prosperous cocoa, coffee and groundnut areas
have attracted migrants from the poorer regions to the north. And men
from Malawi and Mozambique have been migrating to South African
mines for a long time. But some, usually the better-educated, will
migrate to particular cities, and often establish a 'traditional' migration
pattern for their families. Rural–urban migration can thus create a
certain momentum of its own within various ethnic groups, whereby
young men grow up expecting to migrate to a particular urban place.
This is the well-known phenomenon of chain migration. Hence, to
return to an earlier case, the Frafra of northern Ghana exhibit a pattern
whereby

the proportion of extended family members who will migrate from Frafra will depend very much on the number of family members already in the South. Thus, there is something like a multiplier effect, that is the prospects or the gains of migration derived by a family will in turn stimulate others at home to take part in migration. The existence of relatives at destinations . . . weeds away many uncertainties in intending migrants.[22]

A problem with this pattern is that out-migration from backward regions tends to perpetuate their backwardness. The poverty of a region promotes the migration of its abler and younger residents; yet this removal of potentially the most productive and innovative individuals from agriculture heightens the prospect of persistent stagnation. This tendency receives comment in many migration studies. Indeed, this pattern of out-migration sometimes constitutes a net transfer of capital from the poorer to the wealthier regions or the urban areas. In the case of southern Nigeria, for instance, the cost of the education invested in migrants to the cities, combined with the assistance sent to them by rural relatives (in the form of cash and produce), has been shown to outweigh the value of remittances sent to the countryside by employed urban kin. In addition, to the extent that both public and private investment commonly flows disproportionately to wealthier regions, the backwardness of the poor receives reinforcement. Rural inequality, and the resultant migratory movements, are difficult to reverse once created.[23]

Uneven development in the form of rural social differentiation also influences decisions to migrate in complex ways. Commercialization of agriculture in Africa, as elsewhere, has modified pre-capitalist land-tenure systems in the most prosperous regions. Popular (if not legal) acceptance of a person's right to alienate his land has allowed some individuals (often moneylenders) to accumulate large holdings. For example, in certain cocoa-growing areas of western Nigeria, just over 2 per cent of 686 families surveyed as early as 1951 held 20·5 per cent of all the cultivated land (with an average holding of 198·42 acres), whereas 55 per cent of the farmers owned only 19·5 per cent (with an average holding of less than 5 acres). The smaller farms were judged 'not enough to yield more than a bare subsistence'. Even in such a comparatively egalitarian country as Tanzania, land alienation and social differentiation have occurred in the cash-cropping areas since the colonial period. The socialist-minded government has only recently stopped this process by the compulsory formation of 'development villages' among recalcitrant peoples.[24]

Landlessness, an increasingly important determinant of rural–urban migration, generally has roots not only in the explosive growth of rural populations, but also in this process of social differentiation. The extent of landlessness and marginal landholding in Africa is rarely recognized. As William Hance has argued, the popular view that Africa has no land problem stems from the common practice of employing continental or national density statistics in comparative analyses (thus ignoring the carrying capacity of the land), and from the paucity of research on the subject. Hance estimates that almost half of the continent's area and at least half of its population experienced population pressure upon the land in the late 1960s. Forty-eight of the fifty-two African nations experienced some degree of land shortage; of these twenty-three have more or less pervasive problems, while in the rest only specific regions suffered pressure. The areas in tropical Africa where the problem is most severe are: Rwanda, Burundi, the adjacent Kigeze District of Uganda, Iboland in eastern Nigeria and parts of north Nigeria, Upper Volta, the Sahelian countries, many areas of the highlands of East Africa, southern Malawi, Lesotho, and parts of Sierra Leone, Ghana, Togo, Benin, Cameroun, Zambia and Botswana.[25]

Not a country usually regarded as overpopulated, Kenya illustrates the importance of landlessness in fostering urban drift. One of the striking findings of a sample survey in 1976 of 3245 heads of housholds in thirteen spontaneous settlements (six in Nairobi, four in Mombasa, and three in Kisumu) was the extent of landlessness. In Old Pumwani, the original African location in Nairobi, only 36 per cent claimed to own, or possess rights to, land. Of these, about half stated that the land to which they had rights was less than 2·5 acres in area (while 21 per cent claimed not to know the size of their holdings). The survey also included four villages in the increasingly respectable Mathare Valley in Nairobi. The proportion of household heads acknowledging rights to land in these ranged from 6 to about 20 per cent. The pattern again was that a majority of the landed squatters held less than 5 acres – in one village most owned less than one-quarter acre. In the case of the four Mombasa squatter settlements, the proportions with rights to land were in the same range (the lowest proportion with land being 15 per cent). Kisumu, which draws its population much more from surrounding rural areas than either Mombasa or Nairobi, presented a different picture. Between 65 and 80 per cent of the squatters had rights to land, depending upon the settlement. This general pattern of landlessness, with respect to Nairobi's poor at least, has received confirmation in other surveys.[26]

There is no lack of similar studies in other countries. Even in Tanzania, with its relatively low population density, the proportion of landless urban migrants is not insignificant. A survey conducted in 1971 among a sample of 5000 people in Tanzania's seven largest towns and cities found that almost a quarter of the male migrants had no access to land. The landless, moreover, tended to be among the poorest elements. Parts of Nigeria too suffer from population pressure upon the land. The pattern evident there since 1930 has much wider relevance in Africa: 'for the rural areas, the impact of this growth of population was staggering. It led to a sharp reduction of the fallow period and a significant decline in soil fertility. The result was a massive exodus of population from rural to urban areas.'[27]

Population pressures, often exacerbated by inequality in landholding, offer those who can barely survive on the land little choice except migration. Agricultural labour may draw the illiterate, but this is generally unremunerative. Hence, one rural stratum for whom the towns hold promise is the poorest one – or at least the male offspring of the poor. Even if these migrants fail to raise their living standards in the city, they have little or nothing to return to in their rural place of origin. It is not therefore surprising that the landless migrants tend to be among the longest-term residents in the urban areas. Inasmuch as those without land are the most desperate migrants, they must also take whatever income opportunities present themselves. Although little comparative data exists on this subject it appears that the landless are more likely to find themselves consigned to the more marginal occupations than those with access to land. The large-scale Tanzanian urban survey previously referred to, for instance, discovered that only 18 per cent of modern-sector migrant wage-earners were landless, whereas 39 per cent of migrants in the 'informal sector' had this status. In addition, while at least two-thirds of those in the spontaneous settlements of Nairobi and Mombasa had no rights to land, the majority of these earned their livelihoods in informal occupations. It is likely that, in the late 1960s, at least three-quarters of Kenya's industrial workers possessed rights to land. The explanation for this tendency seems to be that those from the poorest rural stratum tend to be the least educated, and are thus largely ineligible for jobs in the modern capitalist bridgeheads.[28]

But it would be incorrect to leave the impression that 'push' factors were the sole, or even predominant, influence upon rural–urban migration in the aggregate. Migrants do not derive overwhelmingly from the backward regions or only (or even mainly) from the poor peasantry. In fact, the migratory stream is highly differentiated. Besides the migrants with negligible or no land and little formal education, there is a larger group who are relatively well educated. The more formal education a person in the rural areas possesses, the more likely he or she will be to move to town. In Tanzania, with an adult literacy rate of about 60 per cent, for example, nearly 90 per cent of all recent urban migrants had some formal education, and two-thirds had received at least five years of schooling. The relationship between education and migration is obvious: those who are best-educated have the best chances of securing a well-paid urban job.[29]

In Africa, as elsewhere in the world, education correlates positively with family income. There is of course no invariable relationship. A common pattern is for a father with negligible land to scrimp in order to provide (at least) his oldest son with a good education; the latter will hopefully then be able to obtain an urban income and assist his deprived family in surviving upon its diminishing per capita landholding. The prevalence of this pattern in overpopulated western Kenya leads one writer to observe that 'parts of Western Province can with justification be described as peri-urban villages, several hundred miles distant from

Nairobi, but yet as closely dependent upon the city for support, school fees and other necessary income as some of the Kikuyu villages near the capital'. Yet, inasmuch as post-primary schooling typically requires the payment of relatively high tuition fees, the children of rich peasants and capitalist farmers generally have better educational opportunities than those of poor peasants. And the jobs for which secondary school educates its pupils are found largely in the towns. Hence, the sons and daughters of the relatively well-to-do move off the land in great numbers. Rural–urban migration is far from a preserve of the poor and dispossessed alone.[30]

'Pull' factors are thus evidently important in explaining the migration process, and they are often reduced to a single dimension: the rural–urban balance of economic opportunities. In the view of the much-cited Todaro model, aggregate rural–urban migration is a function of the differential between expected urban income and expected rural income over a certain period. That is, the rate of migration depends upon the extent to which the average wage in the 'urban modern sector' (often taken as the statutory minimum wage), discounted by the probability of an individual obtaining that income, exceeds the average marginal product in agriculture. This model has generated a great deal of debate. Its strength lies in its recognition of the undoubted primacy of economic motivations in migration decisions, and its reduction of those motivations into several (in principle) quantifiable dimensions. Its basic shortcoming derives from its ahistorical econometric methodology: this is incapable of taking into account some of the complexities of the migratory process mentioned above. If, as I maintain, the logic of decisions to migrate flows from evolving patterns of social differentiation and regional inequality, then these patterns require more explanation than the (rather obvious) logic.[31]

Various rural strata respond to different urban economic opportunities. For the bulk of the poorly educated migrants, the 'average wage in the urban modern sector' is immaterial. Their only opportunity will lie in the so-called informal sector, either through training in the informal apprenticeship system or directly in casual or self-employment.[32] (I shall have much more to say about this later.) The better-educated will more likely aspire to a job in the 'urban modern sector', perhaps hoping to supplement any income from this source with an informal occupation. Even if, as chapter 4 will suggest, the rural–urban income differential is often small when education is held constant, there are still incentives for educated individuals to move to towns. Not only are the jobs for which a person thinks he is qualified more plentiful there, but he will also stand a better chance of promotion and a higher income.

It must be said that the Todaro model implies an unduly narrow concept of man. This approach assumes a person who is perfectly informed about urban employment conditions, always acts rationally, and is concerned only to maximize his earnings over a particular time period. However,

> people decide to migrate to the city (and to a particular city) and to stay or not remain in the city not simply for rational economic considerations, but also because of the quality of life they see the city as offering. Aspects that are important to people in their decision-making come to be embodied in popular stereotypes of the city

Various studies of urban migrants point to various psychic rewards that attract rural people. The desire of young people to enhance their personal independence, the lure of the prestige associated with urban living, and, in general, the view that modernity is associated with urban life, have all received mention in particular cases. Although economic man lives in Africa, Africans are not *only* economic men![33]

The migration which is the consequence of uneven development and popular images is disproportionately to the largest cities. This pattern too has roots in the uneven development of the colonial period. Now, as before independence, there is a concentration of public investment in the capital – a proliferation of governmental bureaucracies and parastatal organizations, and the construction of symbolic independence buildings, conference centres, parliament buildings, stadiums, schools and usually a university. All this activity generates a construction and employment boom. Foreign capital too, for sound political and business reasons, concentrates its industrial investments in the one or two largest cities.

But underdevelopment means that capitalist industrialization is unable to absorb more than a fraction of the labour force generated by massive rural–urban migration. It is now time to explore the nature and implications of this situation.

Dependent industrialization

Although some peripheral capitalist countries in Africa have attained high rates of industrial growth, they are unlikely to duplicate the development path of the advanced-capitalist countries. More specifically, they are unlikely to absorb their burgeoning labour forces into modern productive activities, thereby generating a dynamic internal market and allowing for a rise in the living standards of all classes. In the first place, the labour-absorption problem is more onerous in contemporary Africa than, for example, it was in Western Europe in the early nineteenth century. Movement off the land is occurring in Africa in the context of far higher rates of population growth than those that earlier obtained in Europe. Whereas the annual rate for the former countries is about 3 per cent, that for the latter during the eighteenth and nineteenth centuries was always under 1 per cent. So not only does uneven development furnish positive incentives for rural-urban migration, but increasing population pressure upon the land in some areas makes such movement almost unavoidable for many. In addition, the safety valve of massive emigration to the New World that reduced the surplus population in nineteenth-century European cities has no analogue in tropical Africa today.

In the second place, the conditions that account for the 'successful' industrialization of Western Europe, North America and Japan do not obtain in contemporary Africa. Consequently, a development model imitative of current Western practices is unlikely to prove as transformative. First, a rapid and sustained increase in agricultural productivity – an 'agricultural revolution' – preceded the industrial revolution in the case of the advanced-capitalist countries. But this has not been so in tropical Africa, where oscillating world prices for primary commodities, declining rural–urban terms of trade, and various other urban biases have bedevilled agricultural development. 'Peasanti-zation', not capitalist production, has developed. Secondly, the development of the productive forces in core capitalisms was, in normal times, congruent with the expansion of an internal market for manufactured goods. The antiquated technologies created or borrowed and adapted by the early industrializers absorbed much more labour per unit of capital than the relatively capital-intensive technologies employed by foreign-controlled firms in the Third World. Rising productivity has thus not gone hand-in-hand with a broadening of the internal market in the latter, as it did in the former. Moreover, industrialists in core capitalisms, unlike their counterparts in tropical Africa today, produced a wide range of capital as well as consumer goods; this not only contributed to expanding internal markets in the former, but also permitted firms to innovate and adapt technologies to local environments. Finally, a strong state characteristically devoted to the support of local industrial capital operated in the advanced-capitalist countries, and sought to open up markets abroad. In contrast, the colonial state in African territories actively blocked industrialization until very late in the day. Although some post-colonial states now wish to promote indigenously controlled industrialization, the least risky path – and that most congruent with the interests of the dominant classes – is to continue development along the lines established by the global corporations.

In consequence, industrialization in tropical African countries has not affected a structural transformation of peripheral capitalism. Industrialization is typically belated, limited in scope, and dependent upon foreign technologies and know-how. The capitalist mode of production, though dominant, does not displace petty-capitalist and non-capitalist forms with which it is interconnected. The pattern now to be described has therefore contributed to the crystallization of inegalitarian and impoverished societies.

NATURE AND SCOPE OF INDUSTRIALIZATION

The imperial centres did not favour the development of manufacturing industries in their African colonies until after the Second World War. Colonial policy instead was to foster the extraction of raw materials to supply metropolitan industries. In the case of the British colonies, for instance, the meagre assistance provided them by the British Treasury went into the construction of an infrastructure necessary to export primary products.

Industrialization got under way first in the 1950s in capitals with a substantial concentration of Europeans, such as Dakar, Leopoldville (Kinshasa) and Nairobi. The large dollar deficits accumulated by the colonial powers after the war prompted them to promote the export of raw materials to the United States from their colonies, and to encourage import-substituting industrialization by metropolitan firms behind colonial tariff walls. To foster these ends, the authorities in various colonies extended infrastructure and productivity-related services, and where the initial capital expenditure was heavy, directly invested in enterprises. The British used the Colonial Development Corporation for this last purpose, while many colonial governments created their own industrial development corporation in the 1950s to facilitate industrial growth.[34]

Foreign capital has continued to play an important role in large-scale African manufacturing industries. Indeed, the proportion of direct foreign investment devoted to manufacturing has steadily increased. The total annual flow of investment into the African continent from the advanced-capitalist countries expanded by only 31 per cent between 1967–8 and 1971–2. Yet the annual flow into manufacturing doubled, whereas that into the extractive sector remained constant at about US $450 million. In black Africa, approximately 20 per cent of the total foreign investment in 1967 was in manufacturing (compared to 52 per cent in petroleum, mining and smelting, and 11 per cent in agriculture). The net book value of foreign investment in African manufacturing in 1971 was about US $888 million, though this total underestimates the market value of the relevant assets. The most popular countries for such investment are Nigeria, Zaïre, Kenya, the Ivory Coast and, until recently, Ghana. Another eighteen of the thirty black African countries have received insignificant foreign investment in manufacturing industries; these, as we shall see, are typically the smallest and poorest countries.[35] For those countries that have received considerable foreign investment, economic nationalism has generally become a force to be reckoned with. Post-colonial regimes have sought to augment local control (as I shall discuss in the next chapter) by such means as management contracts with multinational corporations and local equity participation (usually of a minority character in the case of manufacturing).

Industrialization characteristically remains limited in scope. Export-valorization and import-substitution have been the major strategies underlying the belated industrial development. With respect to the former, countries exporting agricultural products have sought to establish processing facilities, such as ginneries for cotton lint production, mills for groundnut and palm oil extraction, canning factories for fruits and vegetables, tanneries for leather, and sawmills for timber. In countries exporting minerals, for instance Zaïre and Zambia, there has been some local processing of ores before export. This has required the construction of smelters and electrolytic refineries. Production of finished goods for export or of components for assembly abroad is rare.[36]

Import-substituting industrialization became the dominant strategy with the approach of political independence. Initially it was argued that this would permit a saving of foreign exchange and generate local employment. Hence, governments designed various incentives to attract foreign investment in manufacturing; the most popular were tariff barriers to protect locally manufactured goods, tax holidays, liberal policies regarding profit repatriation, assurances against nationalization, and the establishment of industrial estates with all the requisite infrastructure.

The results have not been encouraging. For a large number of small, poor countries – for example, Botswana, Burundi, Chad, Gambia, Malawi, Togo and Upper Volta – industrialization has scarcely begun. Such investment as there has been is largely in basic lines like food, beverages and textiles, with perhaps some minimal processing of local primary products for export. Countries with larger populations or other advantages (Nigeria, Ghana, Senegal, Zambia, Zaïre and Kenya) have installed a wider range of industries; but even in these cases the concentration is upon the final manufacture of light consumer goods and export-valorization, with some production of intermediate goods and negligible production of capital goods. Indeed, in the forty 'independent African countries' (excluding principally South Africa) in 1973, the textiles and clothing industries engaged one-third of the total employees, manufacturing, food, beverages and tobacco one-quarter, and fabricated metal products industries only 12 per cent. If we consider only some of the the industrially more advanced countries, then generally between 60 and 75 per cent of gross manufacturing output, and between half and two-thirds of wage-earners in manufacturing are accounted for by the light manufacturing industries (table 2.3). Kenya and Zaïre are partial exceptions to this trend.[37]

The paucity of backward linkages within African economies means that they must import most intermediate and capital goods. The value added, even on the most commonly produced consumer and intermediate goods, is generally limited. For instance, beer, beverages and paint are often made from imported materials; clothing industries rely upon imported cloth; the shoe industry typically depends upon

Table 2.3   *Distribution of manufacturing by industry, 1971*

	Light manufacturing* industries		Heavy manufacturing† industries		Other manufacturing industries		Total manufacturing	
	% of output	no. persons engaged	% of output	no. persons engaged	% of output	no. persons engaged	%	no.
Egypt	74·9	439 910	24·9	211 360	0·2	2 280	100	653 550
Ghana	74·4	43 187	25·2	12 138	0·4	253	100	55 578
Ivory Coast	62·4	27 440	34·5	8 137	3·1	1 210	100	36 787
Nigeria	63·0	101 507	36·2	44 386	0·8	2 665	100	148 558
Senegal	76·7	11 510	23·3	3 150	0·0	—	100	14 660
Zaire	54·4	63 132	44·0	21 496	1·6	1 224	100	85 852
Kenya	57·2	38 615	41·6	35 171	1·2	1 312	100	75 098
Tanzania	73·8	41 103	24·2	6 729	2·0	866	100	48 698
Uganda	72·7	34 558	27·2	6 131	0·1	37	100	40 726
Zambia	63·1	30 998	36·7	17 707	0·2	239	100	48 944
TOTAL independent African countries	67·9	1 263 556	31·2	521 372	0·9	38 936	100	1 823 864

Note:

* 'light manufacturing' includes these industries: food, beverages and tobacco; textiles and clothing; wood and furniture; and paper, printing and publishing

† 'heavy manufacturing' includes the following industries; chemicals, petroleum and plastics; non-metallic mineral products; basic metal industries; and fabricated metal products, machinery and equipment

Source: Computed from ECA, *Survey of Economic Conditions in Africa, 1973* (New York: United Nations, 1975), tables 7 and 8, pp. 90, 91

plastics made from imported raw materials (and sometimes imported
leather or tanning materials too); and most metal products require
imported metal. Studies of manufacturing in middle Africa have also
commented upon the lack of much capital goods production. This
pattern, furthermore, is unlikely to change as long as industrialization
proceeds along the existing lines. It is difficult to see how a capital goods
sector could develop here – even if the multinationals were so inclined –
inasmuch as the heavy engineering and chemical industries are those in
which economies of scale are the greatest. The prospects of creating
common markets to compensate for the small size of most national
markets are dim.[38]

As a result of these factors, industrialization in association with
foreign capital has not transformed, and is unlikely to transform,
tropical African economies. Consider, for instance, the fact that in 1973
the share of the forty African 'independent developing countries' in
world manufacturing was only 0·6 per cent; this proportion had
remained constant since 1960. Indeed, Africa is industrially backward
even in comparison to other continents of the Third World. Not only did
the Third World account for only 7 per cent of the world's
manufacturing output in 1973, but Africa produced only 7 per cent of
the Third World's share (and Latin America, 53 per cent). Some have
argued that industrial growth in Africa, as measured for instance by the
growth of value-added by manufacturing, is remarkable. It is true that
the value-added typically increased in excess of 10 per cent per annum in

Table 2.4 *Proportion of GDP and growth rate attributed to
manufacturing*

	1960	1972	Rate of growth of value added, p.a., 1960–70
Egypt	21·0	22·1	5·1
Ghana	3·7	12·0	13·7
Ivory Coast	7·2	12·3	13·2
Nigeria	4·8	8·4	11·1
Senegal	10·2	15·2	2·5
Zaïre	13·3	19·0	5·9
Kenya	9·6	12·1	9·9
Tanzania	3·0	9·9	19·5
Uganda	6·5	8·4	10·9
Zambia	4·1	10·7	14·4
TOTAL independent African countries*	9·2	11·4	7·3

Note: * excludes Algeria, for all years except 1960, and South Africa
Source: ECA, *Survey of Conditions in Africa, 1973,* table 10, p. 94

Table 2.5 *Distribution of employees by economic activity*

	Agric., forestry, fishing	Mining, quarrying	Manufacturing	Electricity, gas, water	Construction	Trade, hotels, restaurants	Transport, storage, communications	Services (financial, govermental, personal)	TOTAL
Kenya (1978)	26·7	0·3	14·3	1·0	6·1	6·9	5·6	39·3	100·2 (911 600)
Ghana (1971)	11·4	6·0	14·1	4·1	11·0	8·9	8·0	36·5	100·0 (401 600)
Tanzania (1974)	25·6	1·0	13·4	3·3	15·1	5·2	9·3	27·1	100·0 (484 000)
Uganda (1973)	17·6	1·5	15·4	12·8	12·8	4·9	3·4	44·4	100·0 (347 600)
Zambia (1977)	8·7	18·3	11·0	1·5	12·2	10·4	5·7	32·2	100·0 (372 500)

Source: ILO, *Year Book of Labour Statistics*, 1977, 1978, 1979

the 1960s. But this statistic in itself is misleading, insofar as the industrial base in the countries in question is so small. By 1972, as table 2.4 shows, manufacturing accounted for 12 per cent or more of Gross Domestic Product in only five of selected, more dynamic African economies. Moreover, those employed or self-employed in manufacturing industries constituted only 5 per cent or less of the economically active population of the middle African countries in the late 1960s, while in excess of half of the economically active still engaged in agricultural, forestry, fishing and hunting. Even among the salary- and wage-earners of the formal sector, employees engaged in manufacturing characteristically account for less than 15 per cent of the total (see table 2.5). Governmental and personal services are a far more important source of wage-employment, as are agriculture, forestry and fishing, mining and quarrying, and, in particular cases, construction.[39]

COSTS BORNE BY THE POOR

Governments in post-colonial Africa pursuing capital-intensive industrialization have viewed this largely as a strategy by which foreign capital, sometimes (and increasingly) in collaboration with domestic capital or state agencies, would build local factories to produce commodities formerly imported. Implicit in this policy, therefore, has been the assumption that manufacturers would respond to (and shape) the existing skewed pattern of demand originating in the colonial experience. This policy has had certain unfortunate consequences for the poor.

In the first place, neither the goods produced nor the income distribution fostered by this approach is conducive to fulfilling the basic needs of the people. The first point is obvious. Import-substituting manufacturers would, almost by definition, produce commodities they had initially developed for affluent Western markets – processed foods, finely finished clothes and shoes using synthetic materials, international brand-name soaps and detergents, private motor vehicles, and many other items familiar to Western consumers. While in the West people may regard these as necessities, in the context of underdeveloped African countries most of these items constitute luxuries or at least non-essentials. Consider, for example, the impact of transnational manufacturing corporations in reorienting demand towards 'inappropriate' food and soap products in Kenya. *Posho*, made from maize flour using labour-intensive techniques, is a traditional staple. However, effective advertising and packaging has successfully shifted urban demand away from *posho* towards branded, sifted flour; this highly refined product is more expensive, less nutritious, and much more capital-intensive than *posho*. The same trend applies to breakfast foods. Intensive advertising is in the process of replacing demand for the traditional breakfast staples (especially *uji*, made from maize flour) with a demand for more expensive, less nutritious and more capital-intensive Western cereal products, many of which are produced locally under licence. With respect to soap products, a score of locally owned firms satisfied mass demand for these before the entrance of three transnational soap producers in the 1960s. The latter rapidly transformed this industry – with negative consequences:

> Kenya could have a locally-controlled soap industry meeting almost all its needs for common cleaning aids – producing mostly hand-made laundry soap and, perhaps, some simpler non-branded toilet soaps. Such an industry would have higher employment effects, provide better backward linkages, waste fewer scarce resources on advertising and product differentiation, save more foreign exchange, spread regional distribution better, and generate less social inequality. Instead, as a consequence of multinational corporate dominance, Kenya has a soap industry heading in the opposite direction.[40]

The second point flows from the first: the advanced-country technology imported to produce these non-essentials reinforces the distribution of income that determines the pattern of demand. Capital-intensive technologies not only make high incomes for a minority feasible – owing to their relatively high productivity – but also *require* income concentration if there is to be a market for the expensive consumer goods produced. This 'natural tendency' toward income inequality is, of course, typically fortified by the political influence of the emergent classes who benefit by it. I pursue this theme further in the next chapter. Suffice it to say at this point that even where (as in Zambia) state corporations undertake manufacturing investment in concert with transnational corporations, the responsible bureaucrats generally apply normal commercial criteria in their investment decisions. Essentially this implies that state capitalism responds to the existing lopsided pattern of demand; it does not devise social priorities to reorient demand towards the satisfaction of basic human needs. Economic nationalism, manifest in efforts to augment local control over foreign capital, does not then represent a transformation of the existing pattern of capital accumulation and class formation. Indeed, much of the debate about Tanzania has been over the question of whether that country has proceeded past state capitalism to respond to the needs and aspirations of the poor.[41]

In addition, dependent industrialization clearly creates very limited opportunities for productive employment. This is not only because foreign-controlled firms import capital-intensive technologies; locally owned firms too, if they are to be competitive in many product lines, must have recourse to the same sort of technology as the transnationals. This is unfortunate in view of the magnitude of the problem of labour absorption. According to one well-informed estimate, if we assume that the manufacturing sector in a country employs one-fifth of a labour force growing at 3 per cent per annum, employment in this sector would

Table 2.6   *Average annual increase in manufacturing employment, 1963-70*

	%
Ghana	9·3
Nigeria	7·7
Kenya	6·0
Uganda	4·6
Ethiopia	6·4

Source: Calculated from ILO, *Yearbook of Labour Statistics,* various years

need to increase by 18 per cent per year just to absorb the *new* entrants into the labour market. But not even the most successful country in tropical Africa has that high a proportion of its labour force in manufacturing. Moreover, as indicated in table 2.6, not even in the heyday of import-substitution industrialization did manufacturing employment increase at anything like 18 per cent per annum.[42]

The capital-intensity of large-scale manufacturing firms has often been decried. Artificially low interest rates, overvalued exchange rates, preferential licensing of capital equipment imports, investment credits, heavy depreciation allowances, tariff rebates on equipment, and various tax exemptions are the most common policies that have encouraged the substitution of capital for labour by cheapening the former. There might be a rationale for these policies if the industries they helped to establish used domestically produced raw materials and intermediate products as inputs. In this event, industrialization would produce an important indirect effect on employment, absorbing labour once the factories had been constructed. But in practice, as I have already observed, little indirect employment has resulted from import-substitution.

Limited by capital-intensive technologies, few backward and forward linkages, narrow domestic markets and negligible export markets, large manufacturing firms contribute little to the solution of the employment/poverty problem. They are, in fact, part of that problem.

Marginalization

In these circumstances, the variously termed 'traditional', 'informal' or 'non-capitalist' sector of the urban economy must absorb a large portion of the rapidly expanding labour supply. A study for the World Bank based on data from Bombay, Jakarta, Belo Horizonte (Brazil), Lima and eight other Peruvian cities found that the proportion of the labour force engaged in the informal sector varied from 53 to 69 per cent. As table 2.7 shows, this proportion in the African cities for which we possess data is not as high. It is normal, however, for at least one-third of the work force to be engaged (or unengaged) outside the formal sector. This accords with a rough estimate for the major West African cities that those in informal economic activities or unemployed are at least as numerous as the wage-earners in the large-scale sector. Commerce invariably provides the most opportunities in the informal sector – typically at least half of these – followed by petty production (of variable size) and, far behind, urban agriculture.[43]

Given the high rate of urban growth and the low growth of formal employment, the proportion of the economically active population in the informal sector is bound to expand. For instance, with respect to Nairobi, one author has estimated that the proportion of the labour force finding informal economic opportunities will have to rise from 25 to 40 per cent by the year 2000. Already over half of the working populations of spontaneous settlements such as Old Pumwani and Mathara Valley in Nairobi survive in this way.[44]

An important question relates to the prospects of those people who, though superfluous to the labour requirements of the productive capitalist mode, nonetheless work hard to earn a meagre livelihood. On the one hand, there are the economists who regard the informal sector as an important and potentially dynamic part of rural and urban economies. If governments would cease their negative attitude towards these indigenous labour-intensive activities and undertake to foster their expansion, many informal economic activities could absorb more labour more productively. This development would have positive implications not only for employment-generation, but also for national

Table 2.7 *Proportion of the economically active population in the informal sector*

	%
Nairobi (African pop. only, 1972)	25
All Kenyan urban areas (1969)	28–33
Lusaka (1974)	37·9
All Senegalese urban areas (1975)	50
Greater Dakar (1975)	37
Abidjan (1970)	31

Sources: On Kenya, ILO, *Employment, Incomes and Equality*, pp. 54, 225; on Lusaka, R. van der Hoeven, 'Zambia's Income Distribution during the Early Seventies', ILO Working Paper, WEP 2–23/WP 54, March 1977, p. 22; on Senegal, M. P. van Dijk, 'Developing the Informal Sector in Senegal', ILO Working Paper, Jobs and Skills for Africa, Dakar, December 1976, p. 1; and on Abidjan, Heather Joshi *et al.*, *Abidjan* (Geneva: ILO, 1976), p. 1

self-reliance (since fewer inputs would need to be imported), income distribution (greater equality flowing from the spread of opportunities for productive employment), and the production of goods designed to satisfy the basic needs of the masses. On the other hand, there is the 'marginalization' analysis; according to this, the marginal pole of the economy is unlikely to escape from the low productivity/low incomes syndrome owing to the hegemony of the oligopolistic capitalist mode of production. This hegemony with respect to petty-capitalist and non-capitalist forms of production is underpinned by the interests of the dominant classes, as reflected in the economic policies of the state. The consequent model of industrial development is unlikely to be dynamic enough, or to generate sufficient productive employment, to cause the non-capitalist sector to contract within a generation. Hence, the likely future of the marginal pole is neither evolution nor even displacement by the large capitalist firms; it is instead involution, in which more and more poor people share stagnant markets among themselves.[45]

THE INFORMAL SECTOR AND THE EVOLUTIONARY PROSPECT

The 'formal–informal sector' model reflects a dissatisfaction on the part of many development economists with the 'modern–traditional sector' typology. Underlying this original dualistic typology was the notion that, in developing countries, a dynamic, large-scale, highly productive sector coexisted with an isolated, small-scale, minimally or non-productive indigenous sector in town and country. Economists then conceived of economic development as involving a transfer of manpower from 'underemployment' – jobs such as those of petty traders, hawkers, bootblacks or car-washers – to fully productive employment in factories, mines or plantations, for instance. But the main problem was the slow generation of jobs in the modern sector. Hence, the role of the traditional sector in the period of transition was to allow people to subsist while they waited in the queue for modern employment.

The popularity of the 'formal–informal' model in the 1970s mirrors a significant shift in the conventional conception of economic structure. In the first place, the new terminology reflects a refurbishing of the image of the traditional sector. Far from being stagnant and unproductive, some informal economic activities were a potential source of dynamic growth, change and productive employment for the rural and urban masses. However, the informal sector could realize this potential only if governments ceased to neglect or even harass these activities. In the second place, the modern sector in the guise of the formal sector lost much of its former lustre. It was now recognized that the prosperity of the large-scale undertakings owed a great deal to their sponsorship and subsidization by the state, especially with respect to market protection by means of tariffs, quotas, government contracts and trade licences. In sum, the new terminology was beneficial inasmuch as it brought to the fore the role of the state in fostering or hindering the development of each sector.

Nonetheless, the sectors were poorly delineated. This imprecision is evident in the 1972 ILO Report on Kenya, which first employed the distinction. It distinguished the informal from the formal sector on the basis of seven antipodal traits: easy as opposed to difficult entry; reliance on indigenous rather than foreign resources; family in contrast to corporate ownership; small as against large scale of operations; labour-intensive and adapted versus capital-intensive and imported technologies; informally rather than formally acquired skills; and unregulated and competitive, as opposed to protected, markets. Insofar as there is no necessary correlation among the various elements taken to describe each sector, one would be hard pressed to classify many enterprises using this scheme. It is therefore not surprising that the ILO Report (and most subsequent writers on the subject) adopted a simple operational definition that identified the informal sector with establishments unenumerated in official labour statistics. In the case of Kenya (and most other middle African countries), this meant that the informal sector constituted establishments with fewer than ten employees. The conceptual problem, of course, is that the informal sector defined in this way includes many firms that do not fit the syndrome described above. A more sophisticated approach has been to distinguish between the sectors on the basis of self-employment/wage employment. But this is also unsatisfying, owing to the variety of transitional forms lying between the two poles: craftsmen with varying degrees of autonomy over their productive process, including those who hire casual labour but also rely on family labour and work themselves; 'outworkers' who earn a pseudo-wage from capitalist firms, but own their own implements; and casual labourers, journeymen and apprentices. To encompass this diversity in a dichotomic model, one is driven to equivocation. The operational distinction becomes that between 'formal' firms which hire independent labour on a contractual and long-term basis, and 'informal' establishments which depend either solely upon the labour of the head of enterprise and his family, or also upon the labour of a few casual workers (as well as apprentices and journeymen) who often possess particularistic ties to the master.[46]

However defined, the informal sector is clearly large and growing. Many economists have thus come to the view that any attack upon mass poverty must include efforts to stimulate the productivity and expansion of establishments within this sector. In principle, many innovative small entrepreneurs in underdeveloped countries should accumulate enough capital to make the transition into large-scale activities. This organic growth within an economy would enhance poverty-amelioration owing to the characteristic labour-intensity of indigenous enterprise, backward and forward linkages, and the mass-orientated product composition of petty production. Yet this transition rarely occurs in urban Africa; those success stories that do live in local folklore refer mainly to individuals who made their fortunes in trade. Few small producers of goods and services manage to compete successfully with the large firms and expand into large-scale production.[47] The problem, from the viewpoint of the proponents of the informal sector, lies in the onerous structural constraints that obstruct the 'natural' evolution of the indigenous economy.

It will be useful to enumerate these generic constraints, as culled from recent studies of the informal sector in African cities.

1. *Credit*   Informal establishments must finance their own expansion because they can gain credit, if at all, only at high interest rates from moneylenders. Banks as a rule are unsympathetic to the needs of informal enterprises because they lack collateral. But for firms in the formal sector, capital is cheap; local credit is normally readily available to them at relatively low rates owing to their creditworthiness. In addition, multinational firms can draw upon large international resources of technology, skills and finance. Small entrepreneurs are thus at a distinct disadvantage with respect to accumulating the resources for expansion. Even state lending agencies created to foster indigenous enterprise tend to favour the largest (and hence most influential and creditworthy) indigenous enterprises.

2. *Infrastructure*   The services provided by the state flow mainly into the formal sector. Official priorities generally ensure, for instance, that major outlays on water supply, electricity-generation, telecommunications and rail transport benefit the large firms, not the petty producers. These often have to make do without running water or electricity in make-shift quarters in the spontaneous housing settlements.

3. *Regulations*   Typically, there are a myriad of regulations governing informal enterprises that severely restrict their chances of success; these were often designed with the formal sector in mind. In Nairobi and Dakar, for example, even the most marginal self-employment – as bootblack or street vendor – required a licence. In addition, there are regulations governing the proper location of production and trade, hygenic standards, and income tax. Infractions of regulations by poor (and sometimes illiterate) people give police cause to arrest or extract bribes, giving rise to popular feelings of police harassment of small-scale economic activities. The epitome of harassment is the demolition of shanties and kiosks with no provision of alternative accommodation (as has happened periodically in Nairobi).

4. *Markets*   While governments restrict competition with respect to

the goods and services of the large firms via tarrifs, quotas, trade licences and the tendering of government contracts, those in informal economic activities must usually engage in unprotected and highly competitive markets. Thus, profit margins are characteristically low in the latter enterprises. But inasmuch as their expansion depends almost wholly upon the ploughing back of profits, narrow profit margins make an escape from small-scale production or trade difficult.[48]

Although cognizant of these constraints, informal-sector advocates nevertheless regard (or at least declare) as feasible evolutionary change leading to the expansion of an array of informal enterprises. Governments would thereby advance the several important social goals mentioned above. They need only to recognize the errors of their ways by eliminating discriminatory policies and practices against these enterprises, and by fostering informal activities instead. Typical of the usual recommendations were those proposed by a 1977 conference of economists studying the urban informal sector in Africa. The participants called upon governments to recognize

> the need for equality of opportunity for informal sector enterprises in the form of at least equal access to credit facilities, various inputs, training facilities and technology. This means not only that the government and the formal sector should be more responsive to the needs of the informal sector; it also requires the creation of an appropriate policy environment.[49]

The implicit assumption – that the state constitutes a neutral agency dedicated to the public good – requires no elaboration.

THE INVOLUTIONAL PROSPECT

The superiority of the variant of underdevelopment theory propounded here derives from its analysis of the *political* roots of peripheral capitalism. From this perspective, the prospect for the informal sector is neither evolution into larger, more productive enterprises nor even displacement by large capitalist firms. It is instead involution, a situation in which more and more people share stagnant markets among themselves. Petty economic activities will continue to bear the cost of the failure of capitalist industry and commerce to absorb the expanding labour force. Hence, more intensive competition, widespread underemployment (that is, insufficient work to fill the day), instability of employment and, in consequence, low and even declining, real incomes, will be the lot of most of those consigned to marginal activities. The 'hegemony' of the oligopolistic capitalist mode of production accounts for the inability of the marginal pole of the economy to escape from the low productivity/low incomes syndrome. This hegemony is manifest in the manner in which the formal capitalist mode moulds and uses the non-capitalist and petty-capitalist forms to augument capital accumulation. The existing 'articulation' of modes of production thus mirrors the interests of the dominant foreign and domestic classes. Benefiting from the organization of production and the consumption patterns this permits, these classes use their political power to resist costly economic reforms. Any genuine upgrading of the competitiveness of the non-capitalist and petty-capitalist enterprises would constitute such reform by removing the privileged position of the oligopolistic firms.

It follows that reforms in favour of the informal sector are impracticable without a prior shift in political power. Marginalization is a function of the structural constraints upon expansion the informal-sector theorists identify; but this is only a proximate cause. To the extent that the state functions to assist accumulation in the dominant mode, these constraints are not *contingent* but *necessary* elements of the government's economic policy. Therefore, the state discriminates against informal enterprises not because of misconception about the 'traditional' sector, but because of the concrete class interests associated with a certain generic model or pattern of accumulation.

I have stated this thesis in very bold terms.[50] What is needed now is greater specificity concerning the nature of the subordinate forms of production, the manner in which modes of production articulate, and the interests served by such an economic configuration.

In order of decreasing marginality, the subordinate forms in Africa are artisanal, petty-commodity and petty-capitalist production. All of these are contained roughly within the unenumerated or informal sector (operationalized as establishments with fewer than ten employees); the critera distinguishing them are relationship to the market and relations of production.[51]

Consider first the non-capitalist forms. In the case of the artisan, he produces articles in response to the request of particular clients. His only contact with the market is as purchaser (or renter) of his means of production. The classic example is of course the tailor who produces clothing to the specific requirements of a customer who seeks him out. Petty-commodity producers, in contrast, produce for the market and not in response to the direct demand of clients. A carpenter who displays his furniture outside his workplace is such a producer. Both of these forms rely principally for their labour upon apprentices, non-wage family workers and perhaps piece-rate journeymen. The relevant social relations of production (as these obtain in Dakar) have been aptly described as follows:

> the principal aspect is the direct domination of the individual apprentice and his own direct dependence, indispensable to the appropriation of surplus. Relations of personal dependence are of a paternalistic type. The apprentice is closely tied to the master craftsman since the latter often provides housing, food and clothing, in addition to furnishing him with some skills. . . . Apprentices receive occasional pocket-money, especially at religious festivals. Once the apprentice has attained a certain age and competence, it is customary for him to be paid more regularly and substantially, thus

theoretically making the transition from apprenticeship to journeyman. The journeyman is not really a wage-earner; he receives a certain share of the profits from each order, and both he and the apprentices are usually permitted to use the means of production for their own profit during slack periods, and they themselves produce articles for casual sale, or more rarely, to order.[52]

As it is difficult on the basis of most research reports to distinguish between artisanal and petty-commodity producers, I shall refer to both as petty producers.

To the extent that petty producers accumulate capital, they can make the transition to petty capitalism. The main characteristics of this are production solely for the market and the contractual basis of labour commitment. Particularistic relationships between master and employees give way (in principle though rarely fully in practice) to the more impersonal dictates of an independent wage-labour system. Petty capitalism relates to the usually unenumerated establishments in which labour codes and minimum wage laws are rarely respected and employment is insecure. Petty capitalists are obviously better placed to accumulate capital than the petty producers. Yet they too are generally subject to the same structural constraints upon their expansion, especially highly competitive markets. Although the negligible overhead expenses and the super-exploitation of labour and themselves allow small-scale producers to compete successfully in some markets (such as furniture manufacture, automechanics, petty contracting), the pattern is for the oligopolistic capitalist firms to pre-empt the most profitable markets.

There is, in addition, the small-scale distributive sector. The role of petty commerce and transport is to link the various forms of production: market traders dealing with foodstuffs seek out peasants who are not yet, or only marginally, involved in production for sale; transporters owning one or two trucks deliver vegetables grown by peasants to large supermarkets; wholesalers distribute to petty traders commodities produced by the large firms or imported. Indeed, petty traders market goods deriving from all modes and forms of production. The various strata involved in petty commerce, as well as those in production, will receive attention in chapter 5.[53]

The 'modes of production' model, unlike the 'formal–informal sector' one, is dynamic in its conception. The articulation of modes of production is a process that began in Africa two to three hundred years ago, the initial link between externally introduced capitalism and the indigenous pre-capitalist modes appearing only at the level of exchange. In time, capitalism took root. What this has meant is that the capitalist mode has moulded and subordinated the non-capitalist forms. In traditional African cities – Ibadan is an example – petty production was an indigenous pre-capitalist form; in the colonial cities, such as Nairobi, petty production (except blacksmithing) barely existed as an indigenous form. But, regardless of the particular history of petty production, capitalism introduced a demand for new goods and services in the towns; the result has been that some crafts have diversified and expanded (from blacksmithing to metal-working, for example), antiquated crafts have diminished in importance or disappeared (for instance, weavers, tanners, goldsmiths), and new groups of artisans have emerged (such as automechanics, watch or bicycle repairers). Furthermore, the petty production that survived or emerged came to resemble capitalist enterprises – for example in their production for the market, in their increasing willingness to hire casual labourers, and in their reliance upon modern inputs.[54]

The subordination of the non-capitalist and petty-capitalist forms in their relationship to the dominant mode is evident in more than the discriminatory policies of the state. This dependency rests, in the first place, upon reliance on capitalist firms for raw materials – either through purchase or from scavenging industrial or other waste materials. In a sample of petty producers of furniture and construction components in Dakar, for instance, 80 per cent purchased their raw materials from large enterprises, who in turn imported most of these from abroad. Another common pattern is for small-scale manufacturers of such common commodities as kitchen utensils, cooking stoves and mattresses to rely upon a supply of industrial waste materials. In the second place, many craftsmen must purchase or rent their means of production from large concerns. Perhaps the most obvious case is that of seamstresses or tailors who must obtain their sewing machines from the modern sector. There are instances recorded in which small producers have invented their own hand or electrically operated machinery; but these appear rare. Thirdly, in some crafts, a good proportion of producers learn their skills through on-the-job training in capitalist firms. In Dakar, for example, fully 70 per cent of the furniture-makers and 55 per cent of the automechanics in a sample had received their training in this way. Finally, some petty capitalists and petty producers find outlets for their products in large retail stores or (far less frequently) as inputs into large manufacturing firms. Tailors (the most numerous of the craftsmen) often produce for retailers, as do some shoemakers and small furniture manufacturers. Seldom do petty producers provide inputs into industrial establishments; indeed, one common complaint in studies of the urban informal sector in Africa is the paucity of such forward linkages. Most of the goods and services are oriented towards consumers.[55]

The marginality thesis argues not only that the hegemonic capitalist mode subordinates and moulds (though not destroys) the non-capitalist forms, but also that this articulation serves the interests of the former. Note first that it would be absurd to suggest that all those excluded from the modern sector play a functional role. If this were so, the governments of Mexico, Turkey and Algeria would presumably not encourage the emigration of young men to advanced-capitalist countries to seek employment, nor would the United States press birth control upon underdeveloped countries. If an epidemic suddenly swept away the openly unemployed and a good proportion (but how much?) of the most marginally employed, this would be unlikely to disturb accumulation in the dominant mode. It would also be absurd to imply that the marginal pole of the economy is in all respects functional. Nevertheless, there are three ways in which the informal sector assists accumulation in the capitalist mode by lowering operating costs.

In the first place, petty producers and other small entrepreneurs subsidize the consumption of urban workers (and others), thereby lowering the real wages they must receive to sustain themselves. Consider first that wages need cover the costs of workers only while they are employed. Insofar as most African workers still grow up in villages engaged in peasant production and return there upon retirement, the capitalist firms do not have to bear the cost of supporting employees in their unproductive early and late years. In addition, urban workers, while employed, consume many goods and services produced cheaply by petty producers and others. This cheapness is a function of the intense competition in the informal sector and the willingness of small producers and distributers to exploit themselves and others. The result again is to lower the reproduction cost of labour to the large capitalist enterprises. Indeed, the opportunity for employees to supplement their wages with spare-time self-employment also permits employers to offer wages lower than they might have to be in the absence of the marginal pole.[56]

In the second place, the marginal labour force acts to some extent as an 'industrial reserve army'. It may thus constrain wage increases in the modern sector and supply labour during expansionist phases of the economy.

Finally, insofar as capitalist firms subcontract to the self-employed the production of inputs and various services, they can lower costs and raise profits. I have already mentioned that forward linkages between petty producers and large manufacturers appear, as far as one can tell, rare as yet in tropical Africa. More common is the situation in which large firms rely on small contractors to undertake necessary construction or even maintenance work. Since these petty contractors as a rule do not adhere to the labour code in hiring labour, they can pass their low costs on to the employer. As well, firms can lower the distribution costs of their products by reliance upon low-income petty traders (especially women, children and unemployed youth) to peddle these in the streets and market places.[57]

It is obviously difficult to assess the significance of these functions for profitability in the capitalist sector. With respect to labour costs, for instance, both the large employers' desire for labour stability and their ability to pass on costs to consumers mean that wage rates are not closely tied to market conditions. But even if the informal sector's contribution is not a major one, the fact still remains that there exists a rather stable interrelation of modes of production that suits the dominant classes' interests well enough. One dysfunction of this economic configuration, we shall shortly see, is the rampant urban crime it spawns. However, even with respect to the maintenance of the system as a whole, one can argue that the marginal pole is functional. The involutional capacity of this can provide a 'sense of employment' to people who would otherwise be openly unemployed, and hence presumably susceptible to radical appeals to overturn the system.[58]

In sum, there are ample grounds for pessimism about the resolution of the employment/poverty problem. Even under the most optimistic assumption about economic expansion, a large part of the African labour forces would not find productive employment. Reforms within the existing organization of production are unlikely to have much impact; reform of this productive system towards a basic-needs approach probably requires a prior shift in political power. What is at fault is the exclusionary tendency inherent in a certain pattern of capitalist development. I have suggested that the power of the dominant classes and the state underpin this pattern. It is now time to deal directly with this aspect.

Notes

1. ILO, *Employment, Growth and Basic Needs: A One-World Problem* (Geneva: ILO, 1976), p. 17.
2. Baran's book was published in 1957 by Monthly Review Press. For Frank's views, see *Capitalism and Underdevelopment in Latin America* (New York: Monthly Review Press, 1967). A recent piece on underdevelopment theory that retains this stagnationist thesis is M. Harrington, 'Problems and Paradoxes of the Third World', *Dissent* (Fall 1977), pp. 379–89.
3. Critics of early underdevelopment theorists: Bill Warren, 'Imperialism and Capitalist Industrialization', *New Left Review*, 81 (1973), pp. 3–45; Fernando Henrique Cardoso, 'Associated–Dependent Development', in Alfred Stepan (ed.), *Authoritarian Brazil* (New Haven: Yale University Press, 1973), pp. 142–76; C. Leys, 'Underdevelopment and Dependency: Critical Notes', *Journal of Contemporary Asia*, VII, 1 (1977), p. 94; A. Phillips, 'The Concept of "Development"', *Review of African Political Economy*, 8 (1977), pp. 7–20; and G. Palma, 'Dependency: A Formal Theory of Underdevelopment . . .?' *World Development*, VI, 7/8 (1978), pp. 902–4. Conditions facilitating rapid growth: see e.g., C. Leys, 'Capital Accumulation, Class Formation and Dependency – The Significance of the Kenyan Case', *The Socialist Register, 1978* (London: Merlin Press, 1979), pp. 241–66.
4. 'Costs' of capitalist development: S. Lall, 'Is "Dependence" a Useful Concept?', *World Development*, III, 11/12 (1975), pp. 807–9. 'Disturbing studies': see e.g., those reported in K. Griffin and A. Rahman Khan,

'Poverty in the Third World: Ugly Facts and Fancy Models', *World Development*, VI, 3 (1978), pp. 295–304; and M. S. Ahluwalia, 'Income Inequality: Some Dimensions of the Problem', in Hollis Chenery *et al.*, *Redistribution with Growth* (New York: Oxford University Press, 1974), pp. 3–37.

5. Robert Brenner, 'The Origins of Capitalist Development: A Critique of Neo-Smithian Marxism', *New Left Review*, 104 (1977), pp. 25–92, quotes pp. 81, 35.

6. Aidan Foster-Carter, 'The Modes of Production Controversy', *New Left Review*, 107 (1978), p. 51. Marginalization defined: Bryan Roberts, *Cities of Peasants: The Political Economy of Urbanization in the Third World* (London: Edward Arnold, 1978), p. 162. For an indication of the influence of marginalization on development economics, see J. Nugent and P. Yotopoulos, 'What has Orthodox Development Economics Learned from Recent Experience?', *World Development*, VII (1979), pp. 541–54.

7. On 'special reasons', see Irma Adelman and Sherman Robinson, *Income Distribution in Developing Countries: A Case Study of Korea* (Stanford: Stanford University Press, 1978); and the items listed in n. 9, chap. 1. On the limitations of export-oriented manufacturing as a development strategy, see W. G. Tyler, 'Manufacturing Exports and Employment Creation in Developing Countries: Some Empirical Evidence', *Economic Development and Cultural Change*, XXIV, 2 (1976), pp. 355–73.

8. See, e.g., L. Kowarick, 'Capitalism and Urban Marginality in Brazil', in Ray Bromley and Chris Gerry (eds.), *Casual Work and Poverty in Third-World Cities* (New York: John Wiley, 1979), pp. 82–4.

9. Roberts, *Cities of Peasants* (n. 6 above), p. 175.

10. The concept 'dependent urbanization' is developed in Manuel Castells, *The Urban Question: A Marxist Approach*, trans. A. Sheridan (London: Edward Arnold, 1977), pp. 45–59.

11. On the history of pre-colonial African urban areas, see R. W. Steel, 'The Towns of Tropical Africa', in K. M. Barbour and R. M. Prothero (eds.), *Essays on African Population* (New York: Praeger, 1962), pp. 249–78; B. Thomas, 'On the Growth of African Cities', *African Studies Review*, XIII, 1 (1970), pp. 1–8; W. R. Bascom, 'Urbanization as a Traditional African Pattern', *Sociological Review*, VII, 1 (1959), pp. 29–44; A. B. Yusuf, 'A Reconsideration of Urban Conceptions: Hausa Urbanization and the Rural–Urban Continuum', *Urban Anthropology*, III, 2 (1974), pp. 200–21; P. M. Lubeck, 'Contrasts and Continuity in a Dependent City: Kano, Nigeria', in Janet Abu-Lughod and Richard Hay (eds.), *Third World Urbanization* (Chicago: Maaroufa Press, 1977), pp. 281–9; and F. Stambouli and A. Zghal, 'Urban Life in Pre-colonial North Africa', *British Journal of Sociology*, XXVII, 1 (1976), pp. 1–20.

12. See Colin Rosser, *Urbanization in Tropical Africa: A Demographic Introduction* (New York: Ford Foundation, 1972), p. 25; S. Gellar, 'West African Cities as Motors for Development', *Civilisation*, XVII, 3 (1967), p. 255; and J. R. Rayfield, 'Theories of Urbanisation and the Colonial City in West Africa', *Africa*, XLIV, 2 (1974), pp. 163–85. For a study which explains urban expansion and stagnation by reference to a town's incorporation into the world economy, see J. Hinderink and J. Sterkenberg, 'Income Inequality under Changing Urban Conditions in Africa: Cape Coast',

Tijdschrift voor Economische en Sociale Geografie, LXIX, 1/2 (1978), pp. 46–57.

13. The statistics are drawn from Thomas, 'Growth of African Cities' (n. 11 above), pp. 2–3. See also Gellar, 'West African Cities' (n. 12 above), pp. 256–7; and A. Southall, 'The Impact of Imperialism upon Urban Development in Africa', in Victor Turner (ed.), *Colonialism in Africa, 1870–1960*, vol. III (Cambridge: Cambridge University Press, 1971), pp. 216–55.

14. For the statistics on urban growth rates, see Economic Commission for Africa, *Urbanization in Africa: Levels, Trends and Prospects*, 21 July 1972 (Document E/CN.14/POP/67). See also, Kingsley Davis, *World Urbanization, 1950–1970*, vol. II. Population Monograph Series, No. 9, University of California, Berkeley, 1972, p. 170; and William A. Hance, *Population, Migration and Urbanization in Africa* (New York: Columbia University Press, 1970), pp. 230–9.

15. See ECA, *Urbanization in Africa* (n. 14 above), *passim*; and Hance, *Population* (n. 14 above), p. 239.

16. On external impulses, see J. Adams, 'External Linkages of National Economies in West Africa', *African Urban Notes*, VI, 3 (1972), pp. 97–106.

17. The myth of the irrational African is discussed in E. J. Berg, 'Backward Sloping Labor Supply Functions in Dual Economies: The African Case', *Quarterly Journal of Economics*, LXXV (1961), pp. 468–92; and M. Miracle and B. Fetter, 'Backward Sloping Labor Supply Functions and African Economic Behavior', *Economic Development and Cultural Change*, XVII, 2 (1970), pp. 240–1.

18. Much of the information in this and the previous paragraph derives from Miracle and Fetter, 'Backward Sloping Labor Supply Functions' (n. 17 above), pp. 247–50. On the Mossi, see E. Skinner, 'Labour Migration Among the Mossi of the Upper Volta', in Hilda Kuper (ed.), *Urbanisation and Migration in West Africa* (Cambridge: Cambridge University Press, 1965), p. 65; and on Mombasa, K. K. Janmohamed, 'African Labourers in Mombasa, 1895–1940', in B. A. Ogot (ed.), *Hadith 5: Social and Economic History of East Africa* (Nairobi: East African Literature Bureau, 1974), pp. 171–2.

19. For general studies on the use of coercion, see Miracle and Fetter, 'Backward Sloping Labor Supply Functions' (n. 17 above), p. 247: and E. J. Berg, 'The Development of a Labor Force in Sub-Saharan Africa', *Economic Development and Cultural Change*, XIII (1965), pp. 394–412. For case studies on the use of force to create labour markets, see S. O. Osoba, 'The Phenomenon of Labour Migration in the Era of British Colonial Rule', *Journal of the Historical Society of Nigeria*, IV, 4 (1969), pp. 515–26; R. W. Thomas, 'Forced Labour in British West Africa', *Journal of African History*, XIV, 1 (1973), pp. 79–103; Helmuth Heisler, *Urbanization and the Government of Migration: The Interrelation of Urban and Rural Life in Zambia* (London: C. Hurst, 1974), pp. 434–45; Anthony Clayton and Donald Savage, *Government and Labour in Kenya, 1893–1963* (London: Frank Cass, 1974), pp. 95–6, 113–15; and Justinian Rweyemamu, *Underdevelopment and Industrialization in Tanzania* (Nairobi: Oxford University Press, 1973), pp. 17–22.

20. On how these 'facilitating conditions' affected the Frafra, see K. Hart,

'Migration and the Opportunity Structure: A Ghanaian Case Study', in Samir Amin (ed.), *Modern Migrations in Western Africa* (Oxford: Oxford University Press, 1974), p. 332.

21. The most popular ahistorical behavioural approach to the explanation of rural–urban migration is that of Michael Todaro, discussed further below (see n. 31). Examples of the structural–historical approach adopted here are S. Amin, 'Introduction', in Amin (ed.), *Modern Migrations* (n. 20 above), pp. 65–124; and M. Godfrey, 'A Note on Rural–Urban Migration: An Alternative Framework of Analysis', *Manpower and Unemployment Research in Africa*, VIII, 2 (1975), pp. 9–12.

22. John Nabilia, 'The Migration of the Frafra of Northern Ghana: A Case Study of Cyclical Migration', PhD thesis, Michigan State Univeristy, 1974, p. 191. For other cases, see Heather Joshi *et al.*, *Abidjan: Urban Development and Employment in the Ivory Coast* (Geneva: ILO, 1976), p. 44; Richard Sabot, *Urban Migration in Tanzania*, vol. II of the National Urban Mobility, Employment and Income Survey, Economic Research Bureau, University of Dar es Salaam, September 1972, p. 157; and T. S. Weisner, 'The Structure of Sociability: Urban Migration and Urban–Rural Ties in Kenya', *Urban Anthropology*, V, 2 (1976), pp. 199–223.

23. See, in general, D. Byerlee and C. K. Eicher, 'Rural Employment, Migration and Economic Development: Theoretical Issues and Empirical Evidence from Africa', in E. A. G. Robinson (ed.), *The Place of Agriculture in the Development of the Developing Countries* (London: Macmillan, 1974); and W. T. S. Gould, 'International Migration in Tropical Africa: A Bibliographical Review', *International Migration Review*, VIII, 3 (1974), p. 354. For specific cases, see S. M. Essang and A. F. Mabawonku, 'Impact of Urban Migration on Rural Development: Theoretical Considerations and Empirical Evidence from Southern Nigeria', *Developing Economies*, XIII, 2 (1975), pp. 137–49; and Nabilia, 'The Migration of the Frafra' (n. 22 above), pp. 303–4.

24. The statistics and quote are from Osoba, 'The Phenomenon of Labour Migration' (n. 19 above), p. 528. See also, T. Mbagwu, 'Land Concentration around a Few Individuals in Igboland of Eastern Nigeria', *Africa*, XLVIII, 2 (1978), pp. 101–15. For the process of rural differentiation in West Africa, see K. Post, '"Peasantisation" and Rural Political Movements in Western Africa', *European Journal of Sociology*, XIII, 2 (1972), pp. 223–54; and in East Africa, see Rweyemamu, *Underdevelopment and Industrialization in Tanzania* (n. 19 above), pp. 25–30; R. van Zwanenberg, 'The Development of Peasant Commodity Production in Kenya, 1920–40', *Economic History Review*, XXVII, 3 (1974), pp. 442–54; and C. Ehrlick, 'The Uganda Economy', in Vincent Harlow *et al.*, (eds.), *The History of East Africa, Volume II* (Oxford: Oxford University Press, 1965).

25. See, in general, Hance, *Population, Migration and Urbanization* (n. 15 above, pp. 384–6, 420–1; and N. Prothero, 'Continuity and Change in African Population Mobility', in R. W. Steele and N. Prothero (eds.), *Geographers in the Tropics* (Liverpool: University of Liverpool Press, 1964).

26. The survey of Nairobi, Mombasa and Kisumu is James Waweru and Associates, *Progress Report No. 5: Results of the Socio-Economic Survey,*

'Low-Cost Housing and Squatter Upgrading Study', Report to the Government of Kenya and World Bank, August 1976, pp. 10, 22, 33, 43, 50, 64 and 131. A confirming 'Survey of Temporary Structures' in Nairobi is discussed in Andrew Hake, *African Metropolis: Nairobi's Self-Help City* (New York: St Martin's Press, 1977), pp. 98–9. See also, H. Rempel, 'The Rural-to-Urban Migrant in Kenya', *Africa Urban Notes*, VI, 1 (1971), p. 62. Janmohamed treats the historical relationship between land shortage and migration to Mombasa in 'African Labourers' (n. 18 above), pp. 164–7.

27. On Tanzania, see Sabot, *Urban Migration* (n. 22 above), p. 216. On Nigeria, see Akin Mabogunje, *Urbanization in Nigeria* (London: University of London Press, 1968), p. 314. For further cases relating to landlessness of urban migrants, refer to Michael Banton, *West African City* (Cambridge: Cambridge University Press, 1957), p. 62; and Nabilia, 'Migration of the Frafra of Northern Ghana' (n. 22 above), pp. 72–79.

28. The Tanzanian survey is that of Sabot, *Urban Migration* (n. 22 above), pp. 215–16. The information on the occupations of the Kenyan squatters is in Waweru and Associates, *Progress Report No. 5* (n. 26 above), *passim*. See also K. Bissman, 'Industrial Worker in East Africa', *International Journal of Comparative Sociology*, X (March–June, 1969), p. 28.

29. On the propensity of the better-educated to migrate, see, in general, C. Hutton, 'Rates of Labour Migration', in Josef Gugler (ed.), *Nkanga 5: Urban Growth in Subsaharan Africa* (Kampala: Makerere University, 1970), pp. 16–17; and, for specific cases, John Caldwell, *African Rural–Urban Migration: The Movement to Ghana's Towns* (New York: Columbia University Press, 1969), p. 88; R. H. Bates and B. W. Bennett, 'Determinants of the Rural Exodus in Zambia', *Cahiers d'études africaines*, XIV, 55 (1974), p. 550; Henry Rempel, 'Labour Migration into Urban Centers and Urban Unemployment in Kenya' PhD thesis, University of Wisconsin, 1971, p. 30; and R. H. Sabot, 'Education, Income Distribution and Urban Migration in Tanzania', staff paper, Economic Research Bureau, University of Dar es Salaam, 1972.

30. For the relationship between education, family income and migration, refer especially to the review of the literature in Hutton, 'Rates of Labour Migration' (n. 29 above), pp. 16–17. Quote from Kenneth King, *Jobless in Kenya: A Case Study of the Educated Unemployed*, Monograph Series No. 1, Bureau of Educational Research, University of Nairobi, October 1976, p. 5.

31. The primacy of economic considerations in explanations of migration in Africa is demonstrated in J. Gugler, 'On the Theory of Rural–Urban Migration in Africa', in J. A. Jackson (ed.), *Migration* (Cambridge: Cambridge University Press, 1969), pp. 134–55. For the Todaro model (and its development), see M. P. Todaro. 'A Model of Labor Migration and Urban Unemployment in LDCs', *American Economic Review*, LIX, 1 (1969), pp. 138–43; J. R. Harris and M. P. Todaro, 'Migration, Unemployment and Development: A Two-Sector Analysis', *American Economic Review*, LX, 1 (1970), pp. 126–42; and M. P. Todaro, *Internal Migration in Developing Countries* (Geneva: ILO, 1976), especially chap. 2. Useful critiques of this model include K. Hart, 'Migration and the Opportunity Structure: A Ghanaian Case Study', in Amin (ed.), *Modern Migrations* (n. 20 above), pp. 324–33; and E. M. Godfrey, 'Economic

Variables and Rural–Urban Migration: Some Thoughts on the Todaro Hypothesis', *Journal of Development Studies*, x, 1 (1973), pp. 66–78.
32. See, e.g., N. Sudarkasa, 'Commercial Migration in West Africa', *African Urban Notes*, ser. B, 1 (1974–5), pp. 61–103.
33. The quote is from E. Wachtel, 'The Urban Image – Stereotypes of Urban Life in Kenya', Working Paper No. 172, Institute for Development Studies, University of Nairobi, April 1974, p. 2. For a discussion of non-economic variables in rural–urban migration, see D. Byerlee, 'Rural–Urban Migration in Africa. Policy and Research Implications', *International Migration Review*, VIII, 4 (1974), pp. 555–7; Joshi *et al.*, *Abidjan* (n. 22 above), pp. 31–7; and J. Clyde Mitchell, 'African Images of the Town: A Quantitative Exploration', *Manchester Statistical Society* (January 1969), pp. 1–7.
34. See, in general, A. F. Ewing, *Industry in Africa* (Oxford: Oxford University Press, 1968); and A. L. Mabogunje, 'Manufacturing and the Geography of Development in Tropical Africa', *Economic Geography*, IXL (1973), pp. 1–3. For case studies, see N. Swainson, 'The Role of the State in Kenya's Post-War Industrialization', Institute for Development Studies, University of Nairobi, Working Paper 175, September 1976; and L. E. Grayson, 'Manufacturing Development in Ghana, 1920–65', *Economic Bulletin of Ghana*, IV, 3/4 (1974), pp. 61–70.
35. L. L. Rood, 'Foreign Investment in African Manufacturing', *Journal of Modern African Studies*, XIII, 1 (1975), pp. 19–34.
36. See Mabogunje, 'Manufacturing' (n. 34 above), p. 3. Even such a relatively advanced industrializer as Kenya has been unable to develop stable export markets for manufactures; its prospects are further diminished by the demise of the East African Community. See R. C. Porter, 'Kenya's Future as an Exporter of Manufacturers', *East African Economic Review*, IV, 1 (1974), pp. 44–69.
37. The continent-wide statistics are from Economic Commission for Africa, *Survey of Economic Conditions in Africa, 1973* (New York: United Nations, 1975), table 9, p. 93. See also, Mabogunje, 'Manufacturing' (n. 34 above), pp. 4–9; and Ewing, *Industry in Africa* (n. 34 above), pp. 22–3. For case studies of the import-substitution process and of the distribution of industries, see Grayson, 'Manufacturing Development in Ghana' (n. 34 above), pp. 70–86; J. E. A. Manu, 'Import-Substitution in Ghana, 1956–68', *Ghana Social Science Journal*, II, 1 (1972), pp. 50–65; and Kenya, Ministry of Commerce and Industry, *A Guide to Industrial Investment in Kenya* (Nairobi: Government Printer, 1972).
38. See G. Arrighi, 'International Corporations, Labor Aristocracies, and Economic Development in Tropical Africa', in Robert Rhodes (ed.), *Imperialism and Underdevelopment* (New York: Monthly Review Press, 1970), pp. 225–6; Mabogunje, 'Manufacturing' (n. 24 above), pp. 4–8; and Ewing, *Industry in Africa* (n. 34 above), pp. 23–5.
39. The global statistics on manufacturing are from ECA, *Survey* (n. 37 above), p. 88. The statistics respecting the economically active population were calculated using the ILO's *Yearbook of Labour Statistics*, 1971–6.
40. *Posho*: Frances Stewart, *Technology and Underdevelopment* (London: Macmillan, 1977). Breakfast food: R. Kaplinsky, 'Inappropriate Products and Techniques: Breakfast Food in Kenya', *Review of African Political*

Economy, 14 (1979), pp. 90–6. Soap: S. Langdon, 'Multinational Corporations, Taste Transfer and Underdevelopment', *Review of African Political Economy*, 2 (1975), pp. 12–33, quote p. 29.

41.   These paragraphs have drawn generally on Richard Barnett and Ronald Muller, *Global Reach: The Power of the Multinational Corporations* (New York: Simon & Schuster, 1974), chaps. 6 and 7; K. Griffin, 'Multinational Corporations and Basic Needs Development', *Development and Change*, VIII, 1 (1977), pp. 61–76; and N. Girvan, 'Economic Nationalists v. Multinational Corporations: Revolutionary or Evolutionary Change?', in Carl Widstrand (ed.), *Multinational Firms in Africa* (Uppsala: Scandinavian Institute of African Studies, 1975), pp. 26–56. Excellent relevant case studies include A. Seidman, 'The Distorted Growth of Import-Substitution Industry: The Zambian Case', *Journal of Modern African Studies*, XII, 4 (1974), pp. 601–31; M. R. Bhagavan, *Zambia: Impact of Industrial Strategy on Regional Imbalance and Social Inequality*, Research Report No. 44, Scandinavian Institute of African Studies, Uppsala, 1978; Langdon, 'MNCs, Taste Transfer and Underdevelopment' (n. 40 above); and Rweyamamu, *Underdevelopment and Industrialization in Tanzania* (n. 19 above), pp. 166–72.

42.   On the relative capital intensity of foreign and local firms, see P. Streeten, 'Transnational Corporations and Basic Needs', in M. E. Jegen and C. Wilbur (eds.), *Growth with Equity* (Paulist Press, 1979), p. 166. The 'well-informed estimate' is that of D. Morawitz, *Employment Implications of Industrialization in Developing Countries*, World Bank Staff Working Paper, No. 170, January 1974, p. 1. A thorough analysis of the employment effects of manufacturing in Ghana is found in K. Ewusi, *Employment Performance of Ghanaian Manufacturing Industries*, ILO, World Employment Programme; Working Paper WEP 2–23/WP49, January 1977. For further analysis of the negligible impact of manufacturing upon employment, see Bhagavan, *Zambia* (n. 41 above); and A. O. Olaloye, 'Technology Transfer and Employment in Nigerian Manufacturing Industries', *Quarterly Journal of Administration* XII, 2 (1977), pp. 167–76.

43.   The World Bank study is by Dipak Mazumdar, *The Urban Informal Sector*, World Bank Staff Working Paper No. 211, July 1975, pp. 9–11, 12–13. The West African estimates are in David Rimmer, 'Wage Politics in West Africa', Occasional Paper, Faculty of Commerce and Social Science, University of Birmingham, 1970, p. 52.

44.   On Nairobi, see (for the projection) Andrew Hake, *African Metropolis: Nairobi's Self-Help City* (New York: St Martin's, 1977), p. 196; and (for information on the spontaneous settlements) James Waweru and Associates, *Progress Report No. 6: Economic Aspects*, 'Low-Cost Housing and Squatter Upgrading Study', Report to the Government of Kenya and World Bank, August 1976, table 7, p. 15.

45.   The 'informal sector' approach was stated most forcefully in ILO, *Employment, Incomes and Equality: A Strategy for Increasing Productive Employment in Kenya* (Geneva: ILO, 1972). On the marginality thesis, see the version proposed by A. Quijano Obregon, 'The Marginal Pole of the Economy and the Marginalized Labor Force', *Economy and Society*, III, 4 (1974), pp. 393–428. The most open-minded and inclusive summary and critique of this debate is Caroline Moser, *The Informal Sector or Petty*

Commodity Production: Autonomy or Dependence in Urban Development: A Critical Review of Recent Theoretical Models and Policy Proposals in Third World Employment Studies, Working Paper No. 3, Development Planning Unit, University of London, August 1977.

46. See ILO, *Employment* (n. 45 above), p. 6. The key source for the definition and description of the informal sector is K. Hart, 'Informal Income Opportunities and Urban Employment in Ghana', *Journal of Modern African Studies,* xi, 1 (1973), pp. 68–9. A good description of the major informal economic activities is found in P. Halpenny, 'Getting Rich by being "Unemployed": Some Political Implications of "Informal" Economic Activities in Urban Areas Not Represented in Official Indices', paper presented to the Universities of East African Social Sciences Conference, Nairobi, 1972; and N. Nelson, 'How Women and Men Get By: The Sexual Division of Labor in the Informal Sector of a Nairobi Squatter Settlement', in Ray Bromley and Chris Gerry (eds.), *Casual Work and Poverty in Third-World Cities* (New York: John Wiley, 1979).

47. Some petty producers do make the transition to petty-capitalist production. See, e.g., P. Kennedy, 'Indigenous Capitalism in Ghana', *Review of African Political Economy,* 8 (1977), pp. 30–4. In general, however, the foreign-controlled oligopolistic manufacturing firms in Ghana have 'stifled' the expansion of small entrepreneurs. See A. N. Hakam, 'Impediments to the Growth of Indigenous Industrial Entrepreneurship in Ghana, 1948–68', *Economic Bullitin of Ghana,* ii, 2 (1972), pp. 3–31.

48. On constraints, see S. V. Sethuraman, 'The Urban Informal Sector in Africa', *International Labour Review,* cxvi, 3 (1977), pp. 343–52; ILO, *Employment* (n. 45 above), pp. 227–8, 504–5 and *passim*; D. Remy and J. Weeks, 'Employment, Occupation, and Inequality in a Nonindustrial City (Zaria)', in Karl Wohlmuth (ed.), *Employment Creation in Developing Societies* (New York: Praeger, 1973), pp. 296–305; and M. A. Bienefeld, 'The Informal Sector and Peripheral Capitalism: The Case of Tanzania', *Institute of Development Studies Bulletin,* viii, 3 (1975). On state harassment of the informal sector, see I. Inukai, 'The Legal Framework for Small-Scale Enterprise with Special Reference to the Licensing System', in Frank Child and Mary Kempe (eds.), *Small-Scale Enterprise* (in Kenya), Occasional Paper No. 6, Institute for Development Studies, University of Nairobi, 1973, pp. 88–99; and M. P. van Dijk, *Developing the Informal Sector in Senegal*, ILO, Jobs and Skills in Africa, Dakar, December 1976, pp. 19–21, 31. On credit, see especially William Steel, *Small-Scale Employment and Production in Developing Countries: Evidence from Ghana* (New York: Praeger, 1977), pp. 124–30.

49. Report of this conference is in Sethuraman, 'Urban Informal Sector' (n. 48 above), p. 352.

50. In developing this thesis, I have selectively drawn from these sources: Foster-Carter, 'Modes of Production Controversy' (n. 6 above), pp. 47–77; Quijano, 'The Marginal Pole' (n. 45 above); M. Godfrey, 'Surplus Population and Underdevelopment: Reserve Army or Marginal Mass?', *Manpower and Unemployment Research,* x, 1 (1977), pp. 63–9; and Roberts, *Cities of Peasants* (n. 6 above), chap. 7.

51. See Richard Sandbrook and Jack Arn, *The Labouring Poor and Urban*

Class Formation, Occasional Monograph No. 12, Centre for Developing-Area Studies, McGill University, 1977, pp. 24–5.

52. Quote from O. LeBrun and C. Gerry, 'Petty Producers and Capitalism, *Review of African Political Economy*, 3 (1975), p. 25.

53. See S. W. Mintz, 'Men, Women and Trade', *Comparative Studies in Society and History*, XIII, 3 (1971), p. 249; and, for an example of the linkage role played by traders, A. Callaway, 'From Traditional Crafts to Modern Industries', in P. C. Lloyd *et al.* (eds.), *The City of Ibadan* (Cambridge: Cambridge University Press, 1967), p. 162.

54. See, in general, Alison Scott, 'Who are the Self-Employed?', in Ray Bromley and Chris Gerry (eds.), *Casual Work and Poverty in the Third World City* (New York: John Wiley, 1979), pp. 105–29; and in particular, A. Callaway, 'Nigeria's Indigenous Education: The Apprenticeship System', *Odu*, I, 1 (1964), p. 64. Refer also to the references relevant to petty production in chap. 5.

55. On 'articulation' in the case of Dakar, see Chris Gerry, *Petty Producers and the Urban Economy: A Case Study of Dakar*, ILO, Working Paper WEP 2/19/101/1, WP8, September 1974; and van Dijk, *Developing the Informal Sector* (n. 48 above), p. 16. For similar findings elsewhere, see G. A. Aryee, *Effects of Formal Education and Training on the Intensity of Employment in the Informal Sector: A Case Study of Kumasi, Ghana*, ILO, Working Paper WEP 2–18/WP14, September 1976, pp. 2–3; Kenneth King, *The African Artisan: Education and the Informal Sector in Kenya* (London: Heinemann Educational Books, 1977), chaps. 2, 4, 5; and Remy and Weeks, 'Employment, Occupation, and Inequality' (n. 48 above), pp. 300–2.

56. See A. Portes, 'The Informal Sector and the World Economy: Notes on the Structure of Subsidized Labour', *IDS Bulletin*, IX, 4 (1978), pp. 36–8; and Godfrey, 'Surplus Population' (n. 50 above), pp. 67–8. On the function of the rural pre-capitalist mode, see C. Meillassoux, 'From Reproduction to Production', *Economy and Society*, 1 (1972), pp. 93–105.

57. This function is elaborated by Portes, 'The Informal Sector' (n. 56 above), p. 38.

58. On the counter-revolutionary function: W. R. Armstrong and T. G. McGee, 'Revolutionary Change and the Third World City: A Theory of Urban Involution', *Civilisation*, XVIII, 3 (1968), p. 354.

3   The State and Capital Accumulation

How long will Africa be cursed with its leaders? There were men dying from the loss of hope, and others were finding gaudy ways to enjoy power they did not have. We were ready here for big and beautiful things, but what we had was our own black men hugging new paunches scrambling to ask the white man to welcome them onto our backs. These men who were to lead us out of despair, they came like men already grown fat and cynical with the eating of centuries of power they had never struggled for, old before they had even been born into power, and ready only for the grave.

Ayi Kwei Armah, *The Beautyful Ones Are Not Yet Born*, 1968

What is the role of the state in the perpetuation or, alternatively, the alleviation of mass poverty in Africa? An explanation of the roots of poverty requires first an examination of the deleterious consequences associated with a generic pattern of peripheral capitalist development. It then requires a consideration of the *particular strategies of accumulation* implicitly or explicitly pursued by states that reflect the interests of *particular class alliances*. Similarly, useful discussions of poverty-eradication need to specify the various development strategies and related class alliances which, to a greater or lesser extent, may be conducive to the alternative pattern of basic-needs development.

The state in peripheral capitalist societies

Implicit in the writing of many economists on development is the liberal assumption that the state is a neutral and even benevolent arbiter, whose role is to promote the national interest in economic growth, efficiency and social welfare. In prescribing appropriate development policies, economists rarely take into account that these will often differentially affect the conflicting interests of social classes or regional–ethnic groups who dispose of differential political power.[1]

An opposing view conceives of the state as a set of public institutions that reflects in its activities the interests of the dominant social forces rooted in the structure of production. In the Marxist conception the state encompasses more than government: it comprises the executive, bureaucratic, legislative, judicial, coercive, and publicly controlled educational, media, trade-union and party apparatuses designed to protect national security, foster the conditions for capital accumulation, and maintain social control. This class-based model appears more realistic than the 'impartial arbiter' one. For instance, with respect to proposals for upgrading the informal sector, it requires the analyst to dispense with the naive notion that well-informed governments will remove discriminatory policies against informal enterprises in order to advance the public interest in growth, employment-generation, national self-reliance and equity. The state may, in fact, institute and maintain such policies, not out of ignorance of their consequences, but out of a concern to protect the interests of certain dominant classes.

If however this general model of the state is sensible, conceptual problems arise as soon as we seek to make it more precise. Ideally, a framework should be elaborate enough to identify plausible causal interrelationships between state and society, yet open enough not to beg important questions. Unfortunately, however, the current tendency towards highly abstract and deductive reasoning in Marxist studies of the state leaves few questions open to empirical confirmation or disconfirmation.[2]

Consider, for example, the approach of those who write within the Leninist tradition. The mechanistic and economistic notion of the state as a tool of the economically dominant ruling class – a notion reflected in dependency studies in the popular 'neo-colonialism-or-socialism' dichotomy – forecloses the issue of the efficacy of reform. In this model structural reform represents, not victories won by ordinary citizens, but clever manipulations by a far-sighted ruling class to forestall discontent. To be sure, reform *may* constitute manipulation: the liberal-pluralist conception of a neutral government passively responding to the pressures of a multiplicity of interest groups has even less applicability to the Third World than the First. Nevertheless, the conceptualization of the state should not be so rigid as to beg the question of whether, short of a socialist revolution, poor and oppressed people can hope to better their position through political action.[3]

The more flexible view of the capitalist state as possessing a 'relative autonomy' from all socio-economic groupings need to not prejudge this question. However, this concept also raises difficult issues, including the specification of the *limits* of state autonomy in policy formation and the mechanisms which preserve these limits.

Nicos Poulantzas, a prominent Marxist theoretician, provides one popular approach to these issues. In a society dominated by the capitalist mode of production, he argues that the state can, and indeed must, maintain a considerable freedom from the dominant class(es). Such a 'relative autonomy' is necessary if the state is to protect the long-term interests of the power bloc. On the one hand, the dominat classes typically lack cohesion and are therefore unable, on their own, to establish their hegemony in society. The bourgeoisie in particular is susceptible to intra-class conflict, as commercial, financial, industrial and even regionally based fractions struggle to advance their sectional interests. The state in this situation must perforce exercise some autonomy in deciding how to aggregate the interests of the dominant class fractions; policies will therefore necessarily benefit some fractions at the expense of others.

On the other hand, the establishment of capitalist hegemony would be impossible if the dominated classes organized in their own interests to change the system. Hence, the state must seek to reconcile the underclasses to the system and thereby preclude their autonomous organization. This role requires the state to present itself 'as the representative of the political unity of the people-nation'; it obviously cannot do so unless it disposes of some measure of autonomy from the immediate interests of capital. Above all, the state must be able to respond to the pressures emanating from one or more of the dominated classes. But the accommodations it arranges may be contrary to the short-term *or even long-term* economic interests of one or more fractions of the dominant class(es). 'Such compromises and sacrifices are sometimes necessary for the realization of their political class interests' – namely, the maintenance of a system of property relations that benefits the power bloc in general.[4]

Is this rather conspiratorial conception of the relationship between state and society plausible where the capitalist mode of production predominates? More specifically, is it valid to say that the state 'must' (regardless of appearances) act on behalf of the long-run interests of the dominant class(es)? Two observations are apropos. In the first place, Poulantzas' formulation ascribes a remarkable latitude to state personnel in interpreting the 'essential' interests of the bourgeoisie. One can anticipate a situation where associations of the dominant class(es) revile the government for its reformist policies, yet the analyst must still conclude that the state continues to serve their long-term interests. In a society where the bourgeoisie lacks solidarity, the only essential common interest of the various fractions might lie in the preservation of private property and a good 'investment climate' in some major sectors of the economy. But this surely allows considerable scope for reform in response to popular pressures!

In the second place, and despite this latitude for reform, the deductive approach of Poulantzas seems to set arbitrary limits to the role of the state. From his viewpoint, the state 'must' serve the long-run interests of fractions of capital (and perhaps of allied classes based on non-capitalist modes) because of its insertion into a social formation where the capitalist mode of production is dominant. In the present study, in contrast, the relationship between the state and the dominant economic class(es) is taken as *contingent*, not axiomatic. That is, the normal, though not inevitable, tendency of the State in capitalist society is to act on behalf of the capitalist and allied classes. This tendency derives from the operation of certain structural mechanisms. Political leaders, if they are so inclined, are unlikely to succeed for long in segregating political power from economic power by using the state to promote the class interests of the workers and peasants. Should the state undermine 'business confidence', then in all likelihood members of the dominant classes will take certain defensive actions. They will use their economic power to co-opt those who man the state apparatus by means of bribes, offers of lucrative career opportunities or other inducements. Businessmen, whether foreign or local, will refuse to invest and will seek to withdraw their capital from the country; the subsequent economic dislocation (featuring, typically, price inflation, balance of payments crisis, consumer shortages, increasing unemployment) may well destabilize an unrepentant regime. In the last resort, agents of the dominant classes or foreign interests may directly intervene to 'reorient' the state – either constitutionally or unconstitutionally. Nonetheless, a democratic transition to socialism, in those few countries where competitive politics still obtains, is not precluded by definition.[5]

If the state in advanced capitalist countries possesses some autonomy from society, this independence is typically even more pronounced in the circumstances of post-colonial Africa. Dominant classes are not only recent creations here, but they have also depended upon the state for their emergence. Characteristically, there has been an inversion of the usual relationship between economic and political power; those who control, or have influence upon, the state apparatus have often sought to translate their political power into economic power, thereby joining the indigenous bourgeoisie. By the middle 1970s, this process of dominant-class formation was fairly far advanced in some countries: I examine the cases of the Ivory Coast and Kenya below. In other countries, however, a severe fractionalization of the bourgeoisie has reduced its influence upon policy-formation. Nigeria has been an extreme instance of policy incoherence, where vying fractions have pressed conflicting neo-colonial, state-capitalist and private entrepreneurial strategies upon the government.[6]

Of course, nowhere has the executive power complete autonomy to mould the strategy of capital accumulation and thereby the class structure. If the economically dominant classes are weak and divided, the underclasses are weaker still, for reasons this book will explore. Differential class-consciousness and class power tend to limit the state's independence. In addition, the government has obviously to be wary in its treatment of foreign interests. In countries such as the Ivory Coast, Kenya and Zaire, the exigencies of international power politics and the logic determining the flow of foreign investment have combined to reinforce the influence of foreign capital within the political economy. Hostile moves against foreign interests could lead, at the least, to economic dislocation and political instability and, at the most, to covert intervention by imperialist powers to reorient the state in a more acceptable direction.

These general considerations inform this chapter's examination of the state's role in capital accumulation.[7] In particular, I probe the interrelationship between class formation and the state's support of development strategies that perpetuate a marginalizing pattern of accumulation or, alternatively, that foster the structural transformations entailed in a basic-needs approach to poverty eradication. The analysis of class structure continues in the following two chapters. Then chapter 6 considers how, and with what success, the state in peripheral capitalist societies acts to preserve the social order and stability necessary for production in the volatile milieu of urban Africa. However, insofar as the policies to promote accumulation and the state's efforts to generate legitimacy are sometimes in conflict, the dialectical relationship between these two functions must receive some attention in the cases discussed below.

Development strategies and class formation

A development strategy indicates the general orientation of a regime with respect to the accumulation function. First, a development strategy indicates *who* (that is, which class, class fraction or stratum) will take the main responsibility for expanding the economy, and hence benefit from the accumulation of capital. It also suggests, either explicitly or implicity which classes and/or strata will have to bear the major part of the burden of socio-economic change. Secondly, a development strategy prescribes *how* the economy should be run to achieve growth and other operative goals (which may, for instance, include social equity, the raising of mass material welfare and national autonomy). On this score the agencies of the state must seek to assign a balance between private and public property, market versus planning mechanisms, centralized versus decentralized economic decision making, coercion versus popular participation in the promotion of developmental goals, industrialization and agricultural development, and dependency or autonomy in the world economy. If the resolution of all these issues constitutes a society's development strategy at a particular time, where does one look for authoritative pronouncements? The official development strategy, as contained, for instance, in a development plan, states at most a government's intentions; actual practice will often diverge from these. A state divulges its real orientation in the way it implements policies in areas such as incomes and prices, taxes, employment, fiscal expenditures (especially in public investments), money and credit, tariffs and import licensing, foreign investment and property rights.[8]

In this chapter I identify five ideal types of development strategy: neo-colonialism, national developmentalism (with two variants), national populism, bureaucratic collectivism and transition to socialism.[9] Whereas the first two promote a pattern of growth that reproduces mass poverty, the last three may militate for a transcendance of the peripheral capitalist pattern.

In a sense, a development strategy is at the same time a *class* strategy. This is not to say that the former is necessarily a simple reflection of a dominant class's interests. For the reasons mentioned, the state can dispose of considerable autonomy in determining development strategy at certain junctures. However, while the state's policies influence who will generate economic growth and accumulate capital, the process of accumulation in turn obviously shapes class formation and the emergence of classes or class fractions with the economic power to ensure that the state henceforth represents primarily their interests. The independence of the state from indigenous class forces will thus normally diminish after political independence.

The development of classes during the colonial period will obviously have an important bearing on the configuration of political power in the post-colonial era. The imperial power needed local collaborators if its rule in Africa was to be both effective and inexpensive; hence, colonial governments tended to reinforce the power of certain social forces at the expense of others. Depending upon the circumstances, these collaborators would be either European settlers or some influential indigenous class or classes. In either case, state power buttressed any other claim to pre-eminence that the collaborators possessed, and placed them in an advantageous position to accumulate capital.

In West Africa, where peasants and planters cultivated cash crops and metropolitan firms acted as buyers and controlled the import trade, the colonial state depended upon the support of the traditional classes, which it in turn favoured. Consider, for instance the case of what became Senegal:

> The [French] army destroyed the warrior-dominated states and the colonial state enforced the replacement of African traders with European and later Syrian and Lebanese traders in the interior trade. The colonial state prevented peanut hold-ups by producers but allowed cartels by buyers and it organized investment in railroads, roads and ports (including forced labour in the construction and maintenance) to serve the peripheral integration of the economy. The memory of conquest and the repressive power of the state remained as guarantors of the new order but the bureaucratic apparatus established by the French in Saint Louis and Dakar and local representatives in the administrative circles and subdivisions were not adequately informed or supplied to manage the political tensions in their districts. They had to rely on the marabouts, traders, and administrative chiefs who stood at the junction point between villages and the state and market systems.[10]

It is obvious that the colonial state in French West Africa served primarily the interests of French capital. It secured these interests not only by the use or threat of coercion, even in combination with the ideological appeal of 'assimilation', but also by the provision of influential positions and resources to local notables. It is thus not by chance that these notables remain politically influential today.

Alternatively, a colonial regime based itself primarily upon a settler minority and subordinated the interests of indigenous groups to it. This was the pattern, for instance, in Kenya. Here, the colonial state sponsored 'primitive colonial accumulation', a process of squeezing an economic surplus out of subject farm labourers in favour of the property-owning colonists. But even this partisan use of political power did not prevent, as we shall see, the emergence of an indigenous class of capitalists. The settlers did not survive the transition to independence as a dominant class; instead, the British government countenanced their displacement in order to guarantee peaceful decolonization and large-scale British investments.[11]

Divergent colonial experiences favoured the emergence of diverging post-colonial development/class strategies. But whether neo-colonial or national developmental strategies were pursued, there was a marked trend towards authoritarianism of the single-party or military variety.[12] This trend suggests an obvious hypothesis: that the concentration of the benefits of capital accumulation in a small minority was inconsistent with a participatory policy. The authoritarian tendency will receive attention in the case studies to follow.

The neo-colonial model

The least nationalist but most generative of economic growth is the neo-colonial strategy. This is the pattern in which an auxiliary bourgeoisie accepts a subordinate position in relation to foreign capital in order to extract a share of the surplus for itself. The major facets of this policy include:

> coercion, and a demobilized population, open access to raw materials, tax and other 'incentives' to foreign investors. . . . The forms of joint exploitation vary greatly, expressing the differences in bargaining power between the national and imperial bourgeoisie. Under conditions of total foreign control of the economy the national bougeoisie obtains tax revenues. Under conditions of partnership in which majority ownership and management are in foreign hands, the national bourgeoisie obtains a minority share of earnings plus tax revenues. Whatever the specifics, the foreign component is clearly dominant in internal as well as external relations.[13]

Internationally, Taiwan and South Korea were perhaps the most 'successful' early exemplars of this approach, though they have long since evolved in a more nationalist direction. In Africa, with the exception of Zaïre, it has been the smaller or less economically viable countries that have most clearly followed a neo-colonial strategy: the Ivory Coast, Senegal, Upper Volta, Chad, Niger, the Central African Republic and Malawi.

THE IVORIAN CASE

The 'economic miracle' in the Ivory Coast over the past two decades owes much to a neo-colonial strategy. Indicators of economic success include an annual growth rate of over 7 per cent in 1950–75, the highest per capita income in tropical Africa in 1976, an industrial growth rate of about 15 per cent in 1960–75, and positive balance of trade figures owing to the diversification and expanding output of agriculture. The Ivory Coast is now the world's leading producer of cocoa, one of the top three exporters of coffee, and a major exporter of timber, palm oil, bananas and pineapples. Moreover, the government is seeking to shift its industrial strategy from a concentration upon import-substitution to the export-oriented processing of local raw materials.[14]

But, despite the laudatory tone of a recent World Bank report on the Ivory Coast, economic success has come at a price – and not just in palpable external dependency. Data in this report indicate that though immiseration on the Asian pattern has not appeared, marginalization is a concomitant of capital-intensive agricultural and industrial development. In agriculture, the government has conceived of modernization in terms of mechanization where feasible. It has recently been encouraged in this view by actual shortages of labour in some regions at prevailing rates of remuneration. Indeed, the wages paid to agricultural labourers are not only generally wretched, but declined in real terms in certain areas between 1965 and 1975. In consequence, Ivorians tend to shun agricultural employment. The majority of rural labourers are immigrants from parts of surrounding countries which are densely settled, extremely poor, and prone to draught.[15] Intensified exploitation of migrant labour has therefore constituted the basis of capital accumulation on the part of the planter bourgeoisie.

Agricultural concentration, poor rural employment conditions, and the urban bias in the location of amenities and 'modern' employment have led to a rural exodus. The urban population has increased from 13 per cent of the total population in 1955 to 38 per cent in 1980; Abidjan alone had expanded to about 1 million people by 1975, accounting for about half of the urban populace. It is therefore not surprising that urban unemployment was about 15 per cent in 1975, and has probably increased since. In addition, the urban non-capitalist forms of production have burgeoned as more and more migrants, unable to obtain scarce jobs in capital-intensive industrial enterprises or the state, press into the informal sector. In typical fashion this sector 'in several instances has been obstructed by the public sector rather than encouraged'.[16]

The neo-colonial strategy of capitalist development rests upon the emergence of a power bloc whose interests it serves. In particular, the agricultural and bureaucratic fractions of the local bourgeoisie, in league with foreign – largely French – capital, are able to maintain high standards of consumption along with high rates of growth. Other elements pay the price associated with this strategy. Neo-colonialism therefore depends upon a political context in which, owing to an authoritarian government and various subjective and objective hindrances to popular and worker organization, the bulk of the population has no effective means of protest or influence upon policy formation.

Consider first the nature of the neo-colonial strategy. The World Bank has commented approvingly on the Ivorian government's recognition of the necessity for continuity in development policy after independence:

> The government was fully aware that further economic success was dependent on more foreign capital and labor. Political and economic stability and growth, together with a liberal policy towards foreign investors, were considered essential in creating the confidence abroad needed to acquire these production factors. . . . Given the outward-oriented policy chosen by the Ivory Coast, it was important to preserve and to cultivate close economic and political relations with France and with francophone neighbours. The country needed the former for capital, expertise, skilled labor, and markets, and the latter for both unskilled labor and markets.

The Ivorian state has thus willingly continued an 'open door' policy since 1960. Its efforts have included: an abnegation of nationalization; an elaborate system of tariffs and import quotas to protect import-substituting manufacturers; a package of incentives for industrial investment that includes low tax rates, liberal terms of profit and capital transfers, and tariff exemptions for imported machinery and necessary inputs into the manufacturing process; firm controls over labour (including a ban on strikes and relatively low minimum wages); and a high priority to the maintenance of political stability and social control.[17]

In consequence, French interests still dominate the non-agricultural capitalist mode of production, though the government has recently sought to diversify the sources of foreign investment. The large colonial trading houses – Compagnie Française de l'Afrique Occidentale, Société Commerciale de l'Ouest Africaine, Compagnie OPTORG, and Compagnie du Niger Française – continue to organize much of the Ivorian trade with France and the European Economic Community. They have also diversified into local manufacturing. In 1975, foreigners owned 68 per cent of the equity in formal-sector manufacturing industries. Although Ivorian sources provided just over half of the investment in manufacturing in the first part of 1977, all but a small portion of this derived from state corporations, usually in partnership with transnational corporations.[18]

Emblematic of the foreign influence is the size and wealth of the white expatriate population. In 1970, there were 50 000 Europeans in the Ivory Coast, a four-fold increase from the number resident there at independence a decade earlier. While non-Africans formed less than 1 per cent of the labour force in 1970, they accounted for 68 per cent of managerial staff and 61 per cent of supervisors and technicians in the modern economy. European salaries ranged from ten to twenty times the national average, depending upon the economic sector. It is perhaps not surprising, in view of these statistics, that the government adopted a policy of 'Ivorianization' in 1974. Since then, black faces have begun to replace white ones in the large corporations.[19]

The importance of cheap, foreign African labour to peripheral capitalist development requires comment. Almost a quarter of the Ivorian population of 5·065 million in 1970 was composed of African aliens. Most of these immigrants arrived from Upper Volta, Mali and Niger, countries much poorer than the Ivory Coast in per capita income and, particularly in the case of Upper Volta, suffering from population pressure upon the land. Foreign Africans accounted for over 57 per cent of all employees in the formal sector in 1970. The vast majority of these immigrant workers held unskilled or semi-skilled jobs: they accounted for 78 per cent of unskilled primary-sector employees, 49 per cent of unskilled secondary-sector workers, and 52 per cent of unskilled tertiary-sector employees. With respect to income, there is a significant differential in the average earnings of African aliens and Ivorian nationals which reflects their differing skill levels and job opportunities. Hence, in the primary, secondary and tertiary sectors, foreign Africans earned an average yearly wage of 89 000, 195 000 and 382 000 CFA francs respectively, whereas Ivorian nationals earned an average of 172 000, 237,000 and 664 000 CFA francs respectively. Not surprisingly, then, a study of the causes of low industrial productivity in Abidjan concluded that a sense of despair and hopelessness among penurious foreign African employees was the major factor.[20]

Reliance upon the exploitation of foreign labour has certain obvious advantages from the viewpoint of the state and the dominant classes. Not only are impoverished immigrants likely to regard themselves as fortunate to find a job – even at wretched wages – but also, as non-citizens, they possess neither political rights nor a basis for solidarity with nationals. Any disruptive political or industrial activity on their part can lead to immediate deportation.

A dominant class fraction which has facilitated and benefited from this neo-colonial strategy is the rural bourgeoise. It was initially driven into political life *against* the colonial state in the early 1940s owing to the latter's sponsorship of discriminatory policies benefiting French planters. French cocoa and coffee growers received special advantages in the form of cheap forced labour, higher produce prices, lower transport charges and higher subsidies (as in 1944) to encourage the cultivation of more land. The organizational expression of the Ivorian planters during the war was the Syndicat Agricole Africain (SAA), led by Dr Felix Houphouet-Biogny. In 1946 the abolition of forced labour and other privileges for French planters enhanced the nationalist stature of both the SAA and Houphouet-Boigny, then a Deputy in Paris.[21]

But the resolution of this contentious issue did not immediately lead to a reconciliation between the plantocracy and the colonial state. New grounds for animosity arose in the form of an alliance between the Rassemblement Démocratique Africain (RDA), a nationalist movement representing all of the French West African territories, and the French Communist Party (PCF). Houphouet-Boigny, who led the newly formed territorial arm of the RDA in 1946, the Parti Démocratique de Côte d'Ivoire (PDCI), had helped engineer this association. The rationale from Houphouet-Boigny's perspective appears to have been tactical: the PCF possessed the financial and organizational resources to transform the RDA into an effective political movement. When, however, the French Communists left the governing coalition in France in 1947, a new colonial administration in West Africa opened a campaign to suppress all Communist-influenced organizations. The RDA and its territorial members were special targets in this campaign. The administration's efforts to sponsor pliant parties and undermine the PDCI continued until both this party and the RDA dissociated from the Communists in 1950. Thereafter, the PDCI restored its former political strength. Its accession to power following an election in 1952 inaugurated a close relationship with the colonial administration. Indeed, the latter turned its considerable political talents to the destruction of parties competing with the PDCI during the period of the dyarchy. This experience demonstrates that the French 'were concerned only with having a group in power with whom they could work'.[22]

The implicit terms of the accommodation seem straightforward. The French sought an indigenous ruling group upon whom they could rely to safeguard the existing conditions of capital accumulation. The chiefs could not play this role because they lacked both the education and the mass following; their association with such unpopular colonial policies as forced labour vitiated their popular appeal. The Ivorian elite manning the colonial bureaucracy evinced the requisite pliancy – indeed, they had formed the nucleus of the ethnically based *administratif* parties in 1948–51 – but they also lacked popular support. But the planter bourgeoisie suffered from no disability once the PDCI had broken with the Communists. Not only did this emergent class fraction command widespread support, but its involvement with the capitalist system of banking, trading and finance augured well for a 'responsible' economic approach. The plantocracy, for its part, was willing to enter into an accommodation, provided its rural economic base remained inviolable. No real conflict of interests separated the Ivorian planters and the

French in the 1950s; by then, the French planters accounted for only a minuscule portion of the output in cash crops. Therefore, this ascendant class fraction was not averse to protecting French interests in commerce and manufacturing in exchange for certain economic concessions and military support.[23]

The other indigenous element in the power bloc is the bureaucratic bourgeoisie. A state-capitalist thrust is a peculiar feature of the Ivorian neo-colonial strategy. In industry, for example, the share of public investment increased from about 10 per cent of total equity in 1967–8 to 24 per cent by January 1975. Only 8 per cent of total equity was held by Ivorian citizens at the latter date. In agriculture, the government has created state or joint state/private enterprises to develop each of the new cash crops. These enterprises usually control a bloc of plantations, surrounded by plots owned by local peasants and farmers. The latter are subject to considerable state direction in the form of technical assistance, the supply of subsidized fertilizers and pesticides, and the marketing of the produce. State corporations or public shareholding also exist in trade, transport, energy and telecommunications. Concomitant with these changes has been a rapid accumulation of economic power in the hands of state bureaucrats. In familiar fashion, bureaucratic privilege has allowed top officials to build a base in the private economy, principally in real estate and commerce. Moreover, the alliance between the rural and bureaucratic bourgeoisies is likely to remain stable, in part because of close personal connections between the two. The disproportionate access of the children of the plantocracy to the limited colonial educational facilities has meant that a not inconsiderable share of top bureaucrats possess familial links with planters. Consequently, 'through planting, most of the educated elite keep deep roots in the countryside'.[24]

The final support of outward-oriented, dependent development is French capital, backed by the French state. Through military, monetary, economic and cultural mechanisms, France is able to dispose of considerable influence in the Ivory Coast. In the first place, there is a contingent of the French army based in Port Bouët and backed by French aircraft. This is available for use against insurgencies in the Ivory Coast, as in other compliant former French colonies. In fact, Houphouet-Biogny had occasion to make use of the French military presence during a political crisis in 1963. (The President has remained an advocate of a Western military presence in Africa; as a staunch anti-Communist he, along with the leaders of Senegal, Zaïre and Togo, requested such a presence in 1978 to counter that of the Soviet Union and Cuba.) In the second place, the Ivory Coast, in concert with most other French colonies, joined the franc zone at independence. Although Ivorian membership has provided the country with international support for its currency and free convertibility of this into French francs at a fixed exchange rate, the price has been a French capacity to impose conservative fiscal policies upon the members. Finally, France has channelled the bulk of its foreign aid to assist those former colonies who retain close economic and political relations with France. The most obvious cultural impact is perhaps in the area of educational assistance; the French have supplied the Ivory Coast with entire educational systems, including curricula and examinations, to help generate more educated manpower.[25]

The neo-colonial strategy also rests on the demobilization of the masses. Houphouet-Boigny and the leadership of the PDCI have sought to achieve this within the framework of a single-party state. While there is no toleration of competing power centres, departicipation has occurred without more than occasional recourse to brute force. The foreign African population, as already mentioned, presents few problems of social control. With respect to the indigenous population, the President has on several occasions adeptly defused political tensions by holding 'Dialogues' with aggrieved interest groups. Since 1969, he has met with representatives of ethnic and generational groups, civil servants, teachers, students, agricultural workers, religious groups, merchants, postal employees, transport workers, landlords, tenants, bankers, engineers and technicians. 'Participants at these open meetings are encouraged to express criticisms and formulate demands, and the President personally listens, and in each case replies directly and on the spot. As a device to ease political conflict, it appears to be working well, at least for the time being.' Co-optation into plush jobs is also an effective tactic, particularly in silencing dissident university students. 'Former critics seem to turn into enthusiastic and loyal supporters of the regime as a result of this policy.' Moreover, elections to the National Assembly and Presidency continue to be held regularly every five years – though, in the absence of any choice of candidates, these represent plebiscites at best! The party itself also constitutes a useful instrument of demobilization. The organization of the party's urban branches along ethnic lines has meant that 'what political ethnic dissension . . . exists is contained within the party; one might even say it is a system which fosters a certain amount of ethnic dissension to provide the political consensus'.[26]

Nevertheless, the Ivorian state is currently struggling with a contradiction inherent in a neo-colonial strategy. On the one hand, the key to the 'economic miracle' lies in the openness of the economy to foreign capital, expertise and labour. On the other hand, this dependency engenders considerable hostility among nationals. Foreigners are the focus of employment-related grievances and the source of injured national pride. These tensions can lead into a legitimacy crisis for a regime closely associated with foreign influence. Indeed, the Ivory Coast has experienced several xenophobic outbursts. Houphouet-Boigny has tried to deal with this issue by pointing to the Ivorianization legislation as the means to replace foreigners with nationals. But it is probable that this is really the first step towards a more nationalistic strategy; Houphouet-Boigny or a successor may well find himself pushed towards 'national developmentalism'.

The national-developmental model

Neo-colonialism is neither the invariable outcome of peaceful decolonization nor the only accumulation strategy to foster peripheral capitalist development. The 'inevitability thesis' follows from a mechanistic version of underdevelopment theory that conceives of economic processes as determinative. Insofar as foreign capital dominates the capitalist mode of production in post-colonial societies, this economistic view concludes that the state must therefore represent the joint interests of the foreign and auxiliary bourgeoisies. But this is a simplistic and unrealistic assumption. There is no reason to assume that the indigenous business class will always be willing to collude in a subordinate capacity with foreign investors, or that the state will not work to lessen the foreign economic influence. In practice, the pattern in many underdeveloped countries is the invasion of more and more economic sectors (initially the preserve of foreign capital) by local businessmen or state corporations. This pattern is facilitated by increasing indigenous business knowledge and experience and the declining power of advanced-capitalist countries to control events abroad. The potency of economic nationalism and rivalries among the industrialized powers had, by the late 1960s, provided national governments with some latitude in dealing with foreign investors.[27] Yet economic nationalism *per se* is most unlikely to lead to a transformation of peripheral capitalism in a basic-needs direction.

'National-developmental' strategies reflect essentially the desire of domestic bourgeoisies to reduce or eliminate their junior status in relation to foreign capital. The aim of the state is to use its leverage in order to redefine the terms of dependency and secure a larger share of the economic surplus for a bureaucratic and/or private national bourgeoisie. The state squeezes or limits foreign capital by means of taxation policies, selective partial or total nationalizations, the substitution of management contracts for foreign ownership, and 'indigenization', that is, the exclusion of aliens from certain defined economic activities, usually small and medium-scale ones.

Nationalizations are the most dramatic means of local control. Africa, in fact, experienced a greater number of these than any other region in the period 1960–74 – 340 of 875 cases identified by the United Nations. Indeed, Africa led in nationalizations in all economic sectors except petroleum. As one would have expected, the extractive and service sectors have accounted for the bulk of public expropriations. The governments in Tanzania, Zambia, Uganda, Ethiopia, Somalia, Benin,

Guinea and Mali have carried out the most extensive nationalizations, whereas those in Nigeria and Ghana have undertaken selective, though still substantial, takeovers. There have also been wideranging indigenization programmes since the late 1960s in Ghana, Nigeria, Zaïre, Kenya, Uganda and Zambia, and a more minor one in Malawi.[28]

If the general effect of national-developmental policies is to augment the power and independence of the national bourgeoisie, the composition of this bourgeoisie will depend upon the priority assigned to the public or private sector. On the one hand, an emphasis upon nationalization and joint state/foreign ownership of productive assets reflects and enhances the power of a bureaucratic bourgeoisie. On the other hand, indigenization laws and state aid to indigenous businessmen will obviously promote the interests of a private bourgeoisie (and of bureaucrats and politicians only indirectly, to the extent that political power can be converted into economic power within the private sector).

In practice, state capitalism is the more common outcome. The heritage of the post-war colonial practice of employing state corporations and marketing boards to develop the economies, the usual weakness of indigenous capital *vis-à-vis* foreign capital, and a widespread distaste for neo-colonialism all combine to favour this policy. It is moreover, in the interests of those in the state apparatus to promote state capitalism:

> State capitalist oriented social strata lack an independent socio-economic base of any importance. Whatever 'property' they own is incidental to their political and social power.... Given the monopoly control over land, commerce, industry and banking, the probability of advancing through pure private economic activity is quite low. The only available vehicle through which capital accumulation can take place is the state, but only insofar as the principal sources of profits can be taken over or out of the hands of their current benefactors. The expropriation of imperial firms is both an economic necessity to state capital-induced accumulation and a source of political legitimacy: by integrating the resources and capital formerly controlled by foreign firms into a 'national' development effort through the process of nationalization, one of the essential elements of the bourgeois-nationalist revolution is confronted, the formation of the national economy.[29]

But what emerges is still essentially capitalist. To the extent that the hierarchial authority relations at the work place do not change with state ownership, that considerable private property remains, that production continues to respond to the existing skewed pattern of demand, and that profit calculations still determine investment decisions, it is legitimate to speak of state capitalism rather than socialism.

The balance between public and private ownership varies widely. In some cases, the weakness of an indigenous bourgeoisie and the attraction of a socialist rhetoric combine to foster state capitalism to the virtual exclusion of a national private capitalism. This was the pattern in Mali until 1967. Here, the Africans who had been recruited into the colonial bureaucracy used their control over the means of coercion to capture a leadership role in the post-colonial era. This bureaucratic stratum managed to reduce the power and authority of both the traditional rural aristocracy and the town-based but poorly educated indigenous merchant class, and to assume a class-like position via the expansion of state capitalism under the guise of socialism.

> Having been the instrument of the colonial power and having then turned against it to become the mouthpiece of the exploited Malian peasantry, the bureaucracy was gaining (with its access to power) some of the characteristics of a social class: control of the economic infra-structure and use of it as a means of exploitation, control of the means of repression involving a resort to various devices to maintain dominance.[30]

But the more usual pattern is that in which the state-capitalist thrust, though paramount, does not preclude a role for domestic as well as foreign investors. State-capitalist regimes rarely believe that they can afford to dispense with the technical expertise, managerial skills and market access of the transnational corporations. The latter, for their part, can resign themselves to surrendering equity in their local assets, provided the joint ventures and/or management and licensing agreements that they have negotiated leave them with substantial control and a reasonable rate of return. Besides, the continuance of a national private sector can be attractive to state-capitalist strata; accumulation through office-holding can then allow an official to branch out into private ventures. All this points to the possibility of a stable *modus vivendi* characterizing this national-developmental strategy. A central element in creating harmony among capitalists of diverse national origins and the bureaucratic bourgeoisie is the diffusion of capitalist values and outlook. As Richard Sklar has noted in relation to Zambia:

> leading members of the . . . bourgeoisie [that is, in both public and private sectors] are constantly tempted to imbibe the capitalist and managerial attitudes of their foreign business associates. Some . . . may look ahead to careers in the wider business world. Given the obviously bourgeois life styles of individuals in this elite social system, they may be expected to embrace an elitist ideology. . . . The influence of international capitalism functions to reinforce immanent tendencies toward embourgeoisement of the state bureaucratic elite.[31]

This is therefore not a propitious environment for sincere commitment to basic-needs development.

In other cases, the state has assigned priority to the fostering of private entrepreneurship, a decision doubtless reflecting the preponderant influence of the indigenous bourgeoisie. Kenya and Ghana are two such cases, though these countries arrived at a similar accumulation strategy in the early 1970s from divergent origins: by way of state capitalism in the late Nkrumah period (1961–6) in Ghana, and of neo-colonialism in Kenyatta's Kenya. Indeed, there is still much debate over the proper characterization of the state's role in the latter country. An investigation of this case should therefore yield insight into the complex relationship between the state and class forces in the process of peripheral capitalist development.

THE KENYAN CASE

Kenya is another African success story. Its Gross Domestic Product grew at an annual rate of over 7 per cent in constant prices throughout the 1960s; the combination of escalating prices for imported oil and a severe drought in 1974–5 set back the economy, though the annual growth rate in 1970–6 still reached a healthy 4·8 per cent. In addition, the rate of industrial growth in the 1970s has been about 10 per cent per annum, investment flowing largely into import-substitution and the processing of local primary products with the use of advanced-country technology.[32]

Yet this remains a peripheral capitalist pattern of growth. While the absolute living standards of no class may have fallen since independence in 1963, even sympathetic commentators on Kenyan development accept the likelihood of increasing income inequality. The most extensive study of the Kenyan economy, that conducted by an ILO team in 1971, provided evidence of 'rapid "involutionary" growth' in which 'the number of people in the [informal] sector increased faster than incomes, adding to the number of the working poor, if not to unemployment'. This report further argued that this pattern, termed marginalization in the present book, was a long-term phenomenon:

> the growth of the economy along existing lines is unlikely to broaden the base of income-earning opportunities for the majority of the people. Thus a class of poor and disadvantaged persons, already prominent in the Kenyan social scene, may over time be enlarged and suffer further relative impoverishment, in the absence of a strong and coherent strategy for rapid economic growth accompanied by a more egalitarian distribution of the benefits of growth.[33]

If there is a measure of agreement on the pattern of growth, there is less on the relation of the state to class forces in its promotion. One interpretation takes a 'neo-colonial' cast; Colin Leys and Steven Langdon have presented versions of this. More recently, Leys has revised his views and, along with Nicola Swainson and others, contends that the state in the 1970s responded to the interests of a national bourgeoisie in the form of (what James Petras has called) a national-developmental strategy. Each of these interpretations requires elaboration before an assessment is warranted.

In the neo-colonial perspective foreign capital remains the dominant class after 1963. The principal thrust of development policy is thus to rely upon foreign resources and expertise to modernize the economy. This sets severe constraints upon the advancement of local businessmen. For the 'early' Leys, what develops is only an 'auxiliary' bourgeoisie, albeit a prosperous one. The fundamental role of the state (besides maintaining legitimacy) is to mediate between the foreign and local fractions of capital, seeking to manage the manifest contradictions between them in a way that will retain the confidence of foreign investors. Langdon, however, assigns more political influence to the indigenous entrepreneurial group than Leys: the state sometimes decides conflicts between foreign and local capital *against* the interests of the former. Nonetheless, for Langdon, the local bourgeoisie is definitely dependent:

> it is not an *independent* bourgeoisie emerging in Kenya and itself manipulating the state apparatus; rather the state's symbiosis with the MNC [multinational corporate] sector gives it institutional independence vis-à-vis that emerging local bourgeoisie, while at the same time that bourgeoisie remains heavily dependent on the state for its surplus appropriation. This makes it possible for the Kenyan state to enforce the over-riding Kenyan symbiosis with foreign capital, disciplining local businessmen that move too strongly against MNC interests. . . . The auxiliary bourgeoisie remains too state-dependent to extend any opposition to MNC enterprise to destablizing lengths. . . .[34]

The alternative interpretation does not dispute Kenya's ultimate dependency upon international capital. Its major difference with the neo-colonial view lies in the significance attached to the shift of African capital from circulation into agricultural and industrial production. This accelerated throughout the 1970s. Swainson and the revisionist Leys both propose that this shift, taken in conjunction with evidence of the rapid accumulation of capital and skills in indigenous hands, suggests a greater degree of independence from foreign capital on the part of the local bourgeoisie than was previously envisaged. Not an 'auxiliary', 'comprador' or even exclusively 'petty' bourgeoisie has emerged, but in large measure a national bourgeoisie. Furthermore, the state has acted, not as an independent mediator between local and foreign capital, but as a partisan promoter of the interests of the national bourgeoisie against *all* other classes and class fractions. 'The essential function of the state', Leys avers, 'was to displace monopolies enjoyed by foreign capital, and to supplement individual African capitals with state finance capital, and state-secured technology, to enable them to occupy the space created for them in the newly-accessible economic sectors.'[35]

Which view, if either, is correct? It is difficult to arrive at a definitive conclusion because the debate really rests upon the meaning attached to such a vague concept as the dependent or auxiliary position of a particular class. Still, a brief investigation of the evolution of the state-society relationship may justify at least a provisional conclusion on development strategy and class relations in post-colonial Kenya.

From the viewpoint of class formation, the significance of the colonial period derives from the creation of favourable conditions for the later emergence of a national bourgeoisie. This was not an intended consequence. But it was one effect of the colonial state's role in subordinating the pre-capitalist modes of production in order to advance the settlers' interests in the introduced capitalist mode. In retrospect, one can trace the emergence of these conditions favouring national-capitalist development: the creation of a large 'free' labour force accustomed to wage-labour; the construction of essential economic infrastructure on the basis of tax revenues collected largely from Africans; and a substantial concentration of capital in settler hands that indigenous businessmen could, and did, later acquire.[36]

Until the 1950s the colonial regime acted on behalf of settler interests in representations to the Colonial Office, in budgetary allocations on services and infrastructure, in designing labour and tariff legislation, and in the provision of financial relief during the Depression. But the situation was complex owing to the ambivalance of the imperial government. The interests of both Kenya's colonial bureaucracy and the settlers coincided in their concern for capital accumulation in agriculture. However, the imperial government had also to concern itself with its own popularity and the interests of metropolitan firms. These considerations persuaded London occasionally to disallow or delay Kenyan legislation – for example, to ban forced labour after the First World War, and to refuse authority until 1931 for the establishment in Kenya of state-financed, low-interest agricultural loans. The availability of only short-term, high-interest finance, in conjunction with a generally gross lack of farming knowledge and a small scale of operations, meant that most settlers before the Second World War were chronically indebted.

In these uncertain conditions, wage rates paid to labourers were the single factor securely under settler control. Capital accumulation thus required an extreme exploitation of African labour. The colonial state assisted in this exploitation through coercive measures designed to generate an adequate supply of cheaply paid farm workers: forced labour (initially), direct taxation, and the labour recruitment system. Operating in conjunction with land shortages within the 'reserves', these measures presented many Africans with no option but squatting (and working) on European farms. On this basis there developed a large semi-proletarianized work force and (by the post-war period) well-capitalized mixed farms, ranches, estates and plantations.[37]

According to Leys in *Underdevelopment in Kenya*, there was considerable continuity in the pattern of accumulation from the colonial to the post-colonial eras. The Kenyatta regime continued to welcome foreign capital: indeed, there was an influx of this amounting to £41·3 million during 1967–70. This flowed mainly into import-substitution industries, banking, tourism and the wholesale and retail trade. In the early years of independence, much direct foreign investment took the form of wholly owned subsidiaries. Few transnational corporations initially appointed African directors or managers or made shares available to Africans. A superficially contradictory tendency was the state's fostering of African enterprise. Local businessmen, in the 1960s, expanded chiefly into the service sector, especially into trade and transport, while the redistribution of settler land led to an expansion of peasant production of cash crops and of African capitalist farming, at first largely in the mixed-farming sector.[38]

Leys interprets the Kenyan experience as a typical instance of neo-colonialism. His study demonstrates how the state assisted accumulation both on the part of foreign investors (via favourable tax legislation, financing arrangements, tariff protection for local manufacturing, and joint ventures with foreign firms) and on the part of the 'auxiliary bourgeoisie' (via cheap credit, training schemes for aspirant entrepeneurs, preferential tendering of government contracts, and the use of licensing to create monopoly positions in transport and distribution). But there was no real contradiction here. The government could promote the interests of both African and foreign capital as long as the former limited its activities principally to commerce, transport and mixed farming, while the latter remained secure in manufacturing, finance and plantation agriculture. Indeed, the government could even move to reduce external dependency by requiring the Kenyanization of personnel, the local sale of equity in foreign firms, and closer state supervision (including strict exchange controls), without seeming to threaten the essential interests of foreign investors. Leys argues, to the contrary, that 'the nexus between government and foreign capital was an extremely close one' by 1970, with the petty bourgeoisie in an auxiliary position.[39]

Focusing upon more recent events, Swainson and the revisionist Leys deny the applicability of this neo-colonial model to Kenya. They contend instead that the state has shaped the accumulation process to favour the interests of local capital. In agriculture, various agencies of the state assisted in the transfer of settler land (including estates) to indigenous owners by means of land allocation and the provision of credit. Agriculture, moreover, became an important source of further accumulation in 1976–7 owing to the high world prices for coffee and tea. In wholesale and retail trade, the incipient national bourgeoisie gained monopolies not only in the ways Leys had earlier described, but also with the aid of a law in 1975 that prohibited foreign-owned manufacturing firms from handling their own distribution. Finally, the state has facilitated the entrance of African capital into the bastion of foreign control – manufacturing. Swainson notes the growing share in the equity of manufacturing transnationals held by the Industrial and Commercial Development Corporation, and the regulation of direct foreign investment by committees appointed to evaluate the contribution of new projects. She differs with Langdon in holding that these efforts are not intended merely to maintain a neo-colonial system with some local economic involvement; they are genuine attempts to displace foreign investors in lucrative economic activities. Local entrepreneurs have not only invested in foreign industrial concerns or entered into joint ventures with them, but also created their own industrial enterprises in competition with the foreign corporations.[40]

These divergent analyses of the Kenyan case demonstrate either that there is a fluidity in the state's role, or that the intentions of the executive power take some time to unfold. Rather than regard the various formulations as in competition, it is probably more appropriate to conceive of them as accurate representations of the situation at successive historical moments. The state's strategy would therefore evolve from an initial neo-colonialism, through a transitional 'mediating' role, to its current national developmentalism with preponderantly private ownership.

Yet economic nationalism in this country represents only an implicit renegotiation of the terms of dependency, not an economic transformation. Both the forces and relations of production remain substantially unchanged. The interests of the ascendant national bourgeoisie do not lie in revolutionizing the inherited advanced-country technology in order to tap the productive capacities of the marginalized mass.[41] While the existing oligopolistic capitalist mode provides the dominant class with high profits and a 'Western' (or better) life-style, an alternative organization of production might release antagonistic popular energies as well as lower the consumption standards of the latter.

In order to maintain political order in the context of peripheral capitalist development, the regimes headed by Jomo Kenyatta and Daniel arap Moi have favoured the centralization and authoritarian exercise of political power. With respect to the working class, the state has progressively refined and tightened the labour controls bequeathed by the colonial regime. Corporatist policies now include strict controls over the only recognized labour federation, the Central Organization of Trade Unions (since 1966), the delegation to COTU of supervisory powers over the activities of affiliates, and in 1974 the abolition of even the nominal right to strike which unions then possessed. More generally, coercion and departicipation are evident in the use of the security apparatus (including the courts) against political opponents since 1966, the banning of the opposition Kenya People's Union in 1969, the selective use of preventative detention, the alleged involvement of government officials in the assassination of a popular Member of Parliament in 1975, the increasing reliance upon the paramilitary

General Service Unit and the emasculation of the electoral system and the National Assembly in this one-party state. Nationalistic rhetoric and moves against foreign interests have doubtless also allowed the state to displace some part of popular hostility towards foreigners.[42]

Basic-needs development strategies

The purview of this study encompasses a consideration of accumulation strategies that might eradicate mass poverty, as well as those that tend to reproduce marginalization. What are the development strategies and supportive class alliances that might lead to a satisfaction of mass basic needs, and what are the strengths, weaknesses and feasibility of each?

One generic constraint upon basic-needs strategies needs mention at the outset. To implement any such strategy, the state requires a bureaucracy characterized by efficiency, honesty, *élan* and ideological commitment. This is so because any assault on poverty will necessitate extensive state intervention into economic life. Yet exemplary behaviour on the part of public bureaucracies is a rarity. As one writer with long experience in development administration trenchantly observes:

> in much of rural Africa and Asia, the bureaucracy itself has become a caricature, and its performance a drama which would be tragicomic if the substance of the issues were not so important. In these settings, everyone *except the visiting officials and experts from headquarters* understands the underlying hopelessness of the situation. All but the most routine administrative actions become a charade: performed only when superiors are expected.[43]

Indeed, in country after country where state bureaucrats take direct responsibility for development, newspapers and prominent leaders decry bureaucratic incompetence, arrogance, and sometimes corruption.

What are the causes of maladministration?[44] On this there is little agreement. Radical explanations usually focus upon the external, historical factors that have conditioned bureaucratic, as well as socio-economic, underdevelopment. Poor adminstrative performance is attributed first to colonial practices: the neglect of local education in relevant skills, the denial of experience to indigenes in executive positions in the colonial bureaucracy, and the authoritarian tradition in colonial adminstrative decision-making. Maladministration is, furthermore, a function of the decolonization process, whereby the imperial power transferred authority to an indigenous group willing to perpetuate neo-colonial relationships. If, as Issa Shivji argues in the case of Tanzania (see page 107), the post-colonial state is a tool of a dependent bureaucratic bourgeoisie, then one cannot expect bureaucratic rectitude and social commitment until the masses, mobilized by a vanguard party, demand such rectitude.

A contrasting explanation attributes administrative ineffectiveness to the sway of pre-industrial social institutions incongruent with Western-style bureaucratic organization. To advert to the Tanzanian case again, one authority on public administration has contended that the solution to maladministration is not simply further training of administrators in Western management techniques. These techniques are themselves embedded in cultural values and norms that are not readily transferable to a new milieu. In East Africa, for example, 'rational' Western notions of efficiency do not appear so rational. The norms of impersonality that underlie efficiency criteria do not fit well in societies where personal relationships are most highly valued. In short, the solution to administrative disarray must lie in a degree of institutional change to create some congruency between bureaucratic procedures and local values.[45]

This brief survey clearly yields a rather unsatisfying conclusion. Although bureaucratic competence, fairness and commitment is crucial in any basic-needs strategy, the means to foster such a public administration remain uncertain. It is plausible that revolutionary struggle and popular mobilization is the single most important condition in breeding bureaucratic ideological commitment – though not necessarily competence. But one must remain sceptical: Algeria, and even Cuba, China and the Soviet Union, still experience severe adminstrative problems. Moreover, who is to raise the consciousness of the masses, as a check upon the bureaucracy, if not the party bureaucrats whose own behaviour may be at fault? One is driven to the view that maladministration is a function of *both* underdevelopment and pre-industrial social values.[46] But this is of limited use as a general guideline for, of course, the relative importance of each set of factors will vary from case to case.

THE NATIONAL-POPULIST MODEL

Some writers assert the feasibility of an evolution to a basic-needs orientation without drastic changes in property relations. This is the position, for example, of Roger Hansen in a book prepared as part of the (American) Council on Foreign Relations' '1980s Project on North-South Relations' (a project aiming 'to identify norms, goals, and principles that should guide change in political and economic relations between rich and poor nations'):

a basic-human-needs policy surely does not of necessity require a set of policies that merits the label 'a change in control of the means of production'. For better or worse – and the characterization remains a personal choice – one is in the realm of examining, developing, and implementing policies that will gradually change the *structure* of production, the access to crucial production inputs, and eventually the distribution of a much larger base of real assets. Much of this is an incremental process affecting future income flows and governmental expenditures. Except where significant land reform is needed, it does not depend upon redistribution of existing wealth.[47]

Although Hansen does not elaborate this strategy further, the notion of a strong regime reforming the distribution of income and new assets within a capitalist framework suggests a national-populist approach. This is a strategy that has had little currency in Africa. Populist experiments in the Third World have occurred mainly in Latin America, though Ataturk's Turkey and Nasser's Egypt are notable examples elsewhere. Insofar as the conditions that have produced national populism elsewhere may recur in tropical Africa, a study of strategies apparently conducive to assaulting poverty would be incomplete without some reference to its generic features, feasibility and efficacy.

Populism is perhaps the vaguest term in the political vocabulary. I use 'national populism' to refer to a strategy of a regime seeking to articulate an alliance between a fraction of the bourgeoisie or petty bourgeoisie and the working class and/or peasantry, on the basis of a programme of anti-imperialism, rapid modernization (invariably involving industrialization), and a more equitable distribution of income. National populism differs from national developmentalism in that it fosters both the organization (rather than demobilization) of the working class and other dominated classes, and a fairer sharing of the fruits of capital accumulation. But national populism is not socialism, though it may call itself that. The populist state focuses reform upon the nationalization (and sometimes transfer to local private interests) of foreign-owned assets and the distribution of income, not upon a change in the relations of production.[48]

The prospects for such a national-populist programme in any tropical African country appear dim. An obvious necessary condition for this strategy is the emergence of a dissident fraction of the petty bourgeoisie or bourgeoisie determined to capture state power. In Argentina during the first Peronist regime or in Brazil in the 1930s, this oppositional orientation arose at the stage of incipient industrialization when an urban-based industrial bourgeoisie sought to throw off the domination of a conservative landed oligarchy. The political representatives of this rising bourgeoisie therefore appealed to the lower classes for support, on the basis of the programme just discussed, in order to bolster its political position and achieve the requisite policy changes. But in tropical Africa there is generally an absence of either rule by a conservative landed oligarchy or an electoral system that gives the masses some potential political importance. There is therefore little evident motivation for a fraction of the bourgeoisie to attack the state's current sponsorship of oligopolistic conditions, or hope for success if one did. As chapter 5 seeks to show, even the small, competitive capitalists are loath to set themselves against a *status quo* that fetters their expansion. Hence the only possibility is a populist regime of the Nasserist type – that is, a bellicose, reformist and authoritarian state based upon the military in a country where the dissident elements of the middle class or bourgeoisie constitute but a small minority of their classes. Realistically, however, this authoritarianism and the negligible political power of the lower classes would be conducive to the rapid decomposition of national populism into either national developmentalism or bureaucratic collectivism. The actual outcome would obviously depend upon the complexion of the emergent dominant class, in particular whether its power base derives from private wealth or bureaucratic position.[49]

In the unlikely event that a national-populist regime did transpire, would it bring about significant change? It is evident that this hypothethical question can receive only a tentative answer based upon the relevant historical experience. With specific reference to Latin American populism, one finds that views about its social significance vary markedly. On the one hand, there are those who allege either that populism is actually a movement of the *status quo* or that populist regimes provide negligible benefits for the poor in the form of income redistribution or the right to autonomous class organization. Such reforms as are implemented are easily reversed in a right-wing reaction. The problem with national populism, from this viewpoint, is that it short-circuits working-class consciousness through the use of corporatist techniques and an ideology emphasizing charismatic leadership, class reconciliation and reformism. On the other hand, some writers argue that populist movements do aim to change the social structure. Torcuato di Telli, for one, makes a case for the progressiveness of populism on the grounds that the social bases of bourgeois reform in nineteenth-century Europe or revolution in, for instance, Russia, do not obtain in Latin America. Here, the middle classes are too weak and feel too threatened by popular revolution to champion political and social reform. In addition, the working class is too recent – and often too small and disorganized as well – to form the social base for a socialist movement. As a consequence of

the impossibility of forming a strong political movement of a Liberal or Labour type, other combinations have taken the lead on the side of reform (or revolution). They have as a rule been formed by elements drawn from various social classes, and with an ideology more radical than their class composition would have led one to expect.'[50]

These conflicting assessments point out the ambiguity of the phenomenon of populism. On the one hand, populist leaders have been manipulative, seeking to channel and use the potentially dangerous power of an embryonic working class and others (through corporatist political practices, populist ideology, and reforms directed at workers as consumers, not producers). In a sense, national populism has represented a method of organizing power under the hegemony of a rising industrial bourgeoisie. On the other hand, populist regimes have also provided an opportunity for collective self-expression on the part of workers and other dominant classes, in a context where class loyalties are as yet fluid and unformed. Although populist governments have been unwilling to permit autonomous class organization from below, corporatist organizational efforts can nevertheless gain a momentum of their own. Organization, even if controlled, brings workers together; this creates the potential for the demands of workers to transcend the limits set by the authorities. Guillermo O'Donnell writes of this tendency with respect to Argentinian and Brazilian populism:

> When the populist period lost its dynamism and the populist governments had been ousted, in both Argentina and Brazil there remained an urban popular sector with a high degree of organization, political allegiances hostile to the established sectors, and ideological tendencies amenable to more radical formulations than anything proposed by Peron or Vargas during their years in power.

Even in Brazil, often cited as a case where workers gained nothing from populism, recent studies indicate that workers have gained increasingly in solidarity since Vargas' populist regime of the 1930s.[51]

However, even if a populist regime did come to power in Africa and did undertake some necessary reforms, it would be unlikely to survive for long. A regime which bases capital accumulation upon the articulation of an alliance between labour and capital is inherently vulnerable. It is only possible for the state simultaneously to provide benefits for the poor and maintain favourable profit conditions for the dominant bourgeois fraction in the context of rapid economic growth. Yet the dislocations entailed in an anti-imperialistic and redistributive programme are not propitious for economic expansion, at least in the short run. Soon, a government must decide its priorities. 'After the initial redistributive measures and after the initial euphoria over the reduction of the foreign presence, the issue arises as to which of the two national social classes will capitalize the economy: the national bourgeoisie or the workers/peasants.'[52]

The vulnerability of the national-populist strategy, not to mention its questionable efficacy and feasibility, make it an improbable instrument of basic-needs development in Africa.

THE BUREAUCRATIC-COLLECTIVIST AND TRANSITION-TO-SOCIALISM MODELS

Any government seeking to institute a basic-needs approach in an incremental fashion will inevitably confront a dilemma. On the one

THE STATE AND CAPITAL ACCUMULATION   103

hand, the eventual eradication of absolute poverty will require a change in the 'logic' of the economy as manifest in the reorientation of production, consumption and income and asset distribution. On the other hand, poverty-amelioration in any African country will require a high rate of growth to produce the goods, services and jobs for the masses. But it is unrealistic to expect adequate growth when its main generators in the modern sector are seeing their privileges eroded. Any genuine assault on poverty is likely to lead to panic among private firms, and a consequent running down of investment. This would be manageable if the government could rapidly raise the level of public investment and the productive capacity of the poor. But governments with few resources and limited administrative expertise are unlikely to achieve these objectives in the short run.[53] The progressive regime's dilemma is then to retreat from an attack on poverty so as to reassure investors (retaining perhaps the rhetoric of 'basic-needs'), or to forge ahead irrespective of the short-term consequences. The latter course, and the economic dislocation it implies, will tend to push a government towards increasingly radical solutions in an attempt either to mobilize popular support or to consolidate authoritarian rule, and thereby withstand the destabilizing tendencies stemming from economic and social conflict.

Many on the left write as though progression into socialism or retrogression into (state) capitalism are the only options available to a society undertaking a radical development path. This is misleading. Such a society may in practice exit into neither of these modes of production but rather into what Michael Harrington terms 'bureaucratic collectivism'. This is a distinct mode of production and form of class society, of which Stalinist Russia was the prototype, masquerading as socialism. Like socialism, bureaucratic collectivism requires the socialization of the major means of production. Unlike socialism, bureaucratic collectivism is exploitative, in the Marxian sense of the word. That is, a bureaucratic class uses authoritarian methods and control of the economy to extract a surplus from the direct producers and to allocate this between public investment and the enlargement of its own class privileges:

> Where the state owns the means of production, the crucial question is, who owns the state? The people can own the state in only one way: through the fullest and freest right to change its policies and personnel. Therefore, in a nationalized economy exclusion from political power is not something unfortunate that happens in a 'superstructure'; it determines the social and economic base of the system itself, it secures class power to those who 'own' the state, which owns the means of production.

Bureaucratic collectivism is, furthermore, a strategy of accumulation and control that is not restricted to Communist societies. As Communism came to resemble a barracks, there were colonels and generals who suddenly discovered that they were not Rightists but "socialists".'[54]

Tropical Africa has, unfortunately, yielded further illustrations of Jean François Revel's observations that 'any attempt to establish [economic socialism] alongside [political dictatorship] leads either to caricature, or to tragedy'. The Peoples' Republics of Congo/Brazzaville (since 1968) and Benin (since 1974) represent the caricature; Ethiopia since 1975 constitutes the tragedy. In all these cases, the official avowal of Marxism–Leninism followed *coups d'état* that elevated to power late converts to 'socialism'. Both the Congo and Benin presently manifest a vast gap between rhetoric and reality:

> between a stridently vocal concern (especially in Congo) with ideological militancy, vigor, purity, and autocriticism ('Socialist rectitude') and a near-total failure of all leadership strata to direct or control socioeconomic development (in *any* manner, let alone along socialist lines) or to arrest corruption and mismanagement in their own ranks. Indeed, the immense gap between, on the one hand, ideological and ideologically derived policy-goals, incessantly hammered at with an insistence and ferocity reminiscent of the ideological clashes of early Stalinist Russia. . ., and on the other, the pragmatism and continued dependency relations with former colonial powers not only tolerated but encouraged by the ruling elite tempt the critical observer to discount African radical ideology as but 'optium for the masses'.

The *Dirgue*'s rule in Ethiopia represents a closer – and far more murderous – approximation to bureaucratic collectivism. Coming to power in 1974 after a series of military mutinies, popular demonstrations (especially by students) and industrial protests, Colonel Mengistu Haile Mariam duly declared his regime Marxist–Leninist the following year. This action, in the context of an undeniably revolutionary situation, enabled Mengistu to secure Soviet material aid and Cuban military support against the subjugated minorities of the Ethiopian Empire. It also permitted him to exterminate his opponents, including those who had led the initial popular protests: 'more young revolutionaries died under the *Dirgue* than during the reign of Haile Selassie'.[55]

Sadly, in view of these dismal examples, there are grounds for holding that bureaucratic collectivism, not socialism, is the more probable outcome of radical, non-capitalist initiatives in peripheral capitalist societies. These countries generally lack two favourable conditions for socialism identified by Michael Harrington. In the first place, widespread poverty is not conducive to socialist values; only in a highly productive economy is invidious competition and self-seeking rendered unnecessary. Where poverty prevails, a struggle among people to secure the necessities of life will probably emerge. Lacking the requisite material conditions, socialist regimes in underdeveloped countries are tempted to build socialism by demanding exemplary self-denial on the part of the socialist cadres and people. But such demands are unlikely to succeed for long without the application of coercion; the deviation of even a few from ideal behaviour will tend to demoralize the rest and destroy the voluntary collectivist thrust.[56]

A second condition facilitating a socialist path is a proletariat that forms a majority of the labour force and evinces a socialist consciousness. Only then is there likely to exist a secure political base for socialist relations of production – inasmuch as workers typically lack a vested interest in the preservation of private property. Only then, too, will a movement emerge capable of keeping in check the inevitable oligarchical tendencies of the governing elite – owing to the workers' unique propensity for solidarity and organization stemming from their work situation. Where the proletariat is small and weak, socialist movements have sought to substitute some other class for it, usually the peasantry. But these surrogates typically lack both a socialist perspective and a proclivity for solidarity or autonomous class action. They can therefore be manipulated by an oligarchical governing group. 'Actually, the peasants and the urban poor are substitute proletariats only in the heaven of theory', writes Harrington. 'In reality, the party-state, which is a new ruling class, substitutes itself for the proletariat, the bourgeoisie and everyone else.'[57]

But while bureaucratic collectivism is not socialism, it has none-theless in practice revealed its capacity to satisfy basic material needs in some poor countries. Few would deny the success of the Chinese and Cuban Communist regimes in eradicating absolute poverty and reducing relative deprivation by means of land reform and collectivization, socialization of industry and commerce, and policies of equitable social development.[58] It would also be foolish to deny that these social benefits have derived from regimes with scant regard for genuine popular political participation. Bureaucratic collectivism is thus an ambiguous strategy from the viewpoint of the poor: it can handle the dislocations consequent upon a reorientation of the economy towards the fulfilment of basic needs, but at the expense of movement towards basic human rights. For this reason, it is wrong to assume that bureaucratic collectivism is obviously the choice of right-thinking workers and peasants where the alternative is some capitalist approach. The revolution from above may be guided by a Pol Pot as well as by a Castro.

Are bureaucratic-collectivist regimes in tropical Africa – in Somalia and the Republic of Guinea for instance – capable of carrying through an assault on poverty? This would require a regime to confront both national and transnational power centres. In these confrontations, the paucity of economic and political power concentrated in the state will usually prompt revolutionary leaders to temporize with vested interests, thus diluting revolutionary programmes. It is evident, in the first place, that avowedly Marxist–Leninist countries in Africa remain dependent within the world capitalist system – integrated into an essentially colonial division of labour, into an international monetary system in which loans and credits are needed to ward off balance-of-payments problems, and into a pattern of technology transfers that renders the multinational corporations indispensable. If these linkages are to be sundered, some form of regional or sub-regional collective self-reliance among like-minded countries is probably necessary.

In the second place, bureaucratic-collectivist regimes, by themselves, lack the coercive potential to implement rural and industrial collectivization and central planning. The sources of political weakness are obvious. First, a cadre of trained and dedicated revolutionaries sufficiently large to man the party and state apparatuses is typically absent. It is impossible to build bureaucratic collectivism without bureaucratic collectivists (or socialists who don't recognize the difference). Yet it is difficult to generate such a cadre in countries lacking a genuine revolutionary tradition. Without a committed and competent cadre, state control of the economy will engender, as I have already suggested, inefficiency, corruption and widespread popular disillusionment. Secondly, these regimes also characteristically lack a loyal, reliable and disciplined coercive instrument. A reliance upon force under these conditions may well precipitate a *coup d'état* or indisciplined military or police action that alienates the populace from the regime.[59]

In the light of these constraints, it is probable that a bureaucratic-collectivist thrust could successfully satisfy mass basic material needs only in a context of collective self-reliance or sponsorship by the Soviet Union.

Consider next the socialist alternative. Although the objective conditions for socialism in Africa are unpropitious, this is not to say that socialism has no relevance to the solution of the poverty problem there. But the dimensions of the socialist task are awesome. In the first place, the transition phase, whether introduced peacefully or by revolution, must be prolonged – at least several decades – in order to build the material and social base for socialism. The state during this period must, of course, play a decisive role in achieving structural transformation through channelling a large part of the country's economic surplus. However, one would only know whether a transition to socialism was actually under way if the policies of the state also fostered equality, co-operative activities and, above all, mass participation.[60] Popular participation in production units and state arenas is necessary as a means as well as an end of the strategy of transition to socialism: only if the working class, peasantry and labouring poor become the dominant classes in society will oligarchical and bureaucratic tendencies be blunted.

While handling these delicate problems, the state must also manage the dilemma inherent in a reorientation of the economy in a socialist direction. It must not succumb to the temptation either to shelve the socialist project to placate investors, or to undertake a coercive revolution from above, leading to bureaucratic collectivism. The balancing of all these pressures and commitments demands a great deal of any regime – perhaps too much.

In tropical Africa, the most promising cases of socialist transition include Tanzania, Guinea-Bissau and Mozambique. Angola is another possibility, but its continuing civil war disrupts economic reconstruction. The first three countries, though equally integrated into the world economy and equally poor, are blessed with dedicated and able leadership. However, Guinea-Bissau won its independence from Portugal only in late 1974 and Mozambique only in mid-1975; it is thus too early to draw conclusions in these cases about the transition process or the success in attacking mass poverty through socialist policies. The analyst can gain a better perspective on Tanzania, for the regime here moved to the left in 1967. There is, however, heated disputation over the proper characterization of this country's strategy, and concomitantly over the relationship between the state and social classes. A reference to Tanzanian experience and the controversy surrounding it may thus clarify the issues and problems involved in a radical basic-needs approach.

THE TANZANIAN CASE

Is Tanzania a case of a country seeking to eradicate poverty and achieve other social goals by means of a transition to socialism? An overwhelmingly rural, poor (even by the standards of the Ivory Coast) and resource-scarce country, Tanzania seems an odd prospect for such a problematic experiment. Paradoxically, however, under certain conditions economic backwardness can *facilitate* the strategy of transition.

One influential view on the Tanzanian left denies that a socialist transition is in progress. Instead, the reality is the rise of a neo-colonial form of state-capitalism. Issa Shivji is a prominent proponent of this general view. He argues that a section of the weak Tanzanian petty bourgeoisie acceded to state power at political independence in 1961. This fraction, consisting 'mainly of those at the top of the state apparatus – ministers, high civil servants, high military and police officers and such like', he labels a 'bureacratic bourgeoisie'. At first this was only a stratum of the petty bourgeoisie. However, the Arusha Declaration of 1967 allowed the bureaucratic bourgeoisie to emerge as a separate class. It used the ideological guise of socialism to obtain an economic base for itself by the nationalization of the commanding heights of the economy and the gradual undermining of the economic power of the 'commercial bourgeoisie' – which was composed mainly of

Asian wholesalers, retailers and landlords. Shivji thus regards many of the state's interventions into the economy as efforts by a cunning bureaucratic bourgeoisie to displace its rival. The imposition of state control of importing, the strengthening of the co-operative movement, the tightening of foreign-exchange controls, and the nationalizations associated with the Arusha Declaration and of rented houses and offices in 1970, are all interpreted in this light. Eventually, political power and control of property came to reside in the same class; the bureaucratic bourgeoisie then constituted a ruling class. But this remains a *dependent* class, tied into an alliance with foreign capital that requires Tanzania to remain an integral – albeit peripheral – part of the world capitalist system. However, there is still hope, for an ongoing class struggle between the ruling class and the workers and peasants may eventuate in a victory for the latter, and the inauguration of a real transition to socialism under the leadership of a proletarian party.[61]

This analysis, as one critic observes with acerbity, 'extends . . . beyond the credible and into the realm of radical mythology'. Is it credible, in the first place, that bureaucrats who had attained positions of authority only since independence could so rapidly have developed the advanced class solidarity and consciousness that Shivji's interpretation implies? To sustain this view, one has to interpret the *consequences* of certain policies as always intended by the bureaucrats. Hence, the fact that *ujamaa vijijini* (socialist villages) and villagization brought the dispersed peasantry under administrative control, thus facilitating the promotion of cash crops for export and the extraction of a rural economic surplus, can be taken to exemplify the cunning of the emergent ruling class. Alternatively, one can accept as genuine the official aims of this programme, namely that villagization facilitated both the provision of public services and agricultural inputs, and the encouragement of socialist agriculture.[62]

In the second place, Shivji's analysis is simply inconsistent with the evidence of the top bureaucrats' declining relative consumption standards. Why would a bureaucratic bourgeoisie insert a restrictive leadership code into the Arusha Declaration? This code forbade all top and middle-level party officials, politicians and civil servants from owning shares, holding directorships, renting houses or earning more than one salary. The obvious intention, largely realized in practice, was to guarantee that if the state was to be a major source of accumulation, the fruits of this strategy should not flow mainly to officials. In addition, income differentials have narrowed as a consequence of reductions in the salaries of high civil servants and politicians in 1967, the subsequent restriction of salary raises at the top to below the rise in the cost of living, tax reforms, and generous increases in the minimum wage. The ratio between the highest and lowest civil service salary was 26:1 in 1966; this was only 9:1 in 1977. The government by the latter date had also eliminated some of the perquisites of civil servants.[63] If there is a bureaucratic bourgeoisie in Tanzania, it must be one of the most anaemic ruling classes in history!

In contrast to Shivji's simplistic view, there is a more substantial set of analyses that share a refusal to characterize Tanzania's socialist professions as mere deception. John Saul, for instance, represents a more subtle and hopeful Marxist viewpoint than Shivji. He sees (or saw, in 1974) the struggle over the socialist option as taking place largely *within* the state and party apparatuses; there is not yet a cohesive, bureaucratic ruling class. Instead, the bureaucrats constitute an 'unformed class', a group which can still 'opt for different historical alternatives, alternatives which would actually affect in *different* ways their own positions in the production process'. The struggle involves those officials 'who seek to consolidate the neo-colonial set-up and those who are moved, increasingly, to challenge it'. A victory on the part of the radicalized petty bourgeoisie could open the way for the conversion of the Chama Cha Mapinduzi ('Revolutionary Party', until 1977 the Tanganyikan African National Union – TANU) into an ideologically committed movement, and the commencement of a real socialist transition.[64]

Another school of thought, identified by Cranford Pratt as 'democratic socialist', regards this transition as already under way. Rejecting the notion that the building of socialism requires a vanguard party, Pratt holds that 'the state would have a society in transition to socialism if that society were deliberately reshaping itself along more egalitarian and more participatory lines and were promoting co-operative and non-acquisitive motivations amongst men and women in their economic and other interrelationships.' His evidence suggests that public policies are actually advancing these goals, though not without severe problems or outright failures in some areas. But Pratt is implicitly in agreement with Saul on one major issue: it is the considerable autonomy of the state from any dominant class that permitted Julius Nyerere and his followers to undertake the early socialist initiatives.[65]

The roots of this marked autonomy lie in the colonial period. It is now a commonplace observation that the extreme lack of development in Tanzania at independence ironically facilitated the advancement of the socialist option. Owing to the low level of economic and educational development and to the monoplization of the available lucrative opportunities by Europeans and Asians, the traditionally egalitarian African population had undergone only limited social differentiation in most regions. This meant that influential indigenous classes did not exist in 1961 to anywhere near the same extent as in the Ivory Coast or Kenya at independence. There was therefore no powerful political coalition to oppose (or capture) TANU in the early years, and champion a private-capitalist development strategy of the neo-colonial or national-developmental type. Indeed, it was apparently Nyerere's perception of the growing threat to egalitarian and democratic policies posed by embryonic class formation that spurred him to clarify the socialist strategy in 1967.[66]

In addition, the very peripherality of Tanzania in international economic and strategic terms enhanced the state's autonomy. The absence of any crucial raw material, and the extreme poverty and small size of the population, have limited the inflow of foreign investment. Strategically, Tanzania has not been of major importance, except perhaps with respect to its assistance to the liberation movements in southern Africa. And there is always the modest, undogmatic and charming personality of President Nyerere to assuage any Western fears occasioned by his policies. Consequently, the Tanzanian state could undertake wideranging nationalizations in 1967, as part of a socialist programme, without provoking more than mild rebukes from advanced-capitalist countries. Not only has there been no evidence of covert intervention to reorient Tanzanian public policy in a capitalist direction, but the Western-dominated World Bank has looked favourably upon the overall programme (though critical of specific policies). Edmund Clark writes: 'The socialist overtones, far from repelling Western donors, attracted them. Tanzanian socialism was not so strong (at least at this stage) that it challenged the interests of Western capitalism.' Bilateral and multilateral donors actually stepped up the aid they allocated to Tanzania following the Arusha Declaration.[67]

Internal and international conditions thus combined to permit an unusual latitude to the Tanzanian executive in defining the country's development strategy. The state in few other underdeveloped countries can expect to confront such a weakly developed domestic and international structure of vested interests opposed to socialism. If, therefore, Tanzania *is* making a peaceful transition to socialism, its experience will not be directly applicable to circumstances in many other peripheral capitalist countries.

But some contend that the very lack of adverse Western and domestic reaction to Tanzanian policies proves their actual neo-colonial content.[68] Do policy formation and class relations in fact support the proposition that this country is pursuing a socialist strategy dedicated to the satisfaction of mass basic needs and human dignity?

Tanzania has gone far towards realizing the necessary conditions for the building of socialism. In February 1967 the government nationalized all the banks, the major food processors, and the eight principal foreign export trading companies. It also announced its intention to obtain a majority interest in six large manufacturing firms and of the sisal industry. Then, in 1970, the State Trading Corporation took over all import and wholesale trade. In that year, too, the government nationalized all residential and commercial rental buildings valued at over Shs 100 000. The effect of these measures by 1974 was to move four-fifths of the large- and medium-scale firms into the public sector, which thereby generated about 44 per cent of monetary GDP. State corporations created to run the public enterprises include, most prominently, the National Development Corporation in manufacturing industries, the National Bank of Commerce, and the State Trading Corporation. The usual planning apparatus also emerged, though its effectiveness is apparently limited.[69]

A socialist commitment has also influenced social policy. I have already alluded to the impact of the leadership code, incomes policy and tax reforms in enhancing egalitarianism. There has in addition been a sustained effort to provide more equitable territorial and social distribution of such public services as education, health and clean water.[70] All of this accords with a basic-needs approach.

Where the socialist strategy has had least impact is in a reorientation of the system of production. As far as agriculture is concerned, the regime has since 1967 envisaged socialism as entailing a concentration of the dispersed peasantry into villages, and the development in these of both collective ownership and collective working of the land. The pace of villagization was, however, slow until 1972, and the pace of collectivization slower still. At the beginning of 1974 only about 8 per cent of the 5000 existing villages engaged in any degree of collective production. In late 1973 the governing party decided to complete the process of villagization by the end of 1976, a goal that was substantially achieved. Collectivization, however, was to remain a voluntary decision on the part of villagers. Indeed, socialist forms of agriculture have neither received much official encouragement nor made any significant gains since 1974. The reason is not hard to seek. Owing to the disastrous decline in agricultural production in 1974–6 as a result of both drought and the poorly planned and executed programme of enforced villagization, the hard-pressed regime has perforce learned to approach rural policy with considerable caution. Hence,

ujamaa as a concept once intended to convey a social ideal of collective ownership, labour and sharing is reduced to describing a state of affairs in which individual farming is intermittently supplemented by occasional cooperation in such tasks as planting and harvesting. Villagization without socialism is, in effect, the current policy.[71]

If the peasant mode of production remains substantially untransformed, what of the dominant mode? A setback in rural socialism does not in itself signal the demise of a long-term transition process. But if the industrial strategy remains as before, it becomes more difficult to speak of an ongoing transition to socialism.

Industrial development, until 1973 at least, largely continued along the lines instituted by the transnational corporations. Indeed, these continued in partnership with parastatals in many cases. As an extensive study of development expenditures reveals, parastatals 'have concentrated on building enterprises which are often large, capital intensive, and outer directed, and which are not integrated in the rural economy. Far from mitigating the urban/rural dichotomy, they have exacerbated it.' Consequently, the large state-controlled manufacturing enterprises have tended to remain dependent upon advanced-country technology, know-how and imported inputs. Only since 1974 has the government concretely sought to mitigate this marginalizing pattern of industrialization. In 1973 it established the Small Industries Development Organization (SIDO) to promote small-scale, rural-based, co-operatively owned and managed workshops to produce basic capital and consumer goods – for the rural population, in particular. SIDO provides training courses in appropriate industrial arts in various rural centres, soft loans to emergent industrial co-operatives, and extension services. By 1980 there were dozens of co-operative workshops employing labour-intensive techniques scattered in villages throughout Tanzania. Employing between ten and forty workers, these small factories produced such useful items as ox-carts, hoes, spades, bolts of various sorts, buckets and pots. The benefits of this development in terms of appropriate products, employment, backward and forward linkages, saved foreign exchange and urban–rural balance are obvious.[72]

In large-scale industry, however, the relations of production remain essentially capitalist. The Tanzanian state, for readily apparent reasons, has not decisively resolved the inherent dilemma facing all socialist regimes. This dilemma is to reconcile socialist aspirations with the reality of an economy still operating according to capitalist principles. The intentions are to socialize the means of production and reorient them to the satisfaction of basic needs, and to transform the authoritarian relations of production in industry. The economic reality is a dominant mode of production characterized by production for profit, free wage-labour, hierarchical work-place relations, and dependency upon foreign technology, know-how and credits. Hence, on the one hand, the government believes it must respond to certain immediate needs: to ensure a continued inflow of foreign aid, finance capital and production inputs; to generate a surplus through increased production (in part, to finance the state's activities); and, in general, to foster financial stability and economic growth. On the other hand, the commitment to socialism requires public policies which might jeopardize these goals. The government needs to experiment with efficacious forms of worker participation in management and to reshape effective demand and production in order to attack poverty; but these efforts will doubtless panic the remaining local businessmen and the foreign suppliers of capital, assistance and markets, with dire short-term economic consequences.[73]

In the absence of a politically conscious mass base and channels for popular participation, a regime is likely to resolve this dilemma in a non-socialist direction. A transition to socialism is manifest, above all, in the development of a certain hegemonic class alliance.[74] Of course, it would be quite utopian to expect class-conscious workers and peasants to 'own' the Tanzanian state at this early stage; nonetheless, the validity of continuing to speak of a transition must depend upon movement in this direction.

What is the degree of popular participation in the Tanzanian state and socialized industries? In the voluminous literature pertaining to participation in Tanzania, recent evaluations range from the marginally positive to the downright negative. Few deny tendencies towards authoritarianism. These trends include: the declining importance of the National Assembly within this *de jure* one-party state; the elimination of the elected district and urban councils in 1971 (and their replacement by development advisory committees dominated by bureaucrats); the control by state or party of trade unions, co-operatives, newpapers and broadcast media; the failure of workers' councils, introduced in 1970, to become more than weak advisory bodies; the coercive villagization policy of 1974–6; and the growing emphasis upon ideological training at all levels. Cranford Pratt, though cognizant of these barriers to effective democracy, nonetheless tentatively concludes that Tanzania 'does appear to be persisting in its efforts to accomplish a democratic transition to socialism'. He bases this qualified evaluation on the existence of certain counter-tendencies: for example, the effort to introduce elected councils within all villages in 1976, and to make Chama Cha Mapinduzi a more representative, open and powerful party. Joel Samoff, by contrast, does not identify countervailing tendencies in his gloomy assessment of participation in Tanzania:

> Fifteen years of public emphasis on citizen participation, both as an essential characteristic of democratic society and as a necessary foundation for increased productive capacity, as well as a whole series of institutional modifications, seem to have had little impact on the structural exclusion of ordinary citizens from most decision-making settings or on the authoiritarian orientation of administrators.[75]

The minimal political power of the popular classes, it is important to repeat, is not just 'something unfortunate that happens in a "superstructure"' (to requote Harrington). This political fact has implications for the trajectory of the transition strategy. In the absence of pressure from below, bureaucratic interests and short-term considerations may overwhelm the risky, long-term socialist commitments. There are strong pressures towards a retrogression into state capitalism owing to the economic dislocations inherent in a socialist transition and the uncertain outcome of this path. Alternatively, an ascendant vanguard, impatient with the slow pace of the structural change and confident of its own rectitude and the validity of its 'proletarian' ideology, may substitute itself for Tanzanian workers and peasants in carrying through a revolution to sweep away all obstacles to its own socialist vision. This path has normally led to bureaucratic collectivism.

In Tanzania, none of the three options has been decisively foreclosed.

Intellectuals on the left often speak as though the alternatives for underdeveloped countries are neo-colonialism or socialism. This chapter proposes that the more probable alternatives are actually statist-forms of national developmentalism or bureaucratic collectivism. Neo-colonialism is in disrepute in the Third World. Not only do many regimes possess the leverage to renegotiate dependency, but they have the incentive to do so – neo-colonial relationships tend to breed or exacerbate legitimacy crises. National populism emerges only in unusual historical circumstances and is prone to disintegration. And transitions to socialism are rare because the political and economic conditions that facilitate this strategy are rare. National developmentalism, though ascendant in Africa, does not transform the structures of peripheral capitalism, and is therefore unlikely to undo underdevelopment and provide the means for eliminating absolute poverty within a generation. Bureaucratic collectivism under Soviet sponsorship can constitute an assault on poverty, but at the price of authoritarian controls. These are not encouraging conclusions.

If a humane and democratic socialism is to appear on the historical agenda, the development of a cohesive and politically conscious working class is probably essential. But the fashionable 'labour aristocracy' thesis conceives of the leading proletarian sectors as tacitly a part of the dominant class alliance in post-colonial capitalist orders. This thesis, if correct, has obvious implications for the feasibility of various strategies of capital accumulation. It is therefore to the knotty issue of class formation from below, and in particular to the position and role of the working class, that I now turn.

Notes

1. A criticism of development economists made, among others, by K. Griffin and A. Rahman Khan, in 'Poverty in the Third World: Ugly Facts and Fancy Models', *World Development*, VI 3 (1978), p. 302.
2. A striking example of this tendency with respect to the state in underdeveloped countries is W. Zieman and M. Wanzendorfer, 'The State in Peripheral Societies', *The Socialist Register, 1977* (London: Merlin Press, 1978), pp. 143–77.
3. For a useful critique of liberal-pluralist and Leninist models in relation to underdeveloped countries, see Alfred Stepan, *The State and Society: Peru in Comparative Perspective* (Princeton; Princeton University Press, 1978), pp. 7–12, 17–22. For a trenchant critique of the Leninist approach, see A. Wolfe, 'New Directions in the Marxist Theory of Politics', *Politics and Society*, IV, 2 (1974), pp. 135–43.

4. Nicos Poulantzas, *Political Power and Social Classes* (London: New Left Books, 1973), quotes pp. 288 and 285.

5. For a critique of Poulantzas's structuralism and elaboration of 'structural mechanisms', see F. Block, 'The Ruling Class Does not Rule: Notes on the Marxist Theory of the State', *The Socialist Revolution*, VII, 33 (1977), pp. 6–28. For the operation of structural mechanisms in the Third World context, see N. L. Hamilton, 'Mexico: The Limits of State Autonomy', *Latin American Perspectives*, II, 2 (1975), pp 81–108; and E. Henderson, 'The Chilean State after the Coup', *The Socialist Register, 1977*, pp. 121–42.

6. Studies stressing the autonomy of the state in post-colonial African countries, though for different reasons, include: J. S. Saul, 'The State in Post-Colonial Societies: Tanzania', *The Socialist Register, 1974* (London: Merlin Press, 1974) pp. 349–72; T. Turner, 'Multinational Corporations and the Instability of the Nigerian State', *Review of African Political Economy*, 5 (1976), pp. 63–79; and E. A. Brett, 'Relations of Production, the State and the Ugandan Crisis', *West African Journal of Social and Political Science*, I, 3 (1978), pp. 249–84.

7. For a non-Marxist specification of state functions in terms close to those used here, see J. S. Coleman, 'The Concept of Political Penetration', in Lionel Cliffe, James S. Coleman and M. R. Doornbos (eds.), *Government and Rural Development in East Africa* (The Hague: Nijhoff, 1977), pp. 3–10.

8. Compare with Barbara Stalling's discussion of 'development ideologies' in *Class Conflict and Economic Development in Chile, 1958–1973* (Stanford: Stanford University Press, 1978), chap. 1.

9. James Petras develops the first three models with considerable ingenuity in 'New Perspectives on Imperialism and Class in the Periphery', *Journal of Contemporary Asia*, V, 3 (1975), pp. 298–300.

10. J. S. Barker, 'Stability and Stagnation: The State in Senegal', *Canadian Journal of African Studies*, XI, (1977), pp. 32–3.

11. 'Primitive Colonial Accumulation': R. M. A. van Zwannenberg, *Colonial Capitalism and Labour in Kenya, 1919–39* (Nairobi: East African Literature Bureau, 1975). Decolonization: Gary Wasserman, *Politics of Decolonization: Kenya Europeans and the Land Issue, 1960–65* (Cambridge: Cambridge University Press, 1976).

12. See R. Collier, 'Parties, Coups and Authoritarian Rule: Patterns of Political Change in Tropical Africa', *Comparative Political Studies*, XI (April 1978), pp. 62–93.

13. Petras, 'New Perspectives' (n. 9 above) p. 299.

14. Data drawn from World Bank, *Ivory Coast: The Challenge of Success* (Baltimore: Johns Hopkins University Press, 1978), pp. 3, 50; a survey of the Ivorian economy in the *IMF* (International Monetary Fund) *Survey* (22 January 1979), p. 18; and World Bank, *World Development Report, 1978* (August 1978).

15. See, for relevant data and observations, World Bank, *Ivory Coast* (n. 14 above), pp. 40, 139 and 158. See also, A. G. Rondos, 'Ivory Coast: The Price of Development', *Africa Report*, XXIV, 2 (1979), p. 4.

16. See World Bank, *Ivory Coast* (n. 14 above), p. 127 (unemployment), and pp. 196, 202–4 (informal sector). For a radical critique of Ivorian

development: Samir Amin, *Neo-Colonialism in West Africa* (Harmondsworth: Penguin, 1973), chap. 4. A favourable assessment: A. Taylor *et al.*, 'Ivory Coast: Political Stability and Economic Growth', *Focus*, XXVII (1977), part I in no. 3, pp. 1–15, and part II in no. 4, pp. 1–14. On the extent of regional and social inequality, see part I, pp. 13–14, and part II, pp. 2–3 and 5.

17. See World Bank, *Ivory Coast* (n. 14 above), p. 16 for quote, and chap. 3 for policies. On labour controls: Jon Woronoff, *West African Wager: Houphouet v. Nkrumah* (Metuchen, N J: Scarecrow Press, 1972), pp. 220–1.

18. In general, see Rondos, 'Ivory Coast' (n. 15 above), pp. 6–7. Data on foreign ownership: World Bank, *Ivory Coast* (n. 14 above), p. 50. For a case study of foreign influence in cotton and textile production: B. Campbell, 'Neo-colonialism, Economic Dependence and Political Change', *Review of African Political Economy*, 2 (1975), pp. 36–52.

19. Data from Heather Joshi, Harold Lubell and Jean Mouly, *Abidjan: Urban Development and Employment in the Ivory Coast* (Geneva: ILO, 1976), pp. 103, 112.

20. Data from *ibid.*, p. 21, 103, 112 and 12. Industrial study: P.-L. Esparre, 'Le travailleur de Côte d'Ivoire: une intégration difficile à la société industrielle', *Genève–Afrique*, VI, 2 (1967), pp. 181–92.

21. On the colonial policies, see Ruth Schacter Morgenthau, *Political Parties in French-Speaking West Africa* (Oxford: Clarendon Press, 1964), pp. 169–70, 176.

22. Quote: Immanuel Wallerstein, *The Road to Independence: Ghana and the Ivory Coast* (The Hague: Mouton, 1964), p. 64. Information on the PDCI: Aristide Zolbert, *One-Party Government in the Ivory Coast* (Princeton: Princeton University Press, 1964). On the role of the planter bourgeoisie: B. Campbell, 'Social Change and Class Formation in a French West African State', *Canadian Journal of African Studies*, VIII, 2 (1974), pp. 285–306.

23. On the role of the chiefs: Zolberg, *One-Party Government* (n. 22 above), pp. 21, 102. On the role of the educated elite: I. Wallerstein, 'Elites in French-Speaking West Africa: The Social Basis of Ideas', *Journal of Modern African Studies*, III, 1 (1965), pp. 22–3. On the role of the rural bourgeoisie: Campbell, 'Social Change' (n. 22 above), pp. 296–306.

24. On state capitalism: World Bank, *Ivory Coast* (n. 14 above), p. 238; and Taylor *et al.*, 'Ivory Coast' (n. 16 above), Part II, pp. 2–4. On bureaucratic bourgeoisie, see Rondos, 'Ivory Coast' (n. 15 above), p. 8, and Campbell, 'Social Change' (n. 22 above), quote p. 298.

25. See R. Joseph, 'The Gaullist Legacy: Patterns of French Neo-Colonialism', *Review of African Political Economy*, 6 (1976), pp. 4–13.

26. On 'Dialogue' and co-operation, see Taylor *et al.*, 'Ivory Coast' (n. 16 above) part I, quotes p. 12; and Michael Cohen, *Urban Policy and Political Conflict in Africa: A Study of the Ivory Coast* (University of Chicago Press, 1974), chaps. 6 and 7. On the role of the PDCI: Rondos, 'Ivory Coast' (n. 15 above), quote p. 8.

27. Critique of 'economistic' dependency theory: P. Kennedy, 'African Businessmen and Foreign Capital: Collaboration or Conflict?', *African Affairs*, LXXVI, 303 (1977), pp. 177–94. On economic nationalism:

T. H. Moran, 'Multinational Corporations and Dependency', *International Organization*, XXXII, 1 (1978), pp. 86–7.

28. For information on the nature and extent of public expropriations and indigenization programmes: L. L. Rood, 'Nationalization and Indigenization in Africa', *Journal of Modern African Studies*, XIV, 3 (1976), pp. 427–47. Refer also to B. Stefanski, 'Nationalization of Foreign-Owned Assets in Africa', *Africana Bulletin*, XXIII (1976), pp. 47–80.

29. J. F. Petras, 'State Capitalism and the Third World', *Journal of Contemporary Asia*, VI, 4 (1976), p. 436. On the roots of the state-capitalist approach in the colonial experience, see B. van Arkadie, 'Development of the State Sector and Economic Dependence', in D. P. Ghai (ed.), *Economic Independence in Africa* (Nairobi: East African Literature Bureau, 1973), p. 96.

30. C. Meillasoux, 'A Class Analysis of the Bureaucratic Process in Mali', *Journal of Development Studies*, VI (1969–70), pp. 106–7.

31. See Richard Sklar, *Corporate Power in an African State: The Political Impact of Multinational Mining Companies in Zambia* (Berkeley: University of California Press, 1975), pp. 198–207, quote p. 290; and Sklar, 'Postimperialism: A Class Analysis of Multinational Corporate Expansion', *Comparative Politics*, IX, 1 (1976), pp. 75–92.

32. Statistics from World Bank, *World Development Report, 1978*, table 2, p. 78.

33. Sympathetic observer: A. Hazlewood, 'Kenya: Income Distribution and Poverty – An Unfashionable View', *Journal of Modern African Studies*, XVI, 1 (1978), pp. 81–96. ILO, *Employment, Incomes and Equality: A Strategy for Increasing Productive Employment in Kenya* (Geneva: ILO, 1972), pp. 94, 98.

34. Steven Langdon, 'The State and Capitalism in Kenya', *Review of African Political Economy*, 8 (1977), p. 96. This view is elaborated in Langdon, 'Multinational Corporations in the Kenya Political Economy', in Raphael Kaplinsky (ed.), *Readings on the Multinational Corporation in Kenya* (Nairobi: Oxford University Press, 1978), pp. 134–200. 'Early' Leys views: *Underdevelopment in Kenya* (London: Heinemann Educational Books, 1974).

35. See C. Leys, 'Capital Accumulation, Class Formation and Dependency–The Significance of the Kenyan Case', *The Socialist Register, 1978* (London: Merlin Press, 1979), pp. 241–66; and N. Swainson, 'The Rise of a National Bourgeoisie in Kenya', *Review of African Political Economy*, 8 (1977), pp. 39–55. They both acknowledge an intellectual debt to Michael Cowan, whose views appear in Cowan *et al.*, (eds.), *Essays on Capital and Class in Kenya* (forthcoming).

36. See Leys, 'Capital Accumulation' (n. 35 above), pp. 259–60.

37. See van Zwannenberg, *Colonial Capitalism* (n. 11 above). Useful sources on the colonial state: J. Lonsdale and B. J. Berman, 'Coping with the Contradictions: The Development of the Colonial State in Kenya, 1895–1914', *Journal of African History*, XX (1979), pp. 487–505; and B. J. Berman and J. Lonsdale, 'Crises of Accumulation, Coercion and the Colonial State: The Development of the Labour Control System in Kenya, 1919–1929', *Canadian Journal of African Studies*, XIV (1980), pp. 55–81.

38. Leys, *Underdevelopment in Kenya* (n. 34 above), chaps. 4 and 5. On foreign

investment, see also Technical Paper No. 16 in ILO, *Employment* (n. 33 above), pp. 437–57.

39. Leys, *Underdevelopment in Kenya* (n. 34 above), pp. 112–35, 147 (where quote appears).

40. N. Swainson, 'State and Economy in Post-Colonial Kenya, 1963–1978', *Canadian Journal of African Studies*, XII, 3 (1978), pp. 362–81. Similar conclusions are drawn by Leys in 'Capital Accumulation' (n. 35 above) and his complementary article entitled 'Development Strategy in Kenya since 1971', *Canadian Journal of African Studies*, XIII, 1/2 (1979), pp. 295–320.

41. On the persistence of advanced-country technology despite advice (e.g. in the ILO's 1972 Report on Kenya) to encourage the informal sector: F. Stewart 'Kenya: Strategies for Development', in Ukandi Damachi, Guy Routh and A.-R. Ali Taha (eds.), *Development Paths in Africa and China* (London: Macmillan, 1976), pp. 80–111.

42. On the development of labour controls: Richard Sandbrook, *Proletarians and African Capitalism: The Kenyan Case, 1960–1972* (Cambridge: Cambridge University Press, 1975), chap. 2. On departicipation and control: M. Tamarkin, 'The Roots of Political Stability in Kenya', *African Affairs*, LXXII, 308 (1978), pp. 297–320. Allegations regarding the assassination: Kenya, National Assembly, *Report of the Select Committee on the Disappearance and Murder of the. . . Honourable J. M. Kariuki, M. P.*, 3 June 1975.

43. J. Moris, 'The Transferability of the Western Management Tradition into the Public Service Sectors: An East African Perspective', *Taamuli*, VI, 1/2 (1976), p. 60 (emphasis in original).

44. This section draws heavily upon J. R. Nellis, 'Maladministration: Cause or Result of Underdevelopment? The Algerian Example', *Canadian Journal of African Studies*, XIII, 3 (1980), pp. 347–70.

45. Moris, 'Transferability' (n. 43 above).

46. Nellis, 'Maladministration' (n. 44 above), p. 415.

47. Roger D. Hansen, *Beyond the North–South Stalemate* (New York: McGraw-Hill, 1979), p. 273. Compare with the notion of 'reform capitalism' in Irma Adelman and Sherman Robinson, *Income Distribution Policy in Developing Countries* (Stanford: Stanford University Press, 1978), p. 198.

48. On this definition of national populism, see Petras, 'New Perspectives' (n. 9 above), pp. 298, 300; and T. di Telli, 'Populism and Reform in Latin America', in Claudio Veliz (ed.), *Obstacles to Change in Latin America* (London: Oxford University Press, 1965), p. 47.

49. On the conditions for populism, see di Telli, 'Populism' (n. 48 above), p. 54; and K. P. Erickson, 'Populism and Political Control of the Working Class in Brazil', *Proceedings of the Pacific Coast Council on Latin American Studies*, IV (1975), pp. 125–6.

50. Negative view of Latin American populism; L. Hennessy, 'Latin America', in Ghita Ionescu and Ernest Gellner (eds.), *Populism: Its Meaning and National Characteristics* (London: Weidenfeld & Nicolson, 1969), p. 35; and Erickson, 'Populism' (n. 49 above), pp. 121–3. More positive view: di Telli, 'Populism' (n. 48 above), pp. 51–2 (for quote); and A. Stewart, 'The Social Roots', in Ionescu and Gellner (eds.), *Populism*, p. 189.

51. See G. O'Donnell, *Modernization and Bureaucratic Authoritarianism*,

Institute of International Studies, University of California, Berkeley, 1973, p. 59; and A. Mendes de Alemide and M. Lowry, 'Union Structure and Labor Organization in the Recent History of Brazil', *Latin American Perspectives*, III, 1 (1976), pp. 98–119.

52. Petras, 'New Perspectives' (n. 9 above), p. 300.

53. For this argument, see F. Lisk, 'Conventional Development Strategies and Basic-Needs Fulfilment', *International Labour Review*, CXV, 2 (1977), p. 183.

54. Michael Harrington, *Socialism* (New York: Bantam Books, 1972), quotes p. 225, 296. See also, S. Amin, 'Capitalism, State Collectivism and Socialism', *Monthly Review*, XXIX, 2 (1977), pp. 40–1.

55. Quote from J. F. Revel in his *Without Marx or Jesus* (New York: Doubleday, 1971), p. 19. On 'caricatures', see S. Decalo, 'Ideological Rhetoric and Scientific Socialism in Benin and Congo/Brazzaville', in Carl Rosberg and Thomas Callaghy (eds.), *Socialism in Sub-Saharan Africa*, Research Series No. 38, Institute for International Studies, University of California, Berkeley, 1979, pp. 231–64, quote p. 231. On Ethiopia, see M. Chege, 'The Revolution Betrayed: Ethiopia, 1974–9', *Journal of Modern African Studies*, XVII, 3 (1979), pp. 359–80, quote p. 379.

56. Harrington, *Socialism* (n. 54 above), pp. 288–95.

57. *Ibid.*, p. 270.

58. For a well-balanced, recent assessment of poverty-amelioration in China, see three articles by N. Eberstadt entitled 'Has China Failed?', 'Women and Education in China: How Much Progress?' and 'China: How Much Success?' in *New York Review of Books*, XXVI, 5, 6 and 7 and (1979); and in Cuba, see N. Amaro and C. Mesa-Lago, 'Inequality and Classes', in Mesa-Lago (ed.), *Revolutionary Change in Cuba* (Pittsburgh: University of Pittsburgh Press, 1971); Jorge Dominquez, *Cuba: Order and Revolution* (Cambridge, Mass: Belknap, 1978); and Carmelo Mesa-Lago, *Cuba in the 1970s*, rev. edn (Albuquerque: University of New Mexico Press, 1978). For an (ultimately unpersuasive) critique of those (like Mesa-Lago) who depict Cuba as essentially bureaucratic-collectivist, see F. Fitzgerald, 'A Critique of the "Sovietization of Cuba" Thesis', *Science and Society*, XLII, (1978), pp. 1–32.

59. Compare this analysis with that in: T. M. Callaghy, 'The Difficulties of Implementing Socialist Strategies of Development in Africa', in Rosberg and Callaghy (eds.), *Socialism in Sub-Saharan Africa* (n. 55 above), pp. 112–29.

60. For definitions of the socialist-transition strategy, see B. U. Mwansasu and C. Pratt, 'Tanzania's Strategy for the Transition to Socialism', in Mwansasu and Pratt (eds.), *Towards Socialism in Tanzania* (Toronto: University of Toronto Press, 1979), p. 6. See also, Harrington, *Socialism* (n. 54 above), pp. 377–8, 417–8.

61. Issa Shivji, *Class Struggles in Tanzania* (New York: Monthly Review Press, 1976), quote p. 64. In the same vein, see S. Salum, 'The Tanzanian State: A Critique', *Monthly Review*, XXVIII, 8 (1977), pp. 51–7.

62. Quote from Cranford Pratt, *The Critical Phase in Tanzania, 1945–1968: Nyerere and the Emergence of a Socialist Strategy* (Cambridge: Cambridge University Press, 1976), p. 241. On intended consequences, see C. Pratt, 'Tanzania's Transition to Socialism: Reflections of a Democratic

120 THE STATE AND CAPITAL ACCUMULATION

Socialist', in Mwansasu and Pratt (eds.), *Towards Socialism in Tanzania*, pp. 206–7.

63. On reducing salary differentials, see R. H. Green, 'Tanzanian Political Economy Goals, Strategies, and Results, 1967–74', in Mwansasu and Pratt (eds.), *Towards Socialism in Tanzania*, pp. 27–31.

64. See Saul, 'The State in Post-Colonial Societies: Tanzania', (n. 6 above), pp. 357–64.

65. The points at issue between 'Marxist' and 'democratic-socialist' interpretations of Tanzania are brought out brilliantly in a recent polemic between Saul and Pratt. For Saul's views, see *Canadian Journal of African Studies*, XI, 2 (1977), pp. 313–39; for Pratt's views, see the same journal, XII, 3 (1978), pp. 407–26. Quote by Pratt in the introduction to Mwansasu and Pratt (eds.), *Towards Socialism in Tanzania*, (n. 60 above) p. 6. Pratt implicitly assumes a considerable autonomy for the Tanzanian state in his emphasis upon the personality and views of Nyerere in the definition of the socialist strategy. See his *The Critical Phase* (n. 62 above), p. 228.

66. Low degree of class formation: R. H. Green, 'Redistribution with Growth and/or Socialist Development: Some Jottings on Tanzania, 1961–74', *IDS Bulletin*, VII, 2 (1975), p. 26. Nyerere's perception: Pratt, *The Critical Phase* (n. 62 above), p. 226.

67. Lack of significant Western economic or strategic interests: C. Hoskyns, 'Africa's Foreign Policy: The Case of Tanzania', in Lionel Cliffe and John Saul (eds.), *Socialism in Tanzania*, vol. I (Nairobi: East African Publishing House, 1972), pp. 97–8. Foreign aid: W. Edmund Clark, *Socialist Development and Public Investment in Tanzania, 1964–73* (Toronto: University of Toronto Press, 1978), pp. 182–4.

68. See e.g. Salum, 'The Tanzanian State' (n. 61 above), pp. 51–7.

69. See Mwansasu and Pratt, 'Tanzania's Strategy for the Transition to Socialism' (n. 60 above), p. 12; and Green, 'Tanzanian Political Economy Goals' (n. 63 above), p. 19.

70. See Pratt, 'Tanzania's Transition' (n. 62 above), pp. 217–18.

71. Policy on rural socialism: Julius Nyerere, 'Socialism and Rural Development', in his *Ujamaa: Essays on Socialism* (Dar es Salaam: Oxford University Press, 1968), pp. 106–44. For a debate on the responsibility of *ujamaa vijijini* for the decline in agricultural output, see M. F. Lofchie, 'Agrarian Crisis and Economic LIberalisation in Tanzania', *Journal of Modern African Studies*, XVI, 3 (1978), pp. 451–75 (who argues a responsibility); and J. Briggs, 'Villagization and the 1974–76 Economic Crisis in Tanzania', *Journal of Modern African Studies*, XVII, 4(1979), pp. 695–702 (who denies the 'peasant resistance to socialism' thesis). I find Brigg's position firmer. Nonetheless, both agree that the regime has de-emphasized rural socialism in recent years. For data on rural development, see Lofchie's article; also for quote, p. 451. For a survey of the vast literature on this subject, see J. S. Barker, 'The Debate on Rural Socialism in Tanzania', in Bismarck Mwansasu and Cranford Pratt (eds.), *Towards Socialism in Tanzania* (Toronto: University of Toronto Press, 1979), pp. 95–124.

72. Situation to 1974: Clark, *Socialist Development* (n. 67 above), chapters 3, 4, 5. Quote p. 98. Change in orientation since 1974: Pratt, 'Tanzania's Transition' (n. 62 above), pp. 223–4. Information on SIDO provided by

Canadian University Students Overseas (CUSO), a non-governmental organization in Ottawa which has been active in funding SIDO projects.

73.   M. A. Bienefeld ably describes this dilemma in 'Trade Unions, the Labour Process, and the Tanzanian State', *Journal of Modern African Studies*, XVII, 4 (1979), pp. 573–93. Cf. I. Parker, 'Contradictions in the Transition to Socialism: The Case of the National Development Corporation', in Mwansasu and Pratt (eds.), *Towards Socialism in Tanzania*, pp. 60–70.

74.   See C. Bettelheim, 'On the Transition between Capitalism and Socialism', in Paul Sweezy and Charles Bettelheim, *On the Transition to Socialism* (New York: Monthly Review Press, 1971), pp. 16–17.

75.   Pratt's assessment: in his 'Tanzania's Transition' (n. 62 above), pp. 218–22, 230–1. Quote on p. 222. Samoff's assessment: in his 'The Bureaucracy and the Bourgeoisie: Decentralization and Class Structure in Tanzania', *Comparative Studies in Society and History*, XXI, 1 (1979), pp. 30–62. Quote p. 43.

4   Urban Class Formation: the Working Class

And so the strike came to Thiès. An unlimited strike, which, for many, along the whole length of the railroad, was a time for suffering, but for many was also a time for thought. When the smoke from the trains no longer drifted above the savanna, they realized that an age had ended – an age their elders had told them about, when all of Africa was just a garden for food. Now the machine ruled over their lands, and when they forced every machine within a thousand miles to halt they became conscious of their strength, but also of their dependence. They began to understand that the machine was making of them a whole new breed of men. It did not belong to them; it was they who belonged to it. When it stopped, it taught them that lesson.

Ousmane Sembene, God's Bits of Wood, 1970

To what extent do the poor and their putative allies acquiesce in accumulation strategies that reproduce marginalization as well as concentration of wealth? To phrase the question differently: who is going to be the carrier of a poverty-eradicating development strategy? An examination of this strategically important question will necessitate an extensive class analysis. This is undertaken in relation to the urban areas in this and the following two chapters. Chapters 4 and 5 provide an analysis of the socio-economic position, organization and range of political consciousness characteristic of those classes and strata that might benefit from an assault on poverty. Chapter 6 introduces a dynamic element in dealing with forms of urban struggle and social control.

Although the urban focus is a limitation, its justification, as contended in chapter 1, derives from the ubiquity of urban leadership of radical social movements.

The validity of urban class analysis

While social differentiation is a striking feature of African cities, the existence of a process of class formation is more problematic. To assert that classes are forming is essentially to claim that certain urban strata, occupying different positions in the productive and distributive processes, manifest some awareness of their inherently opposed economic interests, and some readiness to act collectively to defend common interests in situations where these are threatened. Implicit therefore in the notion of class formation is the existence of at least two classes which are becoming conscious of their opposed interests. Those who would substitute the less pregnant terms 'social differentiation' or 'stratification' for 'class formation' usually contend that the persistence or indeed broadening of traditional solidarities in the cities obstructs the emergence of class identities.[1] It is probably true that a majority of urban-dwellers in tropical Africa retain strong ties with their rural homes, reinforced by their sense of remaining sojourners in the towns even after a prolonged stay, and by their anxiety to safeguard rights to land through the fulfilment of diverse obligations to kin. It is also likely that many of the better-off urban households continue to integrate within them kinsmen of differing status positions, often in a form of clientage relationship. It would, as well, be unrealistic to deny the saliency of ethnicity as the basis of solidarity in many cities, especially where ethnic cleavages are reinforced by religious or economic ones. But does all this make it illegitimate to speak of classes-in-formation?

Perhaps the most elegant study that might lead us to this conclusion is that of Jean-Marie Gibbal, carried out in Abidjan in the late 1960s. On the basis of extensive surveys and other research in a low-income and a moderate-income residential area (Nouveau Koumassi and Macory), he concludes that one cannot conceive of this urban population as constituting social classes in the Western sense of the term. More precisely, he distinguishes three categories of urban-dwellers who differ in their degree of rural orientation, and hence in the extent to which they can evince a class consciousness transcending parochial divisions. These are: the 'townsmen' (citadins), those who were born in the city and possess moderate incomes (that is, large enough to provide the basic necessities of life for four or five people); the 'new townsmen' (nouveaux citadins), migrants to the city controlling a moderate income; and 'proletarianized peasants' (ruraux prolétarisés), migrants (mainly foreign Africans) with incomes below the poverty line.

He finds that the townsmen manifest greater integration into the city and less of a rural orientation than either the new townsmen or proletarianized peasants. The townsmen, in contrast to the last two categories, tend to interact extensively across ethnic lines with people of the same socio-economic level, feel little obligation to assist members of their extended family, participate rarely in ethnically based associations and frequently in multi-ethnic, urban-based voluntary associations (such as sports', tenants' and trade-union associations), retain few ties to their rural 'homes', and rely little upon 'traditional' explanations of personal misfortune in terms of the supernatural machinations of jealous kin or rivals. In short, although the objective conditions of most of Gibbal's subjects (especially the proletarianized peasants) favour the development of inter-class hostility, their social networks, institutional attachments and village-based ideologies are not conducive to class formation. Ironically, it is the relatively privileged townsmen who were the least subject to these subjective impediments to class identification. But this stratum in any case is proportionally small and possesses no common organizational matrix. Classes are therefore at the moment largely latent, though the future expansion of the ranks of the townsmen will create the conditions for class formation and class conflict.[2]

The problem with even this well-executed study is that it does not treat class formation within a dynamic framework. The formation of classes is neither an all-or-nothing process nor a process that implies the exclusion of non-class identities and loyalties. What this notion does require is the overriding, in certain situations, of other bases of solidarity by an identity deriving from the interests inherent in a common relationship to the means of production.

There are grounds for holding that situations do arise in urban Africa in which class identities are salient, and not just on the part of the more privileged, articulate and easily organized classes. One indication of this is the variety of associations created and sustained by common people to protect specific economic interests. These include not only the obvious case of trade unions, often still dynamic institutions at the level of the shop floor, but also the associations of the petty bourgeoisie, artisans (and associated journeymen and apprentices), petty traders, job-seekers, and even of such supposed elements of the lumpenproletariat as prostitutes and beggars. These we shall describe in this and the next chapter.

Another indicator of class formation is the emergence in African cities of a class terminology, even among peoples whose traditional vocabularies lacked such terms. Consider, for instance, the popular Kiswahili terms used in Nairobi by common people to depict the class structure. In general terms, they speak of the *wananchi* (the people) or *wakini* (poor people) as distinct from the wealthy classes, the *wazungu* (white men). It is indeed congruent with theories of neo-colonialism that black people who adopt European lifestyles after independence should be classed with the former colonizers. The people also draw finer distinctions. They may refer to middle-class Africans as *makarani* (literally 'clerks', that is, educated persons). Even within low-income neighbourhoods like Pumwani, the poor recognize class distinctions. They describe the propertied petty bourgeoisie of landlords and small businessmen as *matajiri* (rich people) or *wananojiweza* (those who can afford), terms which they do not apply to middle-class tenants (*makarani*). In Tanzanian cities, people employ the same or similar words. Indeed, the class vocabulary here is more complex, as TANU-CCM has sought to raise political consciousness by popularizing certain pejorative class terms since 1967. Capitalists are called *wanyonyaji* (from the verb 'to suck') or *wamirija* (from the word for drinking straw); both of these carry the connotation of 'sucking dry' or exploitation. A similar vernacular exists also in other parts of Africa.[3]

A final manifestation of class formation is instances of incipient and mature class conflict. Since an exploration of most of these must await chapter 6, I shall allude only to the major forms here. They include the obvious cases – for instance, industrial action on the part of organized workers seeking to advance their interests *vis-à-vis* employers (and often the state), or the lobbying activities of landlords' associations seeking to win concessions at the expense of tenants in the context of an imminent urban renewal scheme. There are also more spontaneous or subterranean instances in most large cities. An example of the former is the occasional urban riot or demonstration, touched off by a general or 'wildcat' strike; a possible example of the latter type is the mounting incidence of urban crime, among which crimes committed outside the low-income areas by poor people do not necessarily meet with the disapproval of the sub-proletariat.

If the study of urban classes thus appears warranted, what model of the class structure is suitable? This is not an easy choice, inasmuch as this structure is made exceedingly complex by the articulation within African cities of non-capitalist forms of production with the dominant capitalist mode. The existing models or particular descriptions of class structure tend to bypass this complexity by drawing a rich and variegated picture of the classes based upon the capitalist forms, while relegating the strata based upon the non-capitalist mode or unemployed to a residual category. This is variously termed the 'sub-proletariat', 'floating proletariat' or even 'lumpenproletariat'.[4] Few writers have paid much attention to the heterogeneous strata of the non-capitalist and petty capitalist forms, though these together may constitute as much as half or more of the urban labour force. Yet one must understand the extent to which the interests of the various popular classes and strata are seen to be congruent, if one is to begin to understand their potential for collective political action. Therefore, this and the following chapter will devote a good deal of space to a discussion of the relations of production, social interactions, aspirations and political orientations and associations of the modern proletariat, educated unemployed, petty bourgeoisie, petty producers, petty traders, and other strata. I begin with the first.

The limits of proletarianization

The organized working class in most advanced-capitalist countries historically played a dominant role in the political struggles leading to the extension of democratic rights and the 'welfare state'. Elsewhere, the industrial proletariat was a participant in revolutionary upheavals. Is an analogous social democratic or revolutionary role for workers likely in the peculiar circumstances of peripheral capitalism in tropical Africa?

This is not merely an academic question. Some contend that organized labour in certain African countries constitutes a 'labour aristocracy', not an actually or potentially dissident social force. What this implies is the formation of a symbiosis between labour and capital, perhaps mediated by the state. Such a relationship, basing itself upon a mutal respect for the other's economic interests within the existing order, would emerge at the expense of the main victims of peripheral capitalist development, the marginalized masses. The eventual implementation of a basic-needs strategy doubtless requires an alternative class arrangement, whereby organized workers affirm their solidarity with the social marginals in a movement for social justice and equality. Only the workers, owing to the special circumstances of their work situation, are likely to possess the solidarity necessary to spearhead such a movement. Is such a class alliance conceivable?

Consider first the peculiar circumstances of peripheral capitalism as they affect the potential power and perceptions of the incipient working class. Not only is the urban wage-earning force in middle Africa relatively small, but it has also only recently achieved stability and remains only partially proletarianized. Roughly 40 per cent of the population in these countries is typically economically active; the proportion of this in salaried or wage-employment varies considerably – from between a quarter and a third in Zambia to under 5 per cent in Mali and Niger.[5] Between a third and half of the *urban* labour forces are wage-earners in the capitalist or modern sector. It is unusual for more than one half of these to belong to trade unions.

Though small, the urban wage-earning force has become remarkably stable since the 1950s. Circular migration between town and country was the characteristic pattern for the bulk of African workers throughout most of the colonial period; indeed, the colonial authorities resorted to directly or indirectly coercive measures to generate an adequate labour supply until the Second World War. Even in the 1950s, an acute observer could comment that the distinction between 'peasant' and 'worker' was artificial in Africa, in that most men were both at different times or simultaneously. In Walter Elkan's words, 'by and large it is wrong to equate the growth of towns . . . with the growth of an urban proletariat'. However, a variety of factors since the 1950s has encouraged those with jobs to make a career of them – including a long-term need for cash in an increasingly monetarized economy, more attractive wage rates (in particular, scales rewarding long service), burgeoning unemployment, and increasing land shortages. The trend, even in the least developed countries, has been towards labour turnover rates in the modern sector comparable to those in advanced-capitalist countries. For example, a vast urban survey in Tanzania led to the conclusion that

> towns are no longer merely employment centres where a peasant goes for short periods to supplement his income. The urban labour force is now a modern labour force in the sense that its commitment to wage employment is not shared with a commitment to agricultural self-employment. Increasing stability has gone hand in hand with the increasing acquisition of skills, the acceptance of industrial discipline, and specialization, resulting in large part

from the accumulation of experience and on the job training. ... And the towns are no longer mere dormitories for transient workers, but now function as the locus of activity of a growing urban community.[6]

The same observation would apply throughout Africa. Survey upon survey reports that annual turnover rates are now much lower than before 1960 or 1950 (in the order of 5–15 per cent) in the large firms and government, and that the proportion of urban workers resident in town for ten or twenty years is on the increase.[7]

Yet this stable work force remains only partially proletarianized. Proletarianization is the process of creating a 'free' labour market by the separation of individuals from their means of production. But though most urban workers now apparently intend to remain in town for a considerable time, often until retirement, a majority of them still possess rights to land. In East Africa, for instance, roughly three-quarters of samples of industrial workers in the late 1960s and early 1970s acknowledged rights to land. Most workers are therefore not wholly dependent upon selling their labour power to survive (though the land to which many have access is too meagre to support a large family).[8]

This retention of land rights would normally be conducive to the maintenance of a rural orientation. There is in fact substantial evidence regarding the extensive rural links of many urban inhabitants. 'Throughout Subsaharan Africa urban dwellers regularly visit their rural homes where they bring gifts, find wives, maintain land rights, build houses, intend to retire eventually, want to be buried; they receive gifts, offer hospitality to visitors from home, and help new arrivals in town.' Another practice reported in numerous surveys is that of making regular or irregular remittances to rural kin, the sum remitted constituting as much as 10–20 per cent of a worker's take-home pay. In addition, it is not unusual for workers, along with their better-off urban townsmen, to support financially a village improvement society and/or ethnic union located in the city.[9]

Semi-proletarianization, in sum, is evident structurally in the retention by most workers of land rights and culturally in their maintenance of extensive links with their rural homes. These two aspects are closely related. Workers (and urban-dwellers in general) continue to fulfil their traditional obligations partly to ensure their economic security in an uncertain future. City people who intend to retire to their home villages feel constrained to ensure the good will and co-operation of their kin, both to safeguard their rights to land and establish an honoured place for themselves within local society. Furthermore, in the absence of a social welfare system, workers must perforce rely upon the generosity of kin and villagers should they fall upon hard times (occasioned perhaps by unemployment). However, they cannot expect generosity unless they themselves have been generous in the past. A rural orientation thus connotes not the tenacious hold of peasant conservatism upon workers, but a rational response to the exigencies of an insecure existence. Such an orientation is only likely to disappear, as suggested by Gibbal in his fascinating study of Abidjan, among the second-generation townsmen bereft of rural assets. Needless to repeat, this component of the urban population, though now a minority in all cities, is rapidly growing.[10]

If full proletarianization has generally not accompanied labour stabilization, what implications does this have for workers' consciousness? This is a difficult question to answer. On the one hand, to the extent that a worker possesses a continuing interest in the land, he cannot afford to ignore village politics and traditional ties. On the other hand, to the extent that he has made a career in town, he also cannot afford to ignore such urban problems as unemployment, wages and the cost of living. These are the issues that normally engage the attention of trade unions. Semi-proletarianization should therefore not preclude the workers' attachment to collective organization and class solidarity.

But can this solidarity ever take a radical form, or do the circumstances of urban employment encourage militancy but not radicalism? There is little doubt that the preponderant (though not sole) tendency of organized labour in most African countries is to forego any overt political role, besides pressure-group tactics, in favour of concentration upon the defence of its narrow economic interests. This 'trade-union consciousness' makes no connections between socio-political grievances and the workers' specific industrial grievances and protests. Obviously, the political effect of such an orientation on the part of powerful sectors of the working class is to stabilize the development of peripheral capitalism. The explanation of this politically quiescent and even conservative behaviour is often phrased in terms of the 'labour aristocracy' thesis. If this thesis is generally sound, then the radical potential of the leading working-class sectors can be discounted. But is it sound?

A 'labour aristocracy'?

'Labour aristocracy', used descriptively, has long possessed considerable polemical appeal. Considered as a theory of political behaviour, however, it lacks both conceptual clarity and explanatory power. In the first place, ambiguity surrounds the stratum to which the theory refers. Various authors have typified any one of three strata of organized workers as labour aristocrats, while one (Lenin) used the term at various times to apply to all three: the trade-union leadership, the skilled upper stratum, and the whole of the organized (especially urban) working class. In the case of African labour, Frantz Fanon is, of course, the best-known exponent of the view that unionized urban workers as a whole are a relatively pampered and thus conservative force. Giovanni Arrighi and John Saul, on the other hand, initially identified the skilled and semi-skilled workers in international corporations, along with the salariat ('elite' and 'sub-elite'), as the labour aristocracy. The empirical validity of each characterization will receive consideration below.[11]

In the second place, the theory is deficient in explanatory power even when its referent is clear. The original Leninist formulation, at its most elegant, explained the alleged conservatism and Philistinism of certain leading segments of European working classes by reference to both their relatively privileged income position and the security of their employment. Both of these benefits were facilitated by the super-profits derived from the exploitation of non-Western areas by the monopolistic firms who employed the putative labour aristocrats. Translated into the African context, this theory, in its most complex form, can be summarized in three interrelated propositions:

1. The leading segment of the urban working class, employed either by state agencies, state corporations or transnational corporations, has a privileged income position relative to the semi-proletarianized peasants in town and the rural masses.

2. This privileged employment is secure owing to the monopolistic or oligopolistic power of their employers (especially because increased labour costs can typically be passed on to consumers or the public).

3. In these circumstances, the labour aristocrats can see their interests as linked to the persistence of peripheral capitalism and its attendant dominant classes, and as separate from those of the peasants and urban poor. Hence, the leading segment of the working class is both politically quiescent and conservative, and able to impose these orientations upon the labour movement as a whole.

Consider first a methodological problem with this formulation. While working classes at all times and in all places have been internally differentiated and privileged in comparison with other social forces, some of the working classes have assumed a radical orientation and others a conservative one. The fact of income differentials *per se* explains little. For the theory to possess any explanatory power, it must estimate the income differential that allegedly generates, in conjunction with secure employment, complacency and conservatism on the part of workers. Without some rough measure, the thesis easily collapses into a tautology: the labour aristocrats are conservative because they are relatively privileged and secure, and one knows that they are sufficiently priviliged and secure because they are conservative. Only Arrighi and Saul, to their credit, offer a way to avoid tautology, by suggesting that the semi-skilled workers and others of the labour aristocracy earn three to five times the income of the unskilled workers.

But even if one could demonstrate the general applicability of such an income gap (which, I suggest below, is doubtful), the thesis would still be unconvincing. It is simply too crudely materialist in drawing an unmediated link between objective conditions and political behaviour. What counts in understanding the workers' political behaviour is their perception of their place in society and of the desirability and possibility of structural change; it is doubtful that this is a function solely of differentials between a supposed labour aristocracy and those strata and classes below. The consciousness of workers is subject to many other influences – including, for example, the workers' well-being relative to the bourgeoisie and salariat,[12] traditions of struggle or accommodation with the dominant classes, and the existence of a radical party agitating for change.

If the logic of the theory is dubious, its empirical basis with respect to tropical Africa is also generally unconvincing. That is to say, the gap in living standards and lifestyles between a putative labour aristocracy and more deprived classes and strata is, with certain exceptions, too modest to generate in itself conservatism on the part of the workers. Along with the emergence of permanent wage-labour forces in the 1950s and 1960s came the view, with supporters on both the right and the left, that the organized urban workers as a whole were extracting an unduly large share of the potential economic surplus – at the expense of peasants and/or employment-generation.[13] But the evidence now available, sparse as it is, suggests that this conception of African urban workers is largely unwarranted. Arthur Hazlewood's trenchant comment with respect to the Kenyan proletariat can be more widely applied: the view that workers, even skilled ones, are relatively well off could be 'believed only by someone without experience of the way they live or with his nose firmly buried in the figures'.[14]

There is, obviously, not space in this chapter to discuss all the studies bearing upon the contention of relative privilege. Luckily, some fairly exhaustive literature surveys are available which relate to the existence and extent of the urban–rural income differential. One of these, covering the relevant literature to 1971, seeks as far as possible to control cost-of-living differences and size of household in comparing income levels. It concludes, on the basis of evidence from countries as diverse as Senegal, Zaïre, Ghana, Zambia, Kenya, Tanzania and Botswana, that the differentials between urban workers and peasants are (with the exception in particular of Zambia) modest or negligible. Another survey of wage rates in Francophone and Anglophone West Africa supports the notion that urban workers have not prospered. In general,

> the pattern in West Africa since independence has been one of governments restraining changes in money-wages, and allowing real wages to fall, some-
> times steeply and usually for long periods of time, in face of rising prices. Only
> in Nigeria in 1964 was this pattern seriously disturbed and the policy behind it
> seriously breached.[15]

In considering relative well-being, one must recognize, in the first place, that urban workers bear a disproportionate part of the burden of rural poverty. Study after study has reported that these workers remit 20 per cent or more of their income to relatives in the rural areas, and support large households in the towns. In the second place, statistics comparing the real income of peasants and urban workers are misleading, in that they tend to underestimate the value of rural subsistence production (especially housing, food and fuel) and ignore the added expenses of city living – such as transport to work and higher-quality clothing. The net result of these factors is to diminish, or even in some cases eliminate, the per capita household income differential between peasants and workers.[16]

It is in the light of these considerations that the plight of urban workers in various countries is to be understood. In Ghana, for instance, a statistical study found that the real minimum wage fell by 45 per cent throughout the 1960s; by 1970, Accra's labourers were considerably worse off than they had been in 1939. Price inflation has also worked to the detriment of Ghana's skilled workers. Their real earnings in 1967 were only 70 per cent of the 1963 level, and by 1972 they still stood at only 76·7 per cent of the 1963 standard, which was itself below the 1959 real earnings. (Disposable incomes had fallen even more than these statistics would suggest, in that the rise in workers' *money* incomes meant that these became subject to income tax.) This was the context in which Ghana's Ministry of Health made a rather startling discovery in a 1971 survey. Although an average 69 per cent of workers' take-home pay was spent on food purchases, 'many' workers in Accra complained that they often had to rely upon kola nuts to dull their hunger pains after the middle of the month.[17]

In the Ivory Coast, a sample survey of 1000 manual workers in urban food-processing plants arrived at equally distressing conclusions. This survey sought to expose the roots of the low productivity and high rate of absenteeism of the largely immigrant workers from surrounding countries. The most important factor was found to be the workers' general physical debilitation; this was a consequence of nutritional deficiencies, the prevalence of parasitical and endemic diseases and of alcoholism, and a widespread psychological malaise associated with a sense of hopelessness and alienation from work.[18]

But the situation of the skilled and unskilled workers in Kinshasa has probably been the worst. Here, the real minimum wage diminished by more than 50 per cent in the first eight years of independence – and the economy has continued on its downward path since. An intensive, month-long household survey of the income and expenditure of a small sample concluded that workers' households could not survive on the diminishing real wages. Consequently, all of the employed men engaged in spare-time employment or self-employment, all but one of their wives undertook petty trading, and only about half of the school-age children actually attended school. Even so, the workers (skilled and unskilled) and their families could not afford to buy sufficient food (though 62 per cent of total household expenditures went on this item). These families went hungry as often as those in the sample of unemployed.[19]

Of course, not all groups of urban workers are as wretched as these. The Zambian copper miners are perhaps the most clearly privileged workers' group in comparison to peasants. Indeed, one influential study of the comparative returns to agricultural cash production and urban labour in Zambia contended that it did not pay to engage in peasant commercial agriculture. A hard-working peasant who had in 1964 succeeded in attaining an income level equal to that of an urban worker was, by 1968, 30 per cent poorer in absolute terms, and more than twice as poorly off as the non-agricultural wage-earner. While other writers have dismissed this contention as exaggerated on the basis of a new rural cost-of-living index, they still found the rural–urban differential to be substantial. The average real earnings of cash-cropping peasants rose over 32 per cent between 1964 and 1971, whereas those for African wage-earners increased by over 74 per cent. Furthermore, peasants had probably fallen even further behind in 1973–4 owing to poor harvests. Among Zambian wage-earners, it was the miners of the copperbelt towns – whose average income throughout the 1960s was about twice the average for all other industrial sectors – who contributed disproportionately to this rural–urban income differential.[20]

Has the relative privilege of these copper miners induced a conservative and politically quiescent orientation on their part? Yes and no – the evidence is ambiguous. It is the case that the Mineworkers' Union, qua union, played no part in the nationalist struggle. While labour leaders in the 1950s and early 1960s championed nationalist causes in public and the rank-and-file joined the nationalist parties in droves, the miners' union refused to stage politically motivated strikes and resisted efforts by the dominant United National Independent Party (UNIP) to control it. The politicization of the African miners was thus limited (though not absent) during the colonial period. Indeed, the miners have remained a steadfastly economistic lot to the present day, re-sisting attempts at governmental control of their union at branch level and undertaking unofficial strikes in defiance of a ban on work stoppages.[21]

Yet the case is not clear-cut. In the first place, African trade unions catering for workers much less relatively privileged than these miners were also politically inactive during the colonial era; in fact, political quiescence on the part of unions was more the norm than the exception. This had much to do with the repressive power of the colonial state – in particular, the reasonable fear on the part of union leaders and members that political action by their unions would prompt curtailment of labour's collective bargaining and legal rights. In the second place, intensive interviews with a substantial sample of Zambian copper miners have revealed a political orientation that is far from conservative.

These workers clearly do not regard themselves as a beneficiary of a neo-colonial order. Instead, the African miners tend to conceive of

> the union leadership, white management and a black Government as three pillars of a corporate 'power elite' determined to exploit and sap the workers of energy in the pursuit of increased profits to be used as much for their own private benefit as for the development of the country. It is not just that the miner feels 'poverty-stricken' in comparison with the expatriate . . . but also that he feels inadequately treated by his own Government. . . . Their perspectives are coloured by a small black elite competing for higher standards of living in an attempt to emulate the whites.

These attitudes have prompted considerable industrial unrest in the mines, unrest which has increasingly been met by state coercion against the miners' informal leaders. In these circumstances, it is doubtful whether the miners can be regarded as a stabilizing influence within the Zambian political economy. Their political potential remains ambiguous.[22]

If the urban unionized workers as a whole cannot generally by typified as a labour aristocracy, is it more valid to apply this thesis to the skilled workers alone? The existence of a skilled–unskilled wage differential is not at issue; the problem is to determine how wide this income gap must be in order to generate conservatism among skilled workers. Unfortunately, the studies in industrial sociology that would permit one to relate workers' political behaviour to varying skill differentials do not exist. Arrighi and Saul suggest that the complacent labour aristocrats earn three to five times as much as the unskilled migrants. But as table 4.1 shows, the interskill wage differential in Africa is rarely that wide within any sector of economic activity surveyed. Although this differential varies both by activity and time, it is unusual for a skilled worker to earn even twice as much as an unskilled labourer. In a substantial number of cases, the unskilled earn a wage as much as 70 or 80 per cent of that of the skilled worker. This is particularly likely in Greater Accra and Dar es Salaam.

If the secular trend in the interskill wage differential favoured the skilled workers in particular economic activities, then this could also provide some grounds for considering the latter labour aristocrats. Such data do not seem to exist on a comparative basis.[23] One can only tentatively argue that the pressure within most African countries has been towards the *compression* of inter-skill wage differentials. Insofar as most of these countries have suffered from a dearth of skilled manpower and an abundance of unskilled labour, this assertion may sound preposterous. Yet in this area, as elsewhere in economics with widespread state intervention, institutional forces offset market ones. One such force is represented by trade unions. Where unions organize along industrial lines (as is the norm in tropical Africa), union leaders will tend to favour the demands of the less-skilled workers who

Table 4.1   *Interskill wage differentials, most recent year*

	Textile manufacturing unskilled wage × 100 loom fixer's wage	Printing–publishing unskilled wage × 100 machine compositor's wage	Machine manufacturing unskilled wage × 100 machine fitter's wage	Construction labourer's wage × 100 plumber's wage
Dakar, Senegal (1969)	82 (1970)	49	59	62
Abidjan, Ivory Coast (1978)	81	42	69	72
Yaoundé, Cameroun (1978)	89	46	42 (1977)	66
Greater Accra, Ghana (1974)	82	74	88	81
Greater Lagos, Nigeria (1977)	63	58	76 (1970)	60
Lusaka, Zambia (1977)	41	31 (1978)	44 (1976)	53
Dar es Salaam, Tanzania (1972)	88	73	—	62

Source: Calculated from the ILO's, *Bulletin of Labour Statistics,* 1969–79, 2nd quarter, Appendix, part I
Criterion: Hourly wage established by collective agreement or wage-fixing authority for a fully qualified adult worker

constitute the bulk of their members. Collective bargaining can thus lead to the compression of inter-skill differentials.

Governments have represented another important influence on wage rates through minimum-wage legislation, government wage rates and income policy. Claiming to be guided by a 'fair wages policy', official wage-determination agencies have often granted wage rates to unskilled labour higher than those warranted by the market. In the Nigerian Federal Civil Service, for instance, a labourer's minimum wage in 1953 amounted to just 57 per cent of that of the skilled worker; by 1970, this had risen to 77 per cent. In Kenya, the wage guidelines applied by the Industrial Court since August 1973 require higher proportionate increases for the lowest-paid employees. Since then, the real wages of skilled workers have apparently declined, whereas those of the less skilled have, at worst, remained stationary.[24] Efforts by governments to maintain the pretence of their commitment to egalitarian policies have thus tended to favour the unskilled over the skilled wage-earners.

I cannot pretend to have conclusively refuted in these few paragraphs the notion of skilled workers acting as a labour aristocracy. Indeed, it would be ridiculous even to attempt this. In general terms, one can only observe that skilled workers appear to be neither unduly privileged nor enhancing their relative position. There are, of course, exceptions to this general rule. But one must also point out that those studies of African workers' political action which distinguish among skill levels *have not portrayed the skilled workers as politically quiescent and conservative.* The skilled have, indeed, often served either as the informal leaders of radical political action or at least as participants.[25]

There is one further aspect of the notion of a labour aristocracy that requires a brief comment. To constitute this, a group of organized workers must not only be relatively privileged, but also perceive itself as having interests separate from, and indeed opposed to, those of the lower strata or classes. One cannot infer that such a perception exists merely on the grounds of an income differential and the presence of a large industrial reserve army in the towns. Although the situation will vary from place to place, there are certain widely operating social and economic factors tending to associate urban workers with popular interests and grievances, to make them men of the people. These factors are only now receiving the consideration they deserve.

1. *Common residence, lifestyles and aspirations* It must be remembered that those employed in the modern sector in African cities constitute only a half or less of the urban labour force. With the partial exception of miners and railwaymen, urban workers tend to live in the congested and usually unsanitary low-income residential areas side by side with those engaged in petty capitalist and non-capitalist forms of production, in petty commerce, or unemployed. A consistent finding of anthropological studies of these neighbourhoods in West, central and East African cities is the similarity of life-style and perspectives among households headed by wage-earners and non-wage-earners. These similarities are typically as much as a function of intensive interaction as of propinquity:

> ties among members of the same household, among co-tenants of the same building, among kinsmen in neighborhood kin clusters, among women and between women and men in social reproduction, among friends in bars, churches and other consumption activities, among partners in sexual union,

among adults who foster and instruct each other's children, all these social ties knit together in a web of kinship and kithship, white-collar workers, artisans, organized and informal-sector manual workers, petty commodity producers, small businessmen and women, and petty traders. This is the person-to-person context within which political opinion and future action develops.[26]

Workers, in short, are generally not an easily distinguishable or exclusive group within the common people. In addition, urban workers, as much as their self-employed or unemployed neighbours, maintain diffuse links with their rural homes; the effect of this is presumably to promote a perception of the complementarity of workers' and peasants' interests and grievances.

Furthermore, if there is an aristocracy among the common people, it is not usually composed of workers. It was once thought that all self-employed individuals in urban small-scale activities were poor, eking out a living until they could obtain a secure job in the modern capitalist sector. This, we now know, is a myth. Although there is considerable variance even within a single informal occupation, many of the self-employed earn incomes higher than those employed in the modern sector. The best-off are generally the petty bourgeoisie of landlords, traders, transporters, small-scale manufacturers and hotel or bar-keepers. It is little wonder, then, that the successful petty bourgeoisie often constitutes a reference group for their proletarian, sub-proletarian and unemployed neighbours. Numerous studies, especially in West and central Africa, report the prevalence of petty-bourgeois aspirations among both skilled and unskilled workers, who aim to accumulate the initial capital to enter self-employment.[27] This may well be an increasingly unrealizable dream. Nonetheless, the prevalence of popular petty-bourgeois aspirations among even secure workers, combined with their often indistinguishable lifestyle and inclusive social ties, do not represent the sort of conditions conducive to the formation of a labour aristocracy (*or* a radical proletariat).

2. *Multiple job-holding and alternation between wage- and self-employment*   The common practice among urban workers of multiple job-holding and alternation in employment may also dispose them to see their interests as generally congruent with those of the common people. In the first place, many of the urban self-employed are people who had initially been in wage-employment. For instance, 34 per cent of a large sample of self-employed in the eight largest Tanzanian urban areas had proletarian backgrounds. Even if this proportion is lower in other cities, there is doubtless considerable interchange and alternation, especially in those occupations (such as construction and crafts) closely tied to wage-employment opportunities. While some skilled workers become petty producers out of necessity, having been laid off by a large firm, others voluntarily leave wage-employment to set up their own self-financed

establishments. Conversely, petty producers who have fallen upon hard times will naturally seek skilled wage-employment, though not necessarily as more than a temporary expedient.[28]

In the second place, it is common in African cities for a worker's household to contain at least one secondary earner in informal economic activities. This secondary earner may be the worker himself, who devotes part of his spare time to self-employment, or a wife and/or child may contribute a supplementary income by means of petty commerce, manufacturing, or services. One anthropologist studying a neighbourhood in Accra has asserted that 'multiple informal employment – both with and without simultaneous wage-employment – is almost universal in the economic behaviour of Accra's sub-proletariat'. This perhaps is an exaggeration; nonetheless, the practice of multiple job-holding is common enough to receive mention in many detailed studies of African workers' domestic lives.[29] The effect of both multiple job-holding and alternation between wage- and self-employment is to blur the distinction between workers' and non-workers' households. In this way, these practices tend to prevent the separation of a self-conscious labour aristocracy from the sub-proletariat.

This section has sought to suggest that if economism is a common tendency among organized labour in Africa, the labour aristocracy thesis provides no general explanation for it. This theory is, first, generally (though not invariably) empirically unsound in its application to either urban organized workers as a whole or skilled workers as a putative labour aristocracy. Secondly, it is vague conceptually and simplistic in its crude materialism. Political consciousness has more complex roots than the theory allows.

Workers and urban populism

An interim conclusion is that one should not construe economism as implying active support for the peripheral capitalist order. Assent on the part of workers (to the extent that this obtains) it not tantamount to complicity in a class alliance underpinning a neo-colonial or national-developmental state. This is not to say that Africa's urban workers are destined to become a radical force in conjunction with the social marginals. It is rather to assert that one cannot preclude this possibility on the basis of the labour aristocracy thesis.

Is then a progressive political role for African workers precluded by the absence of a vanguard group to politicize and mobilize them? Should one simply agree with Lenin that workers, left to themselves, are capable of only a 'trade-union consciousness'? Indeed, workers in Africa have commonly had to rely inordinately upon their own resources, with precious little institutional support in their confrontations with employers and the state. There is not space here to expatiate upon the sad history of African trade unions; I in any case refer to this in chapter 6. But the typical story, in country after country, of their rise and atrophy requires mention. Trade unions anywhere tend to have contradictory consequences for working-class consciousness. On the one hand, they serve to integrate emergent proletariats into capitalist political economies by working within the rules established for industrial relations and political change. On the other hand, unions broaden and intensify working-class identities in the process of articulating and representing common interests and co-ordinating industrial action on a nation-wide or inter-industry basis. But, in contemporary Africa, national union officials can more often be found stifling rank-and-file initiatives than articulating common grievances or co-ordinating industrial action. Of course, the state's efforts to emasculate organized labour go back to the latter's origins just before the Second World War; post-colonial regimes, regardless of professed political complexion, almost invariably extended and refined the existing panoply of labour controls and sanctions within a few years of independence.[30] Where the state has essentially incorporated trade unions into its structure (above the grass-roots level), workers must perforce find non-institutional forms of protest – and these will inevitably be localized and sporadic.

In addition to the usual atrophy of union movements, working classes in few African countries have been exposed to radical movements. In those few cases where a radical party either assumed power or was permitted an oppositional role, the radical intellectuals have had a profound influence upon working-class action. In the Sudan, for instance, where a Communist party operated openly for a considerable time, its leadership has been regarded as a major determinant of that labour movement's penchant for direct political action (discussed in chapter 6).[31] In Tanzania, since the move to the left in 1967, and especially since the Mwongozo Declaration of 1971, commentators have linked much of Dar es Salaam's industrial protest to TANU–CCM's propagation of such radical notions as the right of workers to participate in management and political decision-making, and to be supervised by individuals who are neither 'arrogant, extravagant, contemptuous nor oppressive'.[32]

It is the case, then, that along with the absence of a revolutionary vanguard went the absence or weakness of radical consciousness among the urban workers. In view of the limited proletarianization of the African labour forces and the weakness of emergent union movements, it is hardly surprising that during the colonial period

the political history of the African worker . . . indicates a locally-based reactive political consciousness and activism rather than a broadly-based class consciousness. At no period during colonialism have African workers revealed such a high degree of political will and organizational skill as to have posed a major threat to colonial rule.[33]

Much the same could be said in general about the post-colonial period. While occasionally general strikes have contributed to the fall of regimes, the working class, possessing neither the requisite cohesion, organization nor consciousness, saw power pass to the army instead of itself.

Yet it is incorrect to conclude from this that African workers, on their own, are capable only of trade-union consciousness. Applied to Africa, Lenin's formulation surely slights the workers' autonomous political role, thus distorting the historical record. The latter, by casting the discussion of workers' consciousness in terms of either 'trade union' or 'social democratic' (that is, revolutionary) types, has obfuscated the range of possibilities. It is more fruitful to adhere to Lenin's more cryptic observation that 'there is consciousness and consciousness'. In some parts of Africa, segments of workers have evolved at least a 'populist', if non-revolutionary, political consciousness that transcends economism. Populism, of course, is not a specifically working-class consciousness. It is instead a mentality of the under-privileged as a whole who no longer accept the legitimacy of the existing distribution of power and wealth. Its prime feature is a tendency to hold an allegedly corrupt and supercilious elite personally responsible for an inegalitarian and oppressive social order, and to invest all virtue and legitimacy in the common people. While such a perspective provides only a limited guideline for effective political action, it is nonetheless a form of consciousness that deserves serious consideration. That this mentality should have been achieved at all is no minor feat, inasmuch as educational and value systems tend to legitimate the *status quo*. That workers apparently manifest a special propensity for populist notions, and indeed for spearheading urban populist protest, requires some explanation.

On what basis can one talk with confidence about the existence of a populist political consciousness in Africa? There are two main methods of gauging the consciousness of particular groups of workers, and each has inherent shortcomings. In the historical approach, the researcher infers consciousness from the actual collective action of workers; but action is often ambiguous. The alternative – more common in Latin American than African labour studies – is the attribution of political orientations on the basis of a sample survey. The shortcomings in this methodology are too well known to require elaboration. Nonetheless, several recent West African studies that have sought to combine interview research with observations have suggested the saliency of populist orientations among the workers they studied.[34]

The historical approach cannot be dealt with so summarily. One must first decide what action will count as evidence of a populist mentality. In more politically developed countries, an oppositional consciousness would be manifested mainly by the workers' support for certain political parties or their participation in mass demonstrations, rallies or riots. But in the circumstances of tropical Africa, radical movements are not tolerated outside of Tanzania and some of the former Portuguese colonies, while mass demonstrations are suppressed and thus infrequent. Hence, the quintessence of workers' populist protest is the general or wildcat strike which supplements its economic demands with a political critique. Although African labour history is still relatively unexplored, it records many instances in which striking workers crystallized the inchoate socio-political grievances of the common people. In these cases, strikes with wide popular support represented essentially ephemeral protest movements.

Before proceeding to an analysis of this populist protest in chapter 6, we need to consider the structure and orientations of other urban elements, especially those swelling the slums and spontaneous settlements. Any popular movement limited to workers is, under current conditions, unlikely to have much long-term impact.

Notes

1. For this view, see M. G. Sautter,' Les ruraux dans les villes: genèse et différentiation des sociétés urbaines', in Centre National de la Recherche Scientifique, *La croissance urbaine en Afrique noire et à Madagascar* (Paris, 1972), vol. I, pp. 77–89; D. Aronson, 'Ijebu–Yoruba Urban–Rural Relationships and Class Formation', *Canadian Journal of African Studies*, v, 3 (1971), pp. 263–80; and R. H. Jackson, 'Political Stratification in Tropical Africa', *Canadian Journal of African Studies*, vii, 3 (1973), pp. 381–400.
2. Jean-Marie Gibbal, *Citadins et villageois dans la ville africaine: l'exemple d'Abidjan* (Grenoble: François Maspero, 1974).
3. On Nairobi: Janet Bujra, *Pumwani: The Politics of Property: A Study of an Urban Settlement in Nairobi*, report on a research project sponsored by the (British) Social Science Research Council, deposited at the University of Nairobi, 1973, pp. 32, 104, 122. For other cases: Richard Sandbrook and Jack Arn, *The Labouring Poor and Urban Class Formation: The Case of Greater Accra*, Monograph No. 12, Centre for Developing-Area Studies, McGill University, 1977, pp. 41–3; R. M. Solzbacher, 'Occupation, Occupational Titles and Status Perceptions in a Manual Workers' Urban Village (Kampala)', Universities of East Africa Social Sciences Conference, Kampala, 1968; and P. C. W. Gutkind, 'The View from Below: Political Consciousness of the Urban Poor in Ibadan', *Cahiers d'études africaines*, xv, I (1975), 5–35.
4. See, e.g., B. Delbard, 'Les classes sociales', in Groupes d'études dakaroises, *Dakar en devenir* (Paris: Présence Africaine, 1968), pp. 423–40; M. H. LeDivelec, 'Les nouvelles classes en milieu urbain', *Civilisations*, xvii, 3 (1967), pp. 240–51; and P. Worsley, 'Frantz Fanon and the

"Lumpenproletariat"', *The Socialist Register, 1972* (London: Merlin Press, 1972), pp. 193–230.

5. K. C. Doctor and H. Gallis, 'Size and Characteristics of Wage Employment in Africa', *International Labour Review*, XCIII, 2 (1966), pp. 150–73.

6. Quote by Elkan in his *Migrants and Proletarians: Urban Labour in the Economic Development of Uganda* (Oxford: Oxford University Press, 1960), pp. 3–4. On Tanzania: Richard Sabot, *Urban Migration in Tanzania*, vol. II of the National Urban Mobility, Employment and Income Survey, Economic Research Bureau, University of Dar es Salaam, September 1972, quote pp. 191–2.

7. Relevant surveys (or reports of surveys): ILO, *Employment, Incomes, and Equality: A Strategy for Increasing Productive Employment in Kenya* (Geneva: ILO, 1972), p. 92n; K. Bissman, 'Industrial Worker in East Africa', *International Journal of Comparative Sociology*, X (March–June 1969), p. 27; R. D. Grillo, *African Railwaymen: Solidarity and Opposition in an East African Labour Force* (Cambridge: Cambridge University Press, 1973), p. 38; Elena Berger, *Labour, Race, and Colonial Rule (in Northern Rhodesia)* (Oxford: Clarendon Press, 1974), pp. 207–10; M. Peil, 'The Unemployment History of Ghanaian Factory Workers', *Manpower and Unemployment Research*, I, 2 (1968), pp. 11–13; K. Hinchliffe, 'The Kaduna Textile Workers: Characteristics of an African Industrial Labour Force', *Savanna*, II, 1 (1973), p. 30.

8. See Bissman, 'Industrial Worker' (n. 7 above), p. 28; H. Rempel, 'The Rural-to-Urban Migrant in Kenya', *African Urban Notes*, VI, 1 (1971), p. 62; and Sabot, *Urban Migration in Tanzania* (n. 6 above), p. 215.

9. There is a wealth of anthropological and sociological literature pertaining to the urbanite's retention of rural links. See in general (and for the quote): J. Gugler, 'On the Theory of Rural–Urban Migration in Africa', in J. A. Jackson (ed.), *Migration* (Cambridge: Cambridge University Press, 1969), pp. 146–7; and J. Aldous, 'Urbanization, The Extended Family and Kinship Ties in West Africa', in Pierre van den Berghe (ed.), *Africa: Social Problems of Change and Conflict* (San Francisco: Chandler, 1965), pp. 107–16. For studies of specific cases: T. S. Weisner, 'The Structure of Sociability: Urban Migration and Rural–Urban Ties in Kenya', *Urban Anthropology*, V, 2 (1976), pp. 199–223; Marc H. Ross, *Grass Roots in an African City: Political Behavior in Nairobi* (Cambridge, Mass: MIT Press, 1975), pp. 44–54; G. P. Ferraro, 'Tradition or Transition: Rural and Urban Kinsmen in East Africa', *Urban Anthropology*, II, 2 (1973), pp. 214–31; Grillo, *African Railwaymen* (n. 7 above), pp. 44–61; Sabot, *Urban Migration in Tanzania* (n. 6 above), pp. 221–4; Abdul-Rahman Taha, 'The Sudanese Labor Movement: A Study of Labor Unionism in a Developing Society', PhD thesis, University of California, Los Angeles, 1970, p. 31; J. Middleton, 'Labour Migration and Associations in Africa: Two Case Studies', *Civilisations*, XIX, 1 (1969), pp. 42–51; John Caldwell, *African Rural–Urban Migration: The Movement to Ghana's Towns* (New York: Columbia University Press, 1969), p. 152; John Nabilia, 'The Migration of the Frafra of Northern Ghana', PhD thesis, Michigan State University, 1974, pp. 265–99; A. Adepoju, 'Rural–Urban Socio-Economic Links: The Example of Migrants in South-west Nigeria', in Samir Amin (ed.) *Modern*

Migrations in Western Africa (Oxford: Oxford University Press, 1974), pp. 127–36; S. Goddard. 'Town–Farm Relationships in Yorubaland: A Case Study from Oyo', *Africa*, XXXV, 1 (1965), pp. 21–9; and A. B. Diop, 'L'Organisation de la famille africaine', in Groupes d'études dakaroises, *Dakar* (n. 4 above), pp. 301–7.

10.   See Gibbal, *Citidins et villageois* (n. 2 above), part II, chap. 2, and part III, chaps. 1 and 2. On the proportion of second-generation townsmen: J. S. La Fontaine, *City Politics: A Study of Leopoldville* (Cambridge: Cambridge University Press, 1970), pp. 106–7; C. N. Ejiogu, 'African Rural–Urban Migrants in the Main Migrant Areas of the Lagos Federal Territory', in J. C. Caldwell and C. Okonjo (eds.), *The Population of Tropical Africa* (London: Longman, 1968), p. 321; and James Waweru and Associates, *Progress Report No. 5: Results of the Socio-Economic Survey*, 'Low-Cost Housing and Squatter Upgrading Study', Report to the Government of Kenya and World Bank, Nairobi, August 1976, pp. 9, 33, 49–50.

11.   Frantz Fanon, *Wretched of the Earth* (London: MacGibbon & Kee, 1965), p. 98; Giovanni Arrighi and John Saul, *Essays on the Political Economy of Africa* (New York: Monthly Review Press, 1973), chaps. 1 and 2. Saul has recently had second thoughts about the utility of this thesis; see his 'The "Labour Aristocracy" Thesis Reconsidered', in R. Sandbrook and R. Cohen (eds.), *The Development of an African Working Class* (Toronto: University of Toronto Press, 1976). Sharon Stichter has recently used the Arrighi–Saul version of the theory in 'Imperialism and the Rise of the Labor Aristocracy in Kenya', *Berkeley Journal of Sociology*, XXI (1976–7). A view close to that of Fanon has been argued by R. Kaplinsky, 'Myths about the "Revolutionary Proletariat" in Developing Countries', *Institute of Development Studies Bulletin*, III, 4 (1971), pp. 15–21.

12.   As Marx and Engels observed long ago, workers could achieve considerable material advances and yet become increasingly disaffected: 'although the enjoyments of the workers have risen, the social satisfaction that they give has fallen in comparison with the increased enjoyments of the capitalist, which are inaccessible to the worker, in comparison with the state of development of society in general. Our desires and pleasures spring from society; we measure them, therefore, by society and not by the objects which serve for their satisfaction. Because they are of social nature, they are of a relative nature.' 'Wage Labour and Capital', *Selected Works*, vol. I (Moscow: Foreign Languages Publishing House, 1955), p. 94.

13.   Perhaps the most influential statement of this view is to be found in H. A. Turner, *Wage Trends, Wage Politics and Collective Bargaining: The Problems of Underdeveloped Countries* (Cambridge: Cambridge University Press, 1966), esp. p. 13.

14.   Arthur Hazlewood, 'Kenya: Income Distribution and Poverty', *Journal of Modern African Studies*, XVI, 1 (1978), p. 90.

15.   The literature survey is C. Allen, 'Unions, Incomes and Development', *Developmental Trends in Kenya*, Proceedings of a Seminar held at the Centre of African Studies, University of Edinburgh, 28–29 April 1972, pp. 61–92. More recent supportive studies include: K. Hinchliffe, 'Labour Aristocracy – A Northern Nigerian Case Study', *Journal of Modern Africa Studies* XII, 1 (1974); J. B. Knight, 'Rural–Urban Income Comparison and Migration in Ghana', *Bulletin*, Oxford University, Institute of Economics

and Statistics, xxiv, 2 (1972); C. Greenhalgh, 'Income Differentials in the Eastern Region of Ghana', *Economic Bulletin of Ghana*, 2nd ser., ii, 3 (1972); and Hazlewood, 'Kenya' (n. 14 above), pp. 90–2. The quote is from D. Rimmer, *Wage Politics in West Africa*, Occasional Paper, Faculty of Commerce and Social Science, University of Birmingham, 1970, p. 50.

16. On this, see (in addition to the references cited in Allen, n.15), Y. Mersadier, 'Les niveaux de vie', Groupes d'études dakaroises, *Dakar* (n. 4 above), pp. 252–4; Charles Elliott, *Patterns of Poverty in the Third World* (New York: Praeger, 1975), p. 295 (data on Yaoundé and Abidjan); ILO, *Employment Incomes and Equality . . . in Kenya*, (n. 7 above), pp. 348–50; Heather Joshi *et al., Abidjan: Urban Development and Employment in the Ivory Coast* (Geneva: ILO, 1976), pp. 40–1.

17. The statistical study: K. Ewusi, *The Distribution of Monetary Incomes in Ghana*, Technical Publication Series No. 14, ISSER, University of Ghana, 1971, pp. 50, 52. On inflation: F. Lisk, 'Inflation in Ghana, 1964–75: Its Effects on Employment, Income, and Industrial Relations', *International Labour Review*, cxiii, 3 (1976), pp. 368–70. For the 1971 survey: N. A. de Heer, 'The Food and Nutrition of the Adult Worker', *Ghana Academy of Arts and Sciences, Proceedings*, x (1972), pp. 79–85.

18. P.-L. Esparre, 'Le travailleur de Côte d'Ivoire: une intégration difficile à la société industrielle', *Genève–Afrique*, vi, 2 (1967), pp. 181–92.

19. C. and J. Houyoux, 'Les conditions de vie dans soixante familles à Kinshasa', *Cahiers économiques et sociaux*, viii, 1 (1970), pp. 99–108. Professor Crawford Young has informed me that his studies of Zaïre support this view of the situation. Recent statistics apparently reveal that real urban wages in Kinshasa were about 25 per cent of the 1960 level and about the same as those prevailing in 1910! On the other hand, rural people are more highly taxed than urban-dwellers, being subjected to export duties, head taxes and semi-legal or illegal extortion.

20. See C. E. Young, 'Rural–Urban Terms of Trade', *African Social Research*, no. 12 (1971), pp. 91–4. The revisionist view is that of J. Fry, 'Rural–Urban Terms of Trade, 1960–73', *African Social Research*, no. 19 (1975), pp. 730–8. See also, F. Maimbo and J. Fry, 'An Investigation into the Change in the Terms of Trade between the Rural and Urban Sectors of Zambia', *African Social Research*, no. 12 (1971), pp. 95–110. For data on the disparities in income between mineworkers and others; ILO, *Report to the Government of Zambia on Incomes, Wages and Prices in Zambia* (Lusaka: Government Printer, 1969), p. 9.

21. See Robert H. Bates, *Unions, Parties, and Political Development: A Study of Mineworkers in Zambia* (New Haven: Yale University Press. 1971), esp. chaps. 7 and 8; and I. Henderson, 'Wage-earners and Political Protest in Colonial Africa: The Case of Northern Rhodesia', *African Affairs*, lxxii (July 1973), pp. 288–99.

22. For the comparative evidence on political quiescence, see E. J. Berg and J. Butler, 'Trade Unions', in James S. Coleman and Carl G. Rosberg (eds.), *Political Parties and National Integration in Tropical Africa* (Berkeley: University of California Press, 1964), pp. 340–81. The relationship between trade unions and the state in Kenya, and the prevalence of 'militant economism' among workers is treated in Richard Sandbrook, *Proletarians and African Capitalism: The Kenyan Case, 1960–72* (Cambridge:

Cambridge University Press, 1975). The quote is in M. Burawoy, 'Another Look at the Mineworker', *African Social Research*, no. 14 (1972), p. 263. More generally, see Burawoy, *The Colour of Class in the Copper Belt* (Manchester: Manchester University Press, 1972).

23. The ILO's *Bulletin of Labor Statistics* has provided tables on wage rates by occupational categories only since 1969, and the data available on any particular African country are either non-existent or discontinuous and incomplete.

24. See, e.g., F. O. Fajana, 'The Evolution of Skill Wage Differentials in a Developing Economy: The Nigerian Experience', *Developing Economies*, XVIII, 2 (1975), pp. 164–5; 151–2; and M. Cowan and K. Kinyanjui, *Some Problems of Income Distribution in Kenya*, Institute for Development Studies, University of Nairobi, March 1977, part II, pp. 12, 13.

25. See, e.g., S. Stichter, 'Workers, Trade Unions, and the Mau Mau Rebellion', *Canadian Journal of African Studies*, IX, 2 (1975); R. D. Jeffries, 'Populist Tendencies in the Ghanaian Trade Union Movement', in Sandbrook and Cohen (eds.), *Development of an African Working Class*; and A. Pearce, 'The Lagos Proletariat: Labour Aristocrats or Populist Militants?', in *ibid*. See also, Maurice Zeitlin, *Revolutionary Politics and the Cuban Working Class* (New York: Doubleday–Anchor, 1970).

26. Roger Sanjek, 'The Organization of Households in Adabraka, Ghana: Toward a Wider Comparative Perspective', unpublished paper, Queen's College, City University of New York, 1979, p. 55.

27. On petty bourgeois aspirations, see Peace, 'The Lagos Proletariat' (n. 25 above), pp. 288–9; M. Peil, 'Male Unemployment in Lagos', *Manpower and Unemployment Research*, V, 2 (1972), p. 20; P. C. Lloyd, *Power and Independence: Urban Africans' Perception of Social Inequality* (London: Routledge & Kegan Paul, 1976), pp. 111–13; P. Lubeck, 'Early Industrialization and Social Class Formation among Factory Workers in Kano, Nigeria', PhD thesis, Northwestern University, 1975, pp. 258–9; O. LeBrun and C. Gerry, 'Petty Producers and Capitalism [in Dakar]', *Review of African Political Economy*, 3 (1975), pp. 23–4; Jeffries, 'Populist Tendencies' (n. 25 above), p. 276; and Sandbrook and Arn, *The Labouring Poor . . . Accra* (n. 3 above), p. 37.

28. For evidence of these patterns: M. A. Bienefeld, *The Self-Employed of Urban Tanzania*, Discussion Paper No. 54, Institute of Development Studies, University of Sussex, May 1974, pp. 34–6; Kenneth J. King, *The African Artisan: Education and the Informal Sector in Kenya* (London: Heinemann Educational Books, 1977), pp. 114–18; T. Mukenge, 'Les hommes d'affaires zaïrois: du travail salarié à l'enterprise personnelle', *Canadian Journal of African Studies*, VII, 3 (1973), pp. 472–5; Lloyd, *Power and Independence* (n. 27 above), pp. 111–13; M. Koll, *Crafts and Cooperation in Western Nigeria* (Gütersloh: Bertelsmann Universitatsverlag, 1969), p. 21; LeBrun and Gerry, 'Petty Producers' (n. 27 above), pp. 23–4.

29. The quote is from K. Hart, 'Informal Income Opportunities and Urban Employment in Ghana', *Journal of Modern African Studies*, XI, 1 (1973), p. 66. See, on the same practice: Joshi *et al.*, *Abidjan* (n. 16 above), pp. 58–9; Sandra Barnes, 'Becoming a Lagosian', PhD thesis, University of Wisconsin, 1974, p. 55; E. Date-Bah, 'Societal Influences on Work

Behaviour and Interaction of Ghanaian Workers: A Case Study', PhD thesis, University of Birmingham, 1974, p. 169; Sandbrook and Arn, *The Labouring Poor . . . Accra* (n. 3 above), pp. 36–7; Houyoux and Houyoux, 'Les conditions de vie . . . Kinshasa' (n. 19 above), p. 107; Mukenge, 'Les hommes d'affaires zaïrois' (n. 28 above), pp. 466–8; Bienefeld, *Self-Employed of Urban Tanzania* (n. 28 above), pp. 34–6; P. Halpenny, 'Getting Rich by Being "Unemployed": Some Political Implications of "Informal" Economic Activities (in Kampala)', paper delivered to Universities of East Africa Social Sciences Conference, Nairobi, 1972, pp. 43–4; and David Boswell, 'Business and Petty Trading in Robert's Compound (Lusaka) in 1964–65 and Reflections on the Situation in 1974', report prepared for the Development Planning Unit, University College, London, March 1975, p. 3.

30. For a comparative analysis of the means used by post-colonial regimes to control labour, the rationales of governments in seeking this, and the extent of their success, see Sandbrook and Cohen, 'Introduction: Contemporary Working-class Action', in Sandbrook and Cohen (eds.), *Development of an African Working Class* (n. 11 above), pp. 195–204. The state's control of unions is discussed further in chap. 6.

31. Taha, 'The Sudanese Labor Movement' (n. 9 above), p. 242.

32. Mwongozo Declaration, Clause 15. See also Clause 28. On the nature of, and background to, industrial unrest in Tanzania in the 1970s, see J. V. Mwapachu, 'Industrial Labour Protest in Tanzania: An Analysis of Influential Variables', *The African Review*, III, 3 (1973), pp. 383–401; and M. A. Bienefeld, 'Socialist Development and the Workers in Tanzania', in Sandbrook and Cohen (eds.), *Development of An African Working Class* (n. 11 above), pp. 250–6.

33. P. C. W. Gutkind, *The Emergent African Urban Proletariat*, Occasional Paper No. 8, Centre for Developing-Area Studies, McGill University, 1974, p. 57.

34. See Richard Jeffries, *Class, Power and Ideology in Ghana: The Railwaymen of Sekondi* (Cambridge: Cambridge University Press, 1978), pp. 201–3; Sandbrook and Arn, *The Labouring Poor . . . Accra* (n. 3 above), chap. 6; Peace, 'The Lagos Proletariat', (n. 25 above), pp. 281–302; and Gutkind, 'The View from Below' (n. 3 above), pp. 11, 19, 20.

5   An Anatomy of the Urban Masses

> The fact was that so far as we low, uneducated people were concerned, they were all the same; they enjoyed the same things, though they attached labels to one another. None of them ever thought of giving up some of their privileges so that we could enjoy a little ourselves. They had, and we didn't have; and the words they talked were meaningless to us. Neither *communasocialism* nor *neocolosciencism* meant that somebody would stop people dying because they didn't have money to go to hospital; or prevent them from living in houses without ceilings, where ten people had to share one room; or give to public toilets and water supplies the same attention as to income tax and propaganda. . . . They did not mean the coming of a time when there would be no more 'high' or 'low' but only people – the people of Ghana.
>
> Cameron Duodu, *The Gab Boys*, 1967

Writing about Paris in the eighteenth century, Jeffrey Kaplow describes the 'laboring poor' in terms that would aptly apply to many in informal occupations in African cities today. The Parisian poor were then mainly recent rural migrants who had faced a bleak or non-existent future on the land. This labouring poor comprised 'a *mélange* of producers and merchants, skilled and unskilled, sedentary and nomadic' – petty traders, casual labourers, artisans, apprentices and journeymen, as well as amateur and spare-time thieves. This population in general apparently evinced a populist orientation: 'an elemental form of consciousness to which we may not even attach the prefix "class", the kind that is capable of identifying only the differences between "us" and "them". . . .' But the *menu peuple* lacked any common organization or internal leadership that could crystallize common discontents and promote collective remedial action. The only 'positive identifications open to them – with a craft, a province, or an occupational group – were always within the larger category of the laboring poor, never encompassing the whole'. Under these conditions, the Parisian poor in the main passively accepted their lot, and sought to make the best of it.[1]

However, owing to divergent patterns of development, the history of African cities is unlikely to resemble that of Paris since the revolution. Competitive capitalism in Western Europe led to the revolutionizing of the forces of production throughout the economy and the eventual absorption of the labouring poor (or 'industrial reserve army') into productive activities. In contrast, a concomitant of peripheral capitalist development in Africa is the marginalization of a substantial portion of the labour force into unproductive, unstable and poorly remunerated livelihoods. The African bourgeoisie – commercial, industrial and/or bureaucratic – is a *conservative*, not a revolutionary force. To obviate the marginalizing tendency, there needs to be an oppositional agent capable of mobilizing support for a development strategy congruent with the basic-needs pattern. *Unfortunately, however, the necessary mass solidarity to transcend peripheral capitalism is obstructed by the very socio-economic conditions that such development fosters.* The proletariat is small, mainly non-industrial, and only semi-proletarianized though not, I have hinted, powerless. Within the informal economy, the relations of production are not conducive to collective action, and the petty bourgeoisie has ever played an ambivalent political role. The urban intelligentsia constitutes a potential source of political activists, though it tends to be a small, upwardly mobile and culturally isolated group.

Nonetheless, the political situation is not hopeless. The anatomy of the urban masses presented below indicates classes and strata with a differential perception of conflicting economic interests and a differential propensity for organization. The nature of urban struggle will be treated later.

Petty capitalists and petty capitalism

Petty capitalism, a form of production of goods and services defined in chapter 2, encompasses a variety of economic activities. The least numerous are the small-scale industrialists employing a handful of (in principle) independent wage-labourers. Constraints such as the limited availability of credit, restrictive legislation, inadequate infrastructural development, and intensive competition, ensure that few small-scale manufacturing firms will survive and expand without special assistance from the state. Yet even indigenization legislation, I suggested in chapter 3, tends to favour the political insider rather than the long-established entrepreneur based in the low-income residential areas. Nevertheless, there are successful industrial entrepreneurs who have experienced considerable intergenerational and individual social mobility in all African cities containing a private sector. Most of these self-made men come from very humble backgrounds.[2]

Far more numerous are the petty capitalists engaged in the production of services (for instance, building contractors, hotel and bar-keepers, landlords, launderers, garage owners) or in the distributive sector as transporters and/or traders. Commerce is indeed the mainstay of the petty bourgeoisie's economic power. Petty-capitalist merchants range from the wholesalers and shopkeepers to the smaller retailers who sell from permanent kiosks or market stalls that they own or lease. Women enter the petty bourgeoisie chiefly in the role of traders. In West African countries, as is well known, women dominate trade, including the lucrative market trade. Their sway is much less in central and East Africa where men tend to monopolize the best commercial opportunities.[3]

Tales of individuals who rose to fortune via trade are legion in African cities, especially in West Africa. Some of these remarkable cases have even been documented. As early as 1950 in Lagos, for example, some Yoruba market women had capital holdings of £20 000 (sterling) or more while those with more than £5000 in holdings were common. In Dakar, too, such instances of success are far from rare. One renowned female fish trader is reputed to have channelled her profits to create a vertically integrated operation – owning three motor launches and their nets, as well as trucks to transport the catch and a taxi. In light of the characteristic illiteracy of market women, these successes are all the more remarkable. Success, moreover, is normally achieved through a diversification of investments. The following testimony of a Kikuyu laundry owner in the Nairobi slum of Old Pumwani epitomizes this unceasing search for new opportunities:

'I'm only 45 but I've done a lot of things. When I first came to the city in 1934 I was a houseboy, then in 1939 I went over to Kariakor and became a mechanic. Finally I saved enough money to go into business, and in 1942 I got my own shop, selling general merchandise. That's where I was when they arrest me [in 1954, during the Emergency]. . . .

'In 1958 I decided to come to Pumwani, but on my way here I was jailed in Thika for 2 months because I didn't have a pass book. Finally I arrived here, and I still had half of the Shs 600/. . . . I bought a laundry over behind the mosque – it was the kind of business that didn't take much capital. After one year I moved over here. Now I have 3 people working for me part time and I generally make over Shs 300/ a month myself.

'I have 3½ acres at home and 2½ acres of this is in coffee – about 800 plants. We started picking last year and already we got 1400 lbs.

'I also have shares in City Breweries and in a hotel [café]. I saw an ad in a magazine telling about the brewery so I bought a share – it cost Shs 20/– plus Shs 1/50 for stamps and envelopes – maybe its higher now. Up to this time I have 10 shares. I'm trying to get 20 so I leave my dividends there.

'The hotel business is with my friends from Fort Hall, and I'm one of the directors. We meet once every month to discuss how the business is going'.[4]

It is important to emphasize the humble origins of the typical self-made small entrepreneur, for these may well shape his political orientations and political influence. Inasmuch as I have already noted the prevalence of petty-bourgeois aspirations within the proletariat, it should now come as no surprise to learn that many petty capitalists began their careers as employees. Of 118 African shopkeepers in Accra in the early 1960s, for example, fully three-quarters of them had accumulated their initial capital in the form of savings from a job. Similarly, 73 per cent of a sample of 568 African 'heads of establishment' in Kinshasa in the 1960s had established their concerns on the basis of income saved from wage- or salary-employment. A similar background was evident among African retailers in two large squatter settlements near Lusaka in 1970–1. Market traders in West African cities are more likely to owe their original stake, not to wage-employment, but to the trader for whom they had acted as market helper or apprentice. Over half the women in a survey of Accra's market traders had started as a small girl helping her mother, aunt, or a successful friend of the family. Although these young helpers and apprentices rarely receive wages for their hard work, their guardian normally provides, besides room and board, an eventual lump-sum payment or assistance in setting-up in trade or (in the case of seamstresses) a craft.[5]

Not all successful entrepreneurs have had such respectable, if plebian, origins. For some women, the road to prosperity has passed through prostitution, sometimes in conjunction with the brewing and sale of alcoholic beverages. Prostitution, I shall argue below, has in the past represented one of the few potentially lucrative income opportunities for women with little education in African towns. Whereas men dominate trade outside West Africa and allegedly restrict women's employment prospects in the modern sector, the sex imbalance prevailing in African towns until recently opened up other prospects for women. It is perhaps understandable then why some of the more prominent women in low-income areas owe their initial capital to prostitution. It is generally by means of house ownership that prostitutes have become well-established members of these communities throughout Africa. Thus, in Old Pumwani, Nairobi, women own almost half of the rental accommodation even though men dominate the Kenyan economy. In nearby Mathare Valley, women also took advantage of the economic opportunities of prostitution and beer-brewing to emerge as a locally influential and relatively well-off group:

> They are landladies of substance and important brewers. Many run a number of small businesses. Their faces appear on the managing committees of more than one association. They are KANU [Kenyan African National Union] leaders and big share-holders in the . . . Building Societies. . . . Because of their powerful position on the various governing bodies of Mathare, it is they who must liaison [sic] with the institutions of the larger society (Nairobi City Council, the District Officer, and the National Christian Council of Kenya) and as a result they are in a position to manipulate these institutions.[6]

House ownership has indeed constituted an important basis of indigenous capital accumulation throughout urban Africa. Property ownership and entrepreneurship tend to go hand in hand. Of 186 Ghanaian small-scale manufacturers, building contractors and storekeepers in the late 1960s, for instance, virtually all owned urban real estate, the holding varying with the overall prosperity of the entrepreneur. One does not need to search far for the reason. In the first place, housing in a rapidly expanding city is an exceedingly remunerative, or at the least secure, source of income. Consequently, house ownership can free a landlord from the constraint of wage-employment, allowing him or her to embark full time on a career or careers as trader, contractor, transporter or industrialist. Nevertheless, the existing studies do not reveal a pattern of concentrated ownership in low-income residential areas. True, in Sabo, the Hausa quarter of Ibadan, about thirty 'business landlords' controlled over half the housing. But a more typical instance is that of Pumwani, Nairobi, where 360 persons owned the 317 (multi-unit) houses in the area, and only one landlord owned as many as four houses. The same dispersed ownership characterized nearby Mathare Valley – until wealthier citizens moved into this housing market in the late 1960s. But, despite this normal dispersion, landlords do tend to be wealthier and more often engaged in informal economic activities than tenants. Only in a study of Dar es Salaam, a city in which the governing party has discouraged African entrepreneurship, did the income of landlords in the large squatter areas not differ significantly from that of tenants.[7]

In the second place, house ownership allows a landlord in some cultures to build a patron–client relationship with tenants. This may be important for a small businessman who wishes to enhance the commitment of his small labour force. This may also be important for a landlord who, in his capacity as merchant, must deal with itinerant traders. It is not unusual in the *zongos* (strangers' quarter) of West African cities for a landlord to expect concessionary rates or other benefits from long-distance traders in exchange for assured (and free) accommodation. For example, the traders from northern Nigeria (especially in cattle) are crucial to the economic success of Hausa merchants in Sabo, Ibadan; in exchange for room, board, and the business-landlord's mediation between the northern seller and the southern buyer, the landlord receives a commission from the latter. The landlord's control over housing not only permits him to attract these traders as clients, but also allows him to acquire the credit necessary to guarantee the transactions. Housing therefore is 'the most important capital asset of a business landlord'.[8]

Finally, house ownership is important in that it is generally a necessary condition for political influence within a residential area. It hardly needs to be added that this influence, in addition to constituting a valuable end in itself, also enhances one's prospects for further economic success. For instance, for those owning property in the cities of West Africa where the law governing land tenure is complex, local influence is essential. People never know when their title to land may come under challenge; in this event, the support of powerful allies for their claim is invaluable. Influence is also an important asset when the authorities place urban renewal or squatter upgrading schemes on the agenda. It is obviously not by chance (as we shall soon see) that landlords are frequently the major beneficiaries of these schemes. More diffusely, a businessman's political prominence can be good for his business. The case of Luo entrepreneurs in Kampala in the early 1960s is illustrative. Here, Luo members of the petty bourgeoisie vied for leadership positions in the Luo Union and other ethnic associations.

> Though it is not suggested there was a conscious manipulation, the structure of leadership and system of communication did have the result that a leader would soon become known as a 'prominent' Luo, might become popular, and find his bar, shop or taxis patronized more than if he did not enter the public eye.[9]

That there is a link for the petty bourgeoisie between property, political influence and economic success should come as no surprise. Yet this discussion does raise an important question: do urban petty capitalists exercise power and advance their interests on a *collective* basis? Is there, in other words, any sociological reality to the notion of the petty bourgeoisie, manifest perhaps in the formation of organizations to defend and promote common goals?

Indeed, there is a good deal more organization than one might have supposed. One sort of association with long historical roots is that catering for the interests of West African market traders. Associations linking all the market women within a city are potentially powerful bodies – a potential arising not merely from numbers (the Market Traders' Council of Lagos had 63 000 members in 1971, for example), but also from the critical distributive function served by these traders, the ease of membership mobilization owing to members' close interaction, and the influence stemming from the traders' constant contact with the populace. Rarely, however, have market women used their potential power to promote the interests of either women as a whole or traders as an occupational group.[10]

This is so even where, as in Lagos, market traders evince a high degree of organizational coherence. This coherence of the Market Traders' Council of Lagos doubtless owes much to the fact that the bulk of the market traders are both Yoruba women and Muslims. The organizational structure reflects a traditional Yoruba origin. At the head is the *Iyalode* ('Mother of the Markets'), an official chieftaincy title second only in traditional status to that of the *oba*, or chief, of Lagos. Below her in the hierarchy are the chairmen (*Alagas*) of the individual markets, the heads of a section of traders in a particular product range (*Iya Egbe Oja*), and at the bottom, the *O-lo'ri Egbe*, each of whom is in charge of the sellers of a specific commodity (such as yams, cassava, peppers, and so on) within a particular market. There is, moreover, considerable organizational vitality, with for instance regular weekly meetings among an inner core of top *Alagas* and other market representatives. Yet, with all these ingredients of political power, the market women remain 'unassertive' politically. The only public policies for which their association has lobbied (and even then not always successfully) relate to the narrowest of economic goals: the expansion of markets and the improvement of their physical facilities, and the reduction of municipal rental fees on market stalls. In addition, the market women wield *indirect* influence, insofar as governments and political parties (when these exist in Nigera) had constantly to bear in mind the latter's likely reactions in devising policy and legislation. Even when the market traders formed women's wings of parties before their abolition in 1966, their role was reactive, not initiative.[11]

Unassertive influence, at best, also characterizes the political impact of market traders elsewhere, in West Africa and beyond. However, their associations rarely attain the organizational strength of that in Lagos. This generalization applies even to Ibadan, where no overarching traders' association existed in the mid-1960s, and some individual markets lacked a market head or even associations for the various product groups. Where traders' associations do exist, they operate almost exclusively as guilds to keep prices uniform, restrict the number of competitors selling a particular commodity within a market, or perhaps administer a savings or revolving credit scheme. But even as guilds, the efficacy of these associations varies widely.[12]

Why have market traders' associations tended not to articulate and actively press the broad interests of traders (or women)? Explanations usually emphasize the illiteracy of their leaders (and members), their adherence to a traditional, personalistic view of politics (especially in southern Nigeria and Ghana), and the tendency in polyethnic market places for ethnic ties to divide the traders. Doubtless each of those factors is significant in particular cases. In addition, a generic limitation for these organizations is that the drive of market traders to succeed in their individual business pursuits is not conducive to the collective pursuit of societal goals. The competition of all against all restricts the potential power of the market traders.

Among other fractions of the self-made petty bourgeoisie, collective power varies from non-existent to substantial. The relatively prosperous African shopkeepers in some new squatter settlements surrounding Lusaka, for example, in no sense constitute part of a self-conscious class. Not only do they lack cohesiveness and mutual organization, but they also do not play, nor are apparently desirous of assuming, a leadership role in community affairs. Instead, they reportedly engage themselves wholly in the quest for individual material security and advancement. In light of their recent entry into business, however, their individualism is hardly surprising. Established European and Asian businesses had obstructed the emergence of an African petty bourgeoisie engaged in trade during the colonial period. Only after the Zambianization legislation of 1968–9 were many of the African shops set up; this curbed competition by non-Zambians and provided some assistance to Africans wishing to enter the retail trade. While solidarity among these new African businessmen is thus understandably low, this situation may change. Their exclusive urban and entrepreneurial commitments may promote a greater identification of common interests and action. As one writer points out, 'only a few of the [83] businessmen maintain farms or houses in their rural areas. Their future security is tied up in their urban situation. They have cast in their lot with the growing urban society of Zambia.'[13]

In other cities, or rather parts of cities, a longer-established African petty bourgeoisie has clearly evolved a recognition of common economic interests and the organization to protect and advance these. Such was the case in Leopoldville (Kinshasa) as far back as the early 1950s. The Belgian policy of encouraging urban commitment laid the foundations for the emergence of an African petty bourgeoisie as well as a working class. In the 1950s, l'Association des Classes Moyennes Africaines emerged as the organizational expression of a new social class of urban traders and petty producers. This group, according to one observer, evinced considerable solidarity in pursuing its goals.[14]

In Pumwani, the oldest African location in Nairobi, landlords, shopkeepers and traders also early developed a considerable cohesion and a leading position among the common people. With a secure base in urban property, these small entrepreneurs become community leaders during the colonial period. Their dominance was evidenced by their position as a reference group among the African poor, their leadership of religious associations (most landlord-businessmen were Muslims), and their central importance in Nairobi's African politics as brokers and intermediaries between the colonial authorities and the people. Their political influence waned in the 1950s, as the educated African politicians and bureaucrats pushed them aside. Yet, as late as 1970, this local petty bourgeoisie was still able to act effectively to protect common interests. They had an opportunity to demonstrate this capacity when, in the face of a decision by City Council to demolish part of Pumwani, their organizations obtained a very favourable position for the displaced landlords in the new housing development. Indeed, the entrepreneurs' two associations, the Pumwani Landlords' Association and the Pumwani Traders' Association (whose membership and even executive have overlapped), are still the most influential organizations within Pumwani (though not within Nairobi as a whole). In the urban-renewal controversy in 1970, to take a case in point, the Landlords' Association put itself forward before the Nairobi City Council as the representative of all of Pumwani. The petty capitalists succeeded in this tactic, in Pumwani as in other urban settlements in Africa, owing to the absence of any community association they did not dominate.[15]

Where the petty bourgeoisie is influential, what is the societal significance of their influence? Are small entrepreneurs necessarily a conservative force, or could they lead or at least join a popular movement for redistribution and social justice? The views of Marx and

Engels on this subject are well known. 'The lower middle class, the small manufacturer, the shopkeeper, the artisan, the peasant, all these fight against the bourgeoisie', they observed with respect to Western Europe, but only 'to save from extinction their existence as fractions of the middle class'. This meant that 'they are therefore not revolutionary, but conservative. Nay more, they are reactionary for they try to roll back the wheel of history'. This observation has considerable relevance to the political orientation of the African urban petty bourgeoisie today.[16]

Consider the contradictory impulses to which the latter is subject. On the one hand, there is evidence that, in some cities at least, the self-made entrepreneurs evince hostility towards foreign capital and the indigenous bourgeoisie. What provokes this is the state's role in subsidizing and fostering large-scale capitalist enterprises at the expense of small indigenous businesses, and/or the unfair advantages provided for entrepreneurs who are 'political insiders'. On the other hand, the petty bourgeoisie is in the uncomfortable position of forming a relatively privileged group within the low-income neighbourhoods, and, moreover, of accumulating their wealth from the labour and consumption of their poor neighbours. What is more, these small businessmen typically live in societies which still place a high value upon commitment to public rather than individual welfare. In principle, a rising entrepreneur is free to obviate these conflicting pressures by removing his household to a higher-income residential area. But this rarely represents a practical option. Not only are rents in the more fashionable areas exorbitant, but the small entrepreneur, often successful only at middle-age and still only semi-literate, would hardly feel at home outside the indigenous ambiance of his old neighbourhood. But if petty capitalists remain embedded within their old networks, they must perforce protect their local dominance while ensuring that popular animosity focuses elsewhere. In short, the exigencies of personal survival suggest that while the petty bourgeoisie may share and indeed foster urban populism, their hostility to the establishment will not debouch into a radical critique or movement.

One can best demonstrate the conservative political implications of the ambivalent position of the petty entrepreneurs by reference to a specific case. Agege, a suburb of metropolitan Lagos containing about 80 000 mostly poor, self-employed and wage-earning Yoruba, is in some respects typical of other low-income areas. There is the familiar pattern of a small group of well-to-do landlord-entrepreneurs who live in the area and dominate its political life. Apparently, the acquisitive activities of these 'Big Men' do not generate among the *mekunnu* (common people) a sense of exploitation and animus. To the contrary, the successful business men are

greatly admired and widely and sincerely deferred to in their neighbourhoods. *Mekunnu* generally greet and salute them such as they would defer to a village headman or senior office holder of the Yoruba political kingdoms from which most people have migrated to Agege over the past 20 or 30 years.

One important basis for this popular respect and even popular emulation is the ostensible adherence of successful businessmen to the traditional Yoruba normative code. That is, they are anxious to impress upon the public their humble origins, the role that hard work and native intelligence played in their success, and their willingness to use their wealth and political influence to advance the interests of the less fortunate as well as themselves. In addition, this petty bourgeoisie fully subscribes to a form of populist ideology that ranges 'we', the local community, against 'them', the supercilious and corrupt military, political and civil service elite who benefits at the expense of the people. The form of solidarity thus fostered pits the local entrepreneurs and the common people against the dominant sectors – but only at the level of popular notions.

There are certain unfortunate consequences of these patterns for class formation and the emergence of popular social movements. It is true that the patronage of the local Big Men represents an important source of support for some among the poor. But these personalistic patron–client ties have the effect of atomizing the poor, hence contributing to a situation where each seeks a personal solution to generic problems of poverty. Moreover, this individualistic tendency is enhanced by

the implicit message which underpins virtually all the performances of the Big Men and the well-to-do is that getting on and getting up (and even getting by) in the modern urban situation can only be achieved through individual endeavour. The ideology which they espouse . . . is that of self-help. It is one which is against collective action and indeed as situationally defined is apolitical. . . . The means to advancement rests in the development of entrepreneurial skills and personal networks. Competitive individualism is held up as the natural order of things as is the social hierarchy emergent from such competition. . . . In sum, in attempting to legitimate their own positions of privilege within the community, they also legitimate the economic system of relationships and declare that system to be right and proper. . . .

Far from being unique to Agege, this pattern or similar patterns have been reported for other West African urban areas such as Mushin, Lagos and the *zongos* of Accra and Kumasi.[17]

In East Africa, too, the urban petty bourgeoisie has had a conservative influence. In Pumwani, Nairobi, there is the same admixture of landlord-entrepreneurs, wage-earners and self-employed as in Agege – though of course the cultural context is much different. Here, too, the successful businessmen seek to define themselves as part of a larger community, as *maskini* (poor people). But the common people in this case manifest some ambivalence towards the material success of the local petty capitalists: they apparently oscillate between regarding the latter as mean and greedy people, and regarding them as 'natural patrons' to whom they can turn in time of difficulty. For their part, the businessmen are generally quite willing to assume the role of patron – dispensing, for instance, credit at their shops, or reductions in, or remission of, rent to those suddenly destitute or too ill to work. But this limited redistribution of wealth to the poor comes at a price. Successful businessmen, as patrons and models for emulation, encourage individualistic strategies of advancement and petty-bourgeois aspirations that, for most, are unrealizable. There is the additional factor that the organizations of landlords and traders, though pretending to speak for the whole Pumwani community, instead undertake political action calculated to advance the narrow economic interests of their members (as in the case of the 1970 urban renewal programme). In short, the small entrepreneurs are

> of necessity supporters of the status quo, since they fear that political change may threaten their vested economic interests. If this support is of a cynical and self-interested kind, this is merely because they are insecure operators in the interstices of an economic and political system of which they are not the full beneficiaries.[18]

The marginalized labouring poor

Much more numerous than the petty bourgeoisie in the low-income neighbourhoods is the labouring poor. This is the term employed by historians to describe the common people of some European cities in the eighteenth and early nineteenth centuries – in the period before capitalist industrialization largely destroyed the pre-capitalist modes of production. The labouring poor comprise, not a single class, but a congeries of strata whose only common trait is a hard and precarious living made outside capitalist production. The occupations in question range from the petty producers, along with their apprentices and journeymen, to the petty traders and providers of petty services, casual labourers, urban cultivators, and illicit and parasitical occupations – prostitutes, bootleggers, dope-peddlers, beggars and petty thieves. Since these strata do not constitute a single social class, they obviously cannot attain a distinctive class consciousness. Indeed, their solidarity is characteristically low. Individuation, both reflected in and fostered by the patron–client relations just discussed, is more fundamentally a function of the individualistic relations of production in which the labouring poor are engaged. Their political consciousness thus remains rudimentary, in the absence of external leadership and organization.

The labouring poor in African cities, unlike their counterparts in nineteenth-century Paris, are not, and are unlikely to become, an industrial reserve army. Even under the most optimistic assumptions about economic expansion in peripheral capitalist economies, the productive capitalist mode is unlikely to absorb more than a fraction of the available labour force in the next generation or so. Although, as we shall see, individuals within the labouring poor both desire to secure 'modern' wage-employment, and will succeed in doing so, the bulk are excluded from such participation on a continuing basis. Not dissolution of non-capitalist forms of production but their conservation in a subordinate position is the hallmark of peripheral capitalism. If this is so, the limited political potential of the marginalized mass has long-term political consequences.

PETTY PRODUCERS, APPRENTICES AND JOURNEYMEN

Opportunities for training and self-employment in petty production attract many rural youths to the towns and cities. Margaret Peil, who has conducted sample censuses in eight urban locations in Nigeria, Ghana and Gambia, estimates that roughly one-fourteenth of the male labour force is composed of self-employed craftsmen. This proportion is higher in cities with negligible large-scale manufacturing; in Ouagadougou, Upper Volta, for example, petty producers constitute 13 per cent of the labour force.[19]

The varieties of petty production are basically three. 'Artistic artisans' are those producing works of art, today largely for the tourist and expatriate populations: woodcarvers, weavers, basket-makers, jewellers and goldsmiths. Petty producers of goods for use are generally many times more numerous than artistic artisans. Among these, the tailors and seamstresses are always the largest single group, followed in numbers usually by carpenters. Shoemakers have everywhere apparently declined in numbers, driven out of business by the ubiquitous import-substituting shoe factories. Other relevant sizeable trades in many cities include masons, metal-workers, printers, furniture-makers, bakers and leather workers. The final sort of petty producers (which Maraget Peil only partially included in her estimates of male craftsmen) is the one providing services, both traditional and modern. Examples of the former type are the *mallams* (Muslim religious teachers) and traditional doctors – herbalists, diviners, or a combination of both. These 'doctors', often well trained (with apprenticeships of three to seven years, depending upon the society), have diminished neither in numbers nor importance with the coming of Western medicine. In Nairobi, there were still an estimated 200–300 *waganga* active in 1970. Among the 'modern' producers of services, the most numerous are normally automechanics, followed by barbers, launderers, watch, radio, television and bicycle repairmen, car-painters, butchers, plumbers, welders and vulcanizers.[20]

Although petty production in its various forms absorbs a good deal of labour, surprisingly little is known about its origins and evolution in tropical Africa. A brief comparison of its history in Nairobi and Ibadan will illustrate the wide range of patterns.

The history of African petty production in Kenya is a recent one. In most of the East African hinterland, there was no pre-colonial tradition of local craft communities and a minimal division of labour. Blacksmithing was a notable exception, an activity which in some communities was a skill passed from father to son. The spread of specialized craft communities was a consequence of Indian immigration. The Asian artisans in building, tin, wood, steel, car repair, and so on, faced little indigenous competition and sought to perpetuate this skill monopoly by restricting their expertise to their own communities. Eventually, however, Asian craftsmen accumulated enough capital to move into the lower reaches of the large-scale capitalist sector; once there, they were willing to train Africans to do the less-skilled jobs. As a consequence, these trained Africans took over the production of cheap goods that had been produced entirely by Asians until the 1940s. By 1960–1, this first generation of (often illiterate) skilled Africans was besieged by primary-school leavers who, no longer able to obtain good jobs owing to the educational expansion, sought instead to acquire a skill in the informal economy. This first generation was quite prepared to accept apprenticeships, in exchange for a variable fee and the free labour of apprentices. Consequently, this indigenous apprenticeship expanded rapidly, and has diffused versatile and sometimes innovative artisans and cheap products throughout Kenya.

Petty producers in Nairobi today operate in highly competitive markets. This in part can be traced to the openness of the informal apprenticeship system. Artisans have not only refrained from restricting competition by limiting the number of apprentices, but also adopted such a brief training period that an apprentice can himself be training other youths within a year. In addition, the petty producers of particular products have not apparently sought to maximize their bargaining power by such form of co-operation as common sales policies, bulk purchases of raw materials, or co-operative production. Nor do they yet possess even a rudimentary association to co-ordinate their activities and protect their interests.[21]

Contrast this situation with that existing in Ibadan. Here, traditional crafts such as blacksmithing, goldsmithing, weaving and woodcarving were conspicuous elements of the economy long before the arrival of the British. The principle of organization in these crafts was descent: members of a lineage followed the same craft and shared a common workplace; and fathers trained their sons. The form of organization was the lineage meeting which (among other things) settled disputes, regulated the relationships among producers, and fixed prices. During the colonial period, however, this traditional organization came under strain with the proliferation of new crafts (for instance, tailoring, shoemaking, laundering, bicycle and car repairing) associated with the introduction of new technologies and opportunities. These new crafts employed a different principle of organization, one that was based upon the guild. The traditional crafts also changed in the same direction owing to the fact that artisans needed, and took on, apprentices who were unrelated by blood. However, the apprenticeship system that evolved for non-relatives is far more elaborate than that in Nairobi. Written contracts (in English) are as common as wholly verbal ones; the duration of the apprenticeship (relatively long at three to five years), the fee and the conditions of service are all stipulated in advance; and the 'graduation' of the apprentice is usually marked by a special freeing ceremony and the conferral of a 'diploma'.[22]

The degree of co-operation among artisans in Ibadan also contrasts markedly with that in Nairobi. In the first place, at least twenty-one functioning associations or guilds existed in Ibadan in 1967 whose purpose was to create a degree of co-operation within a competitive environment. These guilds, established as early as the 1920s, aim to determine apprenticeship rules and the wages of journeymen, fix prices, and settle disputes involving members or customers of members. (But note that they do not seek to restrict entry into the crafts.) The better-organized ones also act as professional associations in dealing with the government. In the second place, there are various patterns of *ad hoc* or permanent co-operation among groups of petty producers. These range from the simple sharing of a shop, to the joint purchase of materials and even co-operative production, sometimes involving a network of market traders to distribute the goods as well.[23]

Ibadan and the other traditional Yoruba towns are perhaps exceptional in their early development of petty production, but the pattern elsewhere in West Africa approximates more closely to that in Ibadan than Nairobi. In the first place, apprenticeship in, for example, Accra, Abidjan, Dakar and Sierra Leonean towns is generally longer (three to five years, depending upon the trade), more rigorous and formalized than in Nairobi. The average number of apprentices per master varies greatly both by trade (for example, automechanics average ten apprentices each, and carvers less than one in Accra) and city. But what varies little is the rigour of the lives of young people who, in addition to working nine- or ten-hour days, must also sometimes undertake household chores or nightwatchman duties for their masters. Consider the life of an apprentice in a wayside workshop in Adabraka, Accra:

> The apprentice earns no wages, and the small amount of 'chop money' and food supplied is barely enough sustenance for anyone doing a full day's work. Working a six and a half or seven day week, for three or four years, is a very rigorous, experience. . . . The training is not only rigorous, but, especially for those who become chief apprentices before freeing themselves, it covers every aspect of the practical side of the trade and wayside shop management. Only a young person who is 'committed' to the trade could go through with it.

Journeymen, skilled workmen who usually work on a piece-rate basis for a master and own some of their own means of production (while saving money to purchase the rest), compose only a small fraction of the apprentices in West Africa.[24]

In the second place, petty producers in West African cities are more likely than their Nairobi counterparts to have organized themselves into guilds or associations. The degree of organization is of course variable. In the Gold Coast (now Ghana), to take one case, the goldsmiths and silversmiths organized a guild as early as 1909 in response to efforts by the colonial authorities to establish a European monopoly of gold and its processing. This quickly became a powerful association in Accra, governed by its own chief and councillors. About the same time, carpenters, masons and blacksmiths each established their own guilds, with elaborate rules governing apprenticeship and mutal assistance. These have since disappeared, for reasons that remain unclear. In Lagos, there were many guilds in the 1970s. However, the proportion of artisans who belong to one of these varied from 95 per cent of goldsmiths and 56 per cent of automechanics, to nil in the cases of shoemakers or radio and watch repairmen. Since few craftsmen in most trades belong to the relevant guild, they are rarely successful in setting prices for a service or commodity. They therefore tend to operate chiefly as benevolent societies and as promoters of co-operation – especially by resolving disputes and forming buyers' or producers' co-operatives. A few in some cities also seek to specify apprenticeship rules and fees, and protest to the political authorities if their members' economic interests are threatened.[25]

Although the history and organization of African petty production exhibit considerable variation, certain structural features remain constant. One similarity lies in the impact of colonial rule. Although the competition of imported goods from the metropolitan country undercut some traditional crafts, the net effect of capitalist penetration and the consequent creation of a wage-labour force is to stimulate the petty production of many new cheap goods and services. Another similarity is the constraints which the colonial (and post-colonial) economy placed upon the expansion of these petty enterprises. Nowadays it is often argued that capital-intensive and frequently foreign-controlled large firms can capture any market developed by artisans, if they consider it potentially profitable. Whether or not this is true in all cases deserves careful investigation. It is a reasonable proposition that large firms cannot displace petty producers from markets restricted to the poor alone, such as that in small paraffin lamps or braziers. Even in other markets (for instance, furniture manufacture and automechanics), petty producers can often compete with the large firms owing to their negligible overheads, long working hours and low labour costs. Irrespective of whether petty producers can survive, however, their prospects of accumulating enough capital to expand their operations to any great extent are, as noted in chapter 2, quite dim.

If the entrepreneurial prospects of artisans are limited, what implication, if any, does this have for their political orientations? This is a difficult question to approach given the lack of relevant research. A common view, expressed here in relation to Ibadan, is that

> the social relations of production in which . . . craftsmen and petty traders are involved, and the forms of social organization to which these relations give rise, do not bring them into solidaristic relations with one another in opposition to their exploiters. Their relations with the merchant traders and the 'haves' generally are mediated through relations of patronage and clientage rather than through impersonal market relations, or corporate forms of social organization.[26]

This doubtless accurately describes the predominant tendency. Relentless competition and the individualism stemming from the diffusion of petty-bourgeois aspirations and values are likely to vitiate a collective challenge to peripheral capitalism. The artisans' guilds and associations, where these exist, restrict themselves to narrow economic aims.

There is, however, one potentially countervailing trend. As I observed in the discussion of the modern proletariat, there is significant interchange between petty production and wage-employment, especially in the building trades. One should not exaggerate the importance of this; the ultimate goal of most petty producers who have taken a job is to return to self-employment when conditions permit. Nonetheless, this interchange may promote a certain homogenization of world-views between the skilled proletariat and some segments of craftsmen. This may be of some significance for, as I argue in the following chapter, skilled and semi-skilled workers are often among the more politicized of urban inhabitants. It may also be germane to recall that artisans were an important component of the revolutionary crowds during the French Revolution.

PETTY TRADE AND PETTY SERVICES

Petty traders neither own or lease permanent facilities, nor hire independent labour. They either sell their goods from a street-side table or temporary (and often illegal) stall, or hawk goods in their hands or from a tray or head-load. Characteristically, they control a limited inventory of goods, acquired usually on a day-to-day basis, which they sell in small quantities at low profits owing to the intensive competition. This competition is a function of the ease of entry into hawking or peddling. Insofar as these activities require little or no capital or special skills and knowledge, persons needing a supplementary or subsistence income can easily undertake them. Indeed, it is incorrect to regard petty traders as entrepreneurs in any real sense; they essentially sell their labour to a wholesaler for a minimal return.

This ease of entry largely accounts for the fact that petty traders constitute the largest stratum of the labouring poor. In Ghana, for example, one-eighth of the labour force has some involvement in trade, the bulk as petty traders. In Adjamé, Abidjan, to take a specifically urban case, one-third of the economically active population in 1970 was in small-scale trade. Most of these traders are women and young men.[27]

The participation of the latter is presumably explicable in terms of their need to eke out a living while searching for a suitable job in the modern sector. But why do women figure so prominently in petty trade? To be precise, women are more evident in petty trade in the cities and towns of West Africa than in those of central or especially East Africa. The difference is partly a consequence of tradition: trade is more likely to be regarded as a women's occupation in West Africa than elsewhere. Also, people in the newer East African towns with unbalanced sex ratios have tended to regard women earning independent incomes as *malaya* (prostitutes). However, the attraction of trade for women – in East as well as West Africa – derives mainly from their limited income-earning opportunities. Less well-educated on average than men and (according to some) typically subject to discriminatory hiring practices on the part of the male-dominated firms of the modern sector, women find in petty trade a relatively accessible niche in the urban economy. In addition, a women who is both wife and mother can more easily reconcile her domestic obligations with self-employment than with wage-employment. Self-employment allows them some degree of control over both the place of work and the hours of work, this assuming considerable importance in the event of family illness or other domestic crisis.[28]

Although little information exists on the sellers of licit petty services – once regarded along with petty trade as the archetypal activity in the 'urban traditional sector' – they are apparently as marginal economic pursuits as hawking. Bootblacks, water-sellers, car-washers, car-parkers, porters, and so on abound in the cities of the Third World. Few capital or skill barriers bar entry into these activities; thus, rewards are generally meagre even with long hours of work. Petty services compete with petty trade as refuges for the job-seeker and those temporarily (or permanently) down on their luck.[29]

For obvious reasons, those engaged in petty trade or services rarely develop solidarity or indeed organizations to advance common economic interests. Nairobi is a case in which several associations of hawkers and peddlers have emerged over the years. Here there is a typical pattern. A literate person, not infrequently motivated by less than the purest intentions, creates an association and appoints himself chief spokesmen for the petty traders. During the year or so that such an organization survives, the leader mobilizes support among his constituency by articulating its grievances with respect to the many regulations that the city council imposes upon small-scale trade. The leader then loses interest in this activity (perhaps because he finds a job), his association disappears, and eventually another entrepreneurial leader arises to create another association for hawkers and peddlers. The political potential of this impoverished but volatile stratum is negligible.[30]

CASUAL LABOURERS

Casual or day-labour, whether for large firms or the petty capitalists, provides another poorly remunerated opportunity for the labouring poor. Those labouring for the petty entrepreneurs are the most wretched, though they do not constitute a large group. In Accra, only about 15 per cent of all those engaged in small-scale manufacturing (that is, in establishments with less than ten employees) are wage-labourers. In Dakar, the proportion of 'free' labourers in petty manufacturing varies from almost 20 per cent in automechanics and metal-working to almost nil in shoemaking and tailoring. In Nairobi, small producers engage proportionately more casual workers, but this is largely because the boundary between apprenticeship and wage-labour is not as clear-cut here as in West Africa. With respect to modern capitalist industries, the proportion of day-labourers in their work forces is highly variable from place to place and industry to industry. It is not unusual in, for example, Dakar, for factory managers to evade some stipulations of the labour code by hiring many long-term employees on an ostensibly casual basis. Still, casuals generally form a minor element in the modern sector: in Nairobi, for instance, casual workers composed only 9 per cent of formal wage-employment in 1974. However, these labourers, as a large-scale survey has shown, congregated in the poorest spontaneous settlements in and around Nairobi, where they constituted 21 per cent of those with employment.[31]

The objective circumstances of day-labourers are inimical to the development of a collective consciousness or organization. Unable to find regular work and unable or unwilling to return to the land, they circulate between casual employment, self-employment and open unemployment. Many unemployed youths first turn to day-labour in desperation, as a means of eking out a livelihood while looking for a job. Almost half of a sample of 200 unemployed men in Kampala and Jinja (Uganda) in 1965, for example, had undertaken some casual work in town. Similarly, a large sample-survey of unemployed Lagosian males in 1971 found that 38 per cent of them had had recourse to labouring during the previous month. Predictably, this survey also discovered that those who had been without a regular job the longest (that is, more than two years) were the most likely to resort to casual labour. When casual work is unavailable, these unfortunate individuals must turn to such unattractive self-employment as hawking or the cultivation of a vegetable plot on an unused piece of urban land. Given these wretched conditions, the casual labourer is likely to have more in common with the petty trader and petty producer than the industrial proletariat.[32]

A 'LUMPENPROLETARIAT'?

For Marx, the lumpenproletariat comprised the drop-outs of all social classes, that 'passively rotting mass thrown off by the lower layers of society'. In Louis Napoleon's France, it included:

> Vagabonds, discharged soldiers, swindlers, mountebanks, *lazzaroni*, pickpockets, tricksters, gamblers, *macquereaus*, brothel-keepers, porters, *literati*, organ-grinders, rag-pickers, knife-grinders, tinkers, beggars – in short, the whole indefinite, disintegrated mass, thown hither and thither, which the French term *la bohème*.

The lumpenproletariat was 'the dangerous class', dangerous not only to the bourgeoisie (mainly as criminals), but also to the proletariat. Lumpenproletarians were duplicitous because, as social rejects, they had no stake in societal development; they were therefore quite capable of selling their services to the established order and joining the counter-revolutionary ranks.[33]

Is a lumpenproletariat in the Marxian sense to be found in African cities? Writers have often used this term very loosely in studies of Africa, sometimes identifying it with the urban unemployed in general. Yet if the term is rigorously applied, the lumpenproletariat appears to form only a minor (though probably growing) segment of urban populations. Certainly the bulk of job-seekers are far from social drop-outs; as we shall shortly see, their overriding goal is to enter the relatively privileged echelons of class-stratified societies. Even beggars and prostitutes – elsewhere prototypical lumpenproletarians – in Africa sometimes deviate from the model by evincing upward mobility, *élan* and organization. The explanation of this divergence from the European model is doubtless complex, but involves at least a recognition of differing cultural norms. Criminals and juvenile delinquents apparently constitute the archetypal lumpenproletarians in Africa; but the typical dearth of overt class conflict in the post-colonial cities has not provided them with much opportunity to exhibit counter-revolutionary behaviour.

The claim that beggars in some areas do not easily fit the lumpenproletarian image is not meant to deny their wretched condition in African cities. But there are cases in which people regard begging as a legitimate and not unremunerative pursuit, and in which beggars lack neither warm personal relationships nor even protective organization. This is most true for Muslim beggars within cities with a large Muslim population. Studies of beggars in, for instance, Ibadan and Accra, reveal that their average income is about the same as that of unskilled workers (though the range is wide), that Muslims regard alms-receiving and giving as virtuous behaviour, and that the more successful beggars share the petty bourgeois aspirations of the petty bourgeoisie and labouring poor. Associations of beggars sometimes emerge to promote common interests – as for instance in Ibadan, where beggars have grouped themselves into no less than three associations on the basis of handicap. Headed by a chief, each of these is formally recognized by the chief of the Hausa quarter. Each assigns routes to beggars and, in the case of the blind, provides a guide. A Beggars' Committee has also been active periodically in Nairobi.[34]

Another supposedly typical lumpenproletarian is the prostitute. In Africa, prostitution has not been as fully commercialized as in the West; only some 'prostitutes' would fit the Western definition of persons who will sell their body to anyone. Others receiving money for sexual services are more selective, either moving from one casual affair to another, or having only a small number of lovers at the same time. The economic rationale for prostitution in the past, when few women had marketable skills, is obvious. It offered 'a strategy for the economic support of women, which is an alternative to marriage and, given the lack of educational background and the general competition for employment, it is a more profitable strategy than trade or wage-labour'. Prostitution, as I have already mentioned, has provided the means for some women to purchase urban property and enter the petty bourgeoisie. But obviously only some prostitutes can achieve this social mobility. In Kinshasa, for example, whereas there are the much-admired *vedettes*, elegantly attired and selective in their choice of clients, there are also the wretched *chambres d'hôtel* who accept any man willing to pay their price, and cater mainly for the workers.

If the prospect of upward mobility distinguishes some prostitutes from a lumpenproletariat, so does their social acceptability and organization. As a rule, little opprobrium attaches to prostitution in the city, at least among the common people. In the Hausa quarter of Ibadan, for instance, devout Muslims regard prostitutes as prime marriage partners, and divorced women not uncommonly become prostitutes. Indeed, the chief of this quarter officially recognizes a 'Chieftainess of the Prostitutes' whose job is to represent, and resolve disputes among, the Hausa prostitutes. Prostitutes' associations elsewhere take a modern form, as in Abidjan and Kinshasa in the 1960s where they were headed by elected officers. In these cases the associations operated partly as benevolent societies and partly as guilds to establish fair prices and resolve disputes. Where no such formal organizations exist, as in the spontaneous settlements of Nairobi, informal ties among prostitutes and other inhabitants provide for mutual security. This mutal protection also exists within communities engaged in the illegal production of alcoholic beverages, an activity that frequently accompanies prostitution.[35]

The group that most closely approximates to Marx's lumpen-proletariat is that composed of juvenile delinquents and criminals. Crime is disproportionately an urban phenomenon, in Africa as elsewhere. Along with burgeoning rates of urban growth has gone a burgeoning crime rate. Popular concern about the dimensions of this problem is reflected in the editorials and letters to the editors of African newspapers. One Sierra Leonean report has contended that 'many large urban areas in some African countries are known to be virtually under a state of seige, and residents are forced by thieves to impose on themselves what is tantamount to a curfew.' In Kenya, for example, although about 90 per cent of the people lived outside the towns and cities in 1970, 43 per cent of all reported offences occurred in urban areas. Part of the explanation for this lies in the bias introduced by the relative concentration of police posts in the towns. Beyond this, however, crime is closely related to the complex social changes accompanying urbanization.[36]

In the first place, the poor may more intensely feel their poverty in the urban than the rural milieu. Absolute poverty appears harder for its victims to bear when they are well placed, as in cities, to draw invidious comparisons with the lifestyles of the conspicuously well-to-do. Criminological studies invariably propose a causal link between poverty and crime, especially in the case of unemployed urban youths. Similarly, a constant theme in the ruminations of the press and politicians of Africa is the attraction of criminal activities for the chronically unemployed. Indeed, a study of nearly 700 secondary-school students in Kenya provides some basis for speculation that this association also exists in the popular imagination. Fully 42 per cent of this sample expressed the fear that a future inability to find a suitable job would lead to a life of crime. The tendency for the poorest areas in African cities to gain reputations as a 'den' or 'school' of thieves may also say something about popular attitudes.[37]

Crime statistics bear out the relationship between unemployment, poverty and crime. Obviously, one has to treat these statistics with some caution. Insofar as the labouring poor are the least likely to possess money for bribes or influential connections, they are the most likely to be pursued and arrested by the police. Nonetheless, the consistency of the findings about the socio-economic background of offenders is striking. A study of the origins and behaviour of male delinquents in Accra, for instance, led the writer to conclude that

> many immigrants . . . to the cities have remained unemployed or partly unemployed. Destitute, living in overcrowded conditions, and desperately seeking subsistence, older boys often resort to subsistence stealing, a pattern of behaviour that frequently characterizes the adaptive techniques of youths as well as adults. A cultural lag exists between the needs of some youths and the lack of institutions to channelize their needs; this discrepancy places these youths in a marginal position and impels them to satisfy their needs through deviant conduct with their peers. . . .

Similarly, a study of almost 6000 males arrested in Kampala in 1968 found that about half were unemployed and a quarter held an unskilled job. Significantly, of those arrested for property crimes, over 60 per cent were listed as unemployed.[38]

Rootlessness is the second aspect of social change that tends to promote criminality. Urbanization can weaken the family as an integrative and socializing institution. Excessive drinking on the part of one or both partners, divorce, and neglect of children are all common manifestations of the pressures of life in the new urban milieu. With the decline of parental influence and the disintegration of the family, youths become susceptible to the sway of a peer group organized into a gang. Indeed, even parents of stable families fear that raising children in low-income urban locations will expose them to 'bad' influences. But, leaving socio-economic status aside, the main trait distinguishing delinquents from control groups of non-delinquents in such diverse cities as Dakar, Lagos, Lusaka and Kampala is the malfunctioning of the family as a source of affection and social control. Hence, the African experience is much the same as that of the West: much of the crime is committed by young, materially deprived males, without adequate employment and adrift in the city with only their gang to sustain them.[39]

If destitution and rootlessness figure prominently in the origins of urban crime, can one legitimately regard some of it as a form of protest, as sublimated class conflict? Can one characterize African offenders in the same terms used by Friedrich Engels to describe the criminals of Manchester of 1844 – 'those members of the "surplus population" who – goaded by their distress – summon up enough courage to revolt openly against society and become thieves and murderers. They wage open warfare against the middle classes, who have for so long waged secret warfare against them'? On the one hand, the wealthier classes clearly feel threatened by criminals in all African cities. The quest for security leads the rich to turn their urban residences into small fortresses, their houses surrounded by high walls, sometimes topped by barbed wire or jagged glass, and protected by night-watchmen (in some cases supplemented by day-watchmen), guard dogs and barred windows. A further indicator of the possible political significance of urban crime is the fragmentary evidence that the common people condone crimes committed outside the low-income areas. Public distrust of the police tends, understandably, to be high in these areas, inasmuch as the unprotected poor must usually bear the brunt of the corruption and arrogance of poorly educated and underpaid police. It is therefore unsurprising that, in a poor *zongo* in Accra, an anthropologist found that

thieves practise openly, but usually outside their home neighbourhood. This explains the paradox (paralleled in traditional justice) that, while respected and even admired by his immediate social milieu as long as his victims are outsiders, the thief is hounded by crowds, beaten up or vilified wherever he is caught.

The same situation apparently obtains in Kisenyi, a poor suburb of Kampala.[40]

On the other hand, it must be borne in mind that the poor are more often the target of crimes against property than the rich. Crime-as-sublimated-class-conflict is, at most, a minor theme. Although some thievery redistributes income from the rich to the poor, it more often transfers income from the poor worker or self-employed individual to the better-off crook. The common man, too, must barricade his home at night – although in this case the 'home' generally consists of one overcrowded and airless room. Crime rates do vary from one low-income area to the next, depending upon whether a vigilante system operates to mete out severe punishment to apprehended muggers, burglars and pickpockets. But in the absence of such a self-help system, crime represents a major hazard for the people. This was the case in Ashaiman (the 'school of thieves'), a workers' suburb outside Tema studied by the author; muggings on the unlit streets were a nightly occurrence. The same was true of two poor neighbourhoods in Kampala where, in 1968–9, one-third of the men in a large sample had been the victim of a property crime within the previous year.[41]

High crime rates within poor suburbs foster an atmosphere of mutual mistrust. A high incidence of crime indicates, and further reinforces, a lack of community that vitiates the collective power of the urban poor. Most urban crime is thus not at all a masked form of class conflict: the criminal elements constitute a lumpenproletariat as dangerous to the workers and labouring poor as to the dominant classes.

Intellectuals and the educated unemployed

'The revolutionary intellectual is a virtually universal phenomenon in modernizing societies', writes Samuel Huntington. Frantz Fanon, an author of antipodal political complexion, also anticipates a leadership role for intellectuals in revolutionary movements incorporating peasants and lumpenproletarians.[42] How accurate are their views with respect to tropical Africa?

The dissident voice of the literary intelligentsia is very much in evidence. Contemporary African novelists, poets and playwrights have presented trenchant critiques of both colonial and post-colonial societies. Concerning the latter, a growing literature protests against acquisitive individualism, the aping of Western culture, corruption, nepotism and political authoritarianism. One of the first novels in this genre was Chinua Achebe's *A Man of the People* (1966). In both depth and vitriol, this work has since been surpassed, most notably (in the English language) by Ayi Kwei Armah in *The Beautyful Ones Are not Yet Born* (1968) and Ngugi wa Thiongo in *Petals of Blood* (1977). Among poets, Okot p'Bitek eloquently expresses popular disillusion with *uhuru* in his *Song of Prisoner* (1971). For the marginalized poor, this disillusion leads to resignation, not rebellion:

> Let me dance
> And forget my sorrow,
> Let me forget
> That I am jobless
> And landless,
> Forget that I am hopeless
> And helpless,
> Let me sweat out my frustrations
> And anger.
> Who wants to know
> That his children
> Will never go to school
> Will never get a job
> Or land
> Or cow
> Or goat!
> Or chicken?
> Let me dance
> And forget!

But what connection can one draw between this angry literature and movements for social change? Written in European languages, the works just mentioned are obviously aimed at other sections of the intelligentsia – and Western audiences. Indeed, when Ngugi wa Thiongo sought in 1977–8 to bring his critical perspective closer to the Kenyan people – by performing plays in Kikuyu for peasant audiences – he was detained by the authorities. Are the 'beautyful ones' then to emerge from the ranks of the university students, elsewhere a stronghold of oppositional sentiment?

It should come as no surprise that, in Africa as in other parts of the world, the majority of university students appear to be neither politically active nor radical. On the basis of a survey of the limited literature and their own cross-sectional research, Judith and William Hanna conclude that most students are 'cynical nationalists':

> the students are concerned about the political future but only moderately interested in the political present; they talk about nationalism, socialism and democracy, but ethnicity, self-interest, and anti-democratic orientations appear to be near the surface; their cynicism appears to be fairly widespread. . . . [I]t seems clear that various political regimes – ranging from democratic to authoritarian, national to sectional – can obtain significant student support.

A study of 1900 university students in Ghana, Tanzania and Uganda in the late 1960s tends to support these observations. A majority of the sample regarded the 'elite/mass gap' as both inevitable and justifiable; insofar as this finding is valid, the production of an indigenous technocratic class conceivably exacerbates social inequities and fortifies political conservatism.[43]

What explains this quietism on the part of the majority? We must begin with the obvious point that these university students are the products of elitist educational systems that train them for leadership positions in the public service or private sector – and that regimes can usually withhold such rewards from malcontents. The students' socialization and the reward structure therefore both pull in the direction of political conformity.[44]

But this is only half the story: there is hardly a country in Africa where the forces of order have not fired upon or beaten students. In any country activists, in fact, rarely form more than a small proportion of student populations. Yet student demonstrations, pacific or otherwise, are far from rare occurrences in African countries. Usually their political impact is minor, inasmuch as they are precipitated by such university-related grievances as threats to the personal freedoms or perquisites of students or the quality of education. Occasionally, these parochial concerns fuse with societal grievances to confront regimes with a widely based spontaneous protest movement. Indeed, student riots and demonstrations have accompanied the overthrow of governments – as in Khartoum in 1964, Tananarive in 1972, and Addis Ababa in 1974-5 – but in these cases other urban elements, especially workers, joined in and the military proved willing to intervene.[45]

Is there any likelihood of some student activists assuming a more politically conscious role as aspirant leaders of mass social movements? If urban intellectuals are to play the part ascribed to them by Fanon, a necessary condition is probably that the supply of suitable jobs for graduates no longer meets demand. This situation, according to some, is at hand. By the early 1970s, in many African countries, university graduates could no longer automatically obtain a job with some authority.[46] Yet, even if a graduate must now settle for less prestigious employment than a few years ago, he still can aspire to move up the hierarchy. It is therefore not clear that the personal frustrations of university students are such as to motivate more than a handful to undertake the onerous task of organizing the poor in post-colonial Africa. This is not only an inherently dangerous vocation; it is also an immensely difficult one in that the educated organizer has to bridge an enormous socio-cultural gap to relate to the common people.

Some have identified the unemployed secondary school-leaver rather than the university graduate as a potentially radical force. It is now clear that of the 10 per cent or so of African urban labour forces who are openly unemployed, a majority are relatively well-educated young people. Commonly, they continue to search for a suitable job in the modern sector until their kin or friends refuse to support them further, or until they become discouraged and sink into a marginal occupation or (if feasible) return to agriculture. Most authorities now accept that almost any interested person can find some minimally remunerative work to do in the informal economy.[47]

Job-seeking is now typically a frustrating and even humiliating experience for a person with secondary schooling. With state-sponsored educational expansion, all African countries have undergone successive devaluations of higher levels of formal qualifications for the same job. An ambitious applicant may consequently need to mark time in a city for a year or more to have any chance of finding appropriate employment. In the meantime the job-seeker must rely upon the hospitality of relatives and friends to survive, or resort to sporadic casual labour or petty thievery. The life of an unemployed individual in town is usually a hard and degrading one, inasmuch as his host may be grudging in his hospitality and eventually turn him out. Then begins a process of 'social circulation', in which the job-seeker solicits help from one relative and friend after another. Those with stable employment may, in time, become less willing to bear the burden of unemployed kin in town. Needless to say, the attenuation of extended-family obligations will both discourage rural–urban migration and foster a turning to crime on the part of desperate job-seekers.[48]

From the standpoint of class formation, a critical question relates to the self-identification of the educated unemployed. Does their predicament (and background) dispose them to identify with the common people? This is an issue about which virtually nothing is known.

One way to approach a tentative answer is by an intensive and longitudinal study of a handful of unemployed young people in town. This is Kenneth King's approach in *Jobless in Kenya*, in which he records his extended conversations with eight job-seekers in Nairobi and their experiences over the course of a year. It seems that these unemployed youths, though subsisting on meagre incomes and thoroughly frustrated, do not consider themselves as part of an exploited sub-proletariat. Until they surrender their high aspirations and settle into low-status jobs (perhaps by passing through an informal apprenticeship), they are unlikely to change their present identification with the 'Big Men' of Kenya.

The roots of these high aspirations and elite identifications are firmly planted in the Kenyan school system. Apparently, the experience of attending a government-run secondary boarding school for four years can itself create a superior self-image. The youths with whom King talked emphasized the vast status difference between primary and secondary schools, accompanied by a drastic change in lifestyle. In King's words, 'he moves from a world where there are bare feet, long walks to and from school, mud floors, indifferent teachers, crowded classes . . . to a world where there are uniforms, stone buildings in a large compound, better qualified teachers and regulation sized classes' (as well as better meals, escape from household chores, and deference from relatives during holidays). If in consequence the aristocracy of the secondary and technical schools regard themselves as 'big people' preparing for supervisory jobs, this is quite understandable.

But what sustains these aspirations in the face of continual rebuffs in their job searches? Perceptively, King notes that his subjects preferred to call themselves 'job-seekers' rather than 'unemployed'. 'Many . . . see themselves not so much as part of a static category of unemployed but as part of a group that is marking time just as they have had to mark time at various critical stages of their school careers.' They accepted the popular view that the main obstacle to securing a good job is not the dearth of openings, but the pervasiveness of such irregular recruitment practices as bribery, nepotism and 'tribalism'. Their task was thus essentially to determine how to beat this system – and this would take some time. Ironically, the popular belief that even mediocre candidates could obtain enviable positions through influence-peddling encouraged job-seekers to persist in cultivating their chances.[49]

One should therefore be sceptical of the once prominent view of the unemployed as 'the shock troops of political discontent'. It has been tentatively proposed, for example in studies of urban job-seekers in Nigeria and Kenya, that the politicization of the unemployed increases with the length of time they spend in unemployment. Some of this work even leaves the impression that the job-seekers' consciousness is rising to the point where they may soon spearhead an insurrection. Hence, in Kenya, we are told,

the conditions supportive of political rebellion as a form of adaptation and response to the frustrations experienced by unemployed school leavers are . . . rapidly forming. It seems likely that unemployment will constitute an increasingly significant source of political instability in Kenya for some time to come.[50]

Other work, including that of King, has cast considerable doubt upon such a likelihood. Instead, authors emphasize the ambivalence with which the unemployed regard the inegalitarian social order. On the one hand, they are critical of the government and the 'Big Men', evincing a considerable degree of frustration and hostility. On the other hand, they seek to link up with one of these Big Men in order to obtain a suitable job through the use of influence. As long as job-seekers believe they may still succeed in their job search and eventually become Big Men, they are unlikely to do more than verbally abuse the system among themselves. The unemployed, in any event, lack any solidarity; a job-search is an individual activity that pits one job-seeker against all the other qualified contenders. By themselves they are unlikely to pose a political threat.[51]

Summary and conclusion

This discussion of class formation from below should have revealed, above all, the complexity of urban class analysis. It would clearly be dishonest, on the basis of such a wideranging synthesis, to present any definitive conclusions regarding the potential alliances of the various urban classes and strata. Definitiveness in such matters depends upon a detailed analysis of specific historical situations. I can only offer some tentative generalizations to guide such analyses.

1. *The influence of the urban petty bourgeoisie is conservative, in contemporary Africa as earlier in Europe* Once established, this class wields considerable influence among the common people. This derives from control over property and patronage, leadership of community organizations, and popular acceptance as a reference group for the values and behaviour of less successful neighbours. The political position of the small entrepreneurs is characterized by ambivalence. On the one hand, kinship ties, social origins and propinquity bind them to the working class and labouring poor, while the state-supported structural constraints upon their businesses foster in them hostility towards the superordinate classes. On the other hand, their relative privilege and prospects, based upon the consumption and exploitation of their poorer neighbours, are threatened by class formation among the urban poor. Their immediate interest is therefore to retain their political pre-eminence among the common people, and legitimate the existing peripheral capitalist order. Such an interest is congruent with a populist, but not a radical, ideology or movement.

2. *The labouring poor, though comparatively lacking in education, property and political influence (and thus destined to remain poor), nevertheless rarely constitute a disaffected, solidaristic group* This typical lack of class consciousness is hardly surprising, insofar as the labouring poor comprise, not a class-in-itself, but a congeries of producers and sellers outside the capitalist mode of production. Highly individualistic and competitive work situations and the atomizing effects of petty-bourgeois aspirations (and often divergent regional, ethnic and religious loyalties as well) combine to restrict the self-identification of members of this social category. However, they may be susceptible to the ideological influence of the modern proletariat (under rare conditions soon to be specified), as well as of the petty bourgeoisie. But where, as in the bulk of cases, working-class consciousness does not penetrate the labouring poor (and indeed the influence is in the opposite direction), they are capable only of a 'we–they' mentality commonly known as populism. This ideology can foster only riots or *jacqueries*, with little or no long-term political significance.

3. *Of the elements typically included in the lumpenproletariat, only the criminals and juvenile delinquents seem fully to fit the classical Marxian description* These are the 'dangerous classes' for both the bourgeoisie and the urban masses within their low-income neighbourhoods. The prevalence of crime in some settlements breeds a mutal mistrust among the residents which constitutes yet another barrier to a mutual defence against oppression.

4. *The radicalization of urban intellectuals, both university students and the educated unemployed, remains a possibility, though there are strong countervailing tendencies* Insofar as both groups apparently harbour aspirations to middle-class status, it is rare for educated individuals to seek to lead, or align themselves with, the poor to destabilize the existing order.

It is now time to move from this static comparative analysis of classes in formation towards a more dynamic analysis of class interaction, control and struggle.

Notes

1. Jeffrey Kaplow, *The Names of Kings: the Parisian Laboring Poor in the Eighteenth Century* (New York: Basic Books, 1972), pp. 28, 100, 169.
2. See, e.g., J. R. Harris, 'Nigerian Entrepreneurship in Industry', in Carl K. Eicher (ed.), *Growth and Development of the Nigerian Economy* (East Lansing, Mich: Michigan State University Press, 1970), pp. 303–15; P. Kennedy, 'Indigenous Capitalism in Ghana', *Review of African Political Economy* , 8 (1977), pp. 21–38; and Peter Marris and Anthony Somerset, *African Businessmen: A Study of Entrepreneurship and Development in Kenya* (London: Routledge & Kegan Paul, 1971).
3. General information on the development of market places: P. Hill, 'Markets in Africa', *Journal of Modern African Studies,* I, 4 (1963), pp. 441–53. On the extent and significance of the dominance of women in market trade: D. McCall, 'Trade and the Role of Wife in a Modern West African Town', in Aidan Southall (ed.), *Social Change in Modern Africa* (Oxford: Oxford University Press, 1961), pp. 286–99; M. Peil, 'Female Roles in West African Towns', in Jack Goody (ed.), *Changing Social Structure in Ghana* (London: International African Institute, 1975), pp. 73–90; Astrid Nypan, *Market Trade: A Sample Survey of Market Traders in Accra*, African Business Series No. 2, Economic Research Division, University College of Ghana, 1960, pp. 7–9, 15; and D. Aguessy, 'La femme dakaroise commerçante au détail sur le marché', in Groupes d'études dakaroises, *Dakar en devenir* (Paris: Présence Africaine, 1968), pp. 395–421.
4. For the Lagos examples, see Gloria Marshall, 'Yoruba Market Traders in Modern Nigeria', paper delivered at the Annual Meeting of the African

Studies Association, 27–30 October 1965; and the Dakar cases, see C. Le Cour Grandmaison, 'Activités économiques des femmes dakaroises', *Africa*, XXXIX (1969), pp. 138–52. For the range of success in market trade in Accra, see Nypan, *Market Trade* (n. 3 above), pp. 42–8; and E. Reusse and R. Lawson, 'The Effect of Economic Development on Metropolitan Food Marketing: A Case Study of Retail Trade in Accra', *East African Journal of Rural Development*, II, 1 (1969), p. 50. Kenyan petty entrepreneur quoted in Kenneth McVicar, 'Twilight of an East African Slum: Pumwani and the Evolution of African Settlement in Nairobi', PhD thesis, University of California, Los Angeles, 1968, pp. 203–4. On the same phenomenon of investment diversification in Ghana, see K. Hart, 'Small-Scale Entrepreneurs in Ghana and Development Planning', *Journal of Development Studies*, VI, 4 (1971), pp. 108–14.

5.   Origins of shopkeepers and 'heads of establishments': Peter C. Garlick, *African Traders and Economic Development in Ghana* (Oxford: Clarendon Press, 1971), p. 36; T. Mukenge, 'Les hommes d'affaires zaïrois', *Canadian Journal of African Studies*, VII, 3 (1973), pp. 472–5; A. Oberschall, 'African Traders and Small Businessmen in Lusaka', *African Social Research*, no. 16 (1973), pp. 490–1. Previous wage-employment is also common among some categories of small African businessmen in Dar es Salaam; see M. A. Bienefeld, *The Self-Employed of Urban Tanzania*, Discussion Paper No. 54, Institute of Development Studies, University of Sussex, May 1974, pp. 58–9. Origins of market women: in Accra: Nypan, *Market Trade* (n. 3 above), pp. 13, 69; R. Sanjek and I. M. Sanjek, 'Notes on Women and Work in Adabraka', *African Urban Notes*, II, 2 (1976), pp. 12–13; C. Robertson, 'Economic Women in Africa: Profit-Making Techniques of Accra Market Women', *Journal of Modern African Studies*, XII, 4 (1974), pp. 658; and N. Sudarkasa, 'Commercial Migration in West Africa, with Special Reference to the Yoruba in Ghana', *African Urban Notes*, ser. B, 1 (1974–5), pp. 79–80. Origins of market traders elsewhere: A. Oberschall, 'Lusaka Market Vendors: Then and Now', *Urban Anthropology*, I, 1 (1972), p. 108; and A. Callaway, 'Nigeria's Indigenous Education: The Apprenticeship System', *Odu*, I, 1 (1964), p. 72.

6.   On prostitution and entrepreneurship: Nicki Nelson, 'Strategies of Female Migration to Mathare Valley', unpublished paper, University of Sussex, 1978, p. 16 (where the quote appears); J. Bujra, 'Women "Entrepreneurs" of Early Nairobi', *Canadian Journal of African Studies*, IX, 2 (1975), pp. 213–34; C. Obbo, 'Women's Careers in Low Income Areas as Indicators of Country and Town Dynamics', in David Parkin (ed.), *Town and Country in Central and Eastern Africa* (Oxford: Oxford University Press, 1975), pp. 288–93; J. La Fontaine, 'The Free Women of Kinshasa', in John Davis (ed.), *Choice and Change: Essays in Honour of Lucy Mair*, London School of Economics, Monograph No. 50, 1974, p. 107; and Ioné Acquah, *Accra Survey* (Accra: Ghana Universities Press, 1972), p. 74.

7.   Data on the Ghanaian businessmen: Kennedy, 'Indigenous Capitalism in Ghana' (n. 2 above), p. 29; on Ibadan: Abner Cohen, *Custom and Politics in Urban Africa: A Study of Hausa Migrants in Yoruba Towns* (Los Angeles: University of California Press, 1969), chap. 3; and on Pumwani: Janet Bujra, *Pumwani: The Politics of Property: A Study of an Urban Settlement in Nairobi*, report on a research project sponsored by the Social

176 AN ANATOMY OF THE URBAN MASSES

Science Research Council, deposited at the University of Nairobi, 1973, pp. 28–30. Other studies treating the dispersion of house ownership and the relation between landlordism and entrepreneurial activities: Marc H. Ross, *The Political Integration of Urban Squatters* (Mathare) (Evanston, Ill: Northwestern University Press, 1973), pp. 140–1; Sandra Barnes, 'Becoming a Lagosian', PhD thesis, University of Wisconsin, 1974, p. 125; Ita Muller, 'Chawama, a Good Place in Lusaka: A Description of an Informal Settlement', Workshop on the Informal Sector, Institute for Development Studies, University of Nairobi, 8–10 November 1976, p. 4; and Richard Stren, *Urban Inequality and Housing Policy in Tanzania* (Institute of International Studies, University of California, Berkeley, 1975), p. 83.

8. See in particular (and for quote), Cohen, *Custom and Politics* (n. 7 above), pp. 71–97; Barnes, 'Becoming a Lagosian' (n. 7 above), *passim*; and E. Schildkrout, 'Economics and Kinship in Multi-ethnic Dwellings [in the Kumasi Zongo]', in Jack Goody (ed.), *Changing Social Structure in Ghana* (London: International African Institute, 1975), p. 171.

9. Most of the items listed in n. 7 mention the connection between property and local politics. Information and quote on Kampala: David Parkin, *Neighbours and Nationals in an African City Ward* (Los Angeles: University of California Press, 1969), pp. 158, and in general, pp. 158–63.

10. On the general political inefficacy of market women's associations see Nancy J. Hafkin and Edna G. Bay, 'Introduction', to Hafkin and Bay (eds.), *Women in Africa: Studies in Social and Economic Change* (Stanford: Stanford University Press, 1976), p. 12.

11. See Pauline H. Baker, *Urbanization and Political Change: The Politics of Lagos, 1917–67* (Los Angeles: University of California Press, 1974), chap. 8; and P. O. Sada and M. L. McNulty, 'Traditional Markets in Lagos: A Study of the Changing Administrative Process and Marketing Transactions', *Quarterly Journal of Administration*, VIII, 2 (1974), pp. 149–65. Margaret Peil makes similar observations with respect to market women's influence in several Nigerian cities in *Nigerian Politics: The People's View* (London: Cassell, 1976), p. 164.

12. Associational activity among market traders in Ibadan, Accra, Abidjan and Lusaka: B. X. Hodder and U. J. Ukwu, *Markets in West Africa: Studies of Markets and Trade among the Yoruba and Luo* (Ibadan: Ibadan University Press, 1969), pp. 55–6; R. Simms and E. Dumor, 'Women in the Urban Economy of Ghana', *African Urban Notes*, II, 3 (1976–7), pp. 58–61; B. C. Lewis, 'Limitations of Group Action among Entrepreneurs: The Market Women in Abidjan', in Hafkin and Bay (eds.), *Women* (n. 10 above), esp. p. 153; and Oberschall, 'Lusaka Market Vendors' (n. 5 above), pp. 130–1.

13. Information and quote: Oberschall, 'African Traders' (n. 5 above), pp. 487–501.

14. See A. van Cauwenbergh, 'Le développement du commerce et de l'artisanat indigènes à Léopoldville', *Zaïre*, X, 6 (1956), p. 654.

15. The references to Pumwani summarize Bujra's excellent study, *Pumwani* (n. 7 above), see esp. pp. 3, 58–9, 74–6. For a similar situation in Kibera, Nairobi, see D. Clark, 'Unregulated Housing, Vested Interest and the Development of Community Identity', *African Urban Notes*, 3 (1978–9),

pp. 33–46; and in a Lagosian suburb, Barnes, 'Becoming a Lagosian' (n. 7 above), chap. 6.

16. Quote from: Ralph Miliband, *Marxism and Politics* (London: Oxford University Press, 1977), p. 37.

17. Agege case study: Adrian Peace 'Prestige, Power and Legitimacy in a Modern Nigerian Town', *Canadian Journal of African Studies*, XIII, 1/2 (1979), pp. 25–52, quotes p. 29 and 50, respectively. For comparable findings on Mushin: Barnes, 'Becoming a Lagosian' (n. 7 above), chaps. 6 and 7; on Nima (Accra): K. Hart, 'Swindler or Public Benefactor? The Entrepreneur in his Community', in Goody (ed.), *Changing Social Structure* (n. 3 above), pp. 15–35; and on the Kumasi Zongo: E. Schildkrout, 'Economics and Kinship in Multi-Ethnic Dwellings', in Goody (ed.), *Changing Social Structure* (n. 3 above), pp. 167–79.

18. Bujra, *Pumwani* (n. 7 above), pp. 31–2, 119–22, quote p. 119.

19. M. Peil, 'West African Urban Craftsmen', unpublished paper, Centre for West African Studies, University of Birmingham, 1977, pp. 22–3; and G. Pallier, 'Les activités du secteur secondaire à Ouagadougou', in Centre Nationale de la Recherche Scientifique, *La croissance urbaine en Afrique noire et à Madagascar* (Paris, 1972), vol. I, p. 905.

20. Discussions of the occupational distribution of petty producers: Peil, 'West African Craftsmen' (n. 19 above), pp. 5–6; M. P. van Dijk, *Developing the Informal Sector in Senegal*, ILO, Skills for Africa Programme, Dakar, December 1976, pp. 4–7 and tables 4 and 5; Heather Joshi *et al.*, *Abidjan* (Geneva: ILO, 1976), pp. 52–4; D. Remy and J. Weeks, 'Employment, Occupation and Inequality in a Non-Industrial City [Kano]', in Karl Wohlmuth (ed.), *Employment Creation in Developing Societies* (New York: Praeger, 1973), pp. 296–9; and Pallier, 'Les activités' (n. 19 above), pp. 907–11. For information on traditional doctors, see the next chapter.

21. Kenneth King, *The African Artisan* (London: Heinemann Educational Books, 1977), pp. 102–4, 48–56, 120–1.

22. See in general, P. C. Lloyd, 'Craft Organization in Yoruba Towns', *Africa*, XXIII, 1 (1953), pp. 30–44; and, in particular, Callaway, 'Nigeria's Indigenous Education' (n. 5 above), pp. 62–79.

23. Michael Koll, *Crafts and Cooperation in Western Nigeria* (Gütersloh: Bertelsmann Universitatsverlag, 1969), pp. 36–58; Lloyd, 'Craft Organization' (n. 22 above), pp. 39–41; and A. Callaway, 'From Traditional Crafts to Modern Industries', in P. C. Lloyd *et al.* (eds.), *The City of Ibadan* (Cambridge: Cambridge University Press, 1967), p. 159.

24. Terence Smutylo, 'Apprenticeship in the Wayside Workshops of an Accra Neighbourhood', MA thesis, University of Ghana, 1973, pp. 157–8 for the quote, Information from: M. Peil, 'The Apprenticeship System in Accra', *Africa*, XL, 2 (1970), pp. 137–50; Joshi *et al.*, *Abidjan* (n. 20 above), pp. 59–60; O. LeBrun and C. Gerry, 'Petty Producers and Capitalism [in Dakar]', *Review of African Political Economy*, 3 (1975), p. 25; and V. R. Dorjahn, 'Tailors, Carpenters and Leather Workers in Magburaka [Sierra Leone]', *Sierra Leone Studies*, XX (1967), pp. 158–72.

25. On goldsmiths in Accra: David Kimble, *A Political History of Ghana* (Oxford: Oxford University Press, 1963), p. 44. The information on guilds in Lagos was kindly supplied by Margaret Peil on the basis of her sample surveys, in a personal communication. For information on guilds

elsewhere, see Chris Gerry, *Petty Production and the Urban Economy: A Case Study of Dakar*, ILO, Working Paper WEP 2/19/101/1, WP8, 1974, pp. 130–1; and J. S. La Fontaine, *City Politics: A Study of Léopoldville* (Cambridge: Cambridge University Press, 1970), p. 156.

26. G. P. Williams, 'Political Consciousness among the Ibadan Poor', in Emmanuel de Kadt and G. Williams (eds.), *Sociology and Development* (London: Tavistock, 1974), p. 122.

27. For the statistics: Reusse and Lawson, 'Effect of Economic Development ... [Accra]' (n. 4 above), pp. 1–26; Joshi *et al., Abidjan* (n. 20 above), pp. 53–4; and McVicar, 'Twilight of an East African Slum' (n. 4 above), pp. 66–7, 208–9.

28. On the role of women in trade in general: Kenneth Little, *African Women in Trade* (London: Oxford University Press, 1973). On the participation of women in petty trade in specific cases, and the reasons why women congregate in the 'informal sector': T. K. Kumekpor, 'Mothers and Wage-Labour Employment [in Accra]', *Ghana Journal of Sociology*, VII, 2 (1974), pp. 68–91; O. J. Fapohunda and E. R. Fapohunda, *The Working Mothers of Lagos* (Ibadan: Ibadan University Press, 1979); D. Parkin, 'Introduction', in David Parkin (ed.), *Town and Country in Eastern and Central Africa* (London: Oxford University Press, 1975), p. 39; and Bienefeld, *Self-Employed of Urban Tanzania* (n. 5 above), pp. 50–2. For the reasons explaining the lesser role of women in East African urban economies: M. N. Kisekka, 'On the Status of Women within the Framework of the Liberation Movement', *African Urban Notes*, II, 3 (1976–7), p. 69.

29. See, e.g., J. T. Mukui, 'Anatomy of the Urban Informal Sector: A Study of Food Kiosks and Shoeblacks in Nairobi', Workshop on the Informal Sector, Institute for Development Studies, Nairobi, 8–10 November 1976. This paragraph is also based on discussions with a non-random sample of shoeshiners in Nairobi and Accra by the author.

30. Information on these associations: Herbert Werlin, *Governing an African City: A Study of Nairobi* (New York: Africana Publishing House, 1974), pp. 270–4; and Andrew Hake, *African Metropolis: Nairobi's Self-Help City* (New York: St Martin's Press, 1977), p. 178.

31. For the cases mentioned: William Steel, *Small-Scale Employment and Production in Developing Countries: Evidence from Ghana* (New York: Praeger Special Studies, 1977), table 3.10, p. 79; Gerry, *Petty Production and the Urban Economy ... Dakar* (n. 25 above), pp. 113–18. Statistics on casual employment in Nairobi's modern sector: drawn from Kenya's Central Bureau of Statistics. The large-scale Nairobi survey: James Waweru and Associates, *Progress Report No. 6: Economic Aspects*, Report to the Government of Kenya and World Bank, Nairobi 1976, pp. 11, 12, 33.

32. For a study making this point: C. Gerry, 'The Wrong Side of the Factory Gate: Casual Workers and Capitalist Industry in Dakar', *Manpower and Unemployment Research*, IX, 2 (1976), pp. 17–28. Studies of the unemployed: C. Hutton, 'How the Unemployed Survive in Town: Kampala and Jinja, Uganda', *Manpower and Unemployment Research in Africa*, III, 2 (1970), pp. 11, 12; and M. Peil, 'Male Unemployment in Lagos, 1971', *Manpower and Unemployment Research in Africa*, V, 2 (1972), p. 23.

33. Marx–Engels, *Selected Works* (Moscow: International Publishers, 1962), vol. I, pp. 294–5.
34. A. Bamisaye, 'Begging in Ibadan', *Human Organization,* XXXIII, 2 (1974), pp. 197–202; Gold Coast, Department of Social Welfare and Community Development, *Report on the Enquiry into Begging and Destitution in the Gold Coast* (Accra: Government Printer, 1955); and Hake, *African Metropolis* (n. 30 above), pp. 190–95.
35. Quote in La Fontaine, 'Free Women of Kinshasa' (n. 6 above), p. 111. On economic rationale for prostitution and degree of organization: see *ibid.,* pp. 89–113; Cohen, *Custom and Politics . . . Ibadan* (n. 7 above), p. 63; V. D. DuBois, 'Prostitution in the Ivory Coast', American Universities Field Staff, *Report,* West Africa Series, X, 2 (1967); J. M. Gachuhi, 'Anatomy of Prostitutes and Prostitution in Kenya', Institute for Development Studies, University of Nairobi, Working Paper No. 113, July 1973; and McVicar, 'Twilight of an East African Slum' (n. 4 above), pp. 239–55. On co-operation among bootleggers: *ibid.,* pp. 224–37; and N. Nelson, 'The Operation and Continuity of Personal Networks in the Process of Buzaa (Beer) Brewing', in Nelson, 'Some Aspects of Informal Social Organisation of Female Migrants in a Nairobi Squatter Neighbourhood', unpublished manuscript, February 1975.
36. Comparative crime statistics: Marshall B. Clinard and D. J. Abbot, *Crime in Developing Countries* (New York: John Wiley & Sons, 1973), pp. 81–3, 92 and 116. Cases: Erasto Mugo, *Crime and Delinquency in Kenya* (Nairobi: East African Literature Bureau, 1975), pp. 9, 37; and D. N. A. Nortey, 'Crime Trends in Ghana', *Ghana Social Science Journal,* VII, 1 (1977), pp. 102–16.
37. Kenya study: E. B. Evans, 'Secondary Education, Unemployment and Crime in Kenya', *Journal of Modern African Studies,* XIII (1975), pp. 55–66. Relevant criminological studies drawing link between crime and poverty: see items cited in next two notes.
38. Ghanaian study quoted: S. K. Weinberg, 'Urbanization and Male Delinquency in Ghana', *Journal of Research in Crime and Delinquency,* II (1965), pp. 85–94. Kampala study cited: Clinard and Abbott, *Crime* (n. 36 above), p. 97. Supporting studies: Hutton, 'How the Unemployed Survive', (n. 32 above), p. 11; Hake, *African Metropolis* (n. 30 above), pp. 205–14; R. Holloway, 'Street Boys in Addis Ababa', *Community Development Journal,* V, 3 (1970), pp. 139–44; and P. Satgé *et al.,* 'Le problème des jeunes', in Groupes d'études dakaroises, *Dakar en devenir* (Paris: Présence Africaine, 1968), pp. 337–8.
39. See, for a study of Kampala, Clinard and Abbot, *Crime* (n. 36 above), pp. 123–7, 159, 210; for a study of Lusaka, W. Clifford, 'Crime and Culture – An African Study', *Canadian Journal of Corrections,* VIII, 3 (1966), pp. 157–66; O. Oloruntimehin, 'A Study of Juvenile Delinquency in a Nigerian City', *British Journal of Criminology,* XIII, 2 (1973), pp. 157–69; and M. C. Ortiques *et al.,* 'La délinquance juvénile à Dakar: Étude psychologique de 14 cas', *Psychopathologie Africaine,* I, 1 (1965), pp. 85–129.
40. Quote by F. Engels in *The Condition of the Working Class in England, 1844* (Oxford: Basil Blackwell, 1958), p. 100. Popular hostility towards the police: Clinard and Abbott, *Crime* (n. 36 above), pp. 24–5, 220; and J. M. N. Wasikhongo, 'The Role and Character of the Police in Africa and Western

Countries', *International Journal of Criminology and Penology*, IV, 4 (1976), pp. 383–96. Quote on Accra: K. Hart, 'Informal Income Opportunities and Urban Employment in Ghana', *Journal of Modern African Studies*, XI, 1 (1973), p. 76. Kisenyi study: Clinard and Abbott, *Crime* (n. 36 above), p. 87.

41. Poor as objects of crime in Kampala and Nairobi: Clinard and Abbott, *Crime* (n. 36 above), pp. 25–6, 152; Hake, *African Metropolis* (n. 30 above), pp. 213–14.

42. Samuel Huntington, *Political Order in Changing Societies* (New Haven: Yale University Press, 1968), p. 290; Frantz Fanon, *The Wretched of the Earth* (Harmondsworth: Penguin, 1967).

43. Hanna and Hanna, 'The Cynical Nationalists', in William John Hanna (ed.), *University Students and African Politics* (New York: Africana Publishing House, 1975), p. 66; Joel Barkan, *An African Dilemma: University Students, Development and Politics in Ghana, Tanzania and Uganda* (Nairobi: Oxford University Press, 1975), pp. 188–9.

44. See W. J. Hanna, 'Systemic Constraints and Individual Activism', in Hanna (ed.), *University Students* (n. 43 above).

45. W. J. Hanna, 'Students, Universities and Political Outcomes', in Hanna (ed.), *University Students* (n. 43 above). For studies of the causes of student activism, see A. R. Zolberg, 'Political Generations in Conflict: The Ivory Coast Case', in Hanna (ed.), *University Students*, esp. p. 130; and R. Buijtenhuijs, 'The Revolutionary Potential of Black Africa: Dissident Elites', *African Perspectives*, 2 (1978), pp. 135–46.

46. On employment opportunities: Ali Mazrui, *Political Values and the Educated Class in Africa* (London: Heinemann Educational Books, 1978), pp. xi–xii.

47. Revisionist view of the 'unemployment problem': K. Hart, 'The Politics of Unemployment in Ghana', *African Affairs*, LXXV (1976). On the preponderance of educated young people among the urban unemployed, see the following surveys: Peil, 'Male Unemployment in Lagos', (n. 32 above), pp. 20–1; Caroline Hutton, *Reluctant Farmers? A Study of Unemployment and Planned Rural Development in Uganda* (Nairobi: East African Publishing House, 1973), pp. 40–102; A. Callaway, 'Education Expansion and the Rise of Youth Unemployment', in P. C. Lloyd *et al.*, *The City of Ibadan* (Cambridge: Cambridge University Press, 1967), pp. 201–2; J. Sween and R. Clignet, 'Urban Unemployment as a Determinant of Political Unrest: The Case Study of Douala, Cameroon', *Canadian Journal of African Studies*, III, 2 (1965), pp. 467, 476; Teshome Mulat, *Educated Unemployment in the Sudan*, ILO Working Paper, WEP 2–18/WP5, July 1975, pp. 8–15; and Elliott Skinner, *African Urban Life: The Transformation of Ouagadougou* (Princeton: Princeton University Press, 1974), pp. 81–2.

48. On how the unemployed survive in town: P. C. W. Gutkind, 'The Energy of Despair: Social Organization of the Unemployed in Two African Cities: Nairobi and Lagos', *Civilisations*, XVIII, 3 and 4 (1967), pp. 186–210 and 380–402 (summary of notion of 'social circulation' on p. 397); Hutton, 'How the Unemployed Survive in Town' (n. 32 above), pp. 10–11; Peil, 'Male Unemployment in Lagos' (n. 32 above), pp. 20–3; D. Brokensha, 'Kofi in Search of a Job', *ODU*, No. 1 (1969), pp. 71–84; Kenneth King,

Jobless in Kenya: A Case Study of the Educated Unemployed, Bureau of Educational Research, Faculty of Education, University of Nairobi, Monograph Series No. 1, October 1976, p. 10, chaps. 3 and 5; and I. M. Shalaby, 'The Psychological Effects of Unemployment on the Unemployed in Khartoum, Sudan', paper presented to Annual Meeting of the African Studies Association, Syracuse, 1973, pp. 8–9. View that obligations to unemployed kin are diminishing: R. Cruise O'Brien, 'Unemployment, the Family and Class Formation in Africa', *Manpower and Unemployment Research in Africa*, VI, 2 (1973), pp. 47–59.

49. King, *Jobless in Kenya* (n. 48 above), *passim*, esp. chaps. 1 and 2, quotes pp. 7 and 4.

50. Unemployed as 'shock troops': W. A. Lewis, *Development Planning: The Essentials of Economic Policy* (New York: Harper & Row, 1966), p. 86. African job-seekers as potentially radical: P. C. W. Gutkind, 'From the Energy of Despair to the Anger of Despair', *Canadian Journal of African Studies*, VII, 2 (1973), pp. 179–98; A. J. McQueen, 'Unemployment and the Future Orientations of Nigerian School Leavers', *Canadian Journal of African Studies*, III, 2 (1969), pp. 458–9; and E. B. Evans, 'Sources of Socio-Political Instability in an African State: The Case of Kenya's Educated Unemployed', *African Studies Review*, XX, 1 (1977), pp. 37–52, quote p. 48.

51. Ambivalence of the unemployed: King, *Jobless in Kenya* (n. 48 above), chap. 6; R. Cohen and D. Michael, 'The Revolutionary Potential of the African Lumpenproletariat: A Skeptical View', *Institute of Development Studies Bulletin*, V, 2–3 (1973), pp. 33–9; and Richard Sandbrook and Jack Arn, *The Labouring Poor and Urban Class Formation: The Case of Greater Accra*, Occasional Monograph No. 12, Centre for Developing-Area Studies, McGill University, 1977, chap. 6.

6   Social Control and Urban Struggle

The sharks of Uhuru
Devour their own children,
The heads
Of their blood brothers
Bash with the battle axes
Of their tails!

I hear
The triumphant song
Of the hero of Uhuru,
Listen to him
Shout his praise name,
Hear his footsteps
As he prances
The mock-fight
Of victory. . . .

Okot p'Bitek, *Song of Prisoner*, 1971

What are the politics of marginalization? How is order maintained in the rapidly growing and conspicuously inegalitarian cities of peripheral capitalist societies? Does conflict express popular dissidence and, if so, with what implications for development strategy?

In the 1960s opinion varied as to the political significance of rapid urban growth in underdeveloped countries. One view was that there was

no more fertile ground for revolutionary propaganda than the beleaguered cities of the underdeveloped nations. Misery, bitterness, and resentment in the teeming slums and squatter colonies, low wages and long hours in the new factories, competition for jobs, and child labor, all recall the scene that made the *Communist Manifesto* an alluring document in nineteenth century Europe.

But the more widely accepted position by the end of the decade, at least among social scientists, was that of Joan Nelson: 'there is little ground for belief that the swelling urban masses of today's developing nations will prove to be politically radical or violent', and hence 'a large mass of marginals persisting over many decades has no necessary political implications.'[1]

While the evidence is more consistent with Nelson's viewpoint, the conventional political analyses of the urban poor require refinement and extension. In the first place, the terms of the debate – 'urban poor', 'migrants', 'established urbanites', 'urban marginals' – are too gross. It is for this reason that I sought to elaborate a finer class analysis in the preceding chapters. In this chapter I shall argue that among the urban underclasses it is the working class, and more specifically certain sectors of it, that tends to form the leading edge of popular political consciousness. In the second place, this chapter avoids the exclusive focus upon political attitudes that informs so many other studies of the urban poor.[2] Attitudes are important (to the extent that they can be validly ascertained); but more important is an understanding of the cultural milieu and economic and political structures that shape them. I thus seek to explain the political behaviour of underprivileged urban elements by locating them within their cultural, economic and political matrix. In particular, I explore the relationship between the material conditions of certain strata and the efflorescence of depoliticizing belief systems, the implications for mass political activity of the tendency for routine political conflict to crystallize around communal and clientelistic identities, and the role of the state in legitimating the peripheral capitalist order and preventing or suppressing political unrest.

Finally, I do not intend to suggest that structural and cultural conditions in societies undergoing a marginalizing pattern of development, 'overdetermine' political quietism among the poor. Political protest sporadically erupts in urban Africa, though the ideology that typically animates this provides little guidance for progressive change.

The cultural milieu

It is natural for an observer from an affluent society (or class) to feel that the material wretchedness and oppressiveness of the life of the poor provide ample grounds for revolution. Yet this rarely occurs. There are obviously subjective factors that mould the perception of objective reality on the part of the underprivileged. One of the most crucial of these is the set of customs, norms and meaning systems that constitute a culture.

URBANISM AND MODERNITY

There is an influential tradition in American sociology that equates urbanization with cultural change. In this view, urbanism is a 'way of life' that encourages a migrant to shed his traditional customs, orientations and behaviour-patterns. Some sociologists, in investigating the process of acculturation, have implicitly carried this framework over into their studies of Third World cities.[3]

Recently, however, this sort of approach has come into question. A massive study of 5500 urban workers and self-employed in six underdeveloped countries, carried out under the direction of Alex

184 SOCIAL CONTROL AND URBAN STRUGGLE

Inkeles and David Smith, refutes the notion of the city as modernizer. Although these authors were initially sympathetic to this proposition, they found no statistically significant evidence that 'might prove that the amount or quality of urban experience, in its own right, played any substantial part in accounting for the individual modernity of the men in [their] samples'. Their evidence therefore contradicts 'not only popular expectations but also the established wisdom of so many theorists for whom the city epitomizes modernizing influences'.[4]

This finding is significant inasmuch as what Inkeles and Smith label 'modern man' is more likely to evince an activist, even a radical, orientation than 'traditional man'. Modern man has a marked sense of efficacy. This is

> reflected in his belief that, either alone or in concert with others, he may take actions which can affect the course of his life and that of his community; in his own active efforts to improve his own conditions and that of his family; and in his rejection of passivity, resignation and fatalism toward the course of life's events.

Traditional man, in contrast, passively accepts his fate, lacks a sense of efficacy, fears innovation, evinces highly parochial loyalties and preoccupations, limits his ambitions to fit narrow goals, and cultivates 'humble sentiments of gratitude for what little one has'.[5] There is obviously a danger here that ideal types become caricatures. Nevertheless, from the viewpoint of social change, the analyst must count it a pity that urbanism does not, in fact, necessarily breed modern man.

But if urban life *per se* does not shape beliefs, norms and behaviour, what does? One fruitful line of analysis stemming from Marxian scholarship explains forms of consciousness by reference to the modes of production in which particular classes and strata are embedded. At the most mechanistic and deterministic, the proposition is that 'economic base determines consciousness'. This is clearly unacceptable. A more open approach holds that the material conditions of specific classes provide a more or less favourable environment for the propagation of particular values, norms and belief-systems. Thus, while material conditions constrain the diffusion of ideologies incongruent with the operative principles of a particular mode of production, free political and ideological activity can nonetheless influence the prevailing forms of consciousness. This is the general approach that I adopt.

With respect to cities, one can then contend that the 'urban–modern' values and orientations identified by Western sociologists actually constitute the forms of consciousness congruent with a highly developed capitalist mode of production.[6] Capitalist production demands regularity, impersonality, and human control of the environment by the application of scientific knowledge. In African cities, however, a large part, sometimes a majority, of the labour force must find income opportunities outside this advanced mode. It is significant that the non-capitalist forms of production and exchange in which these people engage bear a marked resemblance to the peasant mode of production from which they migrated (in most cases). Similarities in the typical reliance upon family labour and primitive technology to earn relatively low incomes are evident, but the resemblance extends beyond these. The existential position of peasant and self-employed or casual worker is similar: both constantly face considerable risks which they cannot control. The nature of these with respect to the labouring poor I have already sketched. For the peasant, insecurities arise in the form not only of natural calamities (drought, pests or diseases), but also of fluctuations in the world price for the goods he produces. If the material conditions of life of many urban-dwellers remain much the same as those of peasants, one should not then be surprised that peasant (or 'traditional') forms of consciousness survive in the cities.

The findings of the Inkeles and Smith study support this interpretation (though they do not draw this implication). While formal schooling and exposure to the mass media foster individual modernity, the most important influence in transforming traditional values, attitudes and behaviour is factory employment. Furthermore, distinctions among factories, such as the relative competence or political orientations of management, matter much less in determining the workers' modernity than the sheer length of time spent in factory work. The longer the term, the higher the individual modernity. In contrast, participation in the informal sector allows traditional patterns to persist. Samples in the Inkeles and Smith study include a control group of 'urban non-industrial workers' (UNI) who had lived in the cities for comparable lengths of time to the industrial workers. In four of the five poor countries in which valid comparisons can be made, the experienced factory workers are significantly more 'modern' than the self-employed and casual workers with whom they are matched. There was no significant difference in individual modernity in the fifth case. In sum, 'the factory is an effective school modernizing men, whereas, taken together, the results indicate that work as a UNI has but little ability to modernize a man.'[7]

TRADITIONAL BELIEF-SYSTEMS

There is a propensity for people in industrialized societies to divide the universe into discrete spheres: material and spiritual, natural and supernatural, scientific and religious. This dichotomous notion was alien to the pre-industrial cosmologies of the diverse societies of tropical Africa. 'Religious' concepts suffused – and for large categories of people continue to suffuse – all areas of life.

But this does not mean that traditional world-views lacked a rational basis. Robin Horton persuasively refutes the notion that 'African traditional thought' is fundamentally dissimilar to Western scientific thought. There are, of course, important differences between the two; these derive from the distinction that traditional thought formed a closed idea-system, whereas scientific theories are open to refutation on the grounds that a new theory explains a wider range of previously anomalous facts. Hence, change in the tenets of the former could come about only gradually, and without acknowledgement. Despite this difference, however, Horton contends that it is quite inaccurate to conceptualize the distinction as causal versus supernatural orientation, or even empirical versus non-empirical. Although traditional cosmology was not scientific because it was not open to alternatives, it was akin to science in seeking to explain, predict and control events in this world. Both, in short, represent a quest for the order underlying apparent disorder.[8]

Considered specifically as theories about the world, traditional belief-systems differ in a major way from scientific theories. While the latter search for explanations in terms of non-personal or material forces, the former rely upon *personalized* explanations. Consider, for instance, the tendency for traditional thought to ascribe disease to disturbed social relationships – in particular, to ancestral wrath or the malice of kin or neighbours. This theory of disease is not simple superstition. In the West, there is a renewed interest in psychosomatic illnesses, and a recognition that disturbances in one's social life can produce mental stress and physiological disturbances. In sum, 'a theory based on gods and spirits pointed to certain causal connections which have proved fruitful in the absence of powerful drugs; and this is so even if the theoretical framework from which the notions derived is not very serviceable as a wider view of the world'.[9]

Of course, traditional cosmologies have rarely survived intact into the present day. Yet the personal idiom of explanations of misfortune and the recourse to thaumaturgical means to predict and ward off misfortune and control events, continue to flourish in the extreme insecurity of peasant life. If the material conditions of life in the informal sector of the cities similarly breed anxiety and uncertainty, then the recrudescence in the urban areas of beliefs in witchcraft and sorcery should appear entirely reasonable. Indeed, those notions are likely to persist even among the workers in the capitalist mode of production; the bulk of workers, after all, were raised in rural societies where, as children, they internalized the basic world-view of personalized misfortune. This socialization will not be undone swiftly. In general, then, as Joan La Fontaine reports for Kinshasa in the early 1960s:

> Urban life produces new anxieties and tensions. Most urban dwellers have no adequate means of subsistence except employment. . . . . For the unskilled or semi-skilled urban workers, the risk of unemployment has been a threat for many years. . . . Town standards measure a man's success by his economic circumstances and responsibility for this lies with the individual. Town life is thus highly competitive and the results of failure are readily apparent.

Conditions in the life of the urban dweller are subject to changes brought about by the economic and political forces that he does not comprehend, but which nevertheless affect him deeply. In his struggle to succeed, the individual is more isolated and dependent on himself than he would be in a traditional setting. Thus, it is not surprising that beliefs in witchcraft, sorcery, and magic continue to flourish in towns.[10]

A major indicator of the survival of thaumaturgical beliefs in the cities is the prevalence and popularity of fetishists, diviners, marabouts, herbalists and traditional doctors. Clients generally approach such people for help with medical, marital or employment problems, or for protection against sorcery or witchcraft. Patients are not only the poor and illiterate. In Ibadan, a study of 100 (of the approximately 900) practising herbalists and diviners in 1963 reports that both 'elite' and poor families had recourse to them, though the former often received treatment from modern doctors as well. In Lusaka, by contrast, an investigation of 1290 patients of twenty-three traditional doctors shows their average educational level to be well below that of the population within their residential area. A similar finding emerges from a study of *waganga* (traditional doctors) in Nairobi. In Kampala, the shrines to (Baganda) traditional spirits apparently attract people from all classes, religious denominations, and even non-Baganda.

For the man in the street [record two anthropologists], whether he be Christian or Muslim, traditional religious beliefs and practices have always been a part of his everyday life and 'world view', even if considerably modified in form. There is for the urban dweller a strong continuity of religious belief with the past and with the present rural society of Buganda.[11]

This perpetuation of pre-industrial belief-systems, albeit in attenuated and mutated (that is, syncretistic) form, is not just an anthropological curiosity. They serve the latent function of reducing or channelling in apolitical directions the social tension inherent in highly inegalitarian societies, and hence fortifying social order. In the first place, by providing an explanation of the misfortunes associated with poverty in personalized terms, these traditional theories thereby militate against a general recognition of deprivation as an aspect of social injustice. There is a propensity to see evil as a consequence of capricious, individual action, not of impersonal class domination and exploitation. Yet a perception of social injustice is probably essential for the development of movements for the eradication of mass poverty. In the second place, such theories prescribe strategies for controlling or changing events in this life which involve individual and thaumaturgical responses, not collective responses. What is needed to destroy evil is not a programme of political action, but the repeated performance of certain rituals or practices. This notion is not propitious for the diffusion of the view that mass poverty is subject to change through human agency. Finally, the emphasis upon personal malevolence inherent in witchcraft and sorcery is bound to exacerbate interpersonal fears and hostilities.[12] These beliefs thus constitute a powerful cultural impediment to cooperation among the deprived to remedy their generic problems.

It would, however, be incorrect to conclude that religious beliefs and practices are invariably inimical to solidarity. There are instances of ethnically based cults that reinforce reciprocity and cohesion among the poor in the face of a common insecurity.[13] In certain circumstances, Christian and Islamic movements may also foster solidarity, though rarely for political ends.

THE MEANING OF CONVERSIONS

Conversion to Christianity or Islam rarely signifies a sharp break with traditional cosmologies. It is often not a simple substitution of one set of theories of evil and its transcendence for another. Instead, religious conversion commonly represents a way of adapting traditional theories to new and unfamiliar social situations – particularly those found in the towns and cities.[14] The direction of adaptation is not without political implications. Where religious notions continue to permeate the life of the common people, there is likely to be a close relationship between religious and socio-political change.[15]

Certain elements of Christian tradition are not incompatible with major themes in African traditional thought. Christianity originally concerned itself, not only with communion with the Supreme Being and the destiny of the soul, but also with the explanation, prediction and control of events in this world. There was (and remains in some Western sects) a belief in miracles, soothsaying and faith-healing. In time, however, the established churches largely replaced these concerns with an emphasis upon communion with God and the saving of souls. What the missionaries brought to Africa was

> the promise of a new source of strength which would enable people to live in and cope with a new world. In the circumstances, it was easy to assume that the promise involved a new system of explanation–prediction–control; and it required a more detailed inside acquaintance with the churches before people could see that all that was being offered them was a new form of communion.[16]

The response was the intermingling of Christian (and/or Islamic) and traditional religious beliefs and rituals which is so widely observed, especially though not exclusively among the poor and less educated. If in Western industrial societies the churches surrendered explanation and control in the face of scientific progress, the poor in African cities continue to seek powerful protection against the vagaries of a precarious existence. There is hence a range of converts: from the person whose ritual approaches to God in church (or mosque) are rare in a religious life dominated by a cult of the lesser spirits, to the one for whom the Supreme Being monopolizes all religious activity.[17]

One potential syncretistic response in the context of mass poverty is millenarianism. Religion, of course, is not invariably an 'opiate of the masses'. Millenarian movements denote the radical face of religious ideologies:

it would seem that the combination of the historical and the meta-historical in the millenial time conception, the vision of the unification of the transcendent and the terrestrial in a completely transformed and holy social order, the merger between individual and social destinies, coupled with a total rejection of the existing order and a view of an imminent final struggle have a powerful revolutionary potential.

As Vittorio Lanternari shows, messianic cults in colonial societies were 'religions of the oppressed', embodying a vision of the future in which the white-dominated social order is inverted. These cults were thus in some colonies progenitors of the nationalist movements. But in the slums and shanty towns of contemporary Africa, millenarian responses are virtually absent. The socio-economic function of religious activity is more in the direction of integrating the poor into the existing social order than challenging prevailing norms, values and goals.[18] This may constitute further evidence that African slums largely constitute slums of hope, not despair.

If millenarian movements are unusual in African cities, syncretistic sects variously described as 'nativist', 'prophetic', 'spiritual' or 'independent' churches abound. They catered for an estimated 6 million adherents in tropical Africa in the late 1960s. Part of the appeal of these churches stems from their willingness to accept the traditional religious concern with this life. Unlike the established Christian denominations, they promise deliverance from evil as manifest in mental or physiological illness and personal misfortune. Faith-healing and anti-sorcery rites generally figure prominently in the liturgy: the power of sorcery and witchcraft is not denied but counteracted. Also attractive to converts in the teeming slums and squatter settlements is the promise of fellowship – 'a new earthly and spiritual home in the midst of a chaotic world of rapid social change'. Spiritual churches typically provide an intense emotional experience, again something that the more austere established churches cannot match. Guenter Lewy writes that 'the Methodist chapel in eighteenth-century England brought a sense of belonging to the uprooted of the Industrial Revolution in a way that was very similar to the way the African separatist churches satisfy the search for community among Africans living in the squalor of shanty towns.' Not surprisingly in view of the simple message of the prophetic churches, their appeal is disproportionately to the poor and illiterate.[19]

The socio-political significance of these sects is difficult to sum up. Positively, such churches provide solace and fellowship for the wretched of the earth. Yet consolation exacts a price. These movements do not mobilize the poor for collective action to remedy generic problems; rather, by reconciling the marginalized masses to their situation and reinforcing personalized explanations of misfortune, they serve as an agent of depoliticization. In the words of a prominent authority on African religions, the independent churches

> reduce popular aspirations to concern with present benefits such as the type of healing they offer, to a sense of the power and presence of the Spirit manifest in the more ecstatic ways, to protection from the traditional spiritual evil powers and the provision of a general sense of social and spiritual security through having a new community in which to feel at home. These benefits do not seem to depend on what the politicians do or fail to do. But as the sights are raised and the full benefits of the modern world come into view more clearly there may come a greater interest in politics, and a disillusionment with the situation after independence. . . . Whether this disillusionment will produce reactions or revolts akin to those prompted by the miseries of colonialism, or a more extreme escapism into 'spiritual' religion cannot be foreseen. . . .[20]

Islam in Africa is an even more complex cultural phenomenon than Christianity. Indeed, Islam is not only a religion but a complete way of life. This accounts in some measure for its attractiveness to urban migrants in those countries where Muslim communities exist. Insofar as Islam offers a common language (Hausa, Kiswahili or Arabic), a form of dress, eating habits, the form of wedding and funeral ceremonies, and rules relating to divorce and inheritance – in addition to religious practices – it constitutes a convenient, ready-made vehicle for integration into urban life. This is especially the case for those in the informal sector, for there is an ancient connection between Islam and trade. Conversion to Islam can thus signify, apart from an apparent change in religious commitment, the adoption of a new, supra-tribal identity and community. The significance of this for political practice I shall allude to in the following section.

The alleged innate conservatism of Islamic doctrine is an important question, but one that is far too intricate to receive a definitive investigation in these pages. Suffice it to say that such an interpretation is over-generalized. There are messianic movements in Muslim as well as Christian societies. In Islamic societies, it is not unusual for sects to form along quasi-class lines – as in Lagos – or even for Islam to form the idiom of class conflict – as in Kano, for instance. In the latter, leaders among the factory workers tend to articulate industrial grievances as violations of Islamic doctrine. This is an effective means available to labour leaders to mobilize workers' support for industrial action and to legitimate such action within Kano society. Islam, after all, would in this case represent virtually the only ideology from which workers could draw in support of class-based protests.[21]

For the purposes of this discussion, the essential point is that Islam represents for many converts a means of adapting traditional cosmologies to a new world. Unlike mission Christianity, Islam has not demanded that converts abandon long-cherished notions regarding explanation, prediction and control. This tolerance, scholars of Islam often observe, facilitates the widespread acceptance of Islam in Africa. A consequence is the emergence of an Africanized Islam or pseudo-Islamic culture at the mass level. As one authority argues:

> There are societies which have adopted some facets of Muslim culture without formally adopting the faith. There are others which have formally adopted the faith but maintained customs which are in contradiction to it. Above all, there are many which have adopted Islam and maintained many of their practices and beliefs while giving them an Islamic (in the broadest sense) colouring.

Among individuals also, the degree of conversion is highly variable. At the most superficial, conversion may mean no more than a convert's adoption of Muslim dress and his recourse to the thaumaturgical powers (divinations, amulets, medicines) of a *mallam* ('lettered man') in the event of personal misfortune, whether illness, theft or economic setback. This sort of conversion is not uncommon among temporary African migrants, according to anthropological reports. For others, Islam suffuses its adherent's world-view – though even in these cases some traditional notions of manipulating the natural and spiritual worlds may persist.[22]

In sum, I have contended in this section that an understanding of urban politics requires a recognition that pre-industrial belief-systems continue to permeate the world-view of at least the labouring poor. In light of their material conditions and common experience of a rural upbringing, the persistence of personalized explanations of misfortune and thaumaturgical methods of manipulating this-worldly events is not irrational or mere superstition. Conversion is often more akin to an adaptation of existing peasant beliefs than their total or immediate abandonment. Needless to add, this cultural milieu is not conducive to notions of structural change or the necessity of human agency to bring this about. It is probable that the tenacious hold of traditional cosmologies among the poor will diminish only with the continued incursion of industrial organization and technology. 'The advent of modern industrial society', Robin Horton avers, 'must sooner or later make for depersonalization of the idiom of all theory. In Africa, as in the West, it seems likely that religion, if it survives, will do so as a way of communion but not as a system of explanation, prediction and control.'[23]

Vertical solidarities and class control

The labouring poor and working class, especially those who are recent migrants, normally engage in little routinized political activity. This was true during the era of open electoral competition; it is even more true in the authoritarian conditions prevalent today. Their forms of political expression have included: sporadic mobilization by other social forces, usually on the basis of communal appeals or the activation of patron–client networks; individual representations to men of power, generally on a clientelistic basis; 'controlled' participation by means of trade unions, neighbourhood associations or branches of governing political parties; and occasional outbursts of uninstitutionalized and sometimes violent mass protest. I shall consider controlled participation and urban unrest later; in this section I focus upon the implications for class formation of the pervasiveness of communalism and clientelism in peripheral capitalist societies.

An accurate conceptualization of communalism or clientelism must avoid two extreme positions. On the one hand, there is the view that ethnicity and/or clientelism should constitute the exclusive focus of political analysis, obviating class analysis. The usual grounds for such an approach is the alleged weakness of class identities in societies where traditional definitions of status and personalistic ties remain strong.[24] On the other hand, there is a Marxist position that tribalism and patron-clientship are simply forms of 'false consciousness' – deliberate attempts by members of dominant classes to promote control by mystifying the relations of dominance and dividing the under-classes.[25] Both viewpoints are misleading.

One can begin to fashion a more adequate framework by recognizing that, from the standpoint of the poor, participation in communal or clientelistic politics is neither wholly irrational nor wholly rational. It is not irrational or false consciousness for the underprivileged to identify their interests in factional or communal terms because some share of the fruits of victory – access to public services and jobs – do 'filter down' to them. Nonetheless, this is not to argue in favour of ignoring the class dimension. The analyst investigating the potential for social change cannot rest content with the subjective view of the participants. From the viewpoint of the *objective* interests of clients and communal actors in eradicating mass poverty and domination, these identifications are not entirely rational. Nothing serves more to preserve peripheral capitalism than the setting of tribe against tribe (except where tribe and class overlap) or faction against faction. But this is not to say that communalism or factionalism, any more than personalized and thaumaturgical belief-systems, are aspects of clever manipulation by a dominant class or classes. Class control, to the extent that communalism and clientelism foster this, is only a latent function.

COMMUNALISM

Communalism is a complex, diverse and fluid social phenomenon. It refers to the sort of political conflict in which the competing groups possess three characteristics: their members share a common culture and cultural identity; they include both sexes and all age groups; and they encompass members with unequal wealth, status and power. The remarkable diversity of forms of communalism in Africa is now widely understood, and hence requires little adumbration. Kano perhaps best exemplifies the complexity of communal politics. Here, depending upon the conflict situation, a person will perceive one of eight potential communal identities as salient: religion, birthplace, ancestral home, clan or family, 'country' (that is, region), language, urban location, or race. Elsewhere, as in Niamey, the capital of Niger, ethnic groups have arranged themselves in a caste-like relationship, so that the division of labour coincides with ethnic categories. Islam in this case represents an important force integrating the various ethnic groups. In other countries, like the Ivory Coast, where a large alien population resides, communal tensions in the cities take the form of anti-foreigner hostility. Periodic xenophobic outbursts there doubtless originate in the popular Ivorian view that foreigners are responsible for widespread unemployment. In cities where Muslims form a majority, as in Bamako, Mali or Lagos. intra-Muslim ethnic splits are common, manifest in the establishment by each major ethnic group of its own mosque. But where Christians predominate, as for instance in Freetown, Accra or Kumasi, Islam can minimize (though rarely eradicate) ethnic identities in the context of a perceived struggle on supra-tribal and religious lines with the regionally based Christians. The permutations of communalism are manifold.[26]

Ethnicity, the most usual form of communalism in Africa, varies in its saliency both among countries and over time. But even where ethnic identity has been highly politicized, as in Nigerian and Kenyan cities, ethnic relations among ordinary people are usually harmonious. The norm in the overcrowded low-income residential areas is ethnic mixing in houses. Typically, landlords evince greater concern about a prospective tenant's financial status, trustworthiness, and tolerance of others, than about his tribe. Neighbours must find ways to get along with one another if life is to be tolerable. Out of day-to-day interaction, inter-ethnic friendships not infrequently emerge, even where tribal stereotyping abounds. Children, as elsewhere, are the great mixers. In a Nairobi slum, for example, 'little frightened Nandi boys who cry when strangers approach become laughing, Swahili-shouting, Pumwani children in a matter of months, roaming far from their mother's verandah with friends of many tribes, playing cards, and listening to the stories of old men far into the night.' Of course, this social harmony rarely connotes the elimination of ethnic identity or of an underlying mutual suspicion. (Membership of ethnic associations remains widespread in the cities, especially among low-income residents.) Politicians can, and often do, play upon latent mistrust and stereotypes to mobilize ethnic followings within particular political arenas. Margaret Peil's observation with respect to Nigerian cities is apropos: 'it is this political manipulation of ethnicity which is most dangerous, because it turns a useful categorization of strangers by people whose socialization has been almost completely in terms of primary relationships into a source of communal conflicts, riots and civil war'.[27]

If the politicization of ethnic identity is a reality in some cities, what is the significance of this for the development of class consciousness and class conflict? In order to gain some specificity, I shall explore this question only in relation to wage-workers. This focus seems justifiable in view of the importance earlier assigned to the working class in the promotion of a basic-needs pattern of development. One current thesis asserts that tribalism or religious animosities obstruct class formation and the solidarity of workers and the deprived. What is one to make of this?

My position is that there is no conflict between class and ethnic (and religious) identities – up to a point. It is common for people to compartmentalize their identities, in the sense that they perceive that different identities are relevant in different social situations.

Thus, it is possible for the same person to join a trade union to advance his occupational interests, a communal association to promote his social or electoral objectives, and a religious interest group to lobby for educational reforms. In short, it is possible for an individual to be both a communal and a non-communal political actor

In some areas of social life the appropriate identity is unambiguous. For instance, a class identity is obviously salient where employees confront a recalcitrant or oppressive employer as workers. In this case the trade union is the natural organizational focus of activities (provided it possesses some autonomy), not an ethnic association or religious group. It is therefore quite understandable why workers drawn from different (sometimes antagonistic) tribes generally evince a high degree of solidarity in industrial disputes. A trade-union consciousness is not incompatible with strongly held ethnic loyalties.[28]

But the relevancy of a particular identity is not so clear cut in all social situations. There are some ambiguous situations that need to be defined; it is here that leadership plays a role in shaping societal conflicts. For instance, it is not inevitable that people in Africa will perceive party politics or *coups d'état* in ethnic terms. Yet this is in fact often the popular perception of political events. Why is it that, in countries such as Nigeria, Kenya or Zaïre, ethnic identities are usually at the centre of the political process?

Much research has gone into the investigation of the conditions under which ethnicity is politicized. It is widely accepted now that ethnic cleavages are the result of much more than merely a clash of incompatible cultural values or traditional hostilities. Rather, a solidarity along cultural–linguistic lines requires at least the following: a culturally plural society; a common arena or arenas of competition for the distribution of scarce resources and power; and a differential impact of economic and educational development along cultural–regional lines. Even then ethnic conflict is not inevitable. Leaders help to politicize ethnicity in the process of mobilizing a popular base for struggles within the dominant class. A symbiotic relationship emerges between politicians, who wish to advance their own positions, and their 'people', who come to fear political domination and economic exploitation by a culturally distinct group allegedly organized for these ends. A politician thus gains a tribal power base by successfully manipulating the appropriate cultural symbols and by articulating and advancing his people's collective aspirations (which he himself probably helped define). Needless to add, national and local political figures will not be tempted to exploit ethnic loyalties where there exists, as in Tanzania, a large number of equally small ethnic groups.[29]

I have stated that ethnic and class identities are compatible only up to a point. It is now time to clarify this. Although a politicized ethnicity can co-exist with a hardy trade-union consciousness (and even, as we shall see, an amorphous populism), it does obstruct the development of a worker consciousness encompassing solidarity in the *political* as well as the economic sphere. The Nigerian general strike of June 1964 and its aftermath aptly illustrates this point. Although there was an impressive inter-ethnic solidarity during this strike, the workers then reverted to their communal political identities in the general election of December. In Port Harcourt, we are informed,

> the same non-Ibo trade unionists who had enjoyed the complete support of Port Harcourt's predominantly Ibo rank-and-file during the general strike in 1964 were deserted when they subsequently transformed themselves from leaders of a protest movement into parliamentary candidates of political parties which were in opposition to the communally oriented NCNC. The moment the strike was concluded, the lines of political cleavage within which Port Harcourt's Ibo workers shared with workers in all Nigeria's urban centres and which for two weeks had shaped the political life of the nation were once again subordinated to the communal identities of region and nationality.[30]

Where ethnic definitions of political life are entrenched it is a difficult task for a social movement to redefine political conflict in class terms. Such redefinition is not impossible. But it is made even more difficult where the state suppresses radical movements and ideas.

In short, a politicized ethnicity is incompatible with a working-class political consciousness, except in those rare cases where class and ethnicity overlap.

CLIENTELISM

Clientelism refers to a form of inter-personal linkage involving three features. It is, first, a relationship between two persons unequal in status, wealth and influence, the archetype being the relationship between a landowner and a peasant working his land. Secondly, the formation and maintenance of the relationship depends upon reciprocity in the exchange of goods and services. The patron offers economic benefits or protection against the exactions of the authorities, while the client reciprocates with more intangible assets, such as demonstrations of esteem, information on the machinations of a patron's enemies, and political support (by voting, joining his faction in some political arena, and so on). Finally, the clientelistic relationship is a personal one, based upon face-to-face contact.[31]

The political significance of clientelism is highly variable in peripheral capitalist societies. Depending upon the situation in a particular country or region, clientelism may reinforce or vitiate ethnic identities, and weaken or occasionally strengthen the processes of class formation and class conflict. If patron–client networks are confined within ethnic (or, more generally, communal) categories, these linkages will tend to enhance communal identities and loyalties. But to the extent that these networks link the politically relevant members of various communal groups, the overall effect will probably be to augment national integration. With respect to class, some scholars argue that the vertical ties and cleavages characteristic of patron-clientship militate against class consciousness among the deprived clients. This may indeed constitute the pre-eminent tendency; but it is not an inevitable consequence. Clientelism can contribute to class formation not only *objectively* – in that a patron's greater bargaining power fosters social differentiation through unequal exchanges – but also *subjectively* – in that the inability or unwillingness of patrons to satisfy the socially prescribed exchanges can crystallize the inchoate hostilities of poor clients. For instance, where the commercialization of agriculture proceeds apace, landlords may become unwilling to continue their paternalistic relationships with tenants. The spur of the market encourages the former to substitute contractual for diffuse and particularistic obligations, in order to extract higher profits from landholdings. Alternatively, natural disasters, such as plague, famine or economic depression, may reduce the capacity of patrons to deliver the goods to clients. This too can raise the level of class tensions (as happened in Ethiopia before the fall of the monarchy).[32]

Nevertheless, the more common effect of patron–client relationships is undoubtedly to impede class formation at the bottom of society. For the poor, clientelism offers, or seems to offer, an individual solution to the generic problems of mass poverty. 'The most urgent needs of the poor', Joan Nelson acutely observes, 'are intensely individual – a day's work, a room, a week's credit, medical aid, someone to fix trouble with the police. Others equally poor and ill-connected usually cannot offer much help. The poor, rural as well as urban, turn for aid to better-established individuals or organizations. ...' But by retarding the development of class loyalties and class-based organization on the part of clients, these vertical, patronage linkages will enhance the control of the dominant classes. This is not to contend that clientelism constitutes clever manipulation by a cunning ruling class. Rather, factional leaders construct their patron–client networks in town and country only in order to augment their personal power and prestige, or to defeat personal, factional or party opponents within particular political arenas. 'Clientelistic systems are regularly strengthened or cultivated for many different reasons, but one of the principal political results is the reinforcement of class control in the system as a whole.'[33]

During the period of competitive party politics (usually covering the years immediately preceding and following independence), clientelism in the urban setting tended to tie into national political structures. Parties, even if ostensibly of the mass-mobilizational type, often operated at the local level as political machines. In some cases the patronage network penetrated deeply into the urban population. This was so, for instance, in the case of the Convention People's Party (CPP) in Accra, as I discovered in the course of field work there. Although the CPP had committed itself in 1962 to a socialist transformation in its 'Programme for Work and Happiness', it continued to base its support upon the mercenary mechanism of patronage. In Accra, ward bosses openly allocated lower-echelon municipal jobs and market stalls on the basis of party (and personal) support. In consequence, 'mass political mobilization [was] hardly possible in this situation. The leadership directly contributed to the largely economic view of politics and reinforced it rather than changing it by responsible political education.'[34]

Existing studies indicate that similar patronage activities occupied parties in Kampala, Lagos and Ibadan, before coups d'état temporarily ended electoral politics. With respect to the last city, for example, an observer in the mid-1960s noted that 'the informal political economy of Ibadan is a strikingly individualistic sphere, catering to the individual needs of a traditional clientele that does not see itself as oppresssed or alienated. In their councillors they find entrepreneurs who can get things done for them.'[35]

With the progressive restriction and frequent elimination of competitive party politics and autonomous parapolitical institutions, the incentive for political leaders to maintain extensive patron–client networks diminishes. The transition to the single-party or military regime usually reduces the political importance of the individual voter. (Of course, if intra-party contests continue, politicians cannot entirely ignore the ordinary citizen.) Concomitantly, the political weight of the 'kingmakers' increases – including normally the top bureaucrats in the public sector, military and perhaps trade unions, party officials (if any), and local notables. There is, in short, a trend towards the attenuation of politically oriented clientelistic networks and their restriction to the

politically relevant stratum of the population. However, this does not
mean that clientelism disappears among the poor. It does mean that
their patron–client linkages are likely to be multiple and apolitical – at
least with respect to national political struggles.

Lagos is an interesting case in point. During the era of party politics,
the patrons in Mushin, a low-income suburb, were Action Group (AG)
politicians. AG politicians who dominated the Mushin County Council
generally made their way into the upper ranks of the local (Yoruba)
chieftaincy system as well. This fusion of roles augmented the power of a
few politicians, increasing their effectiveness as intermediaries with the
state and as patrons.

Soon after the *coup* of 1966 and the abolition of political parties, the
same politicians re-emerged in Mushin.

A party can be outlawed, but politicians live on. Today [1970s] they behave
not as elected officials or as representatives of any partisan organization, but
as leaders who, along with chiefs and councillors, independently know what
to do and how to do it, especially in the time of human need.

All the patrons are landlords and businessmen in Mushin. 'The landlord
who participates in his ward association increases his contacts and
thereby his following; by increasing his following, he may gain enough
support to advance his position in the chieftaincy system (or formerly
the parties) and thus broaden the scope of his contacts.' Owing to the
continuance of the mutually reinforcing relationship between local
political influence and control of economic resources, patrons in
Mushin retain an incentive to persevere in their role, even in the absence
of parties.[36]

Personal, diffuse and reciprocal linkages between people of unequal
wealth and power can therefore persist in a national context of
departicipation, thereby continuing to obstruct the development of a
common cause among poor clients.

Both ethnic and clientelistic solidarities normally promote a
conservative politics. The usual, though unintended, consequence of
both is to fortify class control in highly inegalitarian societies. True,
both sorts of linkages and identities assist some among the poor in
coping with the acute problems of survival. But the particularistic logic
of ethnic and clientelistic systems is profoundly antagonistic to an
assault on poverty. This necessitates a universalistic and programmatic
response on the part of the authorities to transform the economy and
social structure. But change of the sort envisaged would undoubtedly
undermine the power of ethnic or factional leaders. Hence, as René
Lemarchand rightly concludes, 'the preferred alternative [for such
leaders] is to use external resources to further solidify patron-alliances at
the top while . . . retarding by every conceivable means, including force,
the advent or resurgence of mass politics.'[37]

The state and social control

One important function of the state, as I indicated in chapter 3, is to manage political conflict in order to maintain the order and stability necessary for production. This involves, in the first place, efforts to create and maintain the legitimacy of the capitalist system. To this end, agencies of the state may seek to socialize the populace through the diffusion of official ideologies or the propagation of 'appropriate' values and attitudes. Other agencies often attempt to circumscribe and vitiate class conflict by means of the direct or indirect incorporation into the state of political and parapolitical associations, the co-optation of leaders of dissident groups, and the working out of accommodations in the face of effective protest. These efforts do not, of course, always meet with success. In the event of political unrest the state must resort to coercion in order to re-establish political order.

How and with what effect does the state supporting peripheral capitalist development in Africa fulfil the function of social control?

OFFICIAL SOCIALIZATION

'One of the central aims of any dominant class', asserts Frank Parkin, 'is to make the rules governing the distribution of rewards seem legitimate in the eyes of all, including those who stand to gain least from such rules. The greater the extent to which this is achieved, the more stable the political order is likely to be, and the less need for recourse to coercive means.'[38]

Certainly, there is no dearth of portentous, officially sanctioned ideologies in post-colonial Africa. It may be true, as one authority argues, that the utterances of many African leaders are insufficiently systematic and integrated to warrant the appellation 'ideology'. There are, nonetheless, some rather elaborate official philosophies: 'Nkrumahism' (or 'Consciencism'), the 'National Revolution' (National Redemption Council, Ghana), '*Négritude*' (Senegal), 'Humanism' (Zambia), '*Mobutisme*' (Zaïre), 'African Socialism' (Kenya), and so on.

One effort to distill the essence of these basically nationalist ideologies refers to their principal themes as classlessness, sacrifice, order and national unity. One motif is the illegitimacy of class conflict following political independence. Inasmuch as the social and economic problems are clear, all should apply themselves unselfishly to the task of nation-building under the direction of the ruling party (or junta). There are usually parallel exhortations about the necessity for hard work and sacrifice so that all will benefit from future prosperity. Additionally, there is normally a shift in emphasis from liberty to order in the post-colonial era. Order is essential if the nation is to undertake the massive task of nation-building and to confound its several internal ('tribalist') and/or external ('neo-colonialist') enemies. A further common claim relates to an alleged traditional political pattern of consensus, rather than institutionalized conflict. The implication is obviously that open dissent is unwarrantable. Finally, there is an unsurprising stress upon national unity. These themes are only what one would expect from regimes intent upon establishing their legitimacy.[39]

Yet, though such official political ideologies abound, it is unlikely that they are widely influential. It became evident by the late 1960s that scholars writing about single-party regimes had misled their readers by taking ideological pronouncements seriously. In practice, ideology bore little relation to the actual clientelistic or communal basis of routine political life. In Ghana, for instance, the Convention People's Party after 1961 was supposed to engage itself in propagating the precepts of Nkrumahism or African Socialism among the people. The party established a school, the Kwame Nkrumah Ideological Institute, to ensure that its cadres (and leaders in other spheres) would be well versed in this ideology. However, in the author's study with Jack Arn of political orientations among the poor in Accra, we found that few former CPP militants, let alone ordinary citizens, could say what Nkrumahism or the CPP stood for – except jobs for the loyal. 'The fulminations on high by the CPP radicals had apparently left little residue in the minds of the labouring poor.'

A similar judgement would no doubt apply to the effect of *Mobutisme* in Zaïre today. In 1967 the inaptly named Mouvement Populaire de la Révolution (MPR) created a youth wing (JMPR) to inculcate the principles of this ideology among primary and secondary school students. However, a study in the mid-1970s of the JMPR's role in Lisala, a town in north-western Zaïre, reveals the abject failure of this organization as a mobilizing agency. The problem lay partly in the vagueness of the doctrine: even the JMPR leaders in Lisala could not define such key concepts as *révolution* and *radicalisation*, though *authenticité* was reasonably clear. Popular cynicism about politics was also a problem. The response of the JMPR to these impediments was to stress form over substance. In a coercive atmosphere, it organized cheerleading sessions where the assembled students learned party slogans and songs. Mobutu and the MPR thereby demonstrated the power of the state to potential dissidents, though surely not the cogency of the precepts that ostensibly guided the nation's fate.[40]

It is plausible that the operative legitimating ideology in these peripheral capitalist societies is not the fatuous official one but a set of beliefs derivative from the values of social mobility and self-advancement. Albert Hirschman perceptively refers to a 'hope factor' in the process of economic development that fosters acceptance of present inequality and poverty:

> In the early stages of rapid economic development, when inequalities in the distribution of income among different classes, sectors, and regions are apt to increase sharply, it can happen that society's *tolerance* for such disparities will

be substantial. To the extent that such tolerance comes into being, it accommodates, as it were, the increasing inequalities in an almost providential fashion. But this tolerance is like a credit that falls due at a certain date. It is extended in the expectation that eventually the disparities will narrow again. If this does not occur, there is bound to be trouble and, perhaps, disaster.[41]

For this hope factor to operate, the underprivileged must believe that the success of others is due, not to their connections or other special advantages, but to chance, fate, or superior abilities. There is evidence that such a belief continues to prevail in the low-income urban neighbourhoods – and not just in Africa. Among the poor Yoruba in Ibadan and Agege, Lagos, 'inequality is seen as an inevitable feature of society, one's own position in the hierarchy being determined by a not altogether immutable destiny, by one's own character (and hence efforts) and by the good or evil intentions of others – helpers, witches, rivals, and the like.' In Greater Accra, a large-scale survey reveals that 'a popular view prevails among the poor that the class structure is indeed open'. In Lusaka, 'although most respondents [in a squatter settlement] were aware of class distinction . . . relatively few felt that inequalities were unfair. Although their incomes were low and they were squatters lacking almost every urban facility, they expressed very little hostility toward the affluent and privileged "elites".' In Mathare Valley, Nairobi, the people 'accept the basic legitimacy of a stratified social system in which the majority of the rewards go to the highly educated few. Rather than seeking to destroy this elite group, they want their children to become part of it.'[42]

But it is important to note that this 'hope factor' does not just spontaneously emerge and survive: it receives institutional backing via the educational system. Education serves as a mechanism of social control to the extent that it legitimates inequality by fostering acceptance of the applicability of the meritocratic principle. This is the principle that only the best and the brightest will make their way through the school system and, on this basis, into the most highly prized societal positions. 'Because schooling would be open to all, one's position in the social division of labour could be portrayed as a result, not of birth, but of one's own efforts and talents.' Consequently, the educational system inculcates the view that 'failure to do well in this basically just system is an individual problem, not a societal problem'.[43] So long as some individuals of humble origins gain significant social nobility by means of educational success, this notion receives reinforcement.

Consider, by way of illustration, the role of education in the well-researched case of Kenya. Here, according to David Court, the educational catchwords are: expansion, equality of opportunity, and advancement by merit. Expansion of the educational system geared to employment in the modern sector may appear irrational when employment opportunities there are so bleak. But, of course, a political rationale is at work. If equality of opportunity is a major aspect of the meritocratic principle, then education, the key to social mobility for most, must appear to be open to the children of *all* classes and regions. This requires the building of new schools, regardless of employment prospects. The meritocratic principle also requires that scholastic advancement depend only upon merit:

> Tested and certified academic achievement has been chosen as the measure of objectivity in Kenya. Every wage-earning job has a pre-requisite minimum educational qualification. This is true not simply for the entry points to the formal system, but for every type of educational activity, including the University with the sanctity of its degrees, adult education where correspondence courses are geared almost entirely to formal examinations, technical education with the remorseless domination of the London City and Guilds, right down to the village polytechnics which increasingly view success in Trade Tests as their *raison d'être*.[44]

Although the Kenyan government has succeeded quite well in promoting acceptance of the mobility ethic, this does not mean that equality of opportunity actually exists. True, the government has vastly expanded the number of primary and secondary schools, including some in backward regions, and has removed fees for early primary schooling. But there remain glaring regional disparities in the provision of educational facilities and class disparities in access to the highest quality schools (access being regulated by location of the school and by the payment of substantial fees). Furthermore, the *content* of examinations discriminates against the rural and urban poor; the requisite facility in English and familiarity with Western concepts are more likely to develop among the children of the well-off. With respect to class crystallization, the 1972 ILO Report on Kenya concludes:

> Possession of higher education, higher income and of the influential positions that go with it ensures not only that these persons will have preferential access to scarce productive factors, but also that they will be able to transfer the benefits of high quality education to their children. What is merely the beginning of stratification by education and income, could become a rigid and institutional barrier.[45]

Insofar as such constitutive values of the meritocratic principle as equality of opportunity and advancement by merit legitimate peripheral capitalist development, they serve the interests of the dominant classes. These values encourage confidence in the structures of society while deflecting frustrations attendant upon failure onto the victims themselves.

INSTITUTIONAL INCORPORATION, CO-OPTATION AND ACCOMMODATION

Other agencies of the state seek to impede or prevent the autonomous organization of actually or potentially dissident social forces, and to neutralize those that do emerge. The effectiveness of the state in this regard is, of course, quite variable.

Corporatist policies are not unique to Latin America. They appeal to ruling groups around the world who 'fear that the old modes of domination are breaking down' and who therefore search for 'new mechanisms to link the lower classes to the state and new formulas to legitimize such mechanisms'. In consequence, 'organic–statist or corporatist arguments about the need for unity, the legitimacy of the common good over individual or class interests, and the key role of the state in social engineering are as natural a political response for Africans as for Latin Americans'.[46]

A common target of corporatist policies is organized labour. Owing to the familiarity of this process of incorporation and my earlier references to it in the case studies of chapter 3, I shall simply allude to this subject here. The taming of African labour movements predates by far the granting of independence. Corporatist policies toward labour in African countries now typically include: a labour code requiring the registration of all trade unions, registration dependent upon the fulfilment of a set of restrictive conditions; the abolition, *de facto* or *de jure*, of the right to strike; compulsory membership of all unions in one officially recognized and state-supervised centre or federation; some degree of supervision by this centre over the affairs of affiliates or constituent units; and the use of co-optative devices – financial subsidies or assured finances for recognized labour organizations and co-optation of labour leaders into political positions. Repression of labour militancy is also widespread: in many countries there have been more officials detained or jailed since independence than during the entire colonial period.[47]

The degree of union atrophy occasioned by this official manipulation of rewards and penalties varies from country to country. In some, rank-and-file hostility towards national union officials runs so deep that the latter refuse to make an appearance at the site of a wildcat strike, or even seek police protection for the duration of industrial unrest. National unions or union centres or federations, in any event, rarely publicly articulate any broadly based economic or political grievances – except when labour leaders are emboldened by a severe political crisis. Yet it is not unusual for unions at the grass-roots level (generally involving shop stewards or their equivalent) to continue to respond to the immediate economic interests of their members. Militant economism can persist in the face of corporatist policies and the willingness of the state to resort to force to counter unauthorized work stoppages. Wildcat strikes continue, and occasionally debouch into short-lived movements of mass protest, as I shall point out later.

A governing political party, where this exists, provides another means of institutionally incorporating lower-class organizations. In the urban areas a prominent form of such organization are the residentially based associations or development committees. To the extent that the party links the urban poor to the political leadership, especially through neighbourhood associations, this provides the latter with the opportunity to co-opt emergent leaders and discourage oppositional activity, particularly by accommodating the more parochial and limited economic grievances. Where parties are banned or ineffectual, bureaucratic structures, such as departments of urban affairs, may take on the job of incorporating and neutralizing the poor.

Before proceeding further in this discussion, a few words regarding the varying degree of organization and solidarity within low-income residential areas are necessary. At one extreme, little or no effective neighbourhood organization exists; residents remain largely strangers to one another with rampant crime breeding mutual mistrust. At the other extreme, slums and spontaneous settlements manifest remarkable cohesion and generate organizations to cater for most of the residents' needs. For example, in Mathare Valley, Nairobi, one 'village' has evolved a village committee to take executive decisions, a council of elders to resolve disputes, a youth wing to maintain order, a community centre, and a nursery for local children.[48] What accounts for this wide variation?

Probably the most important factor determining the degree of community feeling and organization is the stability of a residential area's population. Transient populations are unlikely to involve themselves in local organizations to secure improved conditions. The attitude among residents in several suburbs of transients in West Africa was: 'Let the government do it. Why should I contribute anything to this place?' In Kenya, a comparative study of squatter settlements in and around Nairobi, Mombasa and Kisumu arrived at parallel conclusions. The longer established a neighbourhood and the larger the core of long-term residents, the higher was the cohesion and sense of involvement among residents.[49] This, of course, is only to be expected.

A second, perhaps equally obvious, factor is the availability of talented leadership. Someone with flair needs to come forward to organize the residents – whether a chief (in West Africa), a headman, religious leader, teacher in a local school, and so on. Most of the successful cases of slum organization seem to have depended upon the galvanizing influence of one or two able leaders. In the case of the previously mentioned village 2 in Mathare Valley, the leader was reportedly a man with extraordinary gifts for leadership. He was responsible for nearly all important decisions, chaired most meetings, oversaw all community-related work, and mediated between the residents and the outside power structure.[50]

Finally, the degree of homogeneity manifest in the population of a residential area doubtless influences the degree of internal cohesion and organization. While ethnic clustering in distinct residential areas is untypical in the burgeoning slums and spontaneous settlements, it does happen. Ethnic heterogeneity is not necessarily an impediment to the development of a sense of community; however, where people perceive many political conflicts in ethnic terms, ethnic stereotypes and tensions will inhibit a co-operative spirit. It is surely no coincidence that the settlement in Mathare Valley that exhibits such a remarkable degree of organization is socially and culturally homogeneous: the bulk of residents are poor, unskilled, and Kikuyu.[51]

Where neighbourhood associations or development committees do spontaneously emerge, the state may well tolerate their independent existence. In the suburbs of Accra, for instance, these committees were ostensibly the local chapters of the 'National Redemption Charter' in 1972–9; but the reality was substantial autonomy from central control. Neighbourhood associations in poor areas rarely present a political threat to governments. Characteristically, their demands, as articulated in letters to the authorities and by delegations, relate to the provision or improvement of basic urban services: the construction of more public toilets, the provision of standpipes, the rehabilitation of a market place, the improvement of local roads and lorry parks, or the building or upgrading of schools. Politicians can easily accommodate this sort of demand – at least at the level of promise of future performance.

But in vestigial electoral systems it is always conceivable that oppositional elements might capture and use neighbourhood associations to mobilize the low-income population. For this reason, and perhaps also out of a generalized fear of the poor on the part of the elite, politicians or agencies of the state often seek to control the local associations of the poor. The governing party is typically the means of institutional incorporation. In Dakar, for instance, it is usual for the community leader (*délégué du quartier*) in each *bidonville* to hold office in the local machinery of the Union Progressiste Sénégalaise as well. Charged principally with transmitting official views and policies to residents, the *délégués du quartier* are reportedly regarded by them as party hacks. In Mathare Valley, Nairobi, there is also a close connection between the committees of the constituent villages and the governing Kenya African National Union (KANU). Not only is there a KANU sub-branch in most villages, but KANU Youth Wingers also act as vigilantes to maintain order. The community leaders, who are also local KANU officials, are well placed to represent the interests of residents to the government. The leader of village 2, for example,

> knows whom to go to for assistance, and how to approach him. His contacts have been tremendously important in gaining informal promises from the government that the community will not be bulldozed, in getting school fees remitted for many villagers, and in obtaining government encouragement for many village development projects.

The relationship between the neighbourhood association and the authorities is clearly based on reciprocity in this case.[52]

206 SOCIAL CONTROL AND URBAN STRUGGLE

One particularly well-researched case of party-incorporation is that of squatter settlements in and around Lusaka. Consider Chawama (meaning a 'fair place', originally called Robert's Compound), a settlement comprising about 23 000 people in 1973.[53] Between its origins in 1948, and the government's purchase in 1966 of the land on which Chawama sits, the European landowners allowed squatters to build houses in exchange for a monthly land rent.

Although Robert's Compound was a stronghold of the opposition African National Congress (ANC) in the early 1960s, this soon changed with the government's purchase of the area. The governing United National Independence Party (UNIP) used the assistance of state agencies, especially the Squatter Control Unit, and its superior ability to secure concessions from the government – along with considerable coercion – to defeat the ANC. The lot of residents was not an easy one during the time of strife between 1966 and 1970. Youth Wingers from both parties went around intimidating those who could not produce their party's membership card, or those who failed to attend their party's public meetings.

After the local defeat of the ANC in 1970 and the inauguration of a one-party state in 1972, the chief function of UNIP in Chawama was to act as a control mechanism. Youth Wingers still expected the residents to attend UNIP's public meetings, even though the party rarely announced in advance the purpose of these. In fact, these gatherings served mainly to relay instructions or information to residents from some level of government; it was unusual for a presiding branch chairman to elicit questions or public discussion of policies. The government also expected local party officials to keep a list of all residents within each section of Chawama; to enforce local government regulations, such as those prohibiting the brewing of some alcoholic beverages or the sale of goods in non-designated areas; to allocate plots to newcomers and ensure conformity with planning guidelines; and to maintain order through the use of Special Constables (most of whom were party militants) and/or the party's Youth Brigade. In practice, law enforcement varied from section to section of the settlement, depending upon the control exercised by a section leader over the Special Constables or Youth Brigade. In some sections in the early 1970s, the enforcers operated something approaching a protection racket whose victims were bootleggers, barkeepers and shopkeepers. Nevertheless, the political contacts of local UNIP leaders apparently did allow them to obtain some local improvements from government departments.

In short, the chairmen of Chawama's two UNIP branches were to act as recognized community leaders as well as party officials. To legitimate this role, the party decreed that regardless of its constitutional requirement that only section leaders elect the party's branch officials, all residents, whether party members or not, would vote for the UNIP branch officials. However, in the branch elections of 1974, only 2 per cent of the eligible voters in Chawama actually turned out to vote. Few were apparently willing to give credence to the charade of popular election where only one or two picked candidates ran for each post.

COERCION

When official socialization, corporatist policies, co-optation of dissidents and accommodation fail to maintain social control, the resort to coercion is usually swift. Governments throughout Africa apparently feel highly threatened by protest demonstrations. Perhaps they fear, not only that violence may ensue, but also that *the very act of protest* may augment the efficacy of groups whose demands cannot be met within the existing system. Official violence may take the form of terror tactics as practised by Idi Amin's Bureau of State Research or the more disciplined but still awesome form of Kenya's General Service Unit. On occasion, regimes call in the army to quell urban unrest – though owing to the military's evident propensity for political power, this is a last resort of hard-pressed governments. Repression, we shall now see, is not always successful. But the main beneficiaries of breakdowns in order are rarely those whose grievances precipitated them.

Urban struggle

A study of the politics of marginalization and its transendence requires an investigation of the nature and significance of class or quasi-class struggle, as well as of the mechanisms of social control. The urban masses are not merely acted upon by other classes; there are instances of popular protest.

These bear a close resemblance to the sporadic riots and rebellions that characterized political life in eighteenth- or nineteenth-century European cities. The 'city mob', as Eric Hobsbawm observes of these cases, was

the movement of all classes of the urban poor for the achievement of economic or political changes by direct action – that is by riot or rebellion – but as a movement which was as yet inspired by no specific ideology; or, if it found expression for its aspirations at all, in terms of traditionalism and conservatism. . . .

Industrial workers, too, formed part of the mob and participated in the amorphous protest movements; preponderantly of the first generation, proletarians had not yet evolved modern forms of organized class protest. Besides workers, the mob comprised hawkers, 'small-dealers', journeymen, apprentices, artisans, the indigent and the petty bourgeoisie. The precipitants for mob activity were generally disastrous economic changes, such as increases in the cost of living or heightened unemployment. But, irrespective of the immediate goals of protest, popular hostility was always directed against the 'rich and powerful'. Recent histories of London and Paris substantially confirm these general observations.[54]

If the 'mob' or 'crowd' in African cities manifests a similar spontaneity and multi-class composition, that is not surprising.[55] These cities are only now beginning the transition to industrial societies, a transition that, owing to the limitations of the imitative model of development, may never be completed. Workers, I contended in chapter 4, play a special role in urban protest during this early stage, their strikes sometimes crystallizing the inchoate grievances of the common people. It is now time to explore the variety and effects of these ephemeral protest movements.

STRIKES AND POPULIST PROTEST

Three generalizations are relevant here. In the first place, solidarity in protest activity among workers from various sectors, as in general strikes, or between a particular group of workers and elements of the labouring poor, job-seekers, intellectuals and petty bourgeoisie, depends upon the combination of a potent workers' grievance with popular political disaffection. In view of the typically rampant inequality, elite insensitivity and political corruption, such a combination of grievances and interests is not uncommon. This is not to contend that disaffection connotes a popular desire for fundamental political, social and economic change. Indeed, urban populism does not involve a rejection of the dominant values – for example, of the notion inherent in such values as equality of opportunity and advancement by merit that any capable person can enter the bourgeoisie – but rather a condemnation of a nepotistic, corrupt and self-aggrandizing elite for its non-conformance with such values.

In the second place, urban-based strikes in Africa can attain an immediate political impact disproportionate to the relatively small number of workers involved. This is due not only to the fragility of regimes where factions and fractions of the dominant classes vie for pre-eminence, but also to the concentration of workers within the urban seats of power, and the propensity of disaffected elements of the common people to join the protest. Such labour protests, however, have only rarely led to any long-term socio-political change.

In the third place, the workers who have manifested the most solidarity and militancy, as measured by their propensity to strike, have been the dockers, railwaymen and miners. In southern Nigeria, for instance, railway employees participated in a third of twenty strikes occurring between 1897 and 1939, dockers and marine workers in a fifth, and coal miners in a fifth. Of the remainder, all but two involved state employees. In Ghana in the 1970s, factory workers have evinced a growing militancy – accounting for almost half the strikes in 1972-6– but earlier mining and 'transport and communications' employees had the highest strike records.[56]

Dockers, railwaymen and miners have also evidenced the highest propensity to act as the leading edge of popular urban protest. This is not surprising. Marx, Engels and many others have observed that the political potential of workers indeed their emergence as a distinct class – required the growth of large-scale enterprises. In the case of the early industrializers, these enterprises were typically factories. But in the peculiar circumstances of peripheral capitalism, the conglomeration of permanent workers initially occurs in mineral extraction, plantations and the public services. The combination of limited industrialization – mostly undertaken in the post-war period and oriented to import-substitution for a small market and raw-material processing – and the common reliance upon capital-intensive technologies, have restricted the size, and hence the power, of industrial labour. However, industrialization is proceeding apace in a few primate cities; in the future industrial workers may play a more central role within labour movements.

Consider briefly the major patterns revealed in the strike literature. General strikes with evident political implications occur infrequently in middle Africa, in part because national union centres or federations have rarely preserved sufficient autonomy from the government to promote them. Nonetheless, general strikes were a major aspect of urban protest that threatened or toppled governments in Senegal in May–June 1968, Ghana in 1950, 1961 and 1971, Nigeria in 1945 and 1964, the Congo-Brazzaville in 1963 and 1968, the Sudan in 1958 and 1964, Madagascar in 1972 and Ethiopia in 1974.[57] In all cases, the workers' solidarity depended upon the fusing of a basic economic grievance to a widespread political disaffection. The political impact of these strikes depended upon their linking up with other protests and demonstrations, especially those organized by university and secondary school students. In four of the countries – Congo-Brazzaville, the Sudan, Madagascar and Ethiopia – general strikes formed part of the background to an overthrow of government; but power eventually passed to the military.

The recent case of Madagascar illustrates why this is the usual outcome. In the Tananarive demonstrations and riots of May 1972, which undercut the authority of President Tsiranana, widely regarded as a tool of French neo-colonialism, students and workers played a central role. A general strike declared on 15 May paralyzed the country's ecnonomy. But it is one thing to weaken and topple a regime, and quite another to install another in its place. The movement to oust Tsiranana was unorganized and poorly co-ordinated. The dominant goals, as expressed by the most militant and articulate elements involved in the revolt, were utopian and populist:

They called for the destruction of hierarchies and for the establishment of equality for everyone. They designated as their objective the setting up of 'the state of little people' . . . in the form of a National Popular Congress which would realize their dream of direct democracy. This utopian construction was to be produced by the simple inversion of the hierarchical society and despotic power they were attacking.

What inevitably happened, however, was that the chiefs of the armed forces picked up the power lying in the street. Appointed Prime Minister by Tsiranana in the midst of the crisis, the head of the General Staff proceeded to smash the power not only of the old regime, but also of the rebels seeking to realize popular power.[58]

Dockworkers throughout the world evince a relatively high level of group solidarity and militancy. In Africa this segment of emergent working classes has instigated and animated many popular urban protests. The Lagos dockworkers had spearheaded a general strike as early as 1897; this, though lasting only three days and concerning only economic grievances, seriously embarrassed the colonial government. Later labour protests in Nigeria also found the dockworkers at the forefront of the confrontation.[59] The workers in ports along the Indian Ocean have also manifested a propensity for developing a group consciousness and leading ephemeral protest movements – in Mombasa, Dar es Salaam and Zanzibar City. For instance, the docker-led 1948 Zanzibar general strike has been characterized as 'Zanzibar's 1905, the first mass demonstration of the Protectorate's urban work force . . . protesting against aspects of the existing social and economic order.'[60]

The railways and railwaymen have also played an important part in the development of African working classes:

Of all the undertakings of the colonial state, it was the railway which demanded the greatest supply of labor. For this reason, in much of Africa we can see the railway as the nursery of the working class. It is true that the earliest forms of labor organization and even some elements of labor consciousness emerged in connection with the African ports which often became capitals. But the growth of a working class in these waterfront towns was severely limited without a complementary growth of modern communication with the hinterland.[61]

Strikes by railwaymen have a long history in most African countries. In Freetown, Sierra Leone, for instance, the first work-stoppage occurred in 1919, with a second instance in 1926.[62] In the immediate post-Second World War period, there was a spate of railway strikes, some of which assumed the form of popular movements against colonial rule. This happened in Douala in 1945, and on the four territorial railway networks in French West Africa in 1947.[63] Indeed, the latter strike was probably the longest in African union history, with many of the workers staying out for five months. Needless to say, these strikers could not have maintained their strike without the unstinting material assistance provided by kin and neighbours. In the Rhodesias during this period, the African railwaymen were also developing solidarity and eventually union organization through strike action and organizational work by labour leaders.[64] But in this case the colonial government's prohibition of political action, backed by the evident will to employ coercion, prevented the combination of workers' grievances and popular urban demands. In the post-colonial period, the railway workers in both Ghana (in 1961 and 1971), and Nigeria (in 1964) have led or unreservedly backed widely supported general strikes which involved a political critique of the existing regime.[65]

Miners are another group noted for their solidarity. As historical studies of strikes by the iron and diamond miners in Sierra Leone, gold miners in the Gold Coast, and copper miners in Northern Rhodesia (Zambia) have shown, some groups of African miners had achieved a remarkable collective consciousness well before the Second World War.[66] It was not unusual even at this early time for economic grievances to be mixed with political ones. In Nigeria, the famous Enugu colliery strike of 1949, though prompted by strictly economic demands, nevertheless attained a symbolic anti-colonial significance with the death by shooting of twenty-one strikers.[67] In Southern Rhodesia, (Zimbabwe), the African miners apparently developed a group consciousness in the earliest days of the mining industry. However, this could not be manifested through the creation of workers' organizations or political action owing to the oppressive milieu of the mining compound. Instead, workers consciousness was evident in two brief strikes before the First World War, and in such covert forms of labour protest as desertion and resistance in day-to-day situations.[68]

Miners have continued to be an obstreperous group in post-colonial societies where authoritarian and hierarchical production relations continue unchanged, though usually with African managers and supervisors gradually replacing expatriates. While the distance of mines from major urban centres typically limits the capacity of miners to spark urban protests, their industrial actions are not infrequently tumultuous (since they are commonly unofficial and illegal) and fraught with political implications.

Consider the actions of Ghanaian gold miners within the context of Ghana's evolving political economy. These workers engaged in a series of wildcat strikes, riots and demonstrations in 1968–9 and again in 1977. In these periods the police fought with and shot miners on several occasions; striking workers threatened and beat mine managers, supervisors and (significantly) union officials; and in 1969 the management of Ghana's richest mine requested the army to intervene to restore order and prevent the mine's closure. Although various specific industrial grievances precipitated the unofficial strikes and demonstrations, an underlying cause was the miners' hostility towards

the Africanized mine management owing to their superciliousness and
conspicuous consumption while the real incomes of the workers
declined. It is true that this was the lot of most Ghanaian workers. But
not all workers possessed the same propensity for solidarity as the
miners, or confronted the state so directly. Since the state owned most of
the gold mines and was demonstrably unsympathetic to workers'
grievances – having used its coercive apparatus to emasculate the
Mineworkers' Union and crush the miners' protests – the strikes took on
an oppositional (though not revolutionary) connotation. Some of the
flavour of this is apparent in the following description of one wildcat
strike at Tarkwa mine in June 1969:

> Before noon workers gathered at the shaft top and smashed doors and
> windows in the mine offices and chased clerical workers from the building.
> They started to march into Tarkwa. The Medical Officer, Mine Secretary and
> Labour Controller were seized and severely beaten. The Managing Director
> was taken from his office, stripped and dressed in a miner's overalls and boots
> and made to carry mining tools at the head of the workers' procession. The
> miners marched into town, according to one witness 'like an invading army'.
> A platoon of police rushed to the mine to subdue what they described as an
> 'insurrection'. Miners clashed with police and after warning shots failed
> to disperse the workers police opened fire and wounded four workers in the
> legs...
>   The following day the strike continued. One thousand workers with bows,
> arrows and other weapons gathered at the shaft top. Again police rushed to
> the mine and clashed with the workers. Tear gas failed to disperse them and
> again police fired on the workers, wounding three. Workers armed with sticks,
> stones and iron rods fought with police at Akoon Gate and eleven more
> workers were arrested.[69]

The suppression of the two phases of wildcat strikes ushered in
periods of acute tension in the mines. Labour protest took the
subterranean forms of loafing on the job, theft, sabotage, and occasional
underground assaults on overzealous supervisors. Miners thus have
manifested a remarkable militancy and solidarity; yet their
consciousness, in the absence of socialist agitational activities, can only
be characterized as 'defensive, heavily laced with cynicism'.[70]
Factory workers, as I have mentioned, are generally a recent and
relatively small addition to African labour forces. Yet there are
indications that in future they may play an important political role. In
Africa, as elsewhere, factory workers have quickly shown themselves
capable of creating considerable solidarity and initiating concerted
action in defence of their interests. Consider the case of Nigeria, a
country with a high industrial potential owing to the size of its market
and its resource endowment. Although industrial workers are by no
means the largest sector of Nigeria's working class, manufacturing and
repairs accounted for about one-third of all the workers involved in
strikes between 1966 and 1971 inclusive. (Transport and

communications supplied the second largest number of strikers.) In terms of the number of trade disputes and number of strikes, the relative militancy of the various sectors remained about the same, with manufacturing and repairs at the top of the list.[71] This militancy is all the more remarkable when one considers that the number of strikes did not diminish among factory workers even after strikes were essentially banned in 1969.

In some instances, it is clear that striking Nigerian factory workers were animated by more than solely economic grievances. This was evident in early 1971, after private firms had refused to grant a cost of living award that a Wages and Salaries Review Commission had awarded to workers in public employment. The initial refusal of expatriate concerns to follow suit prompted the mobilization of industrial workers. For example, in Ikeja, an industrial estate in metropolitan Lagos, the animus underlying the wildcat strikes and occasional violence of 1971 can be traced to the workers' antipathy to a grossly inegalitarian social order, in addition to the specific economic grievance. Moreover, this industrial action won support among Ikeja's self-employed, who obviously shared this same hostility. In Kano, the third largest industrial centre in Nigeria, the initial intransigence of factory employers in 1971 also sparked a solidary reaction on the part of the workers in some factories. This reaction, it should be noted, apparently took place in the *absence* of conditions which favoured class action among Lagosian factory workers; these adverse conditions in Kano included the relatively small size of factories, the paternalistic or even blatantly oppressive labour–management practices of indigenous or Levantine owners, the relatively low educational level of workers, and the absence of trade unions. Yet, even under these circumstances, the Kano factory workers manifested an 'early class consciousness' during the crisis, successfully defending their interests through the development of informal strike committees and the initiation of wildcat strikes.[72]

It is worth emphasizing, in the light of the militancy and occasional populist protest of the first-generation factory proletariat, that their numbers are expanding in some African primate cities. Consider again the striking case of Lagos. Black Africa's largest city (with 3.5 million inhabitants in 1976), metropolitan Lagos exemplifies the national trend of industrial concentration in one or two cities. By 1965 about one third of Nigeria's total manufacturing plants in the modern sector were concentrated in metropolitan Lagos; in the following five years about half of all new manufacturing investment went to this area. Over half of this city's labour force (about 1·4 million people) was occupied in 1976 in informal economic activities – that is, self-employment or employment in enterprises with fewer than ten employees. In the modern sector, the public service was the largest employer. While manufacturing and repair firms engaged only about half as many employees, this number was still considerably larger than those employed in the formal commercial sector. In 1976 an estimated 112 000 employees worked within 332 industrial establishments employing ten or more workers. Between 1965 and 1974 Lagos's formal industrial employment quadrupled; the growth in industrial employment in the 1970s has been at least 8 per cent per annum. By 1980, there were in the order of 138 000 employees within 439 industrial establishments, with an average number of employees each increasing from 266 in 1974 to 314. And there are grounds for believing that such trends will persist. Metropolitan Lagos's share of Nigeria's net investment has increased in the 1970s – to 73 per cent in 1973. Moreover, the port's handling capacity has been markedly increased since 1975, while the Third National Development Plan stated that seven further industrial estates were to be developed by the Lagos State Government. Finally, it is noteworthy that most heavy industry is located in Lagos, accounting for about three-quarters of the value added on such commodities as chemicals, metals and machinery, and paper and printing.[73]

If it is likely that factory workers will assume a more important role in African labour movements and urban protests, what form will this role take? One probable pattern emerges from a study of collective industrial and political action in Cordoba, an industrial city in Argentina. When foreign capital established large automobile factories there in the 1950s to serve the local market, a modern and relatively well-educated proletariat was thereby grafted on to the existing 'traditional' working class employed in indigenously owned small establishments. Subsequently, large-scale rural–urban migration, prompted by the lure of comparatively lucrative factory employment, created a burgeoning and involutionary tertiary sector. In these circumstances, in May 1969 radicalized students and the modern proletariat led a rebellion that received mass support. However, the absence of any clear ideological direction, owing to the predominance of Peronist ideology, weakened the alliance and lessened its political impact.[74] This pattern of urban protest with widespread popular support, linked to a populist ideology and led in part by a modern industrial proletariat, may well become more common in Africa's expanding cities.

FROM POPULISM TO RADICALISM?

Populism, I have asserted, is a consciousness that workers, the petty bourgeoisie and the labouring poor can evince, but it is not a working-*class* consciousness. It is an oppositional mentality in which popular resentment is limited to a vague notion of a rich, powerful and corrupt 'they' who advance themselves by cheating 'we', the people. It connotes rebelliousness, but not revolution.

Richard Jeffries' astute characterization of the 'radical populism' of Ghanaian railwaymen brings its prominent features into relief. First, populism is reformist in orientation; the workers see their role as limited to 'exerting restraint or pressure within a political system controlled by others'. Secondly, the exploiters are identified as a *political* class – politicians and senior civil servants – not as an indigenous and/or foreign bourgeoisie. Indeed, the railwaymen evince negligible hostility towards indigenous entrepreneurs whose success derives from hard work or luck, rather than political contacts. This sympathy is congruent with an evidently widespread aspiration to *embourgeoisement* on the part of these (and other) workers. Thirdly, railwaymen see themselves not as a leading segment of a national working class, but as the 'spokesmen of the people' in their oppositional activities. More particularly, 'the people' for whom they purport to speak are their neighbours in Sekondi-Takoradi or, perhaps, the Fanti living in Ghana's central and western regions. There is therefore a communal element in the railwaymen's political consciousness.[75]

Populism clearly differs from a radical class consciousness. The latter requires, in Marxian terms, the emergence of a notion of a common, economically dominant, class enemy, and a recognition that only the control or transformation of certain economic and political institutions through collective action would bring beneficial change. Is it likely that populist notions will be absorbed in a radical direction?

A radical proletariat has, of course, only emerged anywhere under quite special conditions. True, the necessary condition for working-class formation – the concentration of permanent workers in large-scale workplaces – increasingly obtains in tropical Africa. But the limited proletarianization of a largely first-generation urban wage-earning force doubtless impedes the deepening of worker consciousness. Furthermore, the typical pattern of political suppression of radical movements and ideas nullifies a potential radicalizing influence upon workers in most peripheral capitalist societies. Is populism then to represent the acme of workers' political dissent?

Some would argue that one should never broach this sort of question in the abstract. They would say that worker consciousness can only be understood historically, within the concrete economic, political, social and cultural configuration of a particular country. Guiding this historical analysis would be the proposition that consciousness emerges from, and in turn affects, the workers' experience of class subordination and conflict. This is in general true: indeed, it is a truism. But in any specific case study, one needs to explain why, if workers' experiences on the job are similar, they develop a differential consciousness. Generic politicizing influences operate upon workers, to which political activists need to be sensitive.

1. *Occupational communities and class formation*   Politicization and class formation are functions of what happens off the job, as well as on. The concept of an 'occupational community', found useful elsewhere in the explanation of working-class consciousness, deserves application in studies of African workers. It is not coincidental that two of the most

politically assertive groups of workers – railwaymen and miners – normally constitute such communities, while two other assertive groups – dockworkers and factory workers – sometimes do. Occupational communities are characterized, first, by the tendency for people who work together, or at least share a common occupation and economic activity, to spend their leisure time together. Secondly, these communities tend to be self-enclosed, that is, to act as reference groups for those who belong in matters of behaviour and opinion. The structural bases for their formation include: shift-work, and the consequent throwing together of workers who jointly work awkward hours; physical isolation, as in some mining operations and railway estates; or simply the concentration of workmates within a common residential area.[76] The point is that interaction and communication both on and off the job can reinforce common views of the world and the legitimacy of shared grievances. They can, moreover, facilitate the socialization of new generations of workers in traditions of industrial and labour protest. Indeed, non-workers living in the midst of a residentially based occupational community may also come to share the dominant political orientations of the working-class sub-culture. The little survey research on African workers relating to this topic confirms that the existence of such communities does influence the nature of working-class consciousness.[77]

Not surprisingly, if an occupational community is culturally or ethnically homogeneous, this can reinforce the solidifying effect. This is well illustrated in the case of the militant gold miners in Ghana, who have a long history of labour protest. The dirty and hard underground work has, from the beginning, been left to migrant workers from northern Ghana and francophone West Africa. These miners tend to live in communities around the mines with a high degree of regional–cultural homogeneity. Hence, these workers

> live together, drink *pito* together, intermarry and generally maintain their 'ethnic' lifestyle. Such cultural elements naturally find their way into political culture. This was quite evident when the workers of Tarkwa Goldfields marched into town singing Dagarti war-songs, wielding their hunting weapons and simultaneously wearing their mining hats and boots.[78]

2. *Education and class formation*   Another politicizing factor that is largely unexplored is education in conjunction with other potentially frustrating influences. There has been a significant shift upwards in the educational achievement of urban manual, especially skilled, workers over the past fifteen years. This is one consequence of the successive devaluation of higher levels of formal qualifications. Owing to the disjunction between the expanding output from the schools and the slow growth of job opportunities, many job-seekers wishing to remain in town have had to revise their occupational expectations downwards. At the same time, employers have sought to limit the pressure from job-

seekers by requiring a minimum educational qualification even for unskilled manual work. While the minimum for this required by relatively good employers is now completion of primary school (six to seven years of schooling), the average educational achievement of recent recruits may in fact be higher. This trend is illustrated by a large sample-survey of manual and non-manual labour markets in both rural and urban areas of the Camerouns in 1964–5. Whereas 69 per cent of the younger individuals with a post-primary education were currently engaged in manual work, only 15 per cent of their older counterparts were so employed. In Kaduna, located in educationally underdeveloped northern Nigeria, a survey of textile workers in 1972 arrived at equally striking findings. Fully 72·5 per cent of all the workers, *including daily-paid operatives*, had at least completed primary school. Among Tema's factory workers, a survey in 1975 discovered that the bulk of the skilled (86 per cent) and a majority of the unskilled had at least elementary-school education.[79]

The relationship between workers' educational achievement and politicization is clear in principle. One would expect that the better-educated workers who considered themselves deprived or oppressed would not only feel more frustrated by their situation, but also be more capable of developing a theory of exploitation, than their less-educated colleagues. Whether this proposition is valid remains to be seen. The two surveys of workers bearing upon it – one conducted among Kano factory workers, the other among workers in Greater Accra – tend to confirm the link between education and working-class formation.[80]

Summary and conclusion

If dominant fractions of the bourgeoisie benefit from a precarious hegemony in many African countries, this owes much to the persistence of pre-industrial belief-systems and of the vertical solidarities of communal and clientelistic politics. Personalized explanations of misfortune, divinations of fate, and thaumaturgical approaches to the manipulation of earthly events direct some of the tensions associated with poverty and inequality into apolitical channels. Traditional belief-systems survive in the cities, though usually in syncretistic or mutated forms, owing to childhood socialization and the uncertainty and insecurity of life for 'urban peasants'. In addition, there are the normally divisive influences of patrons and/or communal bosses. In seeking to advance personal or factional ambitions, they accentuate particularistic responses to generic poverty problems and antagonisms among the common people.

There are, in addition, the more deliberate methods by which the state enhances legitimacy and contains dissent. In the realm of ideology, the dominant value system – typically extolling equality of opportunity, the meritocratic principle, individual achievement and social mobility – is usually a more significant buttress to bourgeois hegemony than pretentious official philosophies. Important means of disseminating these values include the school system and the demonstration effect of successful petty-bourgeois patrons. To contain actual or potential class conflict, the state characteristically employs corporatist policies towards organized groups among the lower classes, co-opts emergent popular leaders, and accommodates parochial or limited grievances. Of course, some poor individuals or groups benefit from all these policies – by, for example, the construction of more public latrines and standpipes in low-income neighbourhoods, or the compensation of those forced to relocate as a result of urban renewal projects. Nonetheless, the gains tend to be marginal, not altering the pattern of development that produces marginalization as well as concentrated wealth.

But acquiescence is not overdetermined. Populist protests do sporadically erupt in many countries – and in the rural as well as the urban areas.[81] These are often sparked by economic recessions that depress the living standards of the common man. At the forefront of urban protests are generally the students and the organized workers.

Populism is, however, a vague and limited ideology. It does not reject the dominant value system, but merely demands that this be respected in practice. It thus fosters only protest against a corrupt, nepotistic and self-interested political class, not concerted political action to control or reshape institutions. Its long-term political import is further reduced by the characteristically spasmodic and localized nature of populist protest. Given these features, regimes can normally quell the poorly co-ordinated unrest by means of repression, concessions, and verbal acceptance of populist rhetoric. Populist rebellions do occasionally unseat governments, but then power passes to the only institution ready to exercise it, namely, the military.

In the advanced-capitalist countries, industrialization eventually allowed for the replacement of the city mob by the working class, and the periodic and spontaneous riot by the organized protest of the labour movement. But the peculiar pattern of peripheral capitalist development in most African countries impedes such a prospect. The working class, elsewhere the lynchpin of social reform, is relatively small and recent, only semi-proletarianized, and mainly non-industrial. The bulk of the population continues to engage in non-capitalist and petty-capitalist forms of production and petty trade that obstruct the development of solidarity. Furthermore, radical parties and autonomous labour movements are vigorously suppressed. Nonetheless, national working classes are growing in size and stability and sections of these have, under special conditions, developed a radical, though non-revolutionary, class consciousness. Their influence on development strategy in the future may therefore not be negligible.

Notes

1. Quotes: Charles Abrams, *Man's Struggle for Shelter in an Urbanizing World* (Cambridge, Mass: MIT Press, 1964), p. 287; and Joan Nelson, 'The Urban Poor: Disruption or Political Integration in Third World Cities?', *World Politics*, XXII, 3 (1970), pp. 413, 408. Studies from Latin America and India supporting Nelson's view: W. A. Cornelius, 'Urbanization as an Agent in Latin American Political Instability', *American Political Science Review*, LXIII, 3 (1969), pp. 833–57; and M. Weiner, 'Urbanization and Political Protest', *Civilisations*, XVII, 1 and 2 (1967), pp. 44–50. For an elaboration of the forms of non-radical political participation, see Joan Nelson, *Access to Power: Politics and the Urban Poor in Developing Nations* (Princeton: Princeton University Press, 1979).
2. For evidence of this attitudinal orientation, see the plethora of studies cited in Joan Nelson, *Migrants, Urban Poverty, and Instability in Developing Nations*, Occasional Paper No. 22, Center for International Affairs, Harvard University, September 1969.
3. On the sociological tradition, see L. Wirth, 'Urbanism as a Way of Life', *American Journal of Sociology*, XLIV (1938), pp. 1–24. Evidence of the popularity of this approach in African urban studies: H. Coing, 'Épidémies et endémies en sociologie urbaine', *Cahiers d'études africaines*, XV, 2 (1975), pp. 329–38.
4. Quotes: Alex Inkeles and David H. Smith, *Becoming Modern: Individual Change in Six Developing Countries* (Cambridge, Mass: Harvard University Press, 1974), pp. 226, 227. Also critical of the city-as-modernizer thesis is M. A. Qadeer, in 'Do Cities "Modernize" the Developing Countries? ... The South Asian Experience', *Comparative Studies in Society and History*, XVI, 3 (1974), pp. 266–83.
5. Inkeles and Smith, *Becoming Modern* (n. 4 above), pp. 290, 301.
6. On the Marxist approach to urban values: Coing, 'Épidémies' (n. 3 above).
7. See Inkeles and Smith, *Becoming Modern* (n. 4 above), chaps. 11 and 12, quotes pp. 174, 215.
8. See Robin Horton, 'African Traditional Thought and Western Science', *Africa*, XXXVII (1967), part I, pp. 50–71, and part II, pp. 157–87. See also, Gustav Jahoda, *The Psychology of Superstition* (London: Allen Lane, 1969), pp. 128, 132, 146.
9. Horton 'African Traditional Thought' (n. 8 above), pp. 56–7. For a fascinating discussion of the main elements of West African, especially Ashanti, traditional cosmologies, see M. J. Field, *Search for Security: An Ethno–Psychiatric Study of Rural Ghana* (Evanston, Ill: Northwestern University Press, 1960).
10. J. S. La Fontaine, *City Politics: A Study of Leopoldville, 1962–63* (Cambridge: Cambridge University Press, 1970), p. 182. For similar observations, see: Andrew Hake, *African Metropolis: Nairobi's Self-Help City* (New York: St Martin's, 1977), p. 217; and J. L. Brain, 'Witchcraft in Africa: A Hardy Perennial', in Maxwell Owusu (ed.), *Colonialism and Social Change: Essays in Honour of Lucy Mair* (The Hague: Mouton, 1975), pp. 189–92. For one of the earliest analyses of witchcraft beliefs in town: J. C. Mitchell, 'The Meaning of Misfortune

for Urban Africans', in Meyer Fortes and G. Dieterlen (eds.), *African Systems of Thought* (London: International African Institute, 1965), pp. 192–203.

11. Sources on the various cities: J.-M. Gibbal, 'Relations ville–campagne et interprétations de la malchance en milieu urbain de Côte d'Ivoire", in Centre National de la Recherche Scientifique, *La croissance urbaine en Afrique noire et à Madagascar* (Paris, 1972), pp. 617–24; G. Jahoda, 'Traditional Healers and Other Institutions concerned with Mental Illness in Ghana', *International Journal of Social Psychiatry*, VII, 4 (1961), pp. 245–68; G. Jahoda, 'Social Aspirations, Magic and Witchcraft in Ghana', in P. C. Lloyd (ed.), *The New Elites of Tropical Africa* (Oxford: Oxford University Press, 1966), pp. 199–212; S. K. Weinberg, 'Culture and Communication in Disorder and Psychotherapy in West Africa', *African Urban Notes*, v, 1 (1970), pp. 22–8; Una Maclean, *Magical Medicine: A Nigerian Case Study* (Ibadan) (London: Allen Lane, 1971), esp. p. 133; J. Leeson and R. Frankenberg, 'The Patients of Traditional Doctors in Lusaka', *African Social Research*, 23 (1977), pp. 217–34, data cited, pp. 222–7; W. J. M. van Binsbergen, 'Ritual, Class and Urban-Rural Relations: Elements for a Zambian Case Study (Lusaka)', *Cultures et développement*, VIII, 2 (1976), p. 209; La Fontaine, *City Politics* (n. 10 above), pp. 182–7; Hake, *African Metropolis* (Nairobi) (n. 10 above), pp. 217–24; and P. Rigby and F. D. Lule, 'Continuity and Change in Kiganda Religion in Urban and Peri-Urban Kampala', in David Parkin (ed.), *Town and Country in Eastern and Central Africa* (London: International African Institute, 1975), pp. 213–27, quote p. 216.

12. Discussion of this final tendency (based on a survey of the literature): Brain, 'Witchcraft in Africa', (n. 10 above), pp. 198–9.

13. See, e.g., van Binsbergen, 'Ritual, Class and Urban–Rural Relations' (n. 11 above).

14. For this thesis: R. Horton, 'African Conversion', *Africa*, XLI, 2 (1971), pp. 81–108.

15. The centrality of religious theories in the lives of poor African urban-dwellers is widely commented upon. See, e.g., M. Peil, 'Social Aspects of Religion in West African Towns', *African Urban Notes*, ser. B, 2 (1975), p. 100; Hake, *African Metropolis* (n. 10 above), pp. 222–3.

16. Horton, 'African Conversion' (n. 14 above), p. 97.

17. Coexistence of traditional with Christian religious beliefs and practices: Field, *Search for Security* (n. 9 above), pp. 53–4; Maclean, *Magical Medicine* (n. 11 above), chaps. 2 and 3; Leonard Plotnicov, *Strangers to the City: Urban Man in Jos, Nigeria* (Pittsburgh: University of Pittsburgh Press, 1967), esp. chap. 4; and Rigby and Lule, 'Continuity and Change in Kiganda Religion' (n. 11 above), p. 226. Range of converts: Horton, 'African Conversion' (n. 14 above), p. 104.

18. On the revolutionary nature of millenarianism: Y. Talmon, 'Pursuit of the Millennium: The Relation between Religious and Social Change', *European Journal of Sociology*, III, 1 (1962), pp. 125–48, quote p. 132; and Bryan Wilson, *Magic and the Millennium: A Sociological Study of Religious Movements of Protest among Tribal and Third World Peoples* (London: Heinemann Educational Books, 1973), esp. p. 23.

See also Vittorio Lanternari, *The Religions of the Oppressed:A Study of Modern Messianic Cults* (New York: Mentor Books, 1965), esp. pp. 20, 240–4.

19. Estimated congregation: H. W. Turner, 'African Independent Churches and Economic Development', *World Development*, VIII, 7/8 (1980), p. 523. On the popular appeal of independent churches: Guenter Lewy. *Religion and Revolution* (New York: Oxford University Press, 1974), pp. 196–8. See also, Wilson, *Magic and the Millennium* (n. 18 above), pp. 54–7, 70–2, 91–2; Lanternari, *Religions of the Oppressed* (n. 18 above), pp 60–2; A. Doutreloux, 'Prophetism and Development [in Zaïre]', *Africa Quarterly*, VI, 4 (1967), pp. 334–42; Hake, *African Metropolis* (n. 10 above), chap. 16; M. West, 'Thérapie et changement social dans les églises urbaines d'Afrique du Sud', *Social Compass*, XIX, 1 (1972), pp. 49–62; and K. A. Opoku, 'Traditional Religious Beliefs and Spiritual Churches in Ghana', *Institute of African Studies Research Review* (Legon), IV, 2 (1968), pp. 47–60. Lower-class membership of spiritual churches: Peil, 'Social Aspects of Religion' (n. 15 above), pp. 98–9; J. K. Parratt, 'Religious Change in Yoruba Society – A Test Case', *Journal of Religion in Africa*, II, 2 (1969), p. 126; H. W. Turner, *History of an African Independent Church*, vol. II: *The Life and Faith of the Church of the Lord (Aladura)* (Oxford: Oxford University Press, 1967, p. 19; and La Fontaine, *City Politics* (n. 10 above), p. 91.

20. Turner, 'The Place of Independent Religious Movements in the Modernization of Africa', *Journal of Religion in Africa*, II, 1 (1969), p. 62.

21. On the radical element in Islamic doctrine: Lewy, *Religion and Revolution* (n. 19 above), pp. 49–53. Kano study: Paul Lubeck, 'Early Industrialization and Social Class Formation among Factory Workers in Kano', PhD thesis, Northwestern University, 1975, pp. 11–13. Lagos case: Pauline H. Baker, *Urbanization and Political Change: The Politics of Lagos, 1917–67* (Berkeley: University of California Press, 1974), pp. 109–10.

22. On variations in Islamic commitment, see, in general, J. Spencer Trimingham, *The Influence of Islam upon Africa* (London: Longman, 1968), p. 110; and J. O. Hunwick, *Islam in Africa: Friend or Foe* (Accra: Ghana Universities Press, 1976), quote p. 14. Case studies of varying Islamic commitment in town: J. A. K. Leslie, *A Social Survey of Dar es Salaam* (Oxford: Oxford University Press, 1963), pp. 11–12; B. T. Grindall, 'Islamic Affiliation and Urban Adaptation: The Sisala Migrants in Accra, Ghana', *Africa*, XLIII, 4 (1973), pp. 333–46; C. Dinan, 'Socialization in an Accra Suburb: The Zongo and Its Distinct Sub-culture', in Christine Oppong (ed.), *Changing Family Studies*, Legon Family Research Papers No. 3, Institute of African Studies, Legon, Ghana, 1975, pp. 45–62; Janet Bujra, *Pumwani: The Politics of Property*, report on a project sponsored by the Social Science Research Council, Institute for Development Studies, University of Nairobi, 1973, pp. 33–8; and Kenneth McVicar, 'Twilight of an East African Slum: Pumwani and the Evolution of African Settlement in Nairobi', PhD thesis, University of California, Los Angeles, 1968, pp. 156–62.

23. Quote: Horton, 'African Conversion' (n. 14 above), p. 107.

24. See, e.g. R. H. Jackson, 'Political Stratification in Tropical Africa', *Canadian Journal of African Studies*, VII, 3 (1973), pp. 381–400.

25. See e.g., A. Mafeje, 'The Ideology of "Tribalism"', *Journal of Modern African Studies*, IX, 2 (1971), pp. 253–62.

26. Definition: R. Melson and H. Wolpe, 'Modernization and the Politics of Communalism: A Theoretical Perspective', *American Political Science Review*, LXIV, 4 (1970), p. 1112. Cases: J. Paden, 'Urban Pluralism, Integration and Adaptation of Communal Identity in Kano, Nigeria', in Ronald Cohen and John Middleton (eds.), *From Tribe to Nation in Africa* (San Francisco: Chandler, 1970), pp. 259–68; Suzanne Bernus, *Particularismes ethniques en milieu urbain: l'exemple de Niamey* (Paris: Institut d'Ethnologie, Université de Paris, 1969); Heather Joshi *et al.*, *Abidjan* (Geneva: ILO, 1977), p. 79; H. J. Fisher, 'Separatism in West Africa', in James Kritzeck and W. H. Lewis (eds.), *Islam in Africa* (New York: Van Nostrand, 1969), pp. 128–9; L. Proudfoot, 'Toward Muslim Solidarity in Freetown', *Africa*, XXXI, 2 (1961), pp. 147–56; E. Schildkrout, 'Ethnicity and Generational Differences among Urban Immigrants in Ghana', in Abner Cohen (ed.), *Urban Ethnicity* (London: Tavistock, 1974), pp. 187–222; and K. Hart, 'Migration and Tribal Identity among the Frafras in Ghana', *Journal of Asian and African Studies*, VI, 1 (1971), pp. 1–35.

27. Pumwani: McVicar, 'Twilight of an East African Slum' (n. 22 above), pp. 135–8, quote p. 268. Ethnic relations in Nairobi more generally: Marc H. Ross, *Grassroots in an African City: Political Behavior in Nairobi* (Cambridge, Mass: MIT Press, 1975), esp. pp. 62–8. On Nigerian cities: M. Peil, 'Interethnic Contacts in Nigerian Cities', *Africa*, XLV, 2 (1975), quote p. 121.

28. A. L. Epstein developed the notion of the 'principle of situational selection' in his *Politics in an Urban African Community* (Manchester: Manchester University Press, 1958), pp. 232–40. A useful theoretical discussion based upon this principle is Melson and Wolpe, 'Modernization and the Politics of Communalism' (n. 26 above), pp. 1112–30, quote p. 1127.

29. For this interpretation of tribalism, see P. H. Gulliver, 'Introduction', in Gulliver (ed.), *Tradition and Transition in East Africa: Studies of the Tribal Factor in the Modern Era* (Los Angeles: University of California Press, 1969); and Melson and Wolpe, 'Modernization and the Politics of Communalism' (n. 26 above).

30. Quote: H. Wolpe, 'Port Harcourt: Ibo Politics in Microcosm', *Journal of Modern African Studies*, VII, 3 (1969), pp. 489–90. See also, R. Melson, 'Ideology and Inconsistency: The "Cross-Pressured" Nigerian Worker', *American Political Science Review*, LXV (1971), pp. 161–71.

31. See A. Weingrod, 'Patrons, Patronage and Political Parties', *Comparative Studies in Society and History*, X, 4 (1968), pp. 378–9.

32. See, in general, R. Lemarchand, 'Clientelism, Class and Ethnicity: The Informal Structuring of Community Boundaries', paper delivered to the 1978 Bellagio Conference on Political Patronage, Clientelism and Development. Case of clientelism serving to mitigate both ethnic and class divisions: Nicholas S. Hopkins, *Popular Government in an African Town: Kita, Mali* (Chicago: University of Chicago Press, 1972), chaps. 5–7. On clientelism and class formation, see R. Sandbrook, 'Patrons, Clients and Factions: New Dimensions of Conflict Analysis in Africa', *Canadian Journal of Political Science*, V, 1 (1972), pp. 118–19.

33. First quote from Nelson, 'The Urban Poor' (n. 1 above), p. 406. See also, P. Flynn, 'Class, Clientelism and Coercion: Some Mechanisms of Internal Dependency and Control', *Journal of Commonwealth and Comparative Politics*, XII, 2 (1974), pp. 133–56, quote p. 150.
34. On Accra: Richard Sandbrook and Jack Arn, *The Labouring Poor and Urban Class Formation: The Case of Greater Accra*, Occasional Monograph No. 12, Centre for Developing-Area Studies, McGill University, September 1977, pp. 60–1. Quote on Ghana: Maxwell Owusu, *Uses and Abuses of Political Power: A Case Study of Continuity and Change in the Politics of Ghana* (Chicago: University of Chicago Press, 1970), p. 254.
35. On Kampala: J. D. Greenstone, 'Corruption and Self-Interest in Kampala and Nairobi', *Comparative Studies in Society and History*, VIII, 2 (1966), pp. 208–9; on Lagos: Baker, *Urbanization and Political Change* (n. 21 above), pp. 236–7; and on Ibadan: G. Jenkins, 'An Informal Political Economy', in Jeffrey Butler and A. A. Castagno (eds.), *Boston University Papers on Africa: Transition in African Politics* (New York: Praeger, 1967), pp. 184–90, quote pp. 188–9.
36. See Sandra Barnes, 'Becoming a Lagosian', PhD thesis, University of Wisconsin, 1975, esp. pp. 186–92, quotes pp. 213, 191.
37. Lemarchand, 'Comparative Political Clientelism and the Client State', paper delivered at the XIth Congress of the International Political Science Association, Moscow, 12–18 August 1979, p. 16.
38. Frank Parkin, *Class Inequality and Political Order* (London: MacGibbon & Kee, 1971), p. 48.
39. See C. Clapham, 'The Context of African Political Thought', *Journal of Modern African Studies*, VIII, 1 (1970), pp. 1–14; and, on major themes, C. Ake, 'The Congruence of Political Economies and Ideologies in Africa', in P. C. W. Gutkind and Immanuel Wallerstein (eds.), *The Political Economy of Contemporary Africa* (Beverly Hills: Sage, 1976), pp. 200–6; and J. Mohan, 'Varieties of African Socialism', in *The Socialist Register, 1966* (London: Merlin Press, 1966), pp. 220–66.
40. On the revisionist view of the reality of party and ideology: H. Bienen, 'Political Parties and Political Machines in Africa', in Michael Lofchie (ed.), *The State of the Nations* (Berkeley: University of California Press, 1971), pp. 195–213. On the CPP in Accra: Sandbrook and Arn, *The Labouring Poor* (n. 34 above), pp. 61–2. On *Mobutisme*: M. G. Schatzberg, 'Fidélité au Guide: The JMPR in Zaïrian Schools', *Journal of Modern African Studies*, XVI, 3 (1978), pp. 417–31.
41. Hirschman, 'The Changing Tolerance for Income Inequality in the Course of Economic Development', *Quarterly Journal of Economics*, LXXXVII (1973), p. 545.
42. Popular perceptions respecting social mobility in Latin American cases: W. Mangin, 'Latin American Squatter Settlements', *Latin American Research Review*, II (1967), pp. 84–5; and A. Portes, 'Rationality in the Slums', *Comparative Studies in Society and History*, XIV, 3 (1972), p. 285. African cases cited: P. C. Lloyd, *Power and Independence: Urban Africans' Perception of Social Inequality* (London: Routledge & Kegan Paul, 1974), p. 143; Sandbrook and Arn, *The Labouring Poor* (n. 34 above), p. 58;

T. Seymour, 'Perceptions of Stratification by the Urban Poor: A Report on Research in a Lusaka Squatter Settlement', paper presented to the Universities of East Africa Social Science Conference, 18–23 December 1972, p. 3; and Marc H. Ross, *The Political Integration of Urban Squatters* (Evanston, Ill: Northwestern University Press, 1973), p. 17.

43. Quotes from M. Carnoy, 'The Political Consequences of the Role of Education in Manpower Formation', *Comparative Education Review*, XVIII, 3 (1974), p. 125.

44. D. Court, 'The Educational System as a Response to Inequality in Tanzania and Kenya', *Journal of Modern African Studies*, XIV, 4 (1976), pp. 680–1.

45. Reality and myth of educational access: *ibid.*, pp. 682–7. See also, ILO, *Employment, Incomes and Equality: A Strategy for Increasing Productive Employment in Kenya* (Geneva: ILO, 1972), p. 97.

46. Alfred Stephan, *The State and Society: Peru in Comparative Perspective* (Princeton: Princeton University Press, 1978), p. 58.

47. On mechanisms of state control and responses to these, see Richard Sandbrook and Robin Cohen (eds.), *The Development of an African Working Class* (Toronto: University of Toronto Press, 1976), esp. pp. 130–6. Country surveys of these mechanisms: Wogu Ananaba, *The Trade Union Movement in Africa: Promise and Performance* (New York: St Martin's Press, 1979), part I.

48. On Mathare Valley: Ross, *Political Integration* (n. 42 above), pp. 192–8. Ashaiman, near Accra, is an example of a low-income area in which community cohesion and organization are negligible. See Sandbrook and Arn, *The Labouring Poor* (n. 34 above), pp. 62–6.

49. On West Africa: M. Peil, 'Social Life in the Burgeoning Suburbs', in R. P. Moss and R. Rathbone (eds.), *The Population Factor in Tropical African Studies* (London: Heinemann, Educational Books, 1975). On Kenya: James Waweru and Associates, *Progress Report No. 5: Results of the Socio-Economic Survey*, 'Low-Cost Housing and Squatter Upgrading Study', Report to the Government of Kenya and World Bank, August 1976, pp. 16, 38, 46, 64–5 and 118.

50. On the importance of local leadership: see Peil, 'Social Life' (n. 49 above); and Ross, *Political Integration* (n. 42 above), pp. 197–8. On the role of urban chiefs: P. C. W. Gutkind, 'African Urban Chiefs: Agents of Stability or Change in African Urban Life?' in Paul Meadows and Ephraim Mizruchi (eds.), *Urbanism, Urbanization and Change* (Reading, Mass: Addison-Wesley, 1969), pp. 457–70.

51. Impact of ethnic homogeneity on sense of community: A. B. Chilivumbo, 'The Ecology of Social Types in Blantyre', in David Parkin (ed.), *Town and Country in Central and Eastern Africa* (London: International African Institute, 1978), pp. 314–15; and Ross, *Political Integration* (n. 42 above), pp. 194–7.

52. See, on Dakar, I. M. Dieng, 'The "Redevelopment" of Nimzatt-Anglemouss and its Consequences', *Manpower and Unemployment Research*, IX, 2 (1976), pp. 7–8; and, on Mathare Valley, Hake, *African Metropolis* (n. 10 above), p. 151; and Ross, *Political Integration* (n. 42 above), pp. 111–12, where quote appears.

53. Information from: David Boswell, 'The Growth and Socio-Political Development of Chawama [1948–66]', Working Paper, Development

SOCIAL CONTROL AND URBAN STRUGGLE 225

Planning Unit, University of London, January 1975; Development
Planning Unit, 'Preliminary Report on the Social Organization of
Chawama [1974]', University of London, May 1974; and Ita Muller,
'Chawama, a Good Place in Lusaka: A Description of an Informal
Settlement', Workshop on the Informal Sector, Institute for Development
Studies, University of Nairobi, 8–10 November, 1976.
54. Eric Hobsbawm, *Primitive Rebels* (Manchester: Manchester University
Press, 1959), pp. 108–25. See also, George Rudé *Paris and London in the
Eighteenth Century: Studies in Popular Protest* (New York: Viking Press,
1971), esp. pp. 19–21; and Gareth Stedman Jones, *Outcast London*
(Oxford: Oxford University Press, 1971), pp. 341–5.
55. For an interesting example of the use of the concept 'crowd' in an African
milieu, see F. Furedi, 'The African Crowd in Nairobi: Popular Movements
and Elite Politics', *Journal of African History*, XIV, 2 (1973), pp. 275–90.
56. A. Hughes and R. Cohen, 'An Emerging Nigerian Working Class: The
Lagos Experience', in P. C. W. Gutkind, R. Cohen and J. Copans (eds.),
African Labor History (Beverly Hills: Sage, 1978), pp. 39–40; and J. Kraus,
'Strikes and Labour Power in a Post-Colonial African State: Ghana',
Development and Change, X, 2 (1979), table 1.
57. See, on Senegal, C. Cottingham, 'Class, Politics and Rural Modernization:
A Study of Local Political Change in Senegal', PhD thesis, University of
California, Berkeley, 1972, pp. 208–13, and P. Waterman, 'Towards an
Understanding of African Trade Unionism', *Présence africain*, no. 76
(1970), p. 10; on Ghana, R. D. Jeffries, 'The Labour Aristocracy? A Ghana
Case Study,' *Review of African Political Economy*, 3 (1975), pp. 59–70, and
St. Clair Drake and L. A. Lacy, 'Government vs. the Unions: The Sekondi-
Takoradi Strike, 1961', in Gwendolyn Carter (ed.), *Politics in Africa* (New
York: Harcourt, Brace & World, 1966); on Nigeria, Robin Cohen, *Labour
and Politics in Nigeria, 1945–71* (London: Heinemann, 1974), pp. 157–68;
R. Melson, 'Nigerian Politics and the General Strike of 1964'. in Robert
Rotberg and Ali Mazrui (eds.), *Protest and Power in Black Africa* (New
York: Oxford University Press, 1970), pp. 771–87; and W. Oyemakinde,
'The Nigerian General Strike of 1945', *Journal of the Historical Society of
Nigeria*, VII, 4 (1975), pp. 673–92; on Congo-Brazzaville, W. H. Friedland,
'Paradoxes of African Trade Unionism: Organizational Chaos and
Political Potential', *Africa Report*, X (1965), pp. 6–13, and Waterman,
'Towards an Understanding', pp. 10–11; on the Sudan, A.-R. Taha, 'The
Sudanese Labor Movement: A Study of Labor Unionism in a Developing
Society', PhD thesis, University of California, Los Angeles, 1970, pp. 92–4,
109–22; on Madagascar, G. Althabe, 'Strikes, Urban Mass Action and
Political Change, Tananarive, 1972', in Gutkind *et al.* (eds.), *African Labor
History* (n. 56 above), pp. 205–43; on Ethiopia, John Markakis and Nega
Ayele, *Class and Revolution in Ethiopia* (London: Spokesman Books,
1978), p. 93ff.
58. Althabe, 'Strikes' (n. 57 above), pp. 205–43.
59. A. G. Hopkins 'The Lagos General Strike of 1897', *Past and Present*, no. 35
(1966), pp. 133–55. On the role of dockers in the 1964 Nigerian general
strike: see e.g. Melson, 'Nigerian Politics' (n. 57 above), p. 784. A study
arguing the political *conservatism* of the broader category of portworkers is
P. Waterman, 'Consciousness, Organization and Action among Lagos

Portworkers', *Review of African Political Economy*, 13 (1978), pp. 47–62.

60. See, on Mombasa, two reports issued by Kenya's colonial government: *Report of the Commission of Inquiry Appointed to Examine the Labour Conditions in Mombasa* (Nairobi: Government Printer, 1939), and *Report of the Committee of Inquiry into Labour Unrest in Mombasa* (Nairobi: Government Printer, 1945); on Dar es Salaam, J. Iliffe, 'The Creation of Group Consciousness: A History of the Dockworkers of Dar-es-Salaam', in Sandbrook and Cohen (eds.), *Development of an African Working Class* (n. 47 above), pp. 49–72; on Zanzibar, Anthony Clayton, *The 1948 Zanzibar General Strike*, Research Report 32, Scandinavian Institute of African Studies, Uppsala, 1976, quote p. 43.

61. Michael Mason, 'Working on the Railway: Northern Nigeria, 1907–1912', in Gutkind *et al.*, *African Labor History* (n. 56 above).

62. H. E. Conway 'Labour Protest Activity in Sierra Leone During the Early Part of the 20th Century', *Labour History*, no. 15 (1968), pp. 49–59.

63. See, on Douala, R. Joseph, 'Settlers, Strikers and Sans Travail: The Douala Riots of 1945', *Journal of African History*, xv, 4 (1974), pp. 669–87; and, on the Afrique Occidentale Française, J. Suret-Canalé, 'The French West African Railway Workers' Strike, 1947–48', in Gutkind *et al.*, *African Labor History* (n. 56 above), pp. 129–54; C. Allen, 'Union–Party Relationships in Francophone West Africa', in Sandbrook and Cohen (eds.), *Development of an African Working Class* (n. 47 above), pp. 99–125; and Ousmane Sembène, *God's Bits of Wood* (New York: Anchor Books, 1970).

64. A. Turner 'The Growth of Railway Unionism in the Rhodesias, 1944–1955', in Sandbrook and Cohen (eds.), *Development of an African Working Class* (n. 47 above), pp. 73–98.

65. See Jeffries, 'The Labour Aristocracy?' (n. 57 above); and Melson, 'Nigerian Politics' (n. 57 above) p. 784.

66. Conway, 'Labour Protest Activity in Sierra Leone', (n. 62 above), pp. 59–63; M. Greenstreet, 'Labour Relations in the Gold Coast with Special Reference to the Ariston Strike', *Economic Bulletin of Ghana*, ii, 3 (1972), pp. 30–40; and C. Perrings, 'Consciousness, Conflict and Proletarianization: An Assessment of the 1935 Miners' Strike on the Northern Rhodesian Copperbelt', *Journal of Southern African Studies*, iv, 1 (1977), pp. 33–51.

67. A. Akpala, 'The Background to the Enugu Colliery Shooting Incident in 1949', *Journal of the Historical Society of Nigeria*, iii, 2 (1965), pp. 335–63. For a study of the development of a cohesive coal miners' union, see David R. Smock, *Conflict and Control in an African Trade Union: A Study of the Nigerian Coal Miners' Union* (Stanford: Hoover Institution Press, 1969).

68. C. Van Onselen, *Chibaro: African Mine Labour in Southern Rhodesia, 1900–1933* (London: Pluto Press, 1976).

69. See J. Crisp, 'Union Atrophy and Worker Revolt: Labour Protest at Tarkwa Goldfields, Ghana, 1968–69', *Canadian Journal of African Studies*, xiii, 1/2 (1979), pp. 265–94, quote p. 270. For a similar analysis, see J. Silver, 'Class Struggles in Ghana's Mining Industry', *Review of African Political Economy*, 12 (1978), pp. 67–86.

70. Silver, *ibid.*, p. 85.

71. See the tables in O. Sonubi, 'Trade Disputes in Nigeria, 1966–71', *Nigerian Journal of Economic and Social Studies*, xv, 2 (1973), pp. 228–33.
72. On Ikeja: see A. Peace, 'Industrial Protest at Ikeja, Nigeria', in Emmanuel de Kadt and G. P. Williams (eds.), *Sociology and Development* (London: Tavistock, 1974); and Peace, 'The Lagos Proletariat: Labour Aristocrats or Populist Militants?', in Sandbrook and Cohen (eds.), *Development of an African Working Class* (n. 47 above), esp. pp. 291–8. On Kano: see Paul Lubeck, 'Early Industrialization and Social Class Formation among Factory Workers in Kano, Nigeria', PhD. thesis, Northwestern University, 1975, p. 123. For a discussion of these workers' informal organization, see P. Lubeck, 'Unions, Workers and Consciousness in Kano, Nigeria: A View from Below', in Sandbrook and Cohen (eds.), *Development of an African Working Class* (n. 47 above).
73. All this data is taken from an impressive report by the Lagos Master Plan Project Unit, 'Master Plan for Metropolitan Lagos: Development of Manufacturing Industry in Lagos, 1976', Master Plan Bulletin no. 2, Ministry of Works and Planning, Lagos, December 1976, mimeo.
74. R. Massari, 'Le "Cordobazo"', *Sociologie du travail*, xvii, 4 (1975), pp. 403–19.
75. Richard Jeffries, *Class, Power and Ideology in Ghana: The Railwaymen of Sekondi* (Cambridge: Cambridge University Press, 1978), pp. 201–3.
76. See C. Kerr and A. Siegel, 'The Interindustry Propensity to Strike', in Arthur Kornhauser *et al.* (eds.), *Industrial Conflict* (New York: McGraw-Hill, 1954), pp. 191–4; and M. I. A. Bulmer, 'Sociological Models of the Mining Community', *Sociological Review*, xxiii, 1 (1975), pp. 61–92.
77. See Lubeck, 'Early Industrialization' (n. 72 above), p. 151; Sandbrook and Arn, *Labouring Poor* (n. 34 above), chap. 6; and P. Konings, 'Political Consciousness and Political Action of Industrial Workers in Ghana: A Case Study of Valco Workers in Tema', *African Perspectives*, 2 (1978), p. 80.
78. Crisp, 'Union Atrophy' (n. 69 above), p. 287.
79. R. Clignet, *The Africanization of the Labor Market: Educational And Occupational Segmentations in the Camerouns* (Berkeley: University of California Press, 1977), p. 67; K. Hinchliffe, 'The Kaduna Textile Workers: Characteristics of an African Industrial Labour Force', *Savanna*, ii, 1 (1973), pp. 33–4; and Sandbrook and Arn, *Labouring Poor* (n. 34 above), table 7. See also M. Peil, 'Aspirations and Social Structure: A West African Example', *Africa*, xxxviii, (1968), pp. 71–8.
80. See Lubeck, 'Early Industrialization' (n. 72 above), pp. 250–1; and Sandbrook and Arn, *Labouring Poor* (n. 34 above), pp. 54–7.
81. See K. Post, ' "Peasantisation" and Rural Political Movements in Western Africa', *European Journal of Sociology*, xiii, 2 (1972), pp. 237–54; C. E. F. Beer and G. Williams, 'The Politics of the Ibadan Peasantry', in Gavin Williams (ed.), *Nigeria: Economy and Society* (London: Rex Collings, 1976); and R. C. Fox, W. de Craemer and J. M. Ribeaucourt, 'The Second Independence: A Case Study of the Kwilu Rebellion in the Congo', *Comparative Studies in Society and History*, viii (1965), pp. 78–105.

7   Paths Ahead

The national government, if it wants to be national, ought to govern by the people and for the people, for the outcasts and by the outcasts. No leader, however valuable he may be, can substitute himself for the popular will; and the national government, before concerning itself about international prestige, ought first to give back their dignity to all citizens, fill their minds and feast their eyes with human things, and create a prospect that is human because conscious and sovereign men dwell therein.

Frantz Fanon, The Wretched of the Earth, 1962

'An analysis without policy implications of a strategic nature is no good analysis.'[1] This dictum has especial application to studies of poverty. What, then, is to be done about mass poverty in tropical Africa?

An action programme requires an analysis of *what is wrong with the status quo, what a better social order might look like,* and *how it should be possible to move from the one to the other.* With respect to what is wrong, chapter 1 documented the high incidence of material deprivation and inequality in tropical Africa in general and the cities in particular. Chapter 2 introduced an historical dimension in exploring the roots of mass poverty. These were found in the mode of incorporation of the African territories into the capitalist world economy, and the pattern of peripheral capitalist development (or better, *mal*development) that this set in train. A major aspect of this pattern was technological dependence, manifest mainly in the transfer of modern technologies to African countries by foreign investment. Dependent industrialization, in the context of limited local and foreign demand for the consumer and intermediate goods produced, spawns certain social pathologies. Those emphasized in this book include massive rural–urban migration, marginalization and poverty. But as chapter 3 sought to make clear, technological dependence *per se* is not the primary cause of these maladies. Technological choice itself depends upon the consumption patterns and economic interests of dominant national and transnational classes within a society. Hence, I explored the complex relationships between class, state and development strategy in Africa. The development/class strategies which tend to perpetuate a peripheral capitalist development pattern are neo-colonialism and variants of national developmentalism. In a time of waxing Third World economic nationalism and waning world power of advanced-capitalist countries, national developmentalism is in the ascendancy.

Widespread recognition of the shortcomings of conventional approaches to development has given rise to much rhetoric about a more desirable, alternative pattern. We now have a fairly clear idea of what a better society (and international order) would look like. One major requirement, as I reported in chapter 1, is a reorientation of the productive system away from the provision of a range of non-essential goods for a small, high-income category, and towards the satisfaction of the basic needs of the low-income majority. Implicit in this proposal are further complementary economic changes: a shift in income and asset distribution in a more egalitarian direction; and the displacement of some imported, capital-intensive technologies by locally produced or adapted technologies.

A second major feature of 'Another Development' is a transformation in the orientation of, and access to, public services. A removal of class biases in access to services is of limited use to the poor if their content remains unreformed. The opening of access to health facilities, for example, must be accompanied by their reorientation away from an emphasis on curative medicine using high technology, towards preventive medicine and basic health care. Similarly, profound changes are necessary in educational curricula, housing programmes and public transport. Finally, basic-needs development requires national and collective self-reliance in production and science and technololgy, and popular participation in the definition, implementation and benefits of basic-needs strategies at national and local levels.

This is an extraordinary agenda for change. Yet those who emphasize the importance of non-material basic needs envisage even more elements of the good society. One list includes: 'diversity of satisfying jobs, self-reliance, access to power, political freedom, national and cultural identity, a sense of purpose in life and work'.[2]

Although visions of the good society can be useful in mobilizing support for social change, those that fail to identify practicable processes of change will understandably be dismissed as utopian fantasies. Radical basic-needs approaches presently run such a risk. In addition to designating *what* the goal is and *why*, programmes must delineate *how* the goal may be achieved: by what socio-economic strategies, promoted by what social class or classes, by means of what political action? Obviously, no definitive answers are possible to such questions.

In chapter 3 I dealt *inter alia* with the development strategies that might be conducive to a basic-needs pattern. The conclusions were not encouraging, inasmuch as each potential strategy suffered some major limitation. Chapters 4–6 then followed up this discussion with a consideration of the urban social forces and political struggles that might open the way for one of the basic-needs strategies. It is now time to draw together these strands of the analysis.

My investigation of urban classes and of class or quasi-class conflict turned up some evidence of rebelliousness, but none of revolutionary classes. I know of no evidence that suggests the political situation differs markedly in the rural areas of these countries. However, in the longer term, the working class in conjunction with the urban intelligentsia may prove to be an important agent of social change. The emphasis placed upon the political potential of workers in this study is not simply a matter of proletarian messianism. I am willing to accept the thesis that the proletariat in no country has yet played the revolutionary role that Marx assigned it. Nevertheless, working classes warrant study owing to their propensity for solidarity and collective action, a propensity that has frequently reinforced movements for social reform and, occasionally, revolution. As two economists not known for Marxist proclivities, Irma Adelman and Cynthia Taft Morris have discovered, the relationship between the power of organized labour and egalitarianism applies to the Third World as well as elsewhere. They conclude, on the basis of a cross-sectional analysis of seventy-four 'developing countries', that the strength of the labour movement is one of the six most important variables related to the pattern of income distribution.[3]

As a consequence of the contemporary trend towards the internationalization of production, the potential power of working classes in particular underdeveloped countries is bound to grow. There is no need to repeat the familiar statistics which show that industries involving a considerable labour input are shifting from the advanced-capitalist countries to the low-wage economies of Asia and Latin America in particular.[4] The attractiveness of the latter economies lies not only in the cheapness of labour but also in its docility, a docility fostered by either the enforced absence of labour unions or their control by an authoritarian state. The countries of tropical Africa have so far not played a prominent part in this so-called new international division of labour; industrialization here is still largely of the import-substitution and raw-material-processing varieties. But as wage rates rise or labour militancy increases in the export-orientated industies of South-East Asia and Latin America, the relatively cheaper and more docile labour of some African countries with easy access to European markets may appear more attractive to the multinationals.

I venture to suggest that the future power and orientations of African working classes will have an important bearing on whether, and if so how, assaults on poverty will be undertaken.

In a few post-colonial societies where the industrial proletariat remains small, semi-proletarianized and hence weak, revolutionary *coups d'état* or civil war, may, I suggested, introduce a stunted basic-needs strategy. But this will likely take the form of what has been called bureaucratic collectivism. The absence of a cohesive proletariat to check abuses of power, combined with the active hostility of national and transnational vested interests, and the possessive individualism born of widespread material deprivation, would encourage a revolutionary elite to substitute itself for the proletariat in carrying through a revolution from above. Such an authoritarian road (and some external sponsorship) might lay the basis for the satisfaction of minimum material needs through the uprooting of the existing productive system. It would probably also introduce a new form of class society. In trading off basic human needs against basic human rights, bureaucratic collectivism represents a morally ambiguous development strategy.

Some socialists regard these authoritarian and elitist components as necessary, and therefore justifiable, during the initial period of revolutionary transformation. With the consolidation of the new property relations, society can make the transition to the mass participation and control characteristic of socialism.[5] It must, however, be recognized that the means used to capture power and transform society do not favour this desirable outcome. Vanguardism and 'democratic centralism' do not foster a tolerance of free political activity. Socialists thus confront here an excrutiating dilemma of means and ends. For some predominantly peasant societies, the only hope for progress lies through revolution. Yet the Leninist techniques of revolution and its consolidation, though often the only effective way of opposing rapacious tyranny, tend to contradict the ultimate Marxist goal of human liberation.

If the continuing internationalization of production does create a larger and more powerful industrial working class in a few African countries, what might the future hold? One can envisage one of two divergent tendencies becoming dominant.[6] The first would see the established working class use its power to work out an accommodation with big business, both foreign and locally controlled; such a symbiosis, engineered by a state intent on forging a narrow version of a national-populist development/class strategy, might well transform the established industrial proletariat into a labour aristocracy. Insofar as the secure labour force was both substantial and relatively well remunerated, this accommodation might foster a somewhat more egalitarian income distribution. But the *modus vivendi* might well take place at the expense of the marginalized masses, who would be even more firmly excluded from the fruits of the economy. In any event, an alliance between capital and labour is inherently fragile in underdeveloped countries subject, as they are likely to be, to periodic economic recessions.

Conversely, unionized labour, identifying downwards with the labouring poor and peasantry, may take the forefront in a movement dedicated to social equity and the eradication of absolute poverty. This would obviously provide the most congenial political context for a strategy of the transition to socialism. However, even the flourishing of export-oriented industrialization in an African country would not eliminate the objective conditions that impede a socialist strategy. Further developments of the productive forces should, in principle, lay the foundations for socialism by abolishing poverty and creating a large industrial proletariat. But is is precisely the *incapacity* of peripheral capitalism to revolutionize the productive forces beyond the modern capitalist bridgeheads that poses the objective need for a socialist alternative. Socialists in Africa are necessarily revolutionary voluntarists to some degree. A transition to socialism can probably succeed only under the most stringent circumstances. Even where the objective conditions were not unfavourable to socialism, as in Czechoslovakia in 1968 and Allende's Chile, the transition has foundered owing to external combined with internal reaction. The fate of these short-lived experiments indicates the vulnerability of the socialist path in a world dominated by corporate capitalism and bureaucratic collectivism. One obvious condition for success is the support of a mobilized national working class for a socialist party – a support that is by no means assured where accommodation with corporate capitalism may yield substantial immediate benefits. Another condition for a transition in underdeveloped countries is a considerable measure of regional or international support and co-operation. National labour movements could play an important role in forging such co-operation. In Robert Cox's words:

> The implications for labour movements are fairly clear. Dependent development exacerbates the divisions within the working class between established, non-established and marginals. An option for solidarity bridging these differences through the pursuit of social equity in development would require a break with dependency. In view, however, of the vulnerability of weak countries seeking on their own to break out of the dependency relationship, the social forces that pursue this goal in one country need the concerted support of social forces in other countries, all acting within their respective states to bring about conditions in which self-reliant development becomes possible. An option for solidarity at the national level by a labour movement thus has as its corollary the pursuit of solidarity at the international level among labour movements that have made similar options. This international solidarity will not be outside of and apart from states, . . . but rather directed toward an alteration of the balance of forces within states at the national level in a common anti-imperialism.[7]

At the first glance the prospect for international labour solidarity along these lines seems bleak. Certainly, the major effect in Africa of the transnational activities of the International Confederation of Free Trade Unions (ICFTU), World Federation of Trade Unions (WFTU), British Trades Union Congress (TUC) and AFL-CIO has been to *weaken* national labour movements.[8] Union factionalism occasioned by the competition between the ICFTU and WFTU for national affiliates in the 1960s had this result, as did the propensity of both Western- and Eastern-oriented labour organizations to recognize and buttress allied African unions whose real role was to control labour for the state. Furthermore, the sole functioning pan-African labour organization since 1973, the Organization of African Trade Union Unity, is merely a creature of the member governments of the Organization of African Unity (OAU).

Nonetheless, recent declarations on the part of all major international labour bodies reveal a concern to promote solidarity behind variously conceived world anti-poverty programmes. The Soviet-dominated WFTU continues to muster support for a programme of anti-capitalist and anti-(Western) imperialist transformation. Since the United States withdrew from the ICFTU, this European-controlled organization has adopted a firmer stand *vis-à-vis* corporate capitalism. This is clear in 'Towards a New Economic and Social Order: The ICFTU Development Charter', adopted in May 1978. Identifying the 'historic mission' of the labour movement as a concern for 'fundamental social values', this charter calls for wideranging reform of national and international economic and political orders in order to shift power and income to the 'mass of the population'. This social-democratic programme requires, moreover, the development of an awareness among workers in industrial countries of the need for solidarity with Third World workers. Trade-union education can foster such an awareness by

discovering the interdependence between workers in the light of the internationalization of capital, whereby a worker in an industrial country may work for the same manufacturing company as a worker in a developing country. The ICFTU Development Charter is directed as much to the peoples of the industrialized countries as to the peoples of the developing countries. Development is not something confined to the poor – it is of common concern to all peoples and must be seen in a one-world perspective.

The smaller World Confederation of Labour (WCL), formerly a confederation of Catholic trade unions, adopted a radical socialist perspective in the 1970s. In its 'Forward the Workers' manifesto of 1976, the WCL militantly declared that

the development of people requires [*inter alia*]: the redistribution of economic, monetary and world political power; putting in hand development which is controlled, home-based, integrated, autonomous, not copied from industrialized countries, based on domestic resources and supported by a willingness to depend upon domestic effort to break the ties of dependence upon imperialist decision centres and their intermediaries; [and] a break with the capitalist system. . . . The WCL states firmly to all the workers in the world . . . that only a conquest of political power by the working class can create the conditions required for an integral development of people.

All this might justifiably be dismissed as mere window-dressing by trade-union elites. Are there not good grounds for contending that powerful Western working classes perceive their interests as opposed to, or at least different from, those of Third World workers?

Some writers believe that the very affluence of established workers in post-war Western societies vitiates their radical potential. However, as I argued in chapter 4, there is no direct relationship between workers' living standards and their political orientations. Indeed, chapter 6 showed that the relatively well-off dockers, railwaymen, miners and factory workers are generally at the forefront of industrial and political protest in Africa. Similarly, in advanced-capitalist countries, affluence does not necessarily produce conservative workers. With reference to French workers, one imaginative analysis of extant opinion polls demonstrates that rising living standards have not eroded the workers' Communist political loyalties or distinctive working-class culture and consciousness. Richard Hamilton finds 'little support for the claim that the "labour aristocrat" has conservative or bourgeois attitudes. . . . The "labor aristocrats", again contrary to the expectation, show a higher level of revolutionary sentiment than the medium or poorly paid workers.' He accounts for this anomaly by reference to the higher probability that skilled and affluent workers reside in large cities and labour in large plants than the unskilled, poorer workers. The former are therefore 'more exposed to radical organizations, and informal radical pressures. . . . The deprived workers, in comparison, are located in settings which distance them from such pressures.'[9] One may surmise, on this basis, that the conservatism of Western working classes cannot be assumed.

But would Western working-class radicalism, even if activated, involve a concern for international as well as national transformation? If Western workers see their own advantageous position as linked to the existing inequitable international economic order, they will not favour international labour solidarity to transform that order. Indeed, an argument somewhat along these lines has been used to explain the AFL-CIO's support of a conservative American foreign policy in the post-war period. Ronald Radosh, in a detailed political history, identifies an implicit agreement between organized labour and big business that plausibly holds the key to the behaviour of American labour leaders. In return for supporting the value of high labour productivity and *the expansion of US corporations abroad*, union leaders expected employers to use the resulting super-benefits to reward workers for their loyalty and diligence.[10]

This community of interests had, however, broken down by 1970. By then it was evident to union leaders that Third World investment by American transnational corporations harmed the short-term interests of US workers.[11] Foreign investment by US manufacturing firms was especially pernicious, in that this transferred the labour-intensive stages of productive processes to low-wage, docile-labour economies. In part, labour's response has been purely defensive, and indeed reactionary. The AFL-CIO and some of its affiliates have lobbied to secure legislative curbs on both the outflow of US investment capital and the inflow of some categories of cheap manufactured imports. But a state responsive to business interests has not been wholly sympathetic to these demands. Hence, the logic of the internationalization of capital is pushing the AFL-CIO into support for genuinely autonomous and strong trade unions in underdeveloped countries, unions capable of pressing their demands against both capital and state. The common interest of American (or more generally Western) and Third World labour movements now lies in establishing 'fair labour standards', fostering labour militancy, and controlling the global operations of transnational corporations.[12] Only in this way will the attractiveness of foreign investment in export-oriented manufacturing be diminished.

The strengthening of international labour solidarity on some development issues is thus not as fanciful a notion as it first appears. The real question concerns the nature of the programme around which such North–South solidarity emerges. Will the political power of organized labour advance socialist goals on a national and transnational basis, or will it be used to consolidate a world labour aristocracy of established workers? It has to be conceded that the latter alternative appears more likely. The danger, then, would be that identified in chapter 3: that labour-supported reforms of national and international economic orders, while benefiting established workers, would not mitigate the marginalizing tendency at the periphery.

This discussion raises the critical issue of whether an action programme for 'Another Development' necessitates revolution or whether a process of reform could conceivably realize this goal. One way to approach this is through a brief consideration and critique of the usual terms of debate between 'reformers' and 'revolutionists'.

Revolutionary change to resolve the poverty problem, claims the reformer, appears historically unlikely in most Third World countries; in these, evolutionary prescriptions for ameliorating poverty are the only realistic ones (and, for some, the only desirable ones too). True, an anti-poverty programme featuring, above all, a redistribution of national income (restricted perhaps to 'redistribution from growth') and probably an initial redistribution of assets such as land, will prove impracticable in countries dominated by an entrenched and recalcitrant ruling group. But that still leaves a range of Thirld World countries in which such a strategy may succeed in some form – if only because a regime and its associated class base fear that intransigence may lead to their displacement from power. In short, a reformed national capitalism, providing both growth and social equity, is feasible in some peripheral countries. Some reformers (for instance, the Sussex school of 'structuralist' economists) go much further in tracing the perpetuation of mass poverty to the inequitable rules and institutions of the world economy. For these, the eradication of Third World poverty requires a New International Economic Order. This position therefore entails an enumeration of the necessary changes in the rules and institutions governing international trade, monetary relations and transfers of technology and capital, and reflections upon the strategies to underdeveloped countries in achieving these through collective bargaining.[13]

Revolutionists, on the other hand, contend that a prerequisite for any genuine anti-poverty programme is a transformation of national power structures that currently reflect and underpin the maldistribution of income and assets. In the absence of a shift in power towards the popular classes, reform programmes will either prove abortive or, worse, serve an ideological function in legitimating peripheral capitalism. Legitimation would in this case flow from the central assumption of 'redistribution with growth' or basic-needs development that equitable change within the existing order is feasible. But, in practice, regimes using the rhetoric of poverty amelioration would implement only those marginal reforms required to give credence to the notion of progress.[14] Clearly, the necessity of revolutionary struggle along class lines flows from this analysis. In the uncompromising and dramatic words of Paul Baran, in his classic *The Political Economy of Growth*:

> Since a social organization, however inadequate, never disappears by itself, since a ruling class, however parasitic, never yields power unless compelled to do so by overwhelming pressure, development and progress can only be attained if all the energies and abilities of a people that was politically, socially, and economically disfranchised under the old system are thrown into battle against the fortresses of the *ancien régime*.

Moreover, given the structural connection between underdevelopment and the development of the imperialist countries, the eradication of mass poverty obviously requires (from Baran's perspective) the eventual transformation of the world capitalist system into a socialist commonwealth.

The debate, as just summarized, seems to end at an impasse. On the one hand, the revolutionary Marxists accuse the reformers of utopianism in recommending the implementation of anti-poverty programmes within political structures whose dominant elements are precisely those who would lose through genuine reform. On the other hand, the reformers rejoin that the transformers are either unhelpful in offering no alternative or impractical in advocating revolutionary change when this, even if desirable, appears unlikely in the foreseeable future of most countries.

Is there a way out of this impasse? Perhaps the only escape at the theoretical level is to draw finer distinctions than the popular 'reform or revolution' dichotomy permits, and thereby demonstrate that some reformers and revolutionaries have more in common than would initially appear to be the case.

Consider first the nature of reform. This is presumably any change that shifts resources or power away from the privileged classes in order to enhance the economic and social position of underprivileged groups. But there are actually two sorts of such change: 'structural' and 'non-structural' reform.[15] In principle, non-structural reform refers to changes that are consistent with the rationality of a given system; that is, they challenge neither the relative power of the various classes nor the logic that underpins the productive system. Structural reform then entails changes that do constitute such a challenge. With respect to structural *political* reform, there is obviously no guarantee that empowering materially deprived groups – through their autonomous organization or freer political activity, for example – will produce structural economic reform or pressure for a basic-needs development strategy. Nonetheless, their empowerment does presumably enhance the prospects of these outcomes. Structural *economic* reforms in the present context involve changes that assert social priorities against the logic of the peripheral capitalist pattern of accumulation. Production within this model, outside the export sector, is geared to satisfying efficiently the demand to which a highly unequal distribution of income and assets gives rise. Efficiency in this context normally requires the transfer of sophisticated technologies, and hence managerial skills and knowhow as well, to produce Western-style, highly-specified consumer goods. Structural reforms must contribute to a reorientation of this productive system to respond not to existing demand, but to the poor majority's need for basic consumer and capital goods. This involves, to repeat, changes in income distribution, asset ownership, productive techniques and, of course, public services.

But is it likely that established regimes will carry out structural reform? This is not inconceivable. After all, non-revolutionary governments in South Korea, Taiwan, Sri Lanka and Jamaica have sought to introduce wide-ranging reforms designed, in whole or in part, to enhance equity and meet basic needs. These programmes have, of course, achieved varying success. Nonetheless, it is not hard to predict the response of most governments when presented with a package of proposals for structural and non-structural reform: they will implement selectively those changes that do not alter the relations of power and production. Indeed, this is the implicit message of a survey by the ILO, *Basic Needs Satisfaction in ILO Member States*, carried out in 1978.[16] Only forty-five 'Developing Countries' responded to the ILO's questionnaire, of which fifteen were from Africa. What is significant is how little information on the incidence of poverty those governments possess, and how little in the way of basic-needs oriented policies and projects they have undertaken. They profess the best of intentions. But the two most popular reforms – site-and-services housing schemes for the urban poor and preventive health care for rural dwellers – represent non-structural (though still laudable) change.

Kenya, the subject of the ILO's seminal report in 1972 on the 'employment problem', nicely illustrates the probable fate of programmes to eradicate marginalization through reform.[17] In response to this report, the Kenyan government proclaimed the satisfaction of basic human needs as a major goal in its 1975–8 and 1979–83 development plans. Yet its action fell short of its rhetoric, insofar as the government shied away from structural reform. True, some of the policy changes did adversely affect the vested interests of powerful local and foreign capitalists: for instance, the imposition of tariffs on intermediate and capital goods; the abolition of investment allowances in Nairobi and Mombasa; an increase in the rate of corporation tax on branches of foreign companies and in the rate of witholding tax on dividends paid to non-residents and on all payments to foreign suppliers; a ten per cent tax on all manufactured goods, with essential foodstuffs and agricultural supplies exempted and 'luxury goods' taxed at a higher rate; and the introduction of a capital gains tax. Other recommendations which have been implemented are of more marginal economic significance, though still beneficial to some among the poor. These included the official acceptance of site-and-services housing schemes; the abolition of the tax on traditional liquor and of the licensing of taxi drivers; the elimination of fees for the first four years of primary school; the establishment of a rural public works programme, albeit on a small scale; the institution of some pilot agricultural projects intended to benefit small farmers; and a rise in the rural and urban minimum wage in 1975.

But these proposals entailing *structural* change were implicitly or explicitly rejected. In this category belong the following recommendations: an incomes policy to narrow income differentials, primarily by the imposition of a freeze on the salaries of the better-paid; a reorientation of agricultural policy, prominently involving a progressive land tax and a ceiling on individual landholdings; a termination of state-subsidization of the formal sector and an unblocking of market opportunities for small-scale enterprises in the informal sector; encouragement of appropriate technologies; and reform of the educational system to make schooling relevant to the needs of the majority who leave school before the fifth or sixth year. It is evident that the government, though undertaking some reform, is not genuinely committed to a basic-needs approach. The lesson drawn by Martin Godfrey from this experience is apropos:

> The problem is that the ILO strategy, while perhaps not constituting a totally indivisible package, contains a *core* of mutually reinforcing recommendations. In particular, the recommendations on the structure of rewards, land policy, technology, protection, the informal sector and education seem to be inextricably linked to each other. For example, the educational reforms recommended would not work in the absence of a substantial change in the structure of rewards. Thus partial implementation is likely to be ineffective and may even in some respects make matters worse.[18]

The distinction between types of reform, as illustrated by the Kenyan case, permits a clarification of the actual intentions and prospects of proponents of assaults on poverty. One possibility is that the aim of basic-needs advocates is simply to extract concessions in the shape of non-structural reform from recalcitrant governments. Proposals for socio-economic transformation would then constitute a gambit on the part of reform-mongers whose sights were actually much lower. This is not a dishonourable approach. Some of the policies of the Kenyan government subsequent to the ILO report have, after all, provided benefits for sectors of the poor. Consider, for instance, the shift in public housing policy from conventional housing to squatter upgrading and site-and-services schemes in the late 1970s. While conventional public housing schemes invariably favour the middle class and skilled workers, squatter upgrading and site-and-services schemes can spread the gains to unskilled workers, the labouring poor and petty bourgeoisie. This is significant in that a current scheme, financed by the World Bank, is to benefit over 300 000 people in Nairobi, Mombasa and Kisumu.[19]

But there is one major strategic objection to reform-mongering along these lines. It is that marginal reforms may reinforce the legitimacy of a peripheral-capitalist accumulation pattern that underdevelopment theory identifies as a major cause of mass poverty. Even this legitimating tendency is not certain, however. Since Alexis de Tocqueville wrote, the sociology of revolution has recognized the ambiguity of reformism. Reforms, while often intended as a counter-revolutionary weapon, can generate among their beneficiaries a momentum for more radical demands.

> The subordinates are made better off, if only marginally, but their subordination is made more secure (at least in the short run); rulers secure the stability and legitimacy they need, but are left ultimately to deal with the dynamic they have set into motion, one that is in basic opposition to their fundamental interests.[20]

Alternatively, the advocates of basic-needs approaches may genuinely be working to realize the national and international structural changes they preach. One must wonder, in this event, whether they fully realize the enormity of the political task involved. Whether they know it or not, they are revolutionaries, or close to it – though not necessarily socialist revolutionaries. *Revolution* is usually conceived of as a violent and abrupt change in political institutions, social structure and economic relations. *Reform* presumably differs in the means, pace and scope of change. But in the context of an assault on poverty, the line between structural reform and revolution is hazy indeed. The scope of change necessitated by a basic-needs strategy is vast. There needs to be simultaneous action in the economic sphere (to change the pattern of national growth and the use of productive resources, and perhaps the international economic order), in social structure (as a result of changes in the distribution of assets, income and public services), and, if the goal of popular participation is taken seriously, in the sphere of political institutions as well. If the aim is not to sacrifice economic growth in the pursuit of social equity, then the pace of change would need to be rapid. It would be unrealistic to expect the transnational corporations and national capitalists to continue to invest and expand the economy during a time of intensive redirection of resources and power. Hence, the period of transition must be short to minimize economic dislocation. Finally, it is most unlikely that change of this scope and abruptness could occur without the prod or threat of violent upheaval. Consequently, whether the process of basic-needs development involved revolution or structural reform would be a moot point in many instances.

To this point I have discussed the basic-needs approach as systemic transformation. The immediate prospect in most countries, not surprisingly, is neither revolution nor structural reform in the direction of 'Another Development'. Non-structural reform is another matter: states in search of legitimacy must seem concerned to mitigate the daily hardships of ordinary people. Centrally adminstered public housing programmes, owing to their visibility and the opportunity to exercise patronage, commonly serve this legitimacy function, though the actual beneficiaries are rarely the poorest.[21]

But this is not the end of the story. There is another longer-term, less dramatic basic-needs strategy of change – this aims at grass-roots liberation despite governmental intransigence on national development strategy. It is evident that a government's commitment to popular mobilization provides the optimal context for what is often referred to as 'development participation' or 'participatory development' at the local level. Yet the enterprise of satisfying basic needs, introducing appropriate technologies, building local self-reliance and, above all, fostering popular organization cannot wait for the conversion of regimes to a basic-needs approach. Participatory development projects will not be feasible in all underdeveloped countries. In societies with intense class conflict and/or repressive.regimes, the ruling group will view any autonomous organization of poor people as a potential threat. However, many authoritarian regimes are more relaxed about such co-operative ventures, as long as these appear non-political in intent.[22]

Grass-roots participatory development can prove liberating in two senses.[23] First, such projects can help liberate small communities *from* something. Insofar as the poor share the benefits of projects designed to improve health, educational, housing or sanitary facilities, or production techniques and facilities in agriculture or small-scale industry, they achieve some relief from material deprivation. Development participation may also be liberating in a broader sense.

Through the process of defining their own needs and designing and implementing their own projects, villagers and urban poor educate themselves in organizational dynamics and self-government. The empowerment to which this experience can give rise will presumably, in time, increase popular pressures for transformation of *national* development strategy.

One should not, however, nurture unrealistic expectations. Participation in local development is not a new idea, and authorities have judged the earlier, government-directed experiments in this – 'community development' and *'animation rurale'* – as largely failures.[24] Participatory development, as presently conceived, does avoid the two major pitfalls of these earlier approaches: a centralized administration of community projects that vitiated grass-roots participation in all but the implementation stage; and the establishment of new structures that bypassed locally supported organizations and (in the case of 'community development') local leaders too. But even if participatory development projects circumvent these limitations, success is far from assured:

> Local organization and adminstrative decentralization are not invariably vehicles for greater participation. Local organizations can exist in form only, with little participation and little vitality, or they may be dominated by the more prosperous and privileged minority. Similarly, efforts to decentralize may not be matched by local effort and initiative, and the authority delegated to local levels may be taken over by local elites. Decentralization may produce greater equity and participation, but may also produce neither.[25]

When a state pursuing neo-colonial or national-developmental strategies is directly involved in development participation, the results are likely to be ambiguous at best. Consider, for instance, the case of the Lusaka Squatter and Site and Services Project, undertaken in 1974.[26] This project required co-operation between the World Bank (which provided a loan of US $21·2 million), the Zambian government, the sole legal party (UNIP) and the American Friends' Service Committee (a non-governmental organization – NGO – committed to community development). It was a very ambitious project. The aim was to provide the following: land-tenure rights and loans for building materials to 17 000 householders in order that they might upgrade their premises; basic infrastructure and community services in the four squatter settlements involved; and another 11 000 serviced lots in areas adjacent to the existing settlements.

However, the uniqueness of this project lay not in its scale but in the importance placed upon the squatters' participation in its design and implementation. All the operational staff received some training in the procedures of development participation. For the community development officers, this involved a ten-month training programme (half on the job); other staff engaged in in-service workshops and seminars. There was consequently a genuine element of popular participation. Householders in the various neighbourhoods, through discussions with community development teams, were able to exert influence on a range of issues: 'everything from allocation of water standpipes to which of the jobs might be done with mutual self-help'.[27] Any money saved by the use of voluntary labour in building the infrastructure was subsequently distributed among the participants.

A definitive assessment of the consequences of a project that has just drawn to a close is obviously premature. Nonetheless, a couple of ambiguous effects can be noted. In the first place, participation, inasmuch as it took place through the structures of UNIP, presumably enhanced the control of the state over the inhabitants of the burgeoning squatter settlements. The main partnership has involved UNIP and the major organ of the state, the specially created Housing Project Unit of the Lusaka City Council.[28] For the purposes of the project, the community leaders in the squatter areas were taken to be the heads of the constituency, branch and section levels of the governing party. Still, regardless of the structural context, the mobilization of squatters has led to their empowerment within the existing political system. In the second place, empowerment of the urban squatters, because it occurred in a society where the national development strategy remains unreformed, has accentuated an already evident urban bias in public policy. The dilemma of this sort of project in a country pursuing national developmentalism is that it benefits one segment of the low-income population at the expense of the rural majority.

Now that the urban squatters form the newest cadres entering the party, and are among the most upwardly mobile, what sources of political influence are likely to counter further urban bias in national policy making? And yet who would want to argue that these hard working, newer arrivals to Zambia's polity should join the ranks of those excluded from decision making?[29]

This dilemma aptly illustrates a principle enunciated at the outset in this book. The problems of urban and rural poverty are insoluble in isolation from one another. Insofar as participatory development projects offer some amelioration of pressing problems and the long-term prospect of empowerment of the poor, the bulk of these projects should be located in the rural areas, where most of the poor reside.

Small-scale rural projects constitute one fruitful focus for co-operation on a North–South basis. NGOs in the North are generally far better suited for this sort of project than national aid agencies. Constraints on the latter's effectiveness include: strict bureaucratic procedures governing resource transfers; a proclivity for large, capital-intensive projects that absorb the maximum of funds with the minimum of adminstrative surveillance; and an acute desire to avoid antagonizing the governments of recipient countries. NGOs, on the other hand, are not usually so constrained, as a recent report on the role of Canadian NGOs makes clear.[30] This Science Council of Canada report arrives at a very favourable evaluation (though the criteria of evaluation are quite vague). It ascribes the effectiveness of NGOs in low-cost rural development projects to their employment of highly motivated personnel who respect local institutions and cultures; their freedom to encourage the local development of appropriate technologies owing to the absence of aid-tying requirements; and a positive philosophy of development. The last rejects the notion of foreign assistance as the transfer of resources to supply a certain officially defined need, and favours a conception of development as liberation. In this view external aid is most useful when it helps communities help themselves – by developing higher productivity, greater self-reliance and autonomy at the local level. Inasmuch as the most active NGOs operate with an underdevelopment prespective on mass poverty, their personnel in the field can, in a modest way, also act as *animateurs*. There is no reason to suppose that Canadian NGOs are unique in their approach.

This book has directed attention to the question of how people might tackle underdevelopment and create a more humane future. There has been enough dreaming about the contours of a better society, whether this is conceived as 'Another Development' or socialism. But 'a goal which is not at the same time a process becomes a dogma, a rigid ahistorical final stage of development – hence an absurdity'.[31] To escape this fate, basic-needs approaches cannot avoid consideration of the ineluctable realities of power – of the class alliances and state mechanisms that undergird concrete development strategies, of the social forces that might serve as the carrier of alternative strategies, and of the sorts of political action at the local, national and international levels that basic-needs development entails. It is time for proponents of these attractive approaches to confront the politics of basic needs.

Notes

1. J. Galtung, 'What is a Strategy?', International Foundation for Development Alternatives, *Dossier 6* (April 1979), p. 13.
2. P. Streeten and S. J. Burki, 'Basic Needs: Some Issues', *World Development,* VI, 3 (1978), p. 414. See also, J. Friedmann, 'Basic Needs, Agropolitan Development, and Planning from Below', *World Development,* VII, 6 (1979), pp. 607–13.
3. Adelman and Morris, *Economic Growth and Social Equity in Developing Countries* (Stanford: Stanford University Press, 1973), p. 183.
4. See G. K. Helleiner, 'Manufactured Exports from Less-Developed Countries and Multinational Firms', *Economic Journal* (March 1973), pp. 21–47; and R. Trajtenberg, 'Transnationals and Cheap Labor in the

Periphery', in Paul Zarembka (ed.), *Research in Political Economy*, vol. I (Greenwich, Conn: JAI Press, 1978).

5. J. F. Petras, 'Class and Politics in the Periphery and the Transition to Socialism', *Review of Radical Political Economics*, VIII, 2 (1976), p. 26.

6. Compare with Robert Cox's incisive analysis in his 'Labour and the Multinationals: Elements for Strategic Planning', Working Paper DEE/D/7/i, Instituto Latinamericano de Estudios Transnationales, Mexico City, May 1978.

7. *Ibid.*, p. 32. See also, A. Martinelli, 'Contradictions between National and Transnational Planning: The Role of Labour Unions', International Foundation for Development Alternatives, *Dossier 11* (September 1979), pp. 75–86.

8. See J. P. Windmuller, 'External Influences on Labor Organizations in Underdeveloped Countries', *Industrial and Labor Relations Review*, XVI, 4 (1963), pp. 559–73; Ioan Davies, *African Trade Unions* (Harmondsworth: Penguin, 1966), chap. 9; and G. E. Lynd, *The Politics of African Trade Unionism* (New York: Praeger, 1968), chap. 4.

9. Richard Hamilton, *Affluence and the French Worker in the Fourth Republic* (Princeton: Princeton University Press, 1966), quotes pp. 130–1, 134.

10. Ronald Radosh, *American Labor and United States Foreign Policy* (New York: Random House, 1969), pp. 4–5, 22, 25.

11. See N. Goldfinger, 'A Labor View of Foreign Investment and Trade Issues', in Robert W. Baldwin and J. David Richardson (eds.), *International Trade and Finance* (Boston: Little, Brown, 1974), p. 104.

12. R. Cox, 'Labor and the Multinationals', *Foreign Affairs*, LIV, 2 (1976), pp. 344–65; and N. Weinberg, 'The Multinational Corporation and Labor', in Abdul Said and Luiz Simmons (eds.), *The New Sovereigns* (Englewood Cliffs: Prentice-Hall, 1975), pp. 91–107. For the contrary view, arguing an inherent conflict of interests between workers in advanced and under-developed countries, see A. Emmanuel, 'Myths of Development vs. Myths of Underdevelopment', *New Left Review*, 85 (1974), p. 79.

13. The points at issue between the reformist and revolutionary approaches are nicely brought out in a debate between Richard Jolly, representing a variant of the former, and Colin Leys, the latter. See Leys, 'The Politics of Redistribution with Growth', and Jolly, 'Redistribution with Growth – A Reply', in *Institute of Development Studies Bulletin*, VII, 2 (1975), pp. 4–17. An important statement of an enlightened 'reformist' approach is Hollis Chenery *et al.*, *Redistribution with Growth: Policies to Improve Income Distribution in Developing Countries in the Context of Economic Growth* (London: Oxford University Press, 1974). The position of the 'Sussex School' is that 'relations between the rich and poor countries normally, and in the absence of conscious and deliberate planning to the contrary, work to the disadvantage of the latter'. For a defence of this position, see Dudley Seers and Leonard Joy (eds.), *Development in a Divided World* (Harmondsworth: Penguin, 1971), chap. 2. Two recent influential books arguing for a New International Economic Order, and proposing stratagems to achieve it, are: Gerald Helleiner (ed.), *A World Divided* (Cambridge: Cambridge University Press, 1976); and Jagdish Bhagwati (ed.), *The New International Economic Order: The North–South Debate* (Cambridge, Mass: MIT Press, 1978). A progressive voice from within the

World Bank advocating a world anti-poverty programme requiring reform within both the national and international spheres is Mahbub ul Haq, *The Poverty Curtain: Choices for the Third World* (New York: Columbia University Press, 1976), esp. pp. 148–50, 164–8.

14. Leys suggests that 'Redistribution with Growth' can serve an ideological function in 'The Politics of Redistribution . . .' (n. 13 above), p. 8. He also carries out a trenchant critique of the ILO notion that a reformed, locally controlled, competitive capitalism can be created in a country like Kenya in his 'Interpreting African Underdevelopment: Reflections on the ILO Report on Employment, Incomes and Equality in Kenya', *African Affairs*, LXXII (1973), pp. 419–29. Paul Baran, *The Political Economy of Growth* (New York: Monthly Review Press, 1957), p. 14.

15. Compare the notions of 'reformist' and 'revolutionary' reform in André Gorz, *Strategy for Labor* (Boston: Beacon Press, 1967), pp. 7–12.

16. Torkel Alfthan, *Basic Needs Satisfaction in ILO Member States: Presentation and Analysis of National Responses to a World Enquiry*, ILO, Working Paper WEP 2–32/WP16, April 1979, 57p.

17. There has been a robust debate on the significance for poverty-amelioration of reform in Kenya. See, for a generally positive assessment: A. Hazlewood, 'Kenya: Incomes Distribution and Poverty – An Unfashionable View', *Journal of Modern African Studies*, XVI, 1 (1978), pp. 81–96; and E. S. Clayton, 'Kenya's agriculture and the ILO Employment Mission – Six Years After', *Journal of Modern African Studies*, XVI, 2 (1978), pp. 311–18. For a negative evaluation, see C. Leys, 'Development Strategy in Kenya since 1971', *Canadian Journal of African Studies*, XIII, 1/2 (1979), pp. 295–320. For a detailed 'balance sheet', see M. Godfrey, 'Prospects for a Basic-Needs Strategy: The Case of Kenya', *IDS Bulletin*, IX, 4 (1978), pp. 41–4; and Martin Godfrey, Dharam Ghai and Frederick Lisk, *Planning for Basic Needs in Kenya: Performance, Policies and Prospects* (Geneva: ILO, 1979).

18. Godfrey, 'Prospects' (n. 17 above), p. 41.

19. R. E. Stren, 'Housing Policy and the State in East Africa', paper presented to the Canadian Association of African Studies Conference, Guelph University, 8 May 1980, pp. 21–4.

20. Quote: I. Katznelson, 'Antagonistic Ambiguity: Notes on Reformism and Decentralization', *Politics and Society*, II (1972), p. 325. For a behavioural theory of revolution building on de Tocqueville's insight, see J. C. Davies, 'Circumstances and Causes of Revolutions: A Review', *Journal of Conflict Resolution*, XI (1967), pp. 247–57.

21. L. Peattie, 'Housing Policy in Developing Countries: Two Puzzles', *World Development*, VII, 1/2 (1979), pp. 1017–22.

22. On the variation of official tolerance, see D. Goulet, 'Development as Liberation: Policy Lessons from Case Studies', *World Development*, VII, 6 (1979), pp. 564–5.

23. I lean heavily here on *ibid.*, pp. 556–6, 564.

24. Norman Uphoff, John Cohen and Arthur Goldsmith, *Feasibility and Application of Rural Development Participation: A State-of-the-Art Paper*, Rural Development Committee, Center for International Studies, Cornell University, Ithaca, NY, 1979, pp. 26–8.

25. *Ibid.*, p. 59. For a study illustrating the dominance of self-help by local elites, see Njuguna Ng'ethe, 'Possibilities for and Limits to Peasant Self-Help Development: The Case of Harambee in Kenya', paper delivered at the Canadian Association of African Studies Conference, Guelph University, 8 May 1980.
26. Information from: C. Bryant, 'Squatters, Collective Action, and Participation: Learning from Lusaka', *World Development*, VIII, 1 (1980), pp. 73–85; and D. Pasteur, 'The Management of Squatter Upgrading: The Case of Lusaka', *IDS Bulletin*, x, 4 (1979), pp. 52–5. Both assessments are positive.
27. Bryant, 'Squatters' (n. 26 above), p. 80.
28. Pasteur, 'Management' (n. 26 above), p. 53.
29. Bryant, 'Squatters' (n. 26 above), p. 81.
30. Science Council of Canada, *From the Bottom Up: Involvement of Canadian NGOs in Food and Rural Development in the Third World* (Ottawa: Science Council of Canada, June 1979), pp. 24–7.
31. Galtung, 'What is a Strategy?' (n. 1 above), p. 14.

Index

migration, rural-urban, 18–19, 41–50, 112, 214
modes of production, 36, 85, 97, 103, 112; articulation of, 35, 63–68; and consciousness, 173, 184–6; and marginalization, 37, 59, 63, 66, 157; precapitalist, 35, 36, 41–44 *passim*, 65, 90, 95, 156; and the state, 78, 79; *see also* capitalism, marginalization
Mombasa, 8, 39, 210
Morris, Cynthia T., 230
Mozambique, 25, 44, 107
multiple job-holding, 136–7

Nairobi: classes and strata, 124, 148–50, 153, 158–60, 165, 187; development, 39, 40, 48; informal sector, 62, 65
national developmentalism, 81, 83, 90–8, 100–1, 109, 137, 228, 241–2
Nelson, Joan, 182, 196
neocolonialism, 83–97, 107, 124, 133, 137, 228
Ngugi wa Thiong'o, 168, 169
Niger, 4, 83, 86, 126; *see also* Ouagadougou
Nigeria, 20, 21, 38, 39; classes and strata, 23, 150, 157, 172, 208, 214; economic policies and results, 2, 3, 51–4, 58, 91, 130, 134; ethnicity, 193–5; migration, 45, 46; *see also* Ibadan, Lagos
nongovernmental organizations (NGOs), 241–3

occupational community, 215–16
occupational groups: apprentices and journeymen, 65, 124, 146, 157–61, 207; artisans, 64–6, 124, 146, 154, 157–61, 207; beggars, 124, 156; contractors, 150; hotel-bar keepers, 136; traders, market and shopkeeping, 82, 136, 147–56; prostitutes, 124, 165; traditional doctors, 187, 191; *see also* bourgeoisie, petty bourgeoisie, petty producers, petty traders, workers
O'Donnell, Guillermo, 102
official development assistance, 9
Omdurman, 39
Ouagadougou, 157

Pakistan, 6
Paris, 146, 156, 202
Parkin, Frank, 199
participation, 1, 10, 16, 231, 240, 242
patron-client relations, 150, 155, 161, 195–8, 200
p'Bitek, Okot, 168, 182

peasants, 23, 123, 231; country cases, 88, 92, 108, 113; differentiation and migration, 44, 45, 47, 49–50; mode of production, 66, 111, 185, 186; politics of, 24–5, 79, 82, 100, 102, 105–6, 154, 168, 196; and proletarianization, 126–37
Peil, Margaret, 157, 193
People's Republic of the Congo, 104, 209
Peru, 58
petty bourgeoisie, 165; aspirations, 136, 148, 161, 164; in Kenya, 94, 96; politics of, 11, 100, 124, 147, 151–56, 173, 207, 214, 218
Portugal, 107
Pol Pot, 105
populism, 195, 214, 215; national, 81, 91, 100; urban, 154, 155, 208
Poulantzas, Nicos, 78, 79
poverty, nature and incidence, 2–5, 19–24, 34, 105, 166; *see also* basic-needs approaches, marginalization, underdevelopment
Pratt, Cranford, 109, 113
protest movements, 170, 207–14, 218, 234

Radosh, Ronald, 234
redistribution, 4–7 *passim*, 11, 235
Revel, J.-F., 104
Roberts, Bryan, 37
Rwanda, 25, 46

Sahelian countries, 46
Salisbury, 39
Saul, John, 109, 129, 133
Sekondi-Takoradi, 215
Sembene, Ousmane, 122
Senegal, 20; economic policies and results, 3–4, 53–4, 59, 83, 130; politics of, 82, 88, 199; *see also* Dakar
Shivji, Issa, 98, 107, 108, 109
Sierra Leone, 46, 159, 166, 210, 211
site and service schemes, 237, 238, 241–2
Singapore, 26
Sklar, Richard, 92
Smith, David, 183–5 *passim*
socialism, 7, 13, 100, 102–14, 231, 232, 236, 243
Somalia, 90, 105
South Korea, 5, 36, 83, 237
Soviet Union, 9, 26, 96, 101–6 *passim*
Sri Lanka, 237
the State, 125; and accumulation, 61–8, 77–114; colonial, 50, 82, 86, 87, 132; and social control, 133, 138, 199–207, 217–18, 232; *see also* basic-needs

250 INDEX

Stewart, Francis, 14
strikes, 195, 208–14; *see also* protest movements, trade unions
Sudan, 3, 138, 209; *see also* Khartoum, Omdurman
Swainson, Nicola, 93, 96

Taiwan, 5, 36, 83, 237
Tanzania, 20; classes, 24, 45, 46, 47, 124, 126, 136; economic policies and results, 3–5, 53–4, 55, 57, 90, 130; politics in, 98–9, 138, 140, 169, 195; Zanzibar, 25, 38, 210; *see also* Dar es Salaam
Tarkwa, 216
technology, 11–14 *passim*
Telli, Torcuato di, 101
Tema, 168, 217
Timbuktu, 39
Tocqueville, A. de, 239
Todaro's model, 48
trade unions, 97, 124–5, 132, 138, 194, 232–5
Togo, 46, 52, 88
transnational corporations, 129, 234; and development strategies, 15, 16, 85, 92, 94–7, 106; and industrialization, 51, 54, 57, 111–12; *see also* capitalism
Turkey, 66, 100

Uganda, 20, 46, 169; economic policies and results, 3, 4, 53–4, 55, 58, 90; *see also* Kampala
underdevelopment, 7, 33–7, 39–41, 49, 63, 88, 98–9, 232, 239; *see also* marginalization
United Nations, 20, 90

United Nations Environmental Programme, 7
United States of America, 12, 51, 67, 233
Upper Volta, 3, 42, 46, 52, 83, 86, 157
urbanization, 20, 38–41, 183–4; and poverty, 21–4, 42, 60, 63, 93; *see also* migration, rural-urban

Vietnam, 25

wage-earners, *see* workers
Warren, Bill, 34
workers, 42–3, 131; agricultural, 12, 24, 83; casual urban, 146–7, 156, 163, 185, 207, 209; consciousness, nature and determinants, 183, 190, 214–17; 'industrial reserve army', 67, 146, 157, 167; politics of, 25, 79, 100–2, 124–5, 137–40, 173, 191–8 *passim*, 208–15, 217, 230–1; proletarianization process, 34, 42, 95, 126–8, 136, 161, 218; *see also* labour aristocracy, labouring poor, strikes, trade unions
World Bank, 2, 4, 33, 58; and basic needs, 7–9, 20; and particular countries, 23, 84–5, 239, 241

Yaoundé, 134

Zaïre, 20, 42; economic policies and results, 3, 51–4, 80, 91, 130; politics in, 43, 88, 194, 199–200; *see also* Kinshasa
Zambia, 20, 46; classes, 92, 152–3, 211; economic policies and results, 3–4, 52–7, 90–1, 126, 130, 132; politics in, 132, 133, 199, 206, 241, 242; *see also* Lusaka
Zimbabwe, 25, 38, 41, 44, 211; *see also* Salisbury